TO KNOW AND SERVE GOD

Also by Alister McGrath

The Enigma of the Cross
Evangelicalism and the Future of Christianity
A Journey through Suffering
Roots that Refresh
Understanding Doctrine

To Know and Serve God

A Life of James I. Packer

Alister McGrath

Hodder & Stoughton

LONDON SYDNEY AUCKLAND

First published in Great Britain in 1997

British Library Cataloguing in Publication Data
A CIP catalogue record for this title is available
from the British Library

ISBN 0 340 56571 3

Typeset by Palimpsest Book Production Limited,
Polmont, Stirlingshire
Printed and bound in Great Britain by
Mackays of Chatham PLC, Chatham, Kent

Hodder and Stoughton
A division of Hodder Headline PLC
338 Euston Road
London NW1 3BH

Contents

Contents

Foreword

Some years back, in America, after I had given a talk, a short young lady with a glittering eye came up and – without preliminaries – asked: 'Have you any allergies?' 'No', I replied. 'Have you ever been in counselling?' 'No', I said. 'You are *strange*', said she, and scuttled off, leaving me feeling that, whatever was true of me personally, the world was indeed a stranger place than I had thought.

Leafing through this book renews that feeling. It was entirely the author's idea; he got it, I believe, somewhere near Luton as we rode the bus together from Oxford to Cambridge. It is not an authorized biography, though I gave him all the facts about myself that he asked for, and can vouch for their accuracy. But his interpretation of me, and my place in the strategy of God's kingdom, are all his. Like me, he writes, not to flatter but to teach, and if he thinks he should evaluate me as a mover and shaper, it is not for me to demur. My only comment is that it feels strange.

Robb Wilton, a master of the comedy of incompetence who made his name on British radio as 'Mr Muddlecombe, J.P.', had a rapturous sketch during the Second World War called 'The Air-Raid Warden'. I believe he did it in costume around the halls: certainly, I heard it broadcast many times. It began thus:

The day war broke out, my missus said to me, 'You've got to stop it.' (Pause; giggles.) I said, 'Stop what?' She said, 'The war.' I said, 'Who? Me?' (More giggles.) She said, 'Well, you and a few other blokes.' (Roars of laughter.)

Robb Wilton comes to mind because my Christian calling thus far has felt so much like me 'and a few other blokes' trying to stop

specific falsehoods, nail specific sins, and further the new life in
Christ that Satan seeks to squelch in his ongoing war with the God
of creation, providence and grace. Emotionally and attitudinally, I
have felt at one with Wilton's 'Air-Raid Warden' (*mutatis mudandis*,
you understand) over and over again. Maybe I am strange, after all.
Dr McGrath's readers shall judge! So now read on.

J.I. PACKER

Introduction

'The history of the world is but the biography of great men.'
These famous words of the English literary critic Thomas Carlyle
(1795–1881) point to the importance of individuals in the shaping
of human history. Individual people can make a difference. This
book focuses on one such person, who has made a major long-term
contribution to the shaping of Christianity in the modern world.
James Innell Packer is one of the best-known names in modern
Christianity. *Christianity Today* readers named him one of the most
influential theological writers of the twentieth century, second
only to C.S. Lewis. His books have sold almost three million
copies worldwide, and are cited by many who have read them
as marking turning points in their lives as Christians. His fame
has drawn thousands of students to Regent College, Vancouver,
over the last two decades, which honoured him by establishing
the 'J.I. Packer Chair of Theology', in much the same way as
Princeton Theological Seminary had earlier honoured the great
Reformed theologian Benjamin B. Warfield. In his role as Visiting
Scholar of *Christianity Today*, he has influenced the thinking of an
increasingly literate, articulate and active evangelical readership.
He is regularly cited by evangelical leaders and thinkers as one of
the most important influences on their lives.

Packer's books have excited, challenged and sustained countless
believers in their Christian lives. In July 1996, the Evangelical
Christian Publishers Association awarded him a Gold Medallion
Lifetime Achievement Award in recognition of his outstanding
contribution to evangelical Christian thinking, and to the life of the
church at large. Although Packer – who has always been noted for
his modesty – would never accept the description, he has become

xi

one of the theological and spiritual giants of the twentieth century. His rare combination of theological competence, spiritual wisdom and a clear and accessible style of writing places him alongside the great spiritual writers of the evangelical tradition, such as John Owen, Richard Baxter, Jonathan Edwards and J.C. Ryle. Packer's literary output has concentrated on the interface of popular and academic concerns. For many, Packer is a 'scholar who found his vocation in popular communication, a popular communicator who never abandoned scholarship'.[1] In addition to his writing, he has maintained what seemed to many to be a punishing schedule of speaking engagements in churches, colleges and parachurch organizations throughout North America, and far beyond.

So who is this James I. Packer, who has come to have such influence within evangelicalism? How did he come to be a Christian? What has shaped his thinking and writing? How has he shaped modern evangelicalism? What can be learned from him? This work aims to tell his story, and by doing so, to cast light on the remarkable growth of evangelicalism in the last generation.

Our story opens in an English school playground in 1933 . . .

« 1 »

The Schoolboy: 1926–44

IT WAS 19 SEPTEMBER 1933. A new school year had begun in England. A seven-year-old boy had just started to attend the National School in the English cathedral city of Gloucester. He was shy and uncertain of himself in his new surroundings. He was already being bullied. Another boy chased him out of the school grounds on to the busy London Road outside. A passing bread van could not avoid hitting him. He was thrown to the ground with a major head injury. The young boy was taken to the Gloucester Royal Infirmary and rushed into an operating theatre. He was discovered to have a depressed compound fracture of the frontal bone on the right-hand side of his forehead, with injury to the frontal lobe of the brain. It was potentially very serious.

The resident surgeon at the hospital immediately performed an operation known as 'trefining and elevation'. This can be thought of as extracting fragments of bone from inside the skull, and repairing the damage as much as possible. As it happened, the surgeon in question had just returned from Vienna after an extended period during which he had specialized in this type of surgery. The boy was left with a small hole in his right forehead, about two centimetres in diameter. The injury would remain clearly visible for the rest of his life.

Looking back, this near-fatal accident can be seen to have had a major impact on the life of James I. Packer. As we shall see, it is directly linked to his love of reading and his remarkable ability to write. But perhaps we have allowed ourselves to rush ahead in this narrative. In what follows, we shall set the scene for the events of 1933.

1

Early Family Life

They call it a 'railroad' in North America, and a 'railway' in Britain. Our story concerns a man who had made both of these places his home. As his story begins in England, we shall call it a 'railway'. One of the greatest English engineering triumphs of the nineteenth century was the Great Western Railway. The company of this name was founded in 1835, and set itself the target of providing a direct rail service from London to the great and bustling western port of Bristol. Constructed under the direction of Isambard Kingdom Brunel, the resulting railway system was hailed as one of the great achievements of the Victorian age. It was now possible to travel directly from London's Paddington station to Bristol. The GWR was famous for its early use of 'broad gauge' lines, which were nearly half a metre wider than the more widely used 'narrow gauge' lines found elsewhere in England. The distinct identity of the Great Western would disappear after the Second World War, when the British government nationalized the private railway systems, and reorganized the entire British railway system into a single structure.

The success of the GWR led to its expansion. On 12 May 1845, it established a connection with the city of Gloucester. The city achieved railway fame during the late 1840s, when the 'Gauge Commissioners' arrived with a mandate to achieve uniformity of railway gauge throughout Britain. For many years, Gloucester was notorious on account of the difficulties involved in changing trains, due to the gauge differences between the two railway companies which had established bases in the city. Both the GWR and the Midland Railway built stations in the town; they were adjacent to one another, with a long footbridge connecting them. By the 1910s, Gloucester was established as a busy and important railway junction, served by large numbers of local trains and long-distance expresses. There was also a significant freight business.[1] An inevitable result of this substantial passenger and freight traffic was the need for a good administrative system, able to cope with the many inquiries which resulted.

James Percy Packer (died 1972) found a position as a clerk at the divisional headquarters of the GWR in the 1920s. The Packer family had close links with the land, through farming in the neighbouring county of Oxfordshire. Percy Packer's father, however, ended up as landlord of a tavern in Gloucestershire's Stroud valley, and Percy had joined the GWR straight from school, at the age of fourteen. In 1923 he married Dorothy Mary Harris (died 1965), who had trained as a schoolmistress in Bristol.

Throughout their entire time at Gloucester, the Packer family lived at 109 Dean's Way, in a small semi-detached house which they rented from a local landlord. The house was typical of those built in the Edwardian period in England. Iron railings and a gate separated the small lawn at the front of the house from the street. The back of the house could be reached by a side gate, which led to another lawn and a small kitchen garden.[2] The downstairs section of the house consisted of a front room, resplendent with piano and aspidistra; a dining room, facing to the back of the house; and a kitchen, scullery and small pantry. Upstairs there were three bedrooms and a bathroom. Electricity was installed in the house at some point about 1932; up to then, the Packers had used gas lighting throughout the house.

The couple had two children – a daughter (Margaret, born in 1929), and a son. Our story focuses on that son, named James Innell Packer, who was born in Gloucester on 22 July 1926.[3] Even today, Packer's voice bears traces of his origins in the west country of England in the distinctive 'West Country burr'. He also retains a great affection for the old Great Western Railway, and especially for the grace of its steam locomotives: the passenger greyhounds, Saints, Stars, Castles and Kings particularly. Packer has never lost a sense of mystique at the beauty of steam trains, which he often uses as a symbol of controlled power.

The Accident of 1933

Packer's early years were uneventful. In September 1933, he began to attend a local junior school at the age of seven. Even at an early age, he realized that he was something of a loner, a shy and awkward boy who found it difficult to relate to other children. He did not find it easy or particularly rewarding to play with other children; he would much rather play with his Meccano (a form of construction kit which was then popular in Britain) or his Hornby train set, draw pictures or read books.

Perhaps it was as a result of this difficulty that he became involved in the accident which was to have such a major impact on his life. Looking back, that accident may be seen to have had a significant influence on Packer's subsequent development. At the time, however, it totally disrupted his education. He had to spend three weeks in hospital, and was then ordered to have six months' recuperation away from school. Damage to the frontal lobe of the human brain is a grave matter, and Packer's doctors were seriously concerned that he might have sustained a brain injury. As it happened, the only significant effect appears to have been on Packer's speech. He remembers being told that, for the next three years, he spoke very slowly 'with a drawl'. His family were deeply concerned by the long-term implications of the accident, and tried to ensure that he avoided situations in the future in which his head injury could be made worse.

From then until he went to university, Packer had to wear a protective aluminium plate over his injury, making it impossible for him to join in normal schoolboy games. This reinforced his natural tendency to be a loner. He tended to be on the outside of things at school. He was subjected to bullying. He never joined the schoolboy gangs which were a routine part of school life. He was known to be clever, and would be asked to help others out with their homework. He would find solace in solitary things, particularly reading.

Packer's six months of enforced absence from school meant that he found himself with time on his hands. It was not until the spring of 1934 that he was able to return to the National School. At an early stage in this period of convalescence, his grandmother took him to the south coast resort of Torquay for a week-long holiday. They stayed at a local boarding house. The weather was cold and wet, making it difficult to get out and enjoy the beach and promenades. Packer and his grandmother thus found themselves confined to the guest house. As Packer did not have access to his construction kits or train set, boredom seemed inevitable. However, the boarding house (presumably aware of how tedious a place Torquay could be in bad weather) thoughtfully provided books for their guests. Having nothing much else to do, Packer began to read those he found in his room. He devoured Agatha Christie's *The Hound of Death* (a collection of short stories). His grandmother was also an admirer of Agatha Christie, and began to lend him some of her own books, including *The Mystery of the*

Blue Train and *The Secret of Chimneys*. He came away from his time at Torquay with a new love for reading.

Since then, Packer has freely admitted that he is 'something of a bookworm'. There can be little doubt that one of his many strengths has been the way in which he has read the spiritual classics of earlier generations, particularly of the sixteenth and seventeenth centuries, realized their relevance for today, and campaigned vigorously for their continued use. It is not unreasonable to suggest that Packer's enforced period of convalescence may have contributed significantly to this aspect of his future ministry.

It was not long before his love for reading developed into an interest in writing. How this happened is worth relating in a little detail.

The Typewriter

Packer's father had overall charge of the general office of the Great Western Railway at Gloucester, responsible for handling minor correspondence and inquiries for both passenger and freight services. The office was located in the Northgate Mansions, about 200 metres from the Great Western Railway station itself. Three people worked in the office: Packer's father, a junior clerk, and a typist. The general office had to deal with minor matters which were not regarded as important enough to be channelled directly to other sections of the organization; nevertheless, there still seemed to be a substantial amount of work to be done. By Friday evening, the week's work was usually not complete. Reluctant to make his colleagues work additional hours, Packer's father was in the habit of returning to his office on Saturday, sometimes in the afternoon, and finishing off the work by himself. Packer, who did not have school on Saturday afternoons, would often accompany his father to work. There were two typewriters in the office. Packer's father would use one for his work, and allow his son to play around with the other. Packer – now aged eight – found using a typewriter immensely satisfying, and soon taught himself how to type. He would painstakingly type out poems – such as Longfellow's 'Hiawatha', Southey's 'The Inchcape Rock' and other items.

His parents could not help but note his interest in typewriters. It seemed to them to offer an answer to a question which had been troubling them. Every schoolboy of the period longed for the day when he would own a bicycle of his own. Usually around the age of eleven, at the point when a schoolboy would enter senior school, parents would mark their son's 'coming of age' by giving him a bicycle as a birthday present. Packer dropped heavy hints that he expected to receive a cycle, like all his friends. However, his parents knew that they could not yet allow their son to have a bicycle. If he were to have any kind of accident, the earlier injury could lead to something much more serious, and potentially fatal. But what could they give their son instead?

On the morning of his eleventh birthday, in 1937, Packer wandered down from his bedroom to see what present awaited him. The family had a tradition of placing birthday presents in the dining room of the house. He expected to find a bicycle. Instead, he found an old Oliver typewriter, which seemed to him to weigh half a ton. Although it was old, in was nevertheless in excellent condition. It was not what Packer had asked for; nevertheless, it proved to be what he needed.[4] Surprise gave way to delight, as he realized what he could do with this unexpected gift. It was not more than a minute before he had put paper into the machine, and started to type. It proved to be his best present and the most treasured possession of his boyhood.

With his new acquisition, Packer began to write stories. Like other eleven-year-old boys, he read a variety of weekly publications aimed at his age group, such as *Modern Boy* (which often included stories based on school life and space travel) and *The Magnet* (which was totally devoted to school stories). Packer found these fascinating, and wrote his own stories in the same style. He contributed an illustrated story in this style for the 'hobbies club' in his first year in grammar school, as well as contributing stories to magazines produced by his friends at school. Although he found himself using the typewriter less frequently during his final years in senior school, he had learned a skill which would remain of vital importance throughout his career. Even though virtually all his colleagues at Regent College, Vancouver, used word processors during the 1990s, Packer patiently continues to type all his material on an old-fashioned typewriter. It is perfectly good enough for his needs, and he sees no reason for change.

Packer's celebrated love of jazz dates from slightly later. Packer recalls an evening when, aged thirteen, he was painstakingly doing his school homework, with a radio (invariably called 'a wireless' in Britain at that time) on in the background. There was an interval between two consecutive programmes, which had to be filled in some way. The announcer told his audience that he would play them a record to fill the time. Packer stopped doing his homework. His breath was taken away by what he heard. The record in question – Jelly Roll Morton's 'Steamboat Stomp' – got him hooked on the New Orleans jazz of the Morton era. It turned out that the record in question had been waxed in 1926, just two months after his day of birth.

Early Religious Views

In September 1937, Packer left his local National School, and moved on to the Crypt School in Gloucester. The school had a long and distinguished history going back to 1539, and counted among its former pupils the great English preacher and evangelist George Whitefield (1714–70). At that stage in its history, the school was known as 'the school of St Mary de Crypt'. The Crypt School followed the classic English public school pattern of dividing the school into 'houses', each of which was named after a distinguished alumnus. One of the Crypt School's four houses was named after Whitefield.

At this stage, Packer had no real interest in religious matters, and the name of Whitefield meant little to him. His mother and father attended church regularly at St Catherine's, a local Anglican church, and Packer would join them. His mother had been brought up in circles which had been influenced by the Anglo-Catholic revival of the nineteenth century, but made no attempt to force Packer to attend Sunday school. However, at the age of fourteen, at his mother's instigation, Packer consented to be confirmed in his local church. Confirmation, as the Church of England understands it, marks the point at which an individual chooses to affirm his or her faith on their own behalf, rather than simply rely on promises made on their behalf at their baptism by their parents and godparents. In rural England during the 1930s, there was considerable social pressure for children to be confirmed once they were old enough.

He had made his decision, however, rather late in the day, and thus missed out on the regular confirmation classes offered by the vicar of St Catherine's. It was now 1941, and the Second World War was by then having a deep impact on Britain. One result was that many of the young men who would normally have gone into training for ministry in the British churches chose to enlist in the armed forces or other war-related agencies instead. The result was a shortage of younger clergy. The new curate of the Packers' local church, Mark Green, was one of those who had not joined up. He agreed to teach Packer on a one-to-one basis. He was distinctly nervous about the whole thing: he had only just been ordained, and this was his very first preparation for confirmation. Green's instruction reflected the Anglo-Catholic ethos which was then very prominent in England, focusing on the need for personal devotion and preparation for Holy Communion, and the importance of personal morality. The word 'conversion' was never mentioned, to the best of Packer's recollection. Green recalls Packer as a 'shy and reserved youth', who was 'very receptive and attentive' to what he had to say.

On entering the sixth form, Packer chose to specialize in 'classics' – the study of the language, literature and history of ancient Greece and Rome. He was the only pupil in his year who wished to specialize in this area. As a result, he was taught on a one-to-one basis by the headmaster of the school, David Gwynn Williams. Around this time, Packer began to play chess at school with Brian Bone, the son of a local Unitarian minister. Between their games of chess, Bone attempted to convert Packer to Unitarianism. Packer found Bone's arguments unconvincing, not least on account of the Unitarian understanding of Jesus purely as a religious or ethical teacher; nevertheless, their debates raised in his mind the whole question of truth in Christianity. This interest was heightened still further through one of the English masters, who found himself in charge of Packer's sixth-form year during one of their weekly periods. Looking for a book which might stimulate discussion among his students, he settled on a recently-published title which had attracted a lot of attention. The book? C.S. Lewis's *Screwtape Letters.*

Encounter with C.S. Lewis

By this time, the name of Clive Staples Lewis was becoming increasingly familiar to the British public. Lewis had undergone a conversion experience at Magdalen College, Oxford, in the early 1930s, and had begun to write books on Christian themes which were attracting increasing interest on the part of the public. The idea for the book which Packer and his classmates would study had come to Lewis on Sunday, 21 July 1940, as he walked home from church. He would write a series of letters 'as one devil to another', in which he would explore the psychology of temptation from a devil's point of view. The resulting thirty-one 'Screwtape Letters' were published in the *The Guardian* (a now-defunct church paper) over the period 2 May through to 28 November 1941. The work was published as a book in February 1942, and attracted considerable attention.

Being obliged to study the book at school gave Packer a taste for Lewis; it also reinforced his growing interest in the truth of Christianity. At the age of seventeen, he publicly defended at school the truth of the teachings of the Christian creeds against some of their sixth-form atheist critics. It also aroused his interest in the other writings of this increasingly high-profile Christian writer. In January and February 1942, Lewis gave a series of 'broadcast talks' for the British Broadcasting Corporation, each lasting fifteen minutes. These were subsequently published as three short books: *What Christians Believe, Christian Behaviour* and *Beyond Personality.* These three volumes were finally merged in 1952 into a single book – the bestselling classic now known as *Mere Christianity.* Packer read each of the volumes as they appeared during 1943 and 1944. He found himself drawn to Lewis, seeing in him 'both a fellow schoolboy and a wise old uncle simultanously'.[5] At this stage, Packer did not possess a Bible of his own, and found himself poring over a copy of the King James version which belonged to his grandmother.

Preparing for Oxford University

Packer had, of course, other things on his mind at this time as well, not least the question of what to do after school. His headmaster had studied classics at Oxford University, and had been an undergraduate at Corpus Christi College. Packer was not merely his best classics student; he was his *only* classics student. Williams was convinced that Packer had the ability to gain a place at Oxford, and encouraged him to think along these lines. The idea of Packer following in his headmaster's footsteps to the same university and college was clearly appealing to Williams.

In the March 1943 edition of the *Oxford University Gazette*, details were published of two major scholarships to Corpus Christi College in the specific area of classics.[6] At that time, Oxford University offered two different types of scholarships, all of which were offered on a competitive basis: 'closed' scholarships, restricted to certain types of student (such as former members of Eton College, sons of Anglican clergy, or students from the West Riding of Yorkshire). Others were 'open' – in other words, there were no restrictions on potential applicants. The competition for 'open' scholarships was fierce. Corpus Christi College offered two major open scholarships in classics: the Charles Oldham Scholarship, and the Hugh Oldham Scholarship. Both were worth £100 per annum, a very substantial sum at the time. The scholarships would be awarded on the basis of a competitive examination, which would be held in Oxford on Tuesday 7 September of that year.

So in September 1943, Packer went to Oxford to sit the scholarship examinations over a period of two days. It was the first time he had been to the ancient university city. Afterwards, he felt that he had not performed especially well in the examinations. It was not long, however, before the news came through that he had been awarded the prestigious Hugh Oldham Scholarship.[7] Although most young men were being drafted into military service at the age of eighteen, Packer's head injury made him unsuitable for this purpose. As a result, he would be allowed to proceed directly to Oxford, and defer his military service indefinitely. But he was only coming up to the age of seventeen in the summer of 1943; this was deemed to be too young an age at which to begin university. He was advised to wait until the following year.

This left Packer with the remainder of his third sixth-form year at school with nothing in particular to do. He was appointed Head Prefect, an important honour within the British school system of the period, indicating that the school regarded him as serious, responsible and mature. Always a bookish person, Packer found himself continuing to reflect about whatever reality might underlie the Christian faith. Through visits to his local public library, he worked his way through works by Sigmund Freud and Carl Jung, notably the latter's *Psychological Types* and the former's notorious work *Moses and Monotheism*. He became increasingly convinced that there was something real behind Christianity – something which Freud had failed to explain away. He read some of the novels of the great nineteenth-century Russian writer Fyodor Dostoevsky, including *The Idiot, Crime and Punishment,* and *The Brothers Karamazov*, all of which are noted for their treatment of specifically Christian themes. It seemed increasingly to him that Dostoevsky was dealing with something *real.* Tolstoy, whom he also devoured during this final year, seemed to him less satisfactory.

As has been stressed, Packer was something of a loner at this stage in his life. He was a solitary figure, who found greatest pleasure in reading and studying. This does not mean that he was without friends. There were friends throughout his schooldays; he simply did not attach as much weight to those friendships as others of his age might have done. Nevertheless, one of Packer's schoolboy friends proved to have a major influence on him during his final year at school. Eric Taylor entered the sixth form at the Crypt School in the same year as Packer. After two years in the sixth form, Taylor left to go to the University of Bristol; Packer remained at school, studying for the scholarship examinations at the University of Oxford. While in his first year at Bristol, Taylor was converted to Christianity through the ministry of BIFCU (Bristol Inter-Faculty Christian Union). He wrote Packer a series of letters, in which he tried to explain what had happened to him, and how he had discovered a living faith.

Packer found some of Taylor's letters mystifying, especially a longer letter which included a fairly detailed exposition of the final verses of Romans 3. He found himself bewildered by Taylor's interest in justification by faith. In particular, he was puzzled by Taylor's emphasis on a 'saving faith' – a faith which Taylor clearly believed Packer to lack. As Packer had defended the truth of the Christian creeds publicly in school discussions, he found himself wondering what more might be required.

In the final summer vacation before Packer went up to Oxford in 1944, he met up with Taylor for a series of face-to-face discussions about the Christian faith. Despite Taylor's best efforts, Packer still found himself struggling with understanding what it was that he lacked. Didn't he believe all the right things? What more was needed? Perhaps sensing that he lacked the ability to express himself clearly enough, Taylor suggested that

Packer get in touch with the Christian Union at Oxford when he arrived.

A new chapter was about to open in Packer's life. Its contents would have surprised him enormously, if he had known them in advance. For our story now takes a new turn, as Packer prepared to go up to Oxford University. Many before him – and many since – have found that going to Oxford or Cambridge marked a decisive moment of transition in their spiritual lives. We must now tell how Packer's life took on a new direction and meaning.

« 2 »

Oxford: Corpus Christi
College, 1944–8

IN THE SECOND week of October 1944, Packer left his parents to begin his life as an undergraduate at one of the world's most celebrated universities. He travelled to Oxford by rail, making use of the privilege tickets available to employees of the Great Western Railway and their families. The GWR, it has to be said, did not make the journey from Gloucester to Oxford as easy as might have been hoped. Packer had to travel from Gloucester to Cheltenham, then change trains to travel to Kingham, from where he could catch a train travelling directly to Oxford. The entire journey would normally take him between two and two-and-a-half hours. Most of his baggage having been sent on in advance in a small tin trunk, Packer was able to walk the final mile from the GWR station to Corpus Christi College, carrying only a small suitcase.[1]

Oxford was now a ghost town. The war had been going on for five years, and its effects were being felt deeply at every level. Most able-bodied students and academic staff were serving in the armed forces. Entire sections of colleges had been closed down for the duration of the war. At night, the wartime blackout plunged the entire town into a darkness it had probably not known since the Middle Ages. The *Oxford University Gazette*, whose pages traditionally recorded details of university lectures, academic distinctions and examination arrangements, now included material of a more sombre nature. Issue after issue recorded details of Oxford students and fellows who were known or believed to have been killed in action. Many of them were in their early twenties.

Life at Corpus Christi College was fairly dreary at this stage in its history. Those who were students at the time particularly recall the lack of heat and the poor food. Some students were fortunate enough to have electric fires in their rooms. Most, however, had old-fashioned coal fireplaces at a time when coal was in seriously short supply. The library was one of the few rooms in college to be heated, resulting in the presence there of numbers of students whose interests lay more in the relative warmth of their surroundings than the books which it contained. As St Peter's Hall (later to become St Peter's College) had been requisitioned for wartime purposes, a number of St Peter's students were living at Corpus at this time. There were few eighteen-year-old students studying for normal-length degree courses; most were undertaking six-month courses, before going on to do military service. Packer's injury meant that he was one of a very small number of students who had been classified as unfit for military call-up, with the result that they were free to study full-time.

Packer had chosen to focus his studies on classical literature, history and philosophy. The two-part undergraduate course at Oxford which focused on these areas was popularly known as 'Mods' and 'Greats', although the university preferred it to be known as Classical Moderations and *Literae Humaniores*. While most of Oxford's undergraduate courses lasted three years, the intellectual rigour of classical studies demanded four years. The rigorous linguistic, philosophical and historical training which Packer would receive during his time at Oxford is widely regarded as being reflected in his ability, shown in many of his books, to handle complex arguments with ease and clarity. One of Packer's duties as one of the college's classics scholars was to recite a long Latin grace before formal dinner in Hall. This had to be done from memory; the use of 'prompt sheets' was a later concession to human weakness.

But Packer had other things to ponder in addition to his academic studies. He had promised Eric Taylor that he would make contact with the Christian Union while at Oxford. In the event, as it proved, the Christian Union came looking for him. There was a long-standing tradition in Christian Union circles in Oxford to arrange in each college a 'freshers' squash' on the evening of the Thursday before the university full term began. This was a social gathering at which members of the Christian Union would meet new students (traditionally referred to as 'freshers' – a shortened form of 'freshmen'), and interest them in the work and meetings of the university and college Christian Union. Ralph Hulme, the Corpus Christi representative of the OICCU (the traditional acronym of the Oxford Inter-Collegiate Christian Union) sought Packer out, and invited him to this meeting, which took place on Thursday 12 October. Packer was glad to accept; it was something he had intended to follow up in any case. The meeting turned out not to be particularly memorable. The speaker was C.J.B. Harrison, known to his friends as 'Harry the Bean'. Packer can recall nothing of that talk, except that it failed to excite him.

The OICCU

In view of the importance of the OICCU to our narrative, it is appropriate to explore the origins and goals of this student organization in a little more detail.[2] Students with evangelical views found themselves in a distinct minority at both Oxford and Cambridge during the mid-nineteenth century. All students at both universities were required to assent to the Thirty-nine Articles (the official teaching of the Church of England). At this time, the Church of England was becoming increasingly influenced by the Oxford Movement, which laid particular emphasis upon the catholic inheritance of the church, and stressed the importance of liturgy. The result was that evangelicals within the Church of England found themselves under pressure. This was especially the case at the University of Oxford, within which the Oxford Movement had its origins in the 1830s. Daily worship in college chapels (most of which were non- or anti-evangelical) was compulsory. It became increasingly clear that there was a need to establish some form of fellowship for evangelical students. In 1871, the formal requirement that students assent to the Thirty-nine Articles was abolished, allowing students from outside the Church of England access to Oxford and Cambridge. The evangelical presence at Oxford and Cambridge began to increase, encouraged by the new 'Keswick Convention' and the growing ministry of the American evangelistic preachers Moody and Sankey.

In 1877, the CICCU (Cambridge Inter-Collegiate Christian Union) was founded, to be followed in 1879 by its sister organization at Oxford. Instrumental in the founding of the OICCU was Wycliffe Hall, established in 1877 as an evangelical theological college for the training of Oxford graduates for ministry in the Church of England. The first principal of the Hall, Robert Girdlestone, gave considerable support and advice to the new student organization as it slowly grew and established its reputation. The OICCU saw itself as having both an evangelistic and a pastoral role, organizing central meetings Saturday and Sunday evenings, which were devoted to biblical expositions and evangelistic addresses respectively, and weekly Bible studies and prayer meetings in individual colleges. Each college had an 'OICCU rep.' (short for 'representative'), who was responsible for organizing Christian Union meetings within the college, and encouraging attendance at the central meetings. There was some tension between the OICCU and the Student Christian Movement (SCM), a more liberal student organization which absorbed the OICCU for a period of several years during the 1920s.

The outbreak of the Second World War in September 1939 led to serious difficulties for the OICCU. The number of students at Oxford declined steeply. In some colleges, student numbers were so low that they could not sustain a Christian Union group. Several college Christian Union groups had to merge. There was even talk of closing Oxford University for the remainder of the duration of the war. By October 1944, student numbers had reached their lowest ebb. At Corpus Christi College, the total number of undergraduate students had declined to twenty-four, of which twelve were full-course students, and twelve one-year cadets from the armed forces. (It was not until well after the end of the war, during the academic year 1946–7, that the college reached its operating level of about 120 undergraduate students.) However, under its president, David Mullins (a medical student at Trinity College), OICCU was determined to maintain its evangelistic activities. In addition to a biblical exposition on every Saturday evening during university term, there would be an evangelistic sermon preached on every Sunday evening, traditionally known as the 'Sunday evening sermon'.

It was to these activities that Packer was invited on the evening of Thursday 12 October 1944. In the event, he attended the Saturday evening Bible exposition two days later, which developed the theme of the supremacy of Christ, based on Colossians 1. But, to the disappointment of Ralph Hulme, he did not go to the evangelistic address the next evening. It would be the following Sunday that marked a dramatic turning point in the life of James I. Packer.

The Conversion

The turning point came in one of the churches in Oxford city centre. The OICCU did not possess its own meeting hall at this point in its history, and was in the habit of using local churches for its Sunday evening sermons. From 1934, the sermon was preached at St Peter-le-Bailey, which became the chapel of the newly-founded St Peter's College. At times, the sermon was preached at St Columba's Presbyterian church in Alfred Street. During the war, it was occasionally preached at St Giles' church, during a period when the principal of Wycliffe Hall acted as minister-in-charge of that parish. On the evening of Sunday 22 October 1944 – 'Sunday of Second Week', to use the traditional Oxford way of referring to days during university term – the sermon was preached at St Aldate's church, one of the larger churches in the city, noted for its significant student ministry. At this stage, black-out regulations were still in force, and considerable care had to be taken not to let light out through any windows.

The meeting began at 8.15 p.m. Its high point was a sermon preached by the Revd Earl Langston, an elderly Church of England parson from the south-coast resort of Weymouth. The first half of his sermon (which was preached in a rather ponderous manner) left Packer unmoved. But the second half spoke to him deeply. During the next twenty minutes, Langston told his audience of his own conversion, which took place at a boys' camp. There had been some minor thefts from the camp, and some of the boys and leaders had stayed up all night to ensure there were no further losses. He told of how he had been on this 'night watch' at the camp, and had been challenged by one of the camp leaders as to whether he was a Christian or not. It was this challenge which forced him to the recognition that he was not, as a matter of fact, a Christian, and thus led on to his personal response to Christ. He told his audience of how he had then written to his parents and told them of this momentous decision.

During this narrative, Packer suddenly – and traumatically, as he recalls – realized that he was not a Christian. Though not a person given to thinking in images, he found a picture arising from within his mind. The picture was that of someone looking from outside through a window into a room where some people were having a party. Inside the room, people were enjoying themselves by playing games. The person outside could understand the games that they were playing. He knew the rules of the games. But he was outside; they were inside. He needed to come in. He had never come in. His mind focused on the thought: 'I need to come in.'

The sermon reached its end, and the preacher stressed the need to reach out to Christ, and come to him. As had become traditional in those days, the service ended with the singing of Charlotte Elliot's famous hymn, 'Just as I am', with its constant emphasis on coming to Christ. And so, about 100 feet from where the great evangelist George Whitefield committed himself to Christ in 1735, James I. Packer made his own personal commitment. He went back to his room at Corpus Christi College, and – following Langston's example – wrote to his parents to tell them of what had happened to him.

Packer was quite clear as to what had happened to him. He already knew about the basic elements of the Christian faith. He did not need anyone to explain it to him. He had needed to be challenged to 'come inside' – to make a full personal commitment to Christ. What had happened had thus built on his growing understanding of the nature of the truth and reality of the Christian gospel. In effect, Earl Langston had managed to achieve what Eric Taylor had failed to do during that same summer: convince Packer that he lacked saving faith, and challenge him to respond.

The next day, 'the Bean' called round to see him. Harrison had been meticulously following up all the freshers who had attended the squash of ten days ago. Perhaps he had been working though a list of names arranged alphabetically, and had thus left Packer's name till late in the day. Totally unaware of what had happened the previous evening, he seemed to be taken slightly by surprise by what he discovered. After listening to Packer explaining how he had committed himself to Christ, Harrison briefly wrote down a list of key biblical texts on a scrap of paper, before taking his leave, and (presumably) going on to visit the next name on his list. Packer recalls a small degree of wonder that Harrison should have spent so short a time with him. Perhaps 'the Bean' had correctly discerned that Packer did not need any explanation or teaching about what had happened to him, and so left him to reflect on his own.

A further development of importance took place a few weeks later. Packer's initial attitude to the Bible was fairly typical of someone who had grown up within the generally sceptical outlook of English schools at the time. He tended to think of the Bible as nothing more than 'a mixed bag of religious all-sorts, of which one could not accept more than the general outlines'. Although he read Scripture in a devotional frame of mind, he continued in his 'partial scepticism' for a few weeks. Six weeks after his conversion, he attended an OICCU Saturday evening Bible study, at which a visiting speaker (whom Packer recalls as 'an eccentric old man from Cambridge') presented an exposition of one of the chapters of the book of Revelation.[3] At the beginning of the meeting, Packer was a gentle sceptic; at its end, he was convinced that the Bible was the Word of God. Something had happened to bring him to a conscious realization that Scripture was not human instruction or wisdom about God, but was in fact God's own instruction about himself. Later, having studied Calvin, Packer realized that he had experienced in his own life what Calvin referred to as 'the inward witness of the Holy Spirit'.[4]

And so Packer became an active member of the OICCU. Looking back on his long life, he has no hesitation in affirming that he gained all his spiritual nurture from the OICCU at this stage. He became involved in the daily prayer meetings, regarded by many as the spiritual power-house of the OICCU. He joined Ralph Hulme in worshipping at St Aldate's church. The significance of this point needs to be noted. The Church of England dominated the centre of Oxford. Two of its churches – St Aldate's and St Ebbe's – were evangelical in their commitments. However, the precise form of evangelicalism which each adopted was somewhat different, leading to a certain coolness and degree of suspicion between them. Students who attended St Ebbe's tended to regard those who attended St Aldate's as being 'fundamentally unsound'. The rector of St Ebbe's at this time was John Carpenter, who had been deeply involved in the work of the China Inland Mission, and was firmly committed to a strongly Protestant ethic, which chiefly seemed to consist in the avoidance of contamination by the world. In Packer's view, Carpenter's cool preaching style contrasted unfavourably with that of the rector of St Aldate's, F.E. Lunt, who was noted for his ardent rhetoric. Packer avoided St Ebbe's, feeling that it was a cold and unwelcoming place. Eventually, he also became weary of St Aldate's, feeling that the lack of substance to Lunt's preaching was a cause for concern.

In fact, Packer was angry with the Church of England. Why had it not presented him with the full facts of the Christian faith? Why had it not told him of the need for conversion? In response to this sense of frustration with the Church of England, Packer made a point of attending a local meeting of the Plymouth Brethren at James Street in east Oxford. In fact, during his first two years at Oxford, he was more regularly to be found at James Street than at any Anglican church. Many senior OICCU figures had links with the Plymouth Brethren at this stage – such as James Houston and Donald Wiseman, both of whom went on to achieve prominence in their respective fields.

Yet Packer's continued attendance – however infrequent – at St Aldate's during his first year at Oxford led to his being regarded with suspicion by the more theologically correct senior members of the OICCU. James Houston, a leading member of the Plymouth Brethren, felt that Packer had the ability to join the Executive Committee of the OICCU (usually known simply as 'the Exec'). He was overruled. Not only was Packer too recent a convert to be allowed to bear such a weighty responsibility; he was blackballed by the existing committee as unsound, because he worshipped at *St Aldate's.*

There is another aspect of this matter which should be noted. In one major way, Packer was something of an outsider to the circles from which the OICCU selected its leaders. Many of those who would be active in English evangelical student work had already been involved in what were affectionately known as 'Bash camps' – 'Bash' being the affectionate nickname for the Revd Eric Nash, who had established his 'Varsity and Public School' Camp at Iwerne Minster, with the specific purpose of evangelizing public school boys – 'the best boys from the best schools', as Nash used to put it.[5] John R.W. Stott, who had been a schoolboy at Rugby School (a leading English public school immortalized in the novel *Tom Brown's Schooldays*), was heavily involved in these camps, as was David Mullins, the OICCU president during the critical period 1943–6. Donald Wiseman, who eventually became president of the OICCU, recalls that the OICCU was 'under something of a "Bash" influence' when he arrived in November 1945.

Packer was an outsider here. He had been to a local grammar school, not a public school, and had no links with the 'Bash camps'. Evangelical Christianity at Oxford around this time was somewhat élitist, reflecting similar trends in British society as a whole. In a later reflection on his family background – which he modestly described as 'unspectacular' – Packer spoke of his family as '... a quiet unobtrusive lot, rural in our style ... My great-grandfather was a wealthy man who fell on hard times. My grandfather was successively a farmer, miller and innkeeper – doing poorly at each. And my father was a railway clerk in charge of another clerk and two typists.'[6] This was not the background from which the typical aristocratic 'public schoolboy' came. Packer's humble origins may have counted against him at this point, in that some influential members of the Executive Committee of the OICCU were 'VPS campers'. (Note that 'VPS' was always pronounced 'Veeps'.)

It was not his humble origins, but another aspect of Packer's life which caused concern to Ralph Hulme in the Michaelmas term of 1944. All good OICCU members spent their Saturday evenings at the weekly Bible readings, soaking up the wisdom of learned and godly expositors. Packer spent his Saturday evenings playing clarinet with the Oxford Bandits, a jazz band who found their services much in demand at local dances. For the young Packer, the forms of jazz which emerged from New Orleans and Chicago during the 1920s – such as the music of King Oliver, Jelly-Roll Morton, Sidney Bechet, Louis Armstrong, and Eddie Condon's groups – were one of the most important American contributions to modern culture. Packer held that opinion, not simply as one who enjoyed listening to their music, but as one who played it himself. He found playing jazz a very rewarding emotional experience, and aimed to continue this interest at Oxford. He played jazz 'after a fashion', and found it exhilarating.

Towards the end of the Michaelmas term of 1944, Hulme took Packer aside, and chided him gently. Should he not review his priorities? Surely he ought to be at the OICCU Bible readings, rather than playing in a jazz band. Packer conceded the merit of this point, and 'let folk around me think I shared their view that what I called New Orleans and what they called Dixieland had a devilish influence on its devotees'. His career as a jazzman thus ended. However, Packer's allusions to jazz throughout many of his writings indicates both a continuing knowledge of and a love for this form of music.[7]

At the end of this first Michaelmas term, in December 1944, Packer returned home to Gloucester to spend the Christmas vacation with his parents. Oxford University full terms – during which undergraduate teaching was concentrated – lasted a mere eight weeks. Packer was determined not to waste the time at his disposal. He wanted to get to know more about George Whitefield. He had attended the same school as Whitefield, and had been converted in the same city and university. Whitefield had been a student at Pembroke College, next door to St Aldate's church, where Packer himself had come to faith. Although the name of Whitefield had meant nothing to Packer while at school, he determined to find out more about him. He went to the city library, and borrowed the two volumes of Tyerman's 1876 biography of Whitefield.

As it happened, Packer found himself with more time to read Tyerman than he had anticipated; he came down with bronchitis, and was confined to bed. Even in the midst of his wheezing and coughing, he found himself totally absorbed in what he was reading. The narrative of Whitefield's conversion and ministry excited and challenged him. It was like an 'unction from God', a 'milestone' in his spiritual journey. Packer found in Whitefield something of a role model, especially in relation to ecumenical attitudes and the fixing of priorities.[8] For Packer, Whitefield was an Anglican who did not accept any restrictions on his ministry on account of his denominational affiliation. Whitefield's transdenominational vision was reinforced by Packer's experience of the OICCU (which was an interdenominational organization). From then on, Packer would have no time for 'denominationalism' in an exclusive or self-justifying sense. If denominations have value, it is as service agencies for strengthening and sustaining their members, enabling them to do things better than they otherwise could.

It would not be long before Puritan writers would excite and inform Packer, not least in relation to their approach to one issue which was of concern to him during his time at Oxford – sanctification.

Misgivings over 'Victorious Living'

The OICCU was dominated at this stage by an approach to Christianity which is often known as 'victorious living'. This approach, in various forms, was especially associated with the

'Convention for the Deepening of the Spiritual Life', which had been established at the Lake District town of Keswick in 1875. Ruth Paxson's, *The Wealth, Walk and Warfare of a Christian*, a 'victorious living' standby, was enormously influential in OICCU circles at this time. Some of the Saturday evening Bible expositions seemed to end up becoming Keswick 'consecration sermons'. Neither St Ebbe's nor St Aldate's favoured this teaching; its sole source in Oxford at this stage was the OICCU. For Packer, Keswick had become a 'sacred cow' among many evangelicals, advancing an understanding of the nature of the Christian life which was regarded as self-evidently correct, in its handling of the teaching of Scripture. As the history of evangelicalism suggests, the movement has always been vulnerable to expository novelties that promised deeper spiritual enrichment. The remarkable hold which the Keswick holiness teaching gained on Oxford undergraduates in the 1940s is an excellent illustration of this point. Other examples can easily be provided from more recent evangelical history, both in North America and Britain.

The Keswick approach offered what many Christians longed for: full deliverance from sin, and a closer relationship with Jesus Christ than anything that they had yet experienced. The reason that believers did not have this life in all its fullness, according to the Keswick view, was that they had not totally surrendered to Christ. For the later Packer, looking back on this period in his life, the Keswick teaching encouraged believers to expect too much and too little at one and the same time. It suggested that it was possible to have full freedom from bondage to sin from moment to moment, while failing to note the importance of the need to break free from the powerful influence of sin at the level of our motivation. The key to 'victorious living' was to surrender to Christ, and trust totally in his ability to work his will within you, rather than trust in the 'energy of the flesh'. The notion of 'active energetic obedience' was thus criticized as representing a lapse into legalism, and a dangerous reliance on one's own abilities.

During 1945, Packer found himself deeply troubled by this teaching.[9] He longed for the state of sustained victory over sin which the Keswick preachers described and extolled, and in which Christians would be able to avoid failure and be enabled to achieve things which were otherwise beyond them. Yet he found that his attempts at 'total consecration' seemed to leave him exactly where he was before – 'an immature and churned-up young man, painfully aware of himself, battling his daily way, as adolescents do, through manifold urges and surges of discontent and frustration'. Somehow, he felt, 'it all seemed a long way from the victorious, power-packed life which spirit-filled Christians were supposed to enjoy.'

The only remedy his teachers could offer was to 'let go and let God' – in other words, to repeatedly reconsecrate himself, in the hope that he might eventually identify whatever obstacle he was unwittingly placing in the path of the blessings which awaited him. There was a serious tension between the teaching and his experience. Packer never doubted that he was a Christian, nor did he have any questions over the truth of the Christian faith. Both these matters were settled in his mind. The difficulty concerned the tension he was experiencing between a specific way of understanding the Christian life, and his own experience of that life. At least one was clearly deficient. But which?

In the event, an answer was provided from an unexpected quarter – a dusty pile of books, dumped in the basement of a hall used on occasion by the OICCU.

Discovering the Puritans

C. Owen Pickard-Cambridge, formerly a scholar of Balliol College back in the 1880s, was a clergyman of the Church of England, whose distinguished career had included periods as a missionary in Japan and later as vice-principal of the Bible Churchmen's College in Bristol (which later changed its name to Tyndale Hall). His final period of ministry was spent in Leicestershire, in the English east Midlands. He had built up a large collection of seminal Christian books, many of which were classics dating from the sixteenth and seventeenth centuries. Now in his eighties, his growing blindness forced him to face the question of what to do with his books. He himself could no longer benefit from them. So where should they go? Rather than break up the collection, he decided to give it, in its entirely, to the OICCU in 1944. As a result, the OICCU suddenly found itself with a large acquisition of books.

Initially, nobody in the OICCU seems to have known what to do with them. They were piled up in the basement of the North Gate Hall, a meeting hall on St Michael's Street in central Oxford, just opposite the Oxford Union Society. The North Gate Hall was then used for the daily prayer meetings, which had been held in the vestry of the nearby Wesley Memorial Church until 1938. It was large enough for the needs of the OICCU, and had a basement which could be used for storage purposes. The Senior Librarian of the OICCU was the Revd John Reynolds, then curate of St Clement's church, an evangelical parish just outside Oxford city centre. He recalled that Packer was something of a bookworm, and was interested in books. Why not entrust them to him? So, during his second year at Oxford, Packer became the junior librarian for the OICCU.

As Packer sorted through the dusty piles of old books in the basement of the North Gate Hall, he came across an uncut set of the edition of the writings of the Puritan divine John Owen (1616–83) which had been published in twenty-four volumes by W.H. Goold during the years 1850–5. Although the pages had never been cut open, the contents of each volume were printed on the spine. As Packer browsed through the contents of the series, he was pulled up sharply by the titles of two treatises in volume 6 – 'On Indwelling Sin in Believers' and 'On the Mortification of Sin in Believers'. These titles seemed to promise a very different approach from that offered by the Keswick preachers. At this stage, Packer had become intensely aware of his own failings and character defects, and he felt the inadequacy of the 'victorious living' approach. There was a serious tension between the man he was, and the man he wanted to be – and Keswick had no answers to this dilemma.

Intrigued, Packer began to cut the pages of Owen's writings, and to read what he found.[10] Immediately, he found himself challenged by the realism of Owen's analysis both of the problems arising from 'indwelling sin' and of the means of dealing with it (referred to by Owen as 'mortification'). So important was his discovery that he subsequently went on in his third year to type out a twenty-page précis of Owen's arguments, which he circulated to his friends. Owen, it turned out, did not make quite the same impression on those friends as Packer had hoped. But that was not the point. Here was a writer who spoke to Packer's condition, and offered a realistic solution to his concerns. (It must be appreciated that virtually no Puritan works were in print at this time; the rebirth of interest in Puritanism led to the reprinting of numerous Puritan works from 1957 onwards. Packer could not have made this discovery by browsing in his local bookstore!) The discovery of Owen must be regarded as marking a turning point in Packer's Christian life, and we shall consider its implications in more detail in the following chapter.

Others within the OICCU shared that interest, and began to meet regularly to discuss issues of Christian faith and life. The group began meeting one Wednesday evening in the Michaelmas term of 1946. A group of students who had been to a missionary prayer meeting decided not to return to their respective colleges for dinner; instead, they would go on to the 'British Restaurant' – a post-war institution, located on 'the plain', just across Magdalen Bridge, which offered cheap meals and quick service, and was a great favourite with OICCU members in the late 1940s. The main members of the group – which continued to meet regularly for some time – were Packer himself, O. Raymond Johnston (studying modern languages at Queen's College), and Elizabeth Lloyd-Jones, the eldest daughter of Dr Martyn Lloyd-Jones, a noted Welsh Congregationalist preacher who ministered at the Westminster Chapel in central London, and had led a mission to Oxford undergraduates in 1940.

Another important friendship which Packer established at this stage was with Donald Wiseman, who first met Packer in November 1945, after being released from his wartime position as a Group Captain in the Royal Air Force. Wiseman recalls a conversation he had with Packer as the two of them walked together to an OICCU tea party, held at the home of Montague Goodman in north Oxford. Packer expressed his view that there was not enough good evangelical literature available. Wiseman encouraged him to think further about this, and mentioned some agencies which were concerned to redress the situation.

Academic Success

We must not forget, of course, that Packer's original intention in coming to Oxford was to study classics. At the end of his fifth term in the spring of 1945, Packer sat his first public examination in *Literae Humaniores* (usually referred to as 'Classical Moderations'). He was placed in the first class. Bruce Harris (Balliol, 1946–50) recalls hearing of Packer's awesome academic reputation the moment he arrived at Oxford: he 'had been awarded an alpha in every paper of Classical Moderations'.

Packer's excellent results confirmed the very high estimation in which he was held by his teachers and his fellow students. It is clear that he devoted all his efforts as a student to his work and his Christian activities, and did not get involved in other college activities. Students attending the college at the time recall that he was rarely seen in the Common Room. An examination of the six *Pelican Records* (the college journal) published over the period 1945–7 shows that Packer is only mentioned once – and that was to record his first class honours in Classical Moderations. Robert Murray, who was an exact contemporary of Packer's at Corpus, also reading *Literae Humaniores*, formed the impression that Packer's injury to his head seriously limited the social options available to him; sport, for example, would have been out of the question.

During the period 1944–6, all students at Corpus Christi were allowed to live in rooms in the college for three years. If the course lasted for four years (as was the case, for example, with *Literae Humaniores* or Chemistry), students were then obliged to find their own rooms outside college for their final year. Packer and others on four-year courses thus assumed that they would have rooms in college for the academic year 1946–7. Packer looked forward to remaining in his room (Staircase X1R, according to the college list). However, in the summer of 1946, the college authorities decided that, given the increase in student numbers, those about to enter their third year could not be offered rooms in college. Packer was thus obliged to search for a room. In the event, he found lodging at 24 Lincoln Road, a quiet road off the busy Abingdon Road, leading south from the city centre. There was no other student living in the house, allowing Packer to have the front room, and an upstairs bedroom, for his own use. Not having a bicycle, he generally walked daily from his digs to Corpus Christi. Packer lived in these digs for his last two years at Oxford.

His final public examinations took place in the summer of 1948. During the Trinity term of 1948, Christopher Evans arrived as the new Dean of Chapel at the college. Evans – who subsequently became Professor of New Testament at King's College, London – recalls visiting Packer in his digs around the time of the examinations. Packer was widely expected to gain a double first (in other words, first class honours in both first and second public examinations). In fact, he came very close to achieving this. His written examination papers were close enough to the required standards in both ancient history and philosophy to merit his examiners summoning him for a *viva voce* examination in these subjects. Packer obtained an outstanding second class degree – but not the first class degree he hoped for.

Packer and Evans would meet again in Oxford, as we shall see. But this lies some way ahead. Our narrative now turns to a question which was preoccupying Packer during much of his time at Oxford. What would he do next? One possibility was to become a schoolmaster, teaching classics to sixth-formers in much the same way as David Gwynn Williams had taught him earlier. But what were the alternatives? What place was there within the providence of God for a shy, introverted young man, whose greatest pleasure was to bury himself in a good book? In the next chapter, we shall explore the beginnings of Packer's call to minister and to teach.

«3»
London: Oak Hill College, 1948–9

IN THE MICHAELMAS term of 1945, a year after his conversion, Packer found certain thoughts about his future crystallizing in his mind. Should he consider offering himself for ordination? Others had certainly made this suggestion to him. Even while in his final year in the sixth form at the Crypt School in Gloucester, Eric Taylor's mother (who had a disconcerting clairvoyant gift) had told him that she was sure he would end up in the Christian ministry. Packer was dismissive of this suggestion at the time. What could he offer anyone? He could defend the creed against its sceptical critics. Beyond that, he considered that he had nothing of any significance to say. Nevertheless, Mrs Taylor's words remained in his mind. She had been right about other matters of importance. Why not this one also?

Reflecting on Ministry

However, the call to ministry inevitably raised a question: ministry in which church? For Packer, there could only be one answer: the Church of England. This may seem surprising. As we have seen, Packer felt angry and betrayed by the Church of England immediately after his conversion, on account of the failure of that church in earlier years to present him with the full facts of the Christian gospel. He was also unimpressed by the calibre of the two Oxford rectors whom he knew best. The rector of St Aldate's was an orator who lacked any real substance; the rector of St Ebbe's was cold and unwelcoming. The Brethren congregation at James Street seemed much more attractive to him.

Nevertheless, Packer experienced a growing sense that he was intended for ministry in the Church of England. He was aware of some slight gifts as a teacher, but was far from sure that these would be enough to be able to serve him well and sustain him in a typical English school. His own judgment is that he might well have been a fairly competent teacher of classics to sixth-formers; that competence, however, would steadily diminish if he had to teach younger pupils. For the best part of a year, Packer considered his options. He was convinced that, being shy, he did not relate easily or naturally to other people. In particular, he felt (as he still feels) acute difficulty in speaking to children. This, he argued to himself, was inevitably going to cause him difficulties in ministry. Yet he was convinced that – whatever the difficulties – he wanted to minister to the people of God.

Finally, during his third year at Oxford, in 1946, Packer spent a long Sunday afternoon thinking and praying about his future. In his digs at 24 Lincoln Road, he painstakingly assembled on a sheet of paper all the reasons he could think of for and against being ordained. By the end of the afternoon, he sensed strongly that he should go ahead with exploring the possibility of ordination. Whatever gifts and talents he lacked, he would rely on the Lord to provide. Somehow and somewhere, he was needed in the service of God as a teacher of biblical truth and a preacher of the gospel.

The Selection Process

Packer therefore began the process of applying to be considered for ordination by the Church of England. The section of the church responsible for this was known as CACTM (an acronym for 'Central Advisory Council on Training for the Ministry'). The Candidates' Secretary was the same Revd Mark Green who had prepared Packer for confirmation while he was a curate at St Catherine's, Gloucester. For this reason, it was an easy matter for Packer to approach Green, and set the procedures in motion. Packer was required to provide the names of two referees, and gave the name of his former vicar in Gloucester (who commended him as 'a faithful churchgoer') and Frank Lepper, his ancient history tutor at Corpus, who was also the college dean.

In due course, Packer was invited to a selection conference

early in 1947, at which he was interviewed by a group of selectors concerning his motivation for offering himself for ministry, his pastoral gifts, and his educational achievements. The selection conferences were introduced immediately after the Second World War, and were modelled on the conferences used by the British government to select senior civil servants and officers in the armed forces. Typically, the conference involved three days spent with other candidates and five selectors. The candidate would have private interviews with each of the selectors, after which they would confer and reach a decision on each of the candidates attending the conference. Packer felt happy with the way the conference went. His sense of vocation was so strong that he determined that, if he was turned down, he would reapply at the first available opportunity.

This proved unnecessary. Within a week, he had his answer from Mark Green. He had been accepted.

And so Packer began to prepare to train for ministry in the Church of England. But what sort of church would he be serving? If we are to understand the major contribution which Packer would make to the redirecting of the increasingly influential evangelical wing of the Church of England in the 1960s, we need to gain an understanding of the difficulties it was in during the 1940s. In what follows, we shall survey the sorry state of evangelicalism in the English national church during Packer's student days.

The Church of England in the Late 1940s

The Church of England can be regarded as the result of the massive programme of religious and social change which swept through western Europe in the sixteenth century. The European Reformation witnessed demands for the medieval church to reform its teachings and practices, returning to more biblical models. Martin Luther (1483–1547) and John Calvin (1509–64) were two of the leading lights of this movement, which had a major impact on western continental Europe. England was also affected by the Reformation. Under Henry VIII, a series of reforming measures were put in place. These were consolidated during the reign of Edward VI. After a brief period of reversion to Roman Catholicism under Mary Tudor, the English national church continued its process of Reformation under Elizabeth

I, resulting in the famous 'Elizabethan Settlement' of 1559. The basics of this settlement can be thought of in terms of the Church of England becoming a Reformed national church, with a Protestant set of beliefs (set out clearly in the Thirty-nine Articles of 1563), which were reinforced by a 'Book of Common Prayer' which embodied Reformed understandings of the gospel and the nature of the church and sacraments. Under the Settlement, the Church of England retained the traditional episcopal system of church government and the practice of clergy wearing vestments. Both these issues would become matters of contention with the growing number of Puritans within the church in the late sixteenth and early seventeenth centuries.

However, as time went by, the Church of England gradually lost its close association with the ideas and practices of the Reformation. The rise of Deism and a form of theological liberalism usually known as Latitudinarianism during the eighteenth century eroded the influence of evangelicalism. Although a major evangelical revival developed during that same century, it had faded away by the 1830s. During the remainder of the nineteenth century, the history of the Church of England was dominated by the rise of Anglo-Catholicism (a 'high church' movement, linked with the Oxford Movement), and the growth of modernism and liberalism. Between the First and Second World Wars, the general growth of liberalism within the Church of England was supplemented by the rise of 'Liberal Evangelicalism'. The strongly liberal 'Group Brotherhood', which began meeting in 1907, 'went public' in 1925 with the publication of a work entitled *Liberal Evangelicalism.* The result was that evangelicalism became seriously disunited and fragmented by the eve of the Second World War.

After the Second World War, evangelicalism was in a sorry state in England. It had lost any positions of power it once had in the national church. It was numerically weak. It was treated with something approaching contempt by academics, especially academic theologians. It was dominated by forms of Pietism which stressed the importance of personal intimacy with Jesus, yet discounted as an irrelevance any serious thinking or engagement with theological issues. It was a movement with a distinguished past, but apparently no viable future. Hensley Henson (1863–1947), Bishop of Durham, dismissed it as 'an army of illiterates, generalled by octogenarians'. With exceptions as honourable as they were few, the movement was characterized by an anti-intellectual defensiveness, nourished by a separatist mentality.

For a convinced evangelical, such as Packer, to go into ministry in the Church of England at this stage was rather like a Daniel volunteering to enter the lions' den. It seemed that there was no place and no future for evangelicals inside that church. They were few in number, and were left in no doubt that they were unwanted. In the post-war period, the Church of England witnessed a major surge in the number of men wishing to be ordained, and a growth in its church life at every level. It seemed that its future was secure. The kind of evangelicalism which Packer represented – which at this stage was generally identified with 'fundamentalism' – was widely regarded as immature, simplistic, irrelevant and unreasonably dogmatic. For Packer to choose to minister in such a church was, quite simply, a step of faith. Could things be changed? In the closing years of the 1940s, there were few reasons to think so. But Packer kept his counsel.

The Church of England required its ordinands to study at one of a number of recognized theological colleges.[1] But which one? A number of factors pointed to Wycliffe Hall as a suitable candidate. The then principal of Wycliffe Hall, Julian Thornton-Ducsbury, had earlier been a fellow of Corpus Christi College. In addition to introducing Packer to St Aldate's church, Ralph Hulme also took Packer along to the local meetings of the Church Missionary Society.[2] At the CMS meetings in Oxford, Packer got to know James Hickinbotham, the vice-principal of Wycliffe Hall, along with one or two other Wycliffe students. For reasons such as this, Packer felt that he would fit in reasonably well at Wycliffe.

He was due to graduate in June 1948, and expected to go directly to Wycliffe Hall with effect from September of that same year. Packer had become convinced of the need to take a degree in theology in order to be of maximum service in his future calling as a minister and preacher, and wished to continue studying at Oxford. By special arrangement, he would be allowed to study theology as a second first degree through Corpus Christi College, while residing and being tutored at Wycliffe Hall. But things would not quite work out as Packer expected. A door opened unexpectedly, as we shall see.

Tutor at Oak Hill College

By the late spring of 1948, Packer was beginning to have some misgivings about a direct move from Corpus Christi College to Wycliffe Hall. Surely he needed more experience of the world? And while he loved Oxford, he had the sense that he would benefit from being away from the city and university for a while. After the best part of four years at Oxford, Packer was discovering that he was finding its academic élitism 'stuffy'. To go directly to Wycliffe Hall might well turn out to be like entering an airless room. It was, however, far from clear how he could take a year or so out in this way, or what he would do during it. Then the good providence of God intervened.

Just before his final examinations, Packer happened to meet John Reynolds at one of the daily prayer meetings. Reynolds, as we have already noted, was the Senior Librarian of the OICCU and a curate at St Clement's, Oxford. He had just received a letter from Leslie Wilkinson, the principal of Oak Hill College in north London, who needed a temporary teacher of Latin and Greek for a period of twelve months. For Reynolds, Packer was the obvious person to approach for the job; for Packer, it seemed a heaven-sent opportunity to get away from the cramping world of Oxford. This totally unexpected invitation seemed ideal. He wrote immediately to Wilkinson, expressing interest in the position, and was summoned to Oak Hill for an interview. At the end of the interview, Wilkinson offered Packer the position for a period of one year, at a salary of £200, to which would be added his board and lodging during terms and vacation. This allowed Packer to stay at Oak Hill during vacations, rather than having to return to his parents (which was his custom during his time at Oxford).

Oak Hill College was founded in 1932 with the aim of 'training persons who are desirous of obtaining ordination in the Church of England and are without adequate means'. It was located in Southgate, in the outer London suburb of Enfield. The college took its name from the home of Charles Baring-Young (1850–1928), whose original vision lay behind the college, which was founded after his death. From 1946, the three leading members of the teaching staff of the college were L.F.E. Wilkinson (Principal, but always referred to as 'Wilkie' by the students), Alan Stibbs (Vice-Principal), and J. Stafford Wright (Senior Tutor).[3] The last-mentioned had formerly been vice-principal at the Bible Churchmen's Missionary Society College in Bristol. These were assisted by a number of part-time lecturers, including Alan Cole and (1948–9) James Packer.

It is tempting to pass over this year in Packer's life as an interlude between studying classics at Corpus Christi College, and going on to study theology at Wycliffe Hall. However, this would be to fail to appreciate the importance of this year to Packer's development. In what follows, we shall explore three areas in which the year at Oak Hill was of significance in this regard.

First, the year marked the establishment of significant friendships, which would make an important impact on Packer's growth in confidence and maturity. He was deeply impressed by Alan Cole, who taught Greek and Hebrew, and subsequently went on to exercise a valuable teaching ministry in Australia and Singapore. Alan Cole recalls Packer's 'slow, careful way, Gloucester accent, and methodical argument', which led some at the college to write him off as 'a slow country boy from Gloucester'. Cole himself, however, had no doubt that Packer's thorough, rigorous and systematic approach to theology would make an impression in the evangelical constituency. In particular, Packer formed a close personal friendship with Alan Stibbs (known to the students as 'Stibbo'), who lectured in doctrine and New Testament. Stibbs was highly valued by the students as a fine expositor of Scripture. He was in the habit of illustrating his lectures with 'Stibbean asides', which students noted down and incorporated into their own sermons and talks. Stibbs treated Packer as an equal, and in the course of many long walks in and around the extensive grounds of Oak Hill, encouraged Packer in his thinking about his future ministry and teaching. Packer and Stibbs remained close friends until the latter's death.

Second, Packer discovered that he could teach. Perhaps he inherited something from his mother in this area; she had been a successful teacher of junior pupils (that is, the seven to ten age range) before her marriage. 'I discovered', Packer remarked, 'that nobody needed to teach me how to teach.' Although Packer's main responsibility was to teach Latin and Greek to those students who needed them in order to meet the matriculation requirements of the University of London, he also ended up teaching some philosophy.[4] His students recall his teaching skills with unanimous praise. 'Meticulous' and 'careful' are two adjectives used frequently to describe Packer's teaching style. Even those who were not taught by him personally recall the prevailing impressions of Packer the teacher among the student body. As a person, he was considered a little shy and withdrawn, lacking in self-confidence; as a teacher, he was seen as caring, competent and considerate. 'Jim was an excellent teacher, and got the best out of his students' will serve admirably as a summary of the impression he made.

Packer thus found Oak Hill a profoundly affirming experience, both personally and professionally. At the professional level, it was clear that he had a natural ability to teach. His slow and precise mode of speaking, which in some situations might be a disadvantage, proved to be ideal in the context of lectures. He also found that he was able to develop the number of areas in which he taught. At the formal level, he was qualified to teach Greek and Latin languages, as well as ancient history and philosophy. Yet these soon expanded to include some biblical areas. For example Packer found himself teaching Oak Hill students the text of Ephesians in Greek, in preparation for the General Ordination Examination. He had been a member (along with Bruce Harris and others) of a Greek New Testament reading group, which met regularly at Balliol for a short time; he was thus well familiar with the problems of handling the Greek text of the New Testament, and this unquestionably helped him with this group of students.

As Packer contemplated the future, and wondered what it held for him, it was now quite clear to him that a teaching ministry in a theological college such as Oak Hill was a real – and also an attractive – possibility. But how could he achieve this? As he reflected on his time at Oak Hill, he became increasingly convinced that he should undertake serious theological research. Although he had been impressed by the commitment and energy of many of those whom he had known at Oak Hill, it seemed to him that the future needs of evangelicalism demanded theological rigour and academic respect.

As his thoughts moved on from those staff members whom he knew at Oak Hill, he went over in his mind the academic qualifications of all those whom he knew to be teaching at the evangelical theological colleges within the Church of England. Only one of these staff members, to his knowledge, had a doctorate, and that was in modern languages, rather than theology. This was Geoffrey

Bromiley, who was then tutor in doctrine at the Bible Churchmen's Missionary Society College in Bristol (and who subsequently went on to a distinguished career at Fuller Theological Seminary, in Pasadena, California). The anticipation of the future needs of the church convinced Packer that he should seriously explore the possibility of following up his proposed Bachelor of Arts in theology at Oxford with a research programme leading to the Oxford degree of Doctor of Philosophy. It was unclear how he could raise the necessary funding for this project; however, he decided he would cross this particular bridge when he came to it.

Third, Packer's time at Oak Hill led directly to the establishment of the 'Puritan Conferences', which would have considerable impact on British evangelicalism during the 1950s and early 1960s. The germ of the idea came from Packer and his close friend O. Raymond Johnston.[5] Johnston had left Oxford in the summer of 1947, intending to pursue a career as a teacher of modern languages. As he wished to include a specialization in religious education in his teaching career, he decided to work for a Diploma in Theology at London Bible College during the academic year 1947–8, and follow this during the next academic year (1948–9) by studying at the University of London Department of Education, in order to gain the necessary qualifications to become a teacher of modern languages.

As a result, both Packer and Johnston were working in London for the academic year 1948–9. We have already noted their enthusiasm for the Puritan inheritance, and their conviction that it remained relevant to the spiritual, pastoral and theological needs of the modern church. In the summer of 1948, Johnston published an article entitled 'John Owen: A Puritan Vice-Chancellor'. Such a positive attitude towards the Puritans was, however, definitely a minority viewpoint at this time. However, Packer and Johnston were becoming increasingly aware of a significant voice outside the Church of England, which was championing ideas very similar to their own.

Dr Martyn Lloyd-Jones had succeeded Dr Campbell Morgan as minister of Westminster Chapel in 1943. Although the two men had both been involved in ministry at the Chapel since 1938, Morgan's decision to retire left Lloyd-Jones in charge. Under his ministry, Westminster Chapel was developing a reputation as a leading centre for Reformed preaching in England's capital city. Its Welsh minister had famously been referred to as 'the last of the Calvinistic preachers'. While this comment shows a lack of prescience, given subsequent events, it nevertheless correctly points to the general theological stance adopted in those sermons. Lloyd-Jones's active involvement in student work also ensured that he was well-known as a significant evangelical thinker to a rising generation of students. For example, in December 1946, he spoke on the theme of 'The Authority of the Bible' at the Theological Students' Conference at St Hugh's College, Oxford. Among his audience was the young Packer, who later remarked that he considered the speaker 'grim and austere, but vastly impressive'.

Oak Hill was located in the greater London region of Enfield, within easy reach of central London and its rich church life. Packer already knew the Lloyd-Jones family from hearing Martyn Lloyd-Jones speak at some Inter-Varsity Fellowship meetings, and especially through his friendship with Lloyd-Jones's elder daughter Elizabeth, during their time at Oxford. (The Inter-Varsity Fellowship – later to become the 'Universities and Colleges Christian Fellowship' – was the student evangelical organization which included the OICCU). Johnston had discovered Lloyd-Jones's preaching skills during his year at London Bible College. He had formed the habit of attending All Souls, Langham Place on Sunday mornings (to hear John R.W. Stott, who had become a curate of this church in 1946), and Westminster Chapel on Sunday evenings (to hear Martyn Lloyd-Jones).

Packer went down to London for several weekends during this year, and went along both to tea parties at All Souls, and subsequently to hear Lloyd-Jones at Westminster Chapel. It took little in the way of persuasion for him to become a regular and appreciative member of the congregation of Westminster Chapel on Sunday evenings during his year at Oak Hill. He admired Lloyd-Jones's preaching style, and began to base his own style on that modelled by the great Welsh orator. It was probably inevitable that Packer, Johnston and Lloyd-Jones should form some sort of relationship, given this important common interest and concern. And so the seed which led to the rebirth of interest in Puritanism within British evangelicalism was sown. We will return to this development later in our narrative.

This chapter of Packer's career closes on a strongly positive note. The academic year 1948–9 had been a happy period in his life, as well as offering him formative experiences and insights which helped him clarify his thinking on his future. As he prepared to return to Oxford to begin his theological studies and ministerial preparation, life seemed to offer some very exciting possibilities indeed. The future, under God's good providence, seemed to beckon to him, inviting him onward.

«4»
Oxford: Wycliffe Hall, 1949–52

IN SEPTEMBER 1949, Packer returned to Oxford to begin theological studies at Wycliffe Hall. He knew Wycliffe reasonably well from his time as a student at Corpus Christi College, and had got to know the vice-principal, Jim Hickinbotham, through a shared interest in overseas missionary work. Initially, it seemed that Packer would spend little more than a year at Wycliffe, before going on to ordained ministry in an English parish. However, as we shall see, his academic excellence resulted in a change of plans, with important results for his future career.

Wycliffe Hall

Wycliffe Hall, situated to the north of the university area of Oxford, was established in 1877 to provide evangelical theological education for Oxford graduates wishing to be ordained into the Church of England. During its first forty years, the college maintained a strongly evangelical emphasis, and was closely linked with work amongst students at Oxford University. The OICCU was established at Wycliffe Hall in 1879. After the First World War, Wycliffe Hall began to be affected by the growing influence of liberal evangelicalism, leading to a loss of its evangelical distinctiveness. It was not until the 1970s that the Hall reasserted its evangelical ethos. During the period 1935–70, Wycliffe Hall was widely regarded as a liberal Protestant college, with little genuine evangelical commitment.

OICCU members were a significant minority within the student body at Wycliffe during Packer's time; substantially more students at the Hall were members of the Student Christian Movement (SCM), which was more liberal in its outlook. The general consensus of the students who studied at the Hall around or during the period 1949–52 is that it was middle-of-the-road Church of England, with a definite evangelical bias in some areas, and a distinctively low church ethos which was seen most clearly in the consistent celebration of Holy Communion from the 'north side'.[1]

The principal in 1949 was Julian Thornton-Duesbury. He was a deeply religious man (an 'evangelical monk', in the view of some of his students), who was almost invariably referred to as 'T.D.' (on account of his surname), but was also occasionally referred to as 'the Honk' on account of his larger-than-life laugh. Thornton-Duesbury was widely respected; however, he had close associations with the organization variously known as 'the Oxford Group' or 'Moral Rearmament', which was regarded by evangelicals as being somewhat moralist in its outlook, and having a weak understanding of the achievement of Christ on the cross. This meant that 'T.D.' was regarded with at least some degree of suspicion by many evangelicals at Oxford. (This cannot be regarded as casting any doubt on his Christian orthodoxy. It should be noted that it was at this stage that the reputation of C.S. Lewis was reaching its zenith at Oxford; Lewis, as far as can be ascertained from the records, was never asked to speak at any meeting sponsored by the OICCU, in that he was regarded as slightly unsound by their standards.) Other staff members at this stage included Jim Hickinbotham (vice-principal), Arthur Berry (chaplain), and Douglas Jones (Old Testament). All were regarded by the students as more definitely evangelical (in various degrees) than the principal.

The daily routine at Wycliffe Hall was fairly typical of a theological college of the Church of England at this time. Morning Prayer was said at 7.30 a.m., followed by a Quiet Time at 8.00. After breakfast at 8.30, the morning's programme of lectures would begin at 9.00 with 'G.T.', and end at 1.00. 'G.T.' was a daily Bible exposition; its name derived from the original title 'Greek Testament'. Following the traditional Oxford pattern, lectures were of one hour in duration. Lunch was served at 1.00, leaving the afternoons free for the sporting activities which were a major feature of student life at the time. Wycliffe Hall had its own tennis courts and croquet lawn, and was conveniently close to the University Parks, where other sporting activities could be pursued. Afternoon tea was served at 4.00 (the principal joining the students for this important social event). Evening Prayer was said at 6.30, followed by dinner at 7.00. The remainder of the evening was intended for study. Saturday was regarded as a normal teaching day; Sunday was set aside for practical experience of ministry in local churches. Many of the students were 'returned warriors' (as they were known in Oxford), ex-servicemen of considerable experience, who did not always fit in well with those who lacked such wartime experience.

Life at Wycliffe was grim. The buildings were bare, functional and unheated. The food was a constant source of complaint. The Hall's cook at this stage was a vegetarian, and was prone to dispense nut cutlets, tasting like cardboard. The smell of boiled cabbage somehow managed to permeate much of the area around the kitchen, especially the nearby reading room. Food rationing was in operation for several years after the war had ended, with the result that institutions were seriously restricted in terms of what they could offer. The local 'Joe Lyons' teashop in Cornmarket Street became a regular haunt of food-starved ordinands in those harsh days. One student with access to alternative food sources was Sumner Walters, an American who studied at Wycliffe from 1949 to 1952. Walters, whose father was a bishop in the Episcopal Church in California, wrote home regularly, recording his impressions of life at Wycliffe Hall during this period. The quality of the food is a constant source of comment: the meals were 'mostly potatoes, bread, cereals and soup'. The arrival of food parcels from home did much to relieve his distress. Other Wycliffe students had long since accepted the situation as normal, and learned to cope with the deprivations.

There were fifty-four students at Wycliffe during the year 1949–50, with the result that the Hall community was small enough for everyone to get to know each other. Students of the period remember Packer well. He served as one of the editors of *The Lollard*, the Hall's student newspaper, and for a while was captain of the Wycliffe Hall table tennis team. Packer's room was No. 12, situated in the part of the Hall known as 'Old Lodge'. Ralph Thomas shared a room with Packer in his first year, and recalls being impressed by his intellectual abilities, and his monumental knowledge of the Bible, Christian theology, and the Thirty-nine Articles. Despite his clear academic inclinations, Thomas recalls that 'he was a friend to us all'.

One student with whom Packer formed a particularly close

friendship was John Gwyn-Thomas. Packer met Gwyn-Thomas over their first evening meal together in September 1949 at Wycliffe Hall.[2] All the students were strangers to each other, and conversation was thus 'exploratory, hearty and random'. Sitting opposite Packer in Wycliffe's somewhat austere dining room was Gywyn-Thomas, who Packer recalls as 'a grinning little Welshman'. Packer mentioned that he was a Puritan addict, and explained that he especially valued their thinking on mortification. 'Mortification!', Gwyn-Thomas responded. 'Let's have a talk after the meal.' And so the two of them crossed the road into the University Parks, and spent two hours walking up and down the banks of the River Cherwell, discussing the theme of mortification. Packer explained how John Owen's sixty pages on mortifying sin had helped him cope with 'a popular brand of holiness teaching, which was driving [him] round the bend'. Gwyn-Thomas told of his experiences of forms of Christian perfectionism which failed to take the reality of sin seriously. The conversation confirmed Packer's view of the realism of the Puritan world-view, and his growing determination to develop and apply it further.

But first, he had to study theology at a more general level. His first academic year at Wycliffe Hall was devoted to acquiring a thorough grounding in Christian theology.

Theological Studies, 1949–50

Packer was able to benefit from a provision which allowed graduate students to complete the Oxford University Final Honour School of Theology in one year. He had used his time at Oak Hill well. During college vacations, he had begun some of the academic work which he knew he would have to undertake at Wycliffe Hall. By the time he returned to Oxford, he had virtually completed all the requirements for the Old Testament papers for the Final Honour School of Theology. He had already decided that he would not study Hebrew; there was simply not enough time at his disposal to master another language. His competence in Greek, and familiarity with the text of the New Testament, would make the study of the New Testament relatively easy. He had found time to read enough books on church history to allow him to feel competent in this area. Packer, as we have seen, was something of a self-starter, and was perfectly capable of immersing himself in study without needing constant supervision and guidance.

The vice-principal of Wycliffe Hall, Jim Hickinbotham, was Packer's tutor in early Christian history and thought (usually referred to as 'patristics'). At this stage, Packer tended to think of early Christian writers such as Augustine as at best 'beginners' – enthusiastic but not particularly competent or helpful – and at worst enemies, in that their teaching and ministry led to the emergence of the Catholic church. (One of the changes that Packer noticed taking place during his long career is his growing respect for these writers; he would now tend to think of them as 'wise men', whose wisdom should be heeded.)

Douglas Jones supervised Packer's Old Testament studies. Noting that Packer already seemed to have worked his way systematically through all the necessary material, Jones suggested that he should feel free to continue his studies on his own, and ask him for help as and when he needed it. It was an arrangement which suited Packer perfectly; it also suited Jones, who was busy learning Ugaritic, and needed all the time he could get to master the intricacies of this ancient Near Eastern language.

Not all Packer's teachers were based at Wycliffe Hall. He also decided to take a special paper in the philosophy of religion, building on his expertise in this field gained from studying classical philosophy in his first phase at Oxford. His studies in this area were supervised by the chaplain of Balliol College, F.W.L. MacCarthy-Willis-Bund, who was surprised that an evangelical should be interested in (still more, competent in) analytical philosophy. MacCarthy was especially interested in classical and modern Thomism, which was on the verge of a revival at this stage through the writings of Jacques Maritain and Étienne Gilson.

Packer also recalls attending the lectures by Austin Farrer in this area, and being stimulated by the ideas of this remarkable Oxford philosopher. For Packer, Farrer was a 'class A genius', a philosopher of religion who showed a genuine concern for New Testament scholarship and systematic theology, even if Packer had misgivings concerning his exegetical methods. More significantly, Packer regarded Farrer's Bampton Lectures, *The Glass of Vision*, as coming very close to recognizing the need for propositional revelation, even if Farrer himself stopped short of this idea.

Packer threw himself into his studies with vigour and enthusiasm.

He was never one for last-minute preparation or revision for examinations; all had been done well in advance. The examinations for the Final Honour School of Theology took place in June 1950. Geoffrey Shaw, a fellow student at Wycliffe, was due to sit the same examinations as Packer. Shaw recalls walking round the gardens of Wycliffe Hall shortly before the examinations were due to start. Packer was eating an apple (his lunch, as it turned out). After a while, Shaw looked nervously at his watch, and remarked that he felt he could just manage to fit in some last-minute revision before the examination started. He returned to his room, but noticed that Packer continued to walk round the gardens, eating his apple. Packer clearly did not feel the need for further revision. The examination results were duly published: Packer obtained first-class honours, Shaw was placed in the second class.[3]

One result of this was that Packer was asked to teach biblical theology and philosophy of religion for St Michael's House, an institution of about thirty students run by the Church Society to prepare women for ministry. The House was located at 119 Banbury Road, merely a few minutes' walk from Wycliffe Hall. This experience was especially useful, in that Packer would subsequently teach biblical theology for the same external London qualification – the Diploma in Theology – at Bristol later in his career.

Packer's dazzling performance in theology also solved a problem he had been wrestling with. As we noted, during his time at Oak Hill, Packer had conceived the idea of undertaking doctoral research. But how could he afford this? His parents were poor, and he had no private means. The £200 he had earned for his teaching at Oak Hill was nearly spent. The Church of England had supported him for his first year at Wycliffe Hall, but would not have had any interest in supporting further studies of the kind he had in mind. Now, on the strength of his examination result, came the news that he had been awarded a Liddon Theological Studentship (a source of funds for theological research at Oxford, established and named after the noted nineteenth-century Oxford theologian H.P. Liddon) for two years, as well as a Local Education Authority grant from his home city of Gloucester. These two awards, both of which were confirmed during the summer of 1950, allowed Packer to take his interest in the Puritans further, and made his intellectual abilities crystal clear.

Doctoral Research, 1950–2

Packer's outstanding result allowed him to make the necessary arrangements to begin doctoral research.[4] It was clear that he had the ability to undertake research leading to the degree of Doctor of Philosophy; what remained to be decided was the precise subject area he would research, and the identity of the person who would supervise his studies.

The former issue was relatively easily settled. Packer's growing interest in the theology of the Puritans had led him to explore the writings of Richard Baxter (1615–91). Although primarily noted for his pastoral writings, Baxter was also a theologian of some stature. Packer had noted some points of interest – and especially some points of difficulty of interpretation – in Baxter's writings, and felt that Baxter's understanding of the doctrine of salvation would be both an interesting and academically significant area of research. It thus remained to find a Baxter expert (who would preferably also be a Baxter enthusiast) to oversee his research. Packer had an idea in this regard, but was not sure whether it would be acceptable to the university authorities.

Packer decided to resolve the matter by visiting Claude Jenkins, the ageing Regius Professor of Ecclesiastical History at Oxford. Packer explained that he wanted to undertake research on the doctrine of salvation as set out in the writings of the Puritan theologian Richard Baxter, and suggested that the most appropriate supervisor for this work would be Geoffrey F. Nuttall.

Nuttall had read *Literae Humaniores* at Balliol during the 1930s. He was then ordained as a Congregationalist minister, before beginning a long period as a lecturer at New College, London. His most significant work was *The Holy Spirit in Puritan Faith and Experience*, which was published by Basil Blackwell in 1946. The work, which was based on a long period of work on Puritan writers, was hailed as a masterpiece, and earned Nuttall the Oxford degree of Doctor of Divinity. Packer could have wished for no finer or more knowledgeable academic supervisor. Although the two men were different in temperament and outlook, Nuttall's vast understanding of Puritanism proved invaluable to stimulating Packer's thought. Packer tended to regard Nuttall as a liberal in the mould of F.D.E. Schleiermacher; Nuttall tended to regard Packer as a biblical positivist in the tradition of Karl Barth.

Jenkins was familiar with Nuttall's work; indeed, he had recently acted as an assessor of Nuttall's *Holy Spirit in Puritan Faith and Experience* for the Oxford degree of Doctor of Divinity. However, in Jenkins's view, there was a problem. Nuttall was not a member of the Oxford University Faculty of Theology, and Jenkins thus believed that he could not act as Packer's supervisor. Nevertheless, some arrangement appears to have been arrived at, apparently based on the fact that Nuttall had been awarded an Oxford DD, which was regarded as conferring at least some nominal association with Oxford's Faculty of Theology. It was not long afterwards that Packer received a formal letter on behalf of the graduate studies committee of the Faculty of Theology. His proposed subject of study had been accepted, and Dr Geoffrey Nuttall had been appointed as his supervisor. Packer was asked to get in touch with Nuttall, so that arrangements might proceed. Nuttall recalls that the arrangements for supervision were very unusual, reflecting the fact that he was not formally a member of the Oxford Faculty of Theology. He would meet up regularly each term with Packer at his home or at Dr Williams's Library in London, which was noted for its significant holdings of Puritan literature. As each draft chapter of his thesis was completed, Packer would mail it to Nuttall for his comments.

Work began in earnest in September 1950. Packer thus had seven Oxford terms in which to complete his research. At first, the research was unrewarding. Packer was obliged to work through a substantial body of secondary literature dealing with Baxter and related matters, which seemed to him to fail to penetrate to the core of the matter. It was not an inspiring start to a research project; nevertheless, Nuttall proved a strongly supportive supervisor. It was not long before Packer felt that real progress was being made. By the time he left Oxford in December 1952, Packer had virtually finished his painstaking research. It now remained for him to write up the material in the form of a thesis. The final title of the thesis sums up its theme succinctly: *The Redemption and Restoration of Man in the Thought of Richard Baxter.*

The thesis was long; its 499 pages extend to nearly 150,000 words. (Oxford University would later insist that doctoral theses should not exceed 100,000 words.) The work shows Packer as a scholar with a gift for rigorous analysis and clarity of expression. In this thesis, Packer set himself the task of providing 'a full, sympathetic exposition of Richard Baxter's doctrine of man, created

47

and fallen; of his redemption by Jesus Christ; and of the restoration in him of the image of God through the obedience of faith by the power of the Holy Spirit'. Baxter had often been represented as being muddled or confused in his theology; Packer was able to demonstrate that his entire theological trajectory was governed by a coherent leading principle. As he himself put it, he found in Baxter 'nothing but the dazzling precision of a man who knows exactly what he thinks and how to say it'. In general terms, Packer was able to show that Baxter reflected 'the mediating Calvinism of Cameron, Amyraldus and the Saumur school'.[5] The basic structure of Baxter's doctrine of redemption could be summarized in the statement that 'Christ, by satisfying the lawgiver, procured the new law, which requires faith and confers justification on those who obediently exercise it.'

Oxford University's regulations demanded that the thesis should be handed in after twelve terms, giving Packer until the second week of July 1954 to complete every aspect of producing the thesis. This was not the easiest of matters. From the middle of December 1952, Packer was working as a clergyman in the diocese of Birmingham (a matter to which we shall pass on presently). This left him relatively little time for writing. However, the vicar of his parish was understanding, and arranged for Packer to have Sunday duties only in the month of June 1954, in order to allow him to get the text of the thesis completed, supervise the typing, and proof-read the final version. In the event, Packer managed to hand in the requisite three copies of the thesis at Oxford in July, three days before the university deadline, in the same week as his marriage to Kit (to which we shall also return presently).

Once the thesis had been delivered to the university authorities, the process of arranging examiners and a place and time of examination proceeded. Oxford University virtually closes down for the summer vacation, and it was not until Michaelmas term 1954 that the arrangements for Packer's oral examination were announced.[6] The examiners appointed by the University of Oxford were Dr John Marsh (principal of Mansfield College) and R.L. Child (principal of Regent's Park College). The *viva voce* examination would take place in Oxford, at Regent's Park College, on Wednesday 1 December 1954 at 2.00 p.m.

In the event, the oral examination lasted an hour. Neither Marsh nor Child knew much about Baxter, with the result that the thesis was judged primarily on its literary merit and Packer's ability to defend his arguments and show competence in related areas of theology. Child seemed at his most comfortable when the discussion moved on to the theory of the Atonement associated with the eleventh-century writer Anselm of Canterbury, and the way in which Baxter related to this earlier writer. Packer returned to Birmingham feeling confident about the outcome of proceedings. It was not long before he learned that he had been successful. For Nuttall, the resulting thesis was 'one of the best theses he had ever supervised or examined'. It has always been a matter of regret to him that it was never published.[7]

However, some publications emerged which bore witness to Packer's growing interest and expertise in the field of Puritan studies, and specifically the soteriology of Richard Baxter. In July 1952, Packer's first published article appeared in the July number of *The Evangelical Quarterly*, its theme 'The Puritan Treatment of Justification by Faith'. This was followed by a study in the December 1952 edition of *The Christian Graduate*, which explored Puritan teaching on the matter of sanctification. Finally, Packer published a significant article on Baxter in the May 1953 edition of the then prestigious journal *Theology*.

Packer's interest in the Puritans had by now found expression in an additional direction which would arguably have considerably more influence on British evangelicalism than his excellent research on Baxter. In 1950, the first Puritan Studies Conference was held.

The Founder of the Puritan Studies Conferences

As we have seen, Packer and his close friend O. Raymond Johnston had developed a deep appreciation of the Puritans at a time when such interest was far from fashionable. During the year 1948–9, when Packer was teaching at Oak Hill and Johnston was studying at the University of London Department of Education, they conceived the idea of establishing a 'Puritan Studies Conference' under the auspices of the recently-formed Tyndale Fellowship for Biblical Literature.

The foundation of this Fellowship was unquestionably one of the most important contributing factors to the resurgence of evangelicalism in England following the Second World War. The origins of this movement can be traced back to a committee set up by the Inter-Varsity Fellowship in 1938 to counter the perception that evangelicalism was at best anti-intellectual, if not downright obscurantist. The 'Biblical Research Committee' was duly formed, and set about establishing a wider group, known as the Tyndale Fellowship for Biblical Research, which was concerned with convening study groups, conferences and summer schools.

The key decisions were taken at a meeting held at Oxford during the period 7–10 July 1941, at Kingham Hill School. A number of senior evangelical scholars were present, as well as some rising stars, including F.F. Bruce and John Wenham. A model which proved to have considerable attraction for many present at that conference (especially Dr W.J. Martin, of the University of Liverpool) was provided by St Deiniol's Library, Hawarden (also known as the Gladstone Memoral Library), which combined excellent library facilities with residential accommodation. It was therefore agreed to hold a summer school in July 1942 at St Deiniol's itself, which would allow evaluation of the kind of property which might be appropriate for the proposed research institute.

St Deiniol's was located in an area of rural north Wales, not far from Liverpool, where the nineteenth-century Prime Minister William Gladstone had purchased a property as a summer retreat. Careful thought was given to the location of the proposed new centre. It was eventually decided to acquire a residential base in the university town of Cambridge, to ensure that an evangelical presence would be secured in this university. The stimulus for this choice appears to have been the fact that Oliver Barclay, a rising young evangelical scholar who was then serving as chairman of the Universities Executive Committee of the IVF, reported that a relative was about to offer a suitable property in Cambridge at a very advantageous price. John Laing, head of a large construction company and a prominent member of the Christian Brethren, provided most of the necessary capital, allowing the purchase of the property in Selwyn Gardens to proceed. By 1945, Tyndale House – as it was named – was operational.

As subsequent events proved, the vision of the original committee was more than amply fulfilled. In addition to establishing a major residential study and research centre in Cambridge, a number of study groups were brought into being, each concerned with fostering evangelical scholarship and reflection in areas of importance. Johnston and Packer believed – rightly, as it turned out – that their idea for a conference with a particular focus on Puritan life and thought could be developed as one such Tyndale Fellowship study group. This proposal would therefore need support from within the Tyndale Fellowship in the first place, and a venue at which to meet. It was clear that Dr Martyn Lloyd-Jones was ideally placed to promote the venture, if his support could be secured. Lloyd-Jones had considerable influence within the Inter-Varsity Fellowship, and was clearly sympathetic to the theological and spiritual vision of the Puritans. He had also served on the committee which brought the Tyndale Fellowship into being.

In early 1949, Packer and Johnston therefore decided to approach 'the Doctor' (as virtually everyone seemed to know him), and see how he reacted. Packer and Johnston had already given much thought to the structure of, and likely market for, the proposed 'Puritan Studies Conference', including its association with the Tyndale Fellowship, and the most suitable date (the week before Christmas). Their joint approach to Lloyd-Jones focused specifically on gaining his support for what was in effect a fully-fledged proposal. Johnston also had a further suggestion: that 'the Doctor' might be well disposed towards the idea of hosting the conference himself. Lloyd-Jones was delighted with the idea, especially with the suggestion that Westminster Chapel should host the conference. He immediately put forward the suggestion that the women of the church could be called upon to feed those who attended the conference, and gave his opinion that they would probably do so without charge for their services.

So all was arranged. The first meeting of the newly-founded Puritan Studies Group of the Tyndale Fellowship for Biblical Research (which everyone referred to simply as the 'Puritan Conference') was held in the church parlour of Westminster Chapel, London, on 19 and 20 December 1950. It had been advertised in *The Christian Graduate* issue for June 1950, as follows:

December 19–20, Tyndale Fellowship Conference at Westminster Chapel, 'The Distinctive Theological Contribution of the English Puritans'. Speakers include Rev Dr D. Martyn Lloyd-Jones.

This notice was repeated in the September issue of the same journal, appended to an article by Packer on 'The Doctrinal Puritans and Their Work'. Packer also actively publicized the event within OICCU circles in the Michaelmas term of 1950. In the event, just over twenty people – most of whom were undergraduates – gathered together to hear seven addresses, of which three (including the closing address) were delivered by Packer himself, and one by Lloyd-Jones.

From the outset, the Conferences proceeded on the assumption that the Puritans were to be studied as potential guides for the modern church. As Packer himself wrote:

> The interests of the Conference are practical and constructive, not merely academic. We look on the Puritans as our fellow-Christians, now enabled to share with us, through the medium of their books, the good things which God gave them three centuries ago . . . And the question which we ask is not simply the historical one: what did they do and teach? (though, of course, that is where we start); our questions are rather these: how far is their exposition of the Scriptures a right one? And what biblical principles does it yield for the guiding of our faith and life today? The second half of each session of the Conference is devoted to discussing the contents of the paper that has been read, from the standpoint of these two questions.[8]

There was no question of regarding the Puritans as being above criticism. They were to be seen as a stimulus and resource.

The Conference consisted of the reading of papers, followed by discussion periods, often characterized by free and fierce debate. The first conference attracted twenty; by the middle of the 1950s, sixty were attending; by the year 1960, the number was regularly in excess of a hundred. The growth in numbers meant that the church parlour was no longer adequate to cope; the Conference now took place in the Institute Hall. It now operated under a new name. Although initially referred to simply as the 'Puritan Studies Group' of the Tyndale Fellowship, the name gradually evolved. In 1958, the title was temporarily altered to the 'Puritan Studies Conference'; from 1959 onwards, it came to be known by the rather more weighty title of the 'Puritan and Reformed Studies Conference'. The Conferences settled down to a fixed pattern, meeting annually for two days on the Tuesday and Wednesday in the week before Christmas. Three papers would be read on each of these two days: one in the morning, one in the early afternoon, and one following afternoon tea. This pattern was maintained until the Conferences ended in 1969, for reasons to which we shall return at an appropriate point in this narrative.

The Conferences were invariably chaired by Lloyd-Jones, who moderated the resulting discussions. In 1959, Lloyd-Jones contributed a paper entitled 'Revival: An Historical and Theological Survey'. From 1960 onwards, he invariably contributed the closing address. Occasionally, the titles of these would be announced in advance, as in the case of the important 1965 address '*Ecclesiola in Ecclesia*', to be discussed later in this work (see p. 123).

The importance of these Conferences is clear. A rising generation of theological students and younger ministers were being offered a powerful and persuasive vision of the Christian life, in which theology, biblical exposition, spirituality and preaching were shown to be mutually indispensable and interrelated. It was a vision of the Christian life which possessed both intellectual rigour and pastoral relevance. It was a powerful antidote to the intellectualism which had been rampant within British evangelical circles in the immediate post-war period. The Conferences offered those who attended them theological stimulation, pastoral reflection and Christian fellowship. In effect, the Conference acted as the nucleus of a new and emerging constituency within British evangelicalism. More than twenty years after he and Johnston had the idea for the Conferences, Packer commented thus on their impact:

> Twenty-two years ago, a group of Oxford friends ran the first Puritan Studies Conference. We had Dr D.M. Lloyd-Jones as chairman, and I was organizing secretary, as today. We did not think of ourselves as setting up a rallying-point for a new movement, although in retrospect it now seems that this is what we did; we only knew that the dusty pages of [John] Owen and [Thomas] Goodwin, mouldering on the bottom shelves of the OICCU library, had become a gold mine to us, and we wanted to share the wealth. So we met to read papers and to help each other by discussion to a firmer grasp of the Puritan profundities.[9]

The growth of this increasingly important movement was stimulated further through the formation of the 'Banner of Truth Trust' on 22 July 1957, which aimed to reprint classics of Puritan and

Reformed theology to meet the growing appetite for these works. By October 1958, eleven titles were available; by 1960, this had risen to thirty-five. It was clear that a new wave had emerged.

The emergence of this new grouping within evangelicalism was of considerable significance. First, it included important elements from both the traditional 'free church' constituency and from the Church of England. The Puritans were thus seen as offering evangelicals a potential point of focus which transcended the traditional hostility of denominational boundaries. Second, the new group potentially posed a significant challenge to the 'received wisdom' of British evangelicalism on a series of issues, especially the Keswick doctrine of 'sanctification by faith'. While an older generation looked back to Keswick Conventions for their fellowship and teaching, an emerging generation looked instead to the Puritans. The Puritan and Keswick positions were incompatible. Tensions and conflict were thus virtually inevitable within evangelicalism over this significant matter. In 1955, serious controversy erupted over this issue, sparked by none other than Packer himself.

Packer and the Puritans

It will be helpful to clarify more precisely what is meant by 'Puritanism'. For Packer, the term refers to the movement in sixteenth- and seventeenth-century England which sought further reformation and renewal within the Church of England than that which was actually achieved under the reign of Elizabeth I. The word 'Puritan' had its origin as a term of abuse, used especially during the period 1564–1642, to refer to various overlapping groups of people with particular reforming concerns, who shared common biblical and Calvinist convictions. So what was it about Puritanism that held such an attraction for Packer, Raymond Johnston and others at this time?

This question may be answered in two different, but related, manners. First, we can establish the impact that the Puritans had upon Packer's own spiritual and theological development, and trace the way in which his distinctive Christian mindset was forged by creative analysis and inward appropriation of the Puritan heritage. It is with good reason that Packer has been referred to as 'The Last Puritan'.[10] Second, we can explore the ways in which

Packer believed that Puritanism offers modern evangelicalism both a resource and a challenge. In what follows, we shall adopt both these approaches.

Packer identifies a number of ways in which he benefited personally from his spiritual walk through the 'Avenue of the Giants', in which he came to devour and digest the writings of the Puritans.[11]

One of the most important influences of the Puritans was also their earliest upon him. The Puritans conveyed to Packer a deep sense of spiritual realism, especially in regard to the power and seriousness of indwelling sin. We have already noted how Packer experienced a crisis in his early period as a Christian, due to a serious difficulty in relation to personal holiness (see p. 23). Having been offered what he later realized were inadequate answers to complex questions, he discovered the writings of John Owen. Despite their 'lumbering Latinized idiom', these allowed him to avoid the sense of despair he had previously experienced as a result of the defective view of sanctification which was then in vogue among English evangelicals. 'Without Owen, I might well have gone off my head or got bogged down in mystical fanaticism.'

Packer is noted as a leading and highly articulate defender of the doctrine of limited atonement (also known as 'particular redemption'). He was won over to this position through reading Puritan writers. In particular, his detailed study of Owen's *The Death of Death in the Death of Christ* led him to move away from his early views concerning the extent of Christ's redeeming work.[12] Packer's early work had focused on Richard Baxter, who adopted what can only be described as something approaching an Amyraldist understanding of the atonement (although Baxter does not appear to have derived this viewpoint directly from the writings of Amyraldus: see p. 48). Packer's reflections on Owen's arguments confirmed his Calvinist views on the sovereignty of God and added to them Calvinist belief in the particularity of redemption (which convictions can be discerned throughout his writings from about 1955 onwards).

If Packer moved away from Baxter on the particularity of redemption, he was deeply influenced by the Reformed pastor of Kidderminster on other issues. Baxter enabled Packer to learn the usefulness of 'regular discursive meditation', in which the individual preaches to himself or herself, applying biblical truth from within as if a talented preacher were doing so from outside.

Packer also found that his views on the nature of the pastoral ministry were shaped by reading Baxter's *Reformed Pastor*. Indeed, Packer affirms that his 'churchly identity' (meaning his vision of the interrelatedness and interdependence of theological orthodoxy, liturgy, personal conversion and spiritual nurture, congregational structures and social witness, to name but a few items) had its origins in the Puritan vision.

Packer also notes the importance of the Puritan understanding of the Christian life as a 'gymnasium and dressing room where we are prepared for heaven'. This classic Christian emphasis upon the transitoriness of life has, to a large extent, been lost within modern evangelicalism, which has tended to invest heavily in its commitment to the world. For Packer, there is a need to regain an awareness that a 'readiness to die' is the 'first step in learning to live'. Modern western evangelicals, cosseted by the comforts of modern medicine, household appliances and social security, have been insulated from many of the life pressures which were very real to the Puritans. In their physical discomfort, they kept their eyes focused on heaven as their only true comfort. 'Reckoning with death brought appreciation of each day's continued life.'

And finally – and for many of Packer's readers, most importantly – the Puritans taught him that 'all theology is also spirituality'. The Puritans knew the importance of putting doctrine to use. Spirituality has its origins in the application of theology – and the application of bad theology will simply lead to bad spirituality. 'If our theology does not quicken the conscience and soften the heart, it actually hardens both.' We shall return to this major theme at several points during our narrative (see pp. 183–6; 255–60). For the moment, it is enough to note simply that this insight underlies the approach found in Packer's classic work, *Knowing God*.

So much for the influence of Puritanism on the shaping of Packer's mind. It will be clear that Packer, while no uncritical acolyte of Owen or Baxter, derived an enormous amount from their writings. But what of Packer's view of what others might learn from them? What do the Puritans have to offer modern evangelicalism? The answer, for Packer, can be summed up in a single word – *maturity*. In a famous comparison, he suggested that many modern evangelicals were like dwarfs in comparison with the stature of the Puritans, who tower above others like giant Redwoods. Packer singled out three groups of people within modern evangelicalism whom he felt would benefit from an engagement with the distilled wisdom of the Puritans. Each is deftly portrayed as a vignette, a thumbnail sketch; each corresponds to a recognizable type within evangelicalism who needs gentle and godly correction, as much for their own good as for that of the gospel.

First, there are the 'restless experientialists'. Packer felt that the Puritans offered a powerful and persuasive antidote to the type of experiential individualism which seemed to be increasingly important in western evangelicalism. Packer argued that such people had 'fallen victim to a form of worldliness, a man-centred, anti-rational individualism, which turns Christian life into a thrill-seeking ego-trip'. The Puritan emphasis on God-centredness, personal discipline, humility and the primacy of the mind were of major importance in this matter. Packer stressed the Puritan insight that 'feelings go up and down, and that God frequently tries us by leading us through wastes of emotional flatness'. While not in any way denying that experience has a significant role in the Christian life, Packer points to the Puritan insistence that experience is interpreted correctly. He further points out the importance of discipline, as a means of responding to God's work within us. The role of the Holy Spirit is 'not to give thrills, but to create in us Christlike character'.

Second, there are the 'entrenched intellectualists'. By this, Packer intends us to understand people who present themselves as 'rigid, argumentative, critical Christians, champions for God's truth for whom orthodoxy is all'. Their chief concern is the defence of 'their own view of that truth'. While they invest themselves unstintingly in this task, their total dedication to 'winning the battle for mental correctness' often leads them to have 'little warmth about them'. Such 'fixated Christian intellectualists' are 'spiritually stunted, not in their zeal for the form of sound words, but in their lack of zeal for anything else'. Having grasped the importance of the intellect, they undervalue everything else, including the importance of personal relationships: 'Relationally, they are remote.' Against this arid mental correctness, Packer urges a recovery of the Puritan vision of true religion as embracing the affections as well as the intellect. It is essential to move on from knowing about God to a relational acquaintance with God himself.

Third, there are the 'disaffected deviationists' – by which Packer means those who have become disillusioned with evangelicalism, particularly through 'naïvety of mind' or 'unrealistic expectations'. Evangelicalism, as has often been pointed out, has at least its fair share of walking wounded. For Packer, the Puritan heritage offers a profoundly realistic vision of the Christian life, lacking the simplistic and misleading platitudes found in some evangelistic preaching of today. Packer points out that the Puritans experienced 'spiritual casualties' back in the seventeenth century, and devised biblically-grounded strategies to cope with them. Once more, modern evangelicalism can learn from its forebears at this point.

The time has come, however, to return to our account of Packer's life. We have already seen that Packer moved on from Wycliffe Hall to Birmingham in 1952. It is now time to relate this matter in greater detail.

«5»
Birmingham: St John's, Harborne,
1952–4

In NOVEMBER 1952, the principal of Wycliffe Hall wrote to the Bishop of Birmingham, confirming that James I. Packer had completed all the studies necessary for ordination. Packer went on to be ordained in the middle of December of that year, to serve as a curate at St John's, Harborne, a suburb of Birmingham. Why Birmingham? We must now tell the story of how Packer came to become curate of Harborne.

Although Packer had spent rather longer at Wycliffe Hall than he had originally intended, he had not lost sight of his primary goal. He wanted to be an ordained minister in the Church of England. As his time at Wycliffe Hall drew close to its end, the question of where he would find his first parish appointment became increasingly important. Packer had formed a high opinion of two churches during his year in London: All Souls, Langham Place, and Westminster Chapel. The latter was strongly Congregationalist, the former Anglican. As the time drew near for Packer to think about finding employment, his initial move was to write to John Stott, now rector of All Souls, asking if there was any possibility of becoming a curate there.[1] John Stott's reply was courteous and affirming – but not affirmative. It was clear to Packer that he would have to look elsewhere. He therefore approached the principal of Wycliffe Hall, Julian Thornton-Duesbury, and asked him what his next move should be.

It so happened that Thornton-Duesbury had just learned that a vicar in Cheltenham was looking for a curate. Cheltenham was a stylish town in Gloucestershire, noted for its prominence in the social life of early nineteenth-century England. By the late 1940s, its social status had faded away somewhat. However, Cheltenham was very close to Packer's home town of Gloucester. Packer therefore followed up this suggestion, and travelled to Cheltenham. The vicar in question was a liberal evangelical, similar in outlook to the 'Group Brotherhood'. There was no real meeting of minds, and Packer returned to Oxford convinced that this would not be an appropriate position for him.

This left Packer in a somewhat difficult position, in that there appeared to be no obvious openings for him, and the time for him to leave Wycliffe was drawing near. At this point, Alan Stibbs (whom Packer had come to know and admire during his year at Oak Hill) mentioned that he had heard that William Leathem was looking for a curate to join him at Harborne. Leathem was an active evangelical, with particular links with the Bible Churchmen's Missionary Society. Packer went to Birmingham in the autumn of 1952, and decided immediately that Leathem could offer him the kind of environment in which he could minister. Packer was looking for a conservative evangelical vicar in a conservative evangelical parish, whose ideals he could respect. Bill Leathem was ideal. Packer was offered the job of curate of Harborne, on an annual salary of £325.

Packer then had to face a formal interview with the Bishop of Birmingham before he could be finally accepted for ministry in the diocese. At that time, the bishop in question was the socialistic modernist Ernest W. Barnes, whose appointment in 1924 had been widely seen as reflecting the political views of the then British Prime Minister Ramsay MacDonald. The appointment caused consternation in orthodox circles. The *Church Times* ridiculed his appointment: not only was Barnes a notorious modernist – he had no experience of parish life. Barnes remained Bishop of Birmingham until 1953. He saw himself as having a mission to eliminate medieval superstition from the church, and to make it acceptable to 'the age of science'. He had an especial interest in the Darwinian theory of evolution, which he championed during the 1920s.

But the Barnes who met Packer in the late autumn of 1952 seemed to be little more than a 'doddering old man'. By now aged seventy-eight, Barnes had largely lost his keen intellect. His interview with Packer focused on the importance of evolutionary theory for the modern church. Packer remembers the interview being amiable, even though he was conscious that they both had very different understandings of what they were talking about. That particular insight probably eluded Barnes. The bishop asked Packer to write him an essay on 'The Use of Reason in Theology' for one of his examining chaplains to assess. Barnes later wrote to Packer, confirming that he would ordain him, and mentioning that the examining chaplain had expressed a 'profound distaste' for Packer's theology, which amounted to 'intellectual bulldozing'.

The Church of England has a long tradition of ordaining men at two specific times during the year. These are traditionally known as 'Petertide' (that is, the Sunday nearest to the celebration of the feast of St Peter, usually late June or early July), and Michaelmas (that is, the Sunday nearest to the feast of St Michael and All Angels, which falls in late September. Oxford's 'Michaelmas term' is so called on account of this important date.) The reason for concentrating ordinations at Petertide and Michaelmas is that these dates correspond to the British academic year. Most clergy are ordained at Petertide, a few weeks after the end of the British academic year, when all their formal qualifications are completed. Some are ordained at Michaelmas, which corresponds to the end of the summer vacation. Packer, however, was to be ordained in mid-December, on account of his unusual programme of studies at Oxford. The Church of England refers to ordinations which take place at this time of year as 'Advent ordinations', as they fall in the period of the year immediately before Christmas. In the event, Packer was ordained deacon in the Church of England on 21 December 1952 at Handsworth parish church by Bishop James Henry Linton, acting on behalf of Bishop Barnes, who was seriously ill at the time. He was subsequently ordained priest on 20 December 1953 at Birmingham Cathedral.

So this 'intellectual bulldozer' went into parish ministry. How did he cope? And what effect did it have on him?

Packer the Curate

Packer lived in the vicarage with the Leathem family (and other student lodgers) from December 1952 until his marriage to Kit in July 1954. William Leathem was a complex man, who defies easy categorization. He was originally from Belfast in Northern

Ireland, a region of the United Kingdom noted for its long-standing tension between Protestants and Roman Catholics. Leathem had been converted through the evangelistic ministry of the famous Ulster evangelist 'Willy' Nicholson. His father had died at an early age, leaving Leathem to care for the family until such time as he was able to attend the Bible Churchmen's Missionary and Training College in Bristol during the early 1930s. He subsequently served as vicar of All Saints, Preston, which was then noted for the length and Protestant substance of its sermons. Leathem was proud of his Irish roots, and affirmed these by wearing the hood of Trinity College, Dublin. (This irritated at least one of his acquaintances, who was of the opinion that it was generally thought necessary at least to have attended a college, and preferably to have gained a degree from it, before wearing its hood.)

St John's, Harborne was at that time a 'black gown' church (so-called on account of the clergy following the free church practice of wearing black gowns, rather than the traditional Anglican surplice, when preaching the sermon), with a definite Protestant stance, which both reflected and suited Leathem's outlook. (Shortly after Packer's departure for Bristol, Leathem decided that 'black gowns' had had their day, and abolished them.) The original church building was destroyed during the bombing raids of the Second World War, so that the local Memorial Hall was used for services until the church buildings could be replaced.

Like Packer, Leathem was a voracious reader, and was active in a diocesan reading group. Each morning, Packer and Leathem would get together for an hour. Part of their time together would be taken up with prayer and the reading of Scripture; part would concern the business of the day, determining who would do what; and the remainder (and perhaps, for Packer, the most important) lay in general theological discussion. Leathem was expansive in such discussion, and left Packer in no doubt concerning his competence, interests and general outlook. It was enormously stimulating and affirming for the young curate.

It was an important period for Packer's development of his preaching and speaking styles. He greatly admired the preaching style of Martyn Lloyd-Jones, particularly its expository thoroughness. His first sermon was an exposition of Matthew 5:3, 'Blessed are the poor in spirit'. Packer had intended it to be twenty-five minutes in length; perhaps unaware that he spoke more slowly in practice than in intention, he discovered that the sermon actually lasted thirty-five minutes. The substance of the sermon was the graciousness of God, and particularly the manner in which God lavishes his grace on the undeserving. The sermon prompted Leathem's younger daughter, Gillian, who was then merely six years old, to comment to her mother: 'He's a better preacher than Daddy, isn't he?' It was not exactly how Packer had intended his ministry to begin! Leathem, however, took this in his stride.

In one sense, Leathem was a poor mentor for Packer. He never told his new curate how to take a funeral, or a private communion service, and never offered any advice or guidance in these important areas of ministry. Leathem's method was to allow Packer to find his own level, and he aimed to encourage and enable him, while remaining content to let Packer get on with developing his own ministerial style. In any case, Packer was busy writing up his doctoral thesis, and spent much of his time working away at it in his room in the vicarage. Six months into his curacy, Leathem offered Packer some feedback concerning his sermons. They were too serious. What Packer said was fine; it was just said in a way that people found hard going. He needed to lighten up, to inject some humour into his preaching. It was wise advice, and Packer took the decision to deliberately include material which would raise a smile, if not a laugh.

We have already noted Packer's growing appreciation both of the importance of teaching, and of his own emerging skills as a careful and able teacher. In addition to preaching and general parish duties, Packer initiated a weekly doctrine class, at which he took his small audience of young people through the main points of Christian doctrine. Those who attended (including Leslie Hyett) recall the clarity of those classes. For Packer, the class was the best thing he did in Harborne. He proved to be an excellent unpacker of Christian doctrine. Even those who found themselves struggling with the theology which he set forth from the pulpit (such as Kitty Ismay and Thelma Jones) recall the clarity with which the ideas were set out.

Many have suggested that Packer's clear, methodical, slow and precise style of speaking seemed inappropriate for evangelistic contexts. For many, Packer's gifts lay more in the careful equipping of the converted, rather than in the business of conversion itself. Whatever truth may lie in this suggestion, it must be noted that

Packer himself saw evangelism as of major importance, and had no hesitation in doing what he could in this respect. He was particularly appreciative of Leathem's institution of monthly 'guest services' on Sunday evenings, which were especially directed towards students from nearby Birmingham University. Indeed, Packer preached at such services himself on occasion.[2]

One example from his time at Harborne is of particular interest in casting light on Packer as an evangelist. One of the leading church youth organizations in England at this time was the Boys' Brigade. The 64th Birmingham company of the Boys' Brigade was based at St John's, with Leslie Hyett as its Captain. It was traditional for the Brigade to have a summer camp under canvas, and for the curate of the church to act as chaplain to this camp. And so, in the summer of 1953, Packer went off to the Brigade camp at Sand Bay, near the Somerset seaside resort of Weston-super-Mare. On this occasion, the 64th company were joined by some boys from the 4th company, based in the Birmingham suburb of Edgbaston.

Packer gave the evening addresses at this camp. In effect, the talks were epilogues, which brought the day to a close. After the penultimate such talk, Packer invited any boy who would like to take things further to speak to him afterwards. One of the Edgbaston lads did so. He turned out to have attended a Baptist church for many years, and had developed a fairly full understanding of what the Christian faith was all about. He needed someone to explain that a decision was necessary. (The parallels with Packer's own conversion will be clear.) Packer was able to explain what needed to be done; as a result, the boy made a commitment to Christ. Hyett recalls Packer being thrilled by this, and talking about a 'classic' or 'text-book case'. What is particularly noteworthy, in the light of Packer's own conviction that he was a very poor communicator to children, is that Packer was able to explain things in ways that a young boy could understand.

Looking back on his time in the parish, Packer saw it to have been an affirming experience. It had helped him develop his preaching style. It had also reinforced his perception that, with due effort and concentration, he could communicate Christian teachings to ordinary intelligent lay people. Enid Leathem, who organized the women's meetings in the parish, recalls clearly how popular Packer was with the older members of her group (whom Packer affectionately referred to as Enid's 'old ducks'). Packer had earlier sensed that he found it difficult to initiate and sustain personal relationships; his time in the parish gave him an opportunity to develop this aspect of his personality. (The surprisingly large number of lay people from St John's at this time who continue to keep in touch with Packer after more than forty years may be mentioned here.)

But one particular personal relationship must be noted here: his growing friendship with Kit Mullett.

Marriage to Kit, 1954

Packer never felt he had been 'called to be single'. As a young Christian, he gave considerable thought and prayer to the question of whom he should marry. He met nobody during his time at Oxford, nor during his vacation visits to the family house in Gloucester, who seemed to be right to him. An additional consideration was that he had no money worth talking about, and felt strongly that he ought to have the means to support a wife before entering into a serious relationship.

In 1945, Packer attended a Church Missionary Society summer school near Bath, at which the main speaker was Bishop Stephen Neill. Here he met a girl from Bradford whom he found attractive, and the two entered into a brief correspondence. Nothing came of it. Barbara – who subsequently married Roy Barker, who had a distinguished career in England as a pastor and evangelist – later recalled that she 'couldn't understand a word' of Packer's letters.

In the late spring of 1952, however, happenstance (or should we say divine providence?) intervened. John Harwood was due to speak at a weekend conference of Combined Christian Unions of St Bartholomew's Hospital, London. (There were two separate Christian Unions at the hospital at this stage, one serving the doctors, the other the nurses; on this occasion, they would meet together.) The meeting had been arranged by Dr Gaius Davies, who worked at Bart's (as the hospital was invariably known) 1947–53; others who were active in the group at that time included Dr Howard A. Gretton and Dr Alan Bapty. Davies was Welsh, and had been active in Welsh evangelical circles before his move to London. In particular, he had been involved in an Inter-Varsity Fellowship evangelistic campaign in Wales, at the village of Ammanford in Dyfed, which had led to the conversion of Kit Mullett.

The weekend conference, attended by about thirty people, had been arranged to take place at a Methodist camping centre on the North Downs, in rural Surrey, near the railway station at Abinger Hammer. However, Harwood discovered that he had double-booked himself, and could not speak in two places at once. He approached Packer, and asked if he could speak to the Bart's group in his place. At this stage, Packer was still a student at Wycliffe Hall, with a reasonable amount of spare time at his disposal. He packed his clothes and a set of four talks on Paul's letter to the Philippians, and headed off to Surrey.

At the end of his first talk on the Friday evening, Packer found that he was left on his own at the speaker's table at the far end of the room, while all the others gathered into small groups to chat. They all clearly knew each other; Packer, however, was something of an outsider. One of the trainee nurses felt sorry for the speaker, and went up to talk to him. She explained that she was a great admirer of the preaching of Dr Lloyd-Jones, whom she heard regularly at Westminster Chapel. Packer's expository style, she commented, was just like that used by Lloyd-Jones. In fact, she had never heard an Anglican speak like this before.

The nurse in question was Kit Mullett. She should really have been on ward duty; however, she had a minor eye infection, which had resulted in her being excused this duty, thus allowing her to slip away for the weekend to attend the conference. Kit was from Llandebie, in Dyfed, and had been converted at the IVF campaign of 1946 at the nearby town of Ammanford.[3] (It was for this reason that she knew Dr Gaius Davies particularly well.) On the Saturday, the group went for a walk along some trails on the North Downs, which allowed Packer and Kit further time together. Finally, the conference came to an end on the Sunday afternoon, and Packer returned to Oxford.

Packer found he could not sleep that night. He could not stop thinking about Kit. He lay awake in his room in the Old Lodge of Wycliffe Hall, wondering whether – and how – he should take things from here. At about 2 a.m., he got out of bed, turned on the light, and read through Proverbs 31:10–31. This did not help him to sleep! After some thought, he decided he would devise some way of getting in touch. They began to correspond. In the meantime, the Michaelmas term of the academic year 1952–3 began at Oxford. This was to be Packer's last term at Wycliffe Hall. He arranged to meet Kit at London's Paddington station on Saturday. However, at this stage, he was concerned to keep his friendship with Kit a secret.

Packer's stratagem for secrecy was, however, nearly totally wrecked that day. As he waited at Oxford station for the train to London, he realized that someone he knew was waiting for exactly the same train. Ailsa Knox (wife of D.B. Knox, then teaching at Wycliffe while writing his DPhil thesis, and subsequently principal of Moore College, Sydney) was on her way to London for a professional singing lesson. Packer's heart sank. As soon as they greeted each other, Packer knew that some difficulties might lie ahead. It would have been unthinkable for the two of them not to sit together in the train on the way to London. Packer therefore spent the journey to London talking animatedly to Ailsa, while at the same time wondering how he could lose her at Paddington, and keep his assignment with Kit without being noticed.

Packer made his excuses to Ailsa – he 'had to rush' – and managed to meet Kit unobserved. They spent a happy day wandering around Kensington Gardens. Their next meeting took place in Oxford, at Wycliffe Hall on a Saturday in November, during a period of heavy snow. Packer met Kit at the railway station, and they walked to a bus stop together. Kit was wearing old shoes which failed to keep out the snow. As a result, by the time the couple arrived at Wycliffe, her feet were soaking. Packer gallantly prepared a bowl of hot water in his room, to allow Kit to warm her cold and wet feet. While this healing process was proceeding, David G. Fountain of St Peter's Hall – who played a prominent role in organizing the Puritan Conference – dropped in to visit Packer. He was clearly taken aback, not merely to find a *woman* in Packer's room, but a woman *with her feet in a bowl of water.* Embarrassed, he withdrew.

In December, Packer moved to Harborne, to live with the Leathems. By this stage, Packer was sure that he was called to the married state, and that Kit was the right person to be his wife. It was only a matter of finding the right place and time to propose. The opportunity came later that same month, when he travelled to London to attend the Puritan Conference at Westminster Chapel.

Packer was scheduled to play a prominent role in the 1952

meeting of the 'Puritan Studies Group' (as it was then known). Six papers would be discussed, of which Packer presented two. On the Tuesday, he spoke on 'Richard Baxter as a Theologian', drawing on his doctoral research at Oxford. On the Wednesday, he spoke on 'Antinomian Theology'. But perhaps the most important event of that conference did not appear on its programme. Packer arranged to borrow a friend's apartment for the Tuesday evening of the conference, and used this opportunity to propose to Kit. She accepted. Later that evening, Packer happened to meet Elizabeth Lloyd-Jones on the platform of Lancaster Gate tube station, and broke the news to her. Packer recalls that she was so thrilled that she nearly fell on to the track in excitement. Her father, as it turned out, would hear the news the next day.

On the Wednesday, Kit came along to hear Packer speak at the Puritan Conference at Westminster Chapel (which, as we have noted, was her normal place of worship). Noticing Kit and one other woman in the audience, Lloyd-Jones complained of their presence to Packer. At the time, they were enjoying a cup of tea in the chapel vestry, and planning the next year's conference. 'They don't come here to study the Puritans!' he remarked. 'They're only here for the men! I know one of them, she's a member of my church.' 'Well, Doctor,' Packer replied, 'as a matter of fact, I'm going to marry her.' Packer recalls that Lloyd-Jones's reply was: 'Well, I was right about one of them. Now what about the other?'

At this stage, Packer was living with William and Enid Leathem and their family. Enid had no idea that Packer had a girlfriend. The first she knew about it was one evening, on which her husband and Packer were both out of the vicarage attending a meeting of the Parochial Church Council. There was a phone call for Packer. Enid explained he was out at a meeting, and asked if she could take a message. 'Tell him it's Kit.' On Packer's return, Enid passed on the message, and asked who 'Kit' was. 'Oh, she's my fiancée', Packer replied. It was the first Enid had heard of this. However, the Leathems were formally introduced to Kit in the spring of 1953.

In the summer of 1953, Kit completed her qualifications as a nurse, and obtained a position as a staff nurse at St Chad's Hospital, some two miles from Harborne. She remained in this position until she married Packer during the summer of 1954. The marriage took place on 17 July in the local Memorial Hall, which was then still acting as a temporary church for St John's,

Harborne. Leathem officiated; Alan Stibbs preached. The service lasted nearly two hours, partly on account of a substantial sermon, and partly because the service included Holy Communion. The Packers subsequently adopted three children: Ruth, Naomi, and Martin.

As we have seen, Packer's time as a curate in Birmingham was important in shaping his future ministry. But what form would that ministry take? And where would it be based? We have already noted Packer's strong conviction that he was called to be a theological educator. Packer's roots were in the west country of England, and Kit's in south Wales. In 1954, a position opened up which seemed to be exactly right for the Packers. One of the leading evangelical theological colleges of the Church of England – Tyndale Hall, Bristol – needed a lecturer in theology. And Bristol was in the heart of England's west country, close to the Welsh border. The scene was set for Packer's decisive rise to fame as a leading evangelical thinker in England.

«6»

Bristol: Tyndale Hall, 1955–61

BRISTOL IS THE leading city of England's west country. It had important historical associations with the rise of Methodism; John Wesley made it a base for preaching during the great Evangelical Revival of the eighteenth century. Once a great port, it was given a new importance with the completion of the Great Western Railway, which allowed a direct rail link with London. Despite its regional importance, the city was late in having any forms of theological education established by the Church of England.[1] The foundation of an Anglican theological training centre is to be traced back to the 1920s, and to the tensions which emerged within British evangelicalism in the aftermath of the First World War.

Tyndale Hall

The origins of Tyndale Hall lie in the great revival of concern for mission within the British churches towards the end of the nineteenth century. Evangelism at home and abroad was seen as an issue of major importance by most evangelicals. After the devastation of the First World War, serious consideration was given to ways in which the quality of those training for mission, whether at home or abroad, could be enhanced. One mission agency which had a long history of involvement in this area was the London-based Church Missionary Society, which was originally founded in 1799. The rise in liberal evangelicalism within the Church of England following the end of the war led to tensions developing within the CMS over the issue of the authority of Scripture. In 1922, it became clear that the tension could no longer be contained. A breakaway body was formed, which affirmed its intention to be more faithful to central evangelical doctrines than its parent body. The new society was known as the Bible Churchmen's Missionary Society (BCMS). Its journal, the *Bible Churchmen's Missionary Messenger*, emphasized that the society would be 'biblical, Protestant and evangelical'. It affirmed its intention to 'become the rallying ground for true scriptural evangelicalism at home and in the mission field'.[2]

From its outset, the BCMS recognized the importance of theological education for its work of mission and ministry. In 1925, the society acquired a property in a Bristol suburb through the generosity of Dame Violet Wills, and founded the Bible Churchmen's Missionary and Training College. Its first principal was Dr Sydney Carter. The college was situated directly opposite the Downs, a picturesque area of parkland extending for more than a mile from the college, which offered uninterrupted views of the Avon Gorge and Bristol Channel. In 1927, the college was recognized by the Church of England as a theological college, thus opening the way to the preparation of men for ministry in the English national church at Bristol. In response to the number of women wishing to train for missionary service, the BCMS opened a new establishment in Bristol, named Dalton House.

In 1931, the college was shaken by a dispute whose aftermath would linger for a generation. A serious disagreement arose between the principal of the college and the executive committee of the BCMS over matters of discipline. The following year, the principal and the staff resigned, and moved a short distance from the original building to establish a new college, which was named 'Clifton Theological College'. By 1934, the original college had recovered from this dispute, and had rebuilt both its staff and student bodies. Yet from this moment there were three evangelical institutions of theological education within a very short distance of each other in the Bristol area, with a history of suspicion and mistrust between two of them.

J. Stafford Wright had been educated at the Bible Churchmen's Missionary Society College before the split of 1932; he returned in 1934 as a tutor on the staff of the college under the new principal, W. Dodgson Sykes (principal 1932–51). Following a disagreement, Stafford Wright spent a period on the staff of Oak Hill College, after which he returned to Bristol to succeed Sykes as principal in 1951. In 1952, the college changed its name to Tyndale Hall, after the English reformer and Bible translator William Tyndale (1494?–1536). By doing this, the college stressed both its commitment to biblical studies, and also its connections with the west of England, where Tyndale had been born. The individual 'houses' within the college, within which students were accommodated, were also named after reformers (such as Cranmer, Latimer, and Ridley). The college retained its close connection with the BCMS, with the result that Tyndale Hall was responsible to two governing bodies: the Hall Council, and the executive committee of the BCMS. In the first years of the principalship of J. Stafford Wright, Tyndale Hall began to establish a reputation for excellence.

One major contributing cause for that excellent reputation was Tyndale Hall's tutor in theology, Geoffrey W. Bromiley. Bromiley (who eventually went on to become a professor at Fuller Theological Seminary in Pasadena, California) had an earned doctorate in modern languages.[3] At this time, it was most unusual for members of theological college staffs to have such advanced qualifications. Tutors at theological colleges were generally enthusiastic amateurs, who would serve between three and five years in theological colleges before returning to parish ministry. Bromiley was a professional in a world dominated by amateurs, and may well have felt that he needed to move on to greater things. There were also tensions over some issues within the staff body at Tyndale, which would resurface in a more serious form in the second half of the 1960s. In 1954, Bromiley announced his intention to move on.[4] Who could replace him?

In one sense, the answer was obvious. Packer held an Oxford doctorate in theology, and already had a year's teaching experience at a Church of England theological college. However, in those days, positions such as this were not advertised. Search committees were virtually unknown. The 'old boy' network was thus of considerable importance in theological college appointments at this time. Principals of theological colleges generally relied on contacts and word of mouth to ascertain who was available and suitable. In the case of Tyndale Hall, the BCMS would also provide a network of contacts which might identify potential candidates for this important position. It is at this point that we need to emphasize the importance of William Leathem. Since 1945, Leathem had served on various committees of the BCMS. He was well aware of Tyndale's need at this particular moment, and felt he was in a position to help. In addition, Leathem himself commuted to Bristol regularly, to lecture to Tyndale students in the general area of the Book of Common Prayer and Anglican worship.

Tyndale needed a tutor in theology from September 1954; as a result, Stafford Wright invited Packer and Kit down to Bristol to discuss possibilities with him. However, Packer had served only eighteen months in his parish, at a time when two years was considered the minimum for curacies in the Church of England. If this norm was to be enforced rigidly, the earliest date at which Packer would be available would have been late in December 1954. Leathem, however, gave Packer permission to be a 'visiting lecturer' at Tyndale with effect from September 1954. As a result, Packer was able to continue his ministry in Birmingham, while spending the best part of two days a week teaching at Bristol. He would take the first train to Bristol from Birmingham in the morning, and stay overnight at Tyndale, returning the following day.

Packer then joined the staff on a full-time basis as a 'resident lecturer' in January 1955. The records of the Diocese of Birmingham note that Packer formally left employment in the diocese on 8 January 1955, to take up a position at Tyndale Hall, Bristol. It was a cold winter day when the Packers left Harborne in the first week of January, travelling down through sleet and snow to Bristol. Not owning a car, they chose to travel down in the van which was transporting their personal effects and furniture.

Packer and Kit lived in the first-floor apartment in Ridley House, which was the name given to the original building of 1925, on the corner of Pembroke Road. This apartment (which included a large room which Packer was to use as a study) was located above the chapel and lecture rooms, and underneath student accommodation for six or seven students. Whether by accident or design, those living above the Packers generally turned out to be among the quieter members of the student body. There were two flights of stairs within this building, and it was agreed that the Packers would have the use of the front set of stairs, and the students the back set.

Packer was required to teach Reformation history and theology for the University of Bristol Bachelor of Arts in Theology,[5] early church history and biblical theology for the external University of London Bachelor of Divinity; and biblical theology for the University of London Diploma in Theology. He was also involved for a while in the teaching of doctrine for the General Ordination Examination, which was the recognized qualification for ministry in the Church of England at this time.

Tyndale Hall had a student body numbering about fifty-five to sixty during most of the period during which Packer was on the teaching staff. Most of the students were Church of England ordination candidates. Although the missionary origins of the college were still in evidence – at least two students around this time (Dr Peter Cox and Dr Maurice Heyman) were in training to serve overseas as missionaries – it is clear that the focus of the college was very much on preparation for ministry at home in the Church of England. As many of the parishes which supported BCMS were in the north of England, there were a disproportionate number of genial Lancashire Protestants to be found in the student body at this time. The college year followed the normal pattern of the British academic year, consisting of three terms of ten weeks. The daily college routine was fairly standard for Church of England theological colleges of the period. Morning Prayer was said in chapel from 7.30 to 8.00 a.m., followed by a Quiet Time from 8.00 to 8.30. After breakfast at 8.30, the teaching programme occupied the period 9.00 to 1.00.

The staff team at Tyndale during this period was unusually talented, and several of their names feature prominently in the development of evangelicalism in England, especially within the Church of England, from the 1950s to the 1980s. There were three residential members of staff. The principal was J. Stafford Wright, a shy and conscientious man with a dry sense of humour, who was much liked by the students. His area of expertise was Old Testament, although he had a particular interest in cults. John Wenham served as vice-principal, and was especially noted for his clear teaching of New Testament Greek. His textbook on this subject, published by Cambridge University Press, became the standard text in England for a generation of theologians and ordinands.

Tyndale Hall was run on a shoestring at this time. Its limited budget and assets meant that it made extensive use of part-time tutors. Richard J. Coates combined his part-time teaching of liturgy at Tyndale with the incumbency of Christ Church, at the nearby seaside resort of Weston-super-Mare. He was a warm-hearted Irish Protestant, and a close friend of William Leathem's. Richard E.

Higginson, who was vicar of Redland (a Bristol suburb) taught church history part-time. Dennis Tongue taught New Testament, also in a part-time capacity.

Most Tyndale students of the late 1950s were quite convinced that they had the strongest teaching staff of any theological college in the country, and regarded Packer as the best among them. It is clear that Packer was the main reason for many students choosing Tyndale Hall in preference to other possible colleges. Although the teaching staff did not share lunch with their students, Packer was in the habit of joining the students for breakfast. Colin Maunsell in particular recalls Packer's remarkable gift for dealing with complex theological questions at a time of day when most were still half asleep. The students would allow Packer to finish his first cup of coffee, and then ask their profound theological question of the day. Packer would put his coffee cup down, put his hands to his head, wait for about ten seconds, and then reel off a remarkably clear and comprehensive answer (usually involving at least three points, and sometimes five).

One feature of Packer's teaching which has remained characteristic of him ever since became particularly clear at Bristol. Packer never seemed to quite manage to fit all his lecture material into the time available. He was also convinced of the importance of answering students' questions, and devoted considerably more time to this than the other members of staff. Packer's belief was that it was important, not only to answer a student's question, but to help the student see how the answer was arrived at. In consequence, his answers were often comprehensive to the point of being encyclopedic. Some students grumbled because the course material was never quite completed; others found the question times challenging and stimulating.

During his time at Tyndale, Packer became heavily involved in the work of the Inter-Varsity Fellowship. It was no accident that his two earliest books were the direct result of addresses given to student groups, or that they address issues which were of major concern in IVF circles. At least two or three times a term, Packer would travel to speak at Christian Unions around the country. He was also engaged on a number of writing projects during this period of his life, most notably a series of articles for the *New Bible Dictionary*. This major work traced its origins back to a proposal of 1953, which noted the need for a new Bible 'dictionary and/or encyclopedia'. Initially, the publishing division of the IVF considered updating an existing American work, before deciding that a completely new work was required. J.D. Douglas was duly appointed as editor, with Packer, F.F. Bruce, R.V.G. Tasker and D.J. Wiseman as consultant editors. It proved a major undertaking, both in terms of planning the structure of the work, and in commissioning the articles themselves. The work was not published until 1962, when it established itself as a major resource.[6]

Packer's reputation as a lecturer and speaker grew steadily. For a substantial part of the student body, Tyndale *was* Packer. His appeal to students was due to two factors. First, irrespective of the theological perspective of the students, there was a general consensus that Packer was the best-informed member of staff, who took considerable care and trouble over his teaching. In particular, students appreciated the way in which he answered their questions, even when those questions were hostile or critical. Second, perhaps between one quarter and one third of the student body was at least sympathetic to the Calvinistic (the term most widely used within the student body to refer to this approach) line developed by Packer during his teaching. The high regard in which Packer was held by the students may have led to some tension within the staff body. Students at the time suspected that at least one staff member was irritated by Packer's high standing within the student body. But nothing was ever said directly.

A lot was said in public, however, in a controversy which broke out during Packer's first year as a residential tutor at Tyndale, and which came close to costing him his job.

The Attack on Keswick

Evangelicalism, both in North America and in Britain, has tended to allow certain individuals, movements or institutions to have considerable authority in defining what evangelicalism actually is. As a result, a criticism of these individuals, movements or institutions is often seen or portrayed as an attack on evangelicalism itself – whereas the point at issue in fact is whether evangelicalism needs to redefine itself in relation to them. By the late 1940s, British evangelicals had, probably without fully realizing it, come to regard the Keswick teaching on sanctification as being, not merely correct, but also of defining importance. In other words, the Keswick teaching had come to be seen as a distinctive article of evangelical belief. To criticize Keswick was thus to attack evangelicalism. The same pattern is repeated regularly in evangelical history.

It must be noted that there were significant evangelical critiques of the Keswick teaching on sanctification in the nineteenth century. Perhaps the most trenchant was offered by Bishop J.C. Ryle, the Anglican Bishop of Liverpool who had an especial regard for the Puritans. Ryle's *Holiness* (1877) can be seen as a clear criticism of the Keswick approach, especially in regard to its weak concept of sin. Nevertheless, by about 1900 the Keswick Convention had become a rallying-point for evangelicals throughout Britain, attracting support from as distinguished evangelical writers and thinkers as Handley C.G. Moule, Bishop of Durham. As Keswick gained in stature, so criticism of its basic ideas became an increasingly hazardous business for any evangelical wishing to remain on good terms with the mainstream of the movement.

As we noted earlier, Packer had encountered the 'Keswick' teaching concerning 'victorious living' during his time at Oxford as a young Christian (p. 22). Initially, his misgivings concerning it had primarily to do with its failure to meet his spiritual condition. However, Packer's growing appreciation of the Puritans and those who had been influenced by them (such as J C Ryle) had by now led him to a much more fundamental criticism of the Keswick movement's teaching: that it was based on a series of theological errors. In 1952, a book appeared which seemed to Packer to reproduce all the old Keswick errors, but which was written in a manner which would allow the teaching a new lease of life. The book in question was Steven Barabbas's *So Great Salvation*. He resolved to counter this book through an extended critical review of it in the leading evangelical journal, *The Evangelical Quarterly*. The fifteen-page review appeared in the July 1955 edition of the journal.

Packer had no doubts about what needed to be done with the old Keswick teaching: he wanted 'to kill it dead'. He also had no doubt about where Keswick's fatal weak spot was to be found – in the idea of the human ability to make the critical decisions necessary to sanctification. For Packer, this was an uninformed Pelagianism, which took a hopelessly optimistic view of fallen human nature. His review abandoned the tact of diplomacy in favour of a full frontal assault. For Packer, 'Keswick offers a salvation which, far from being "so great", is in reality attenuated and impoverished . . . Its teaching rests on a theological axiom which is false to Scripture and dishonouring to God.' This was strong language, inflamed still further by his argument that the Keswick teaching was Pelagian, in that it diminished the role of God and falsely elevated the role of human will and freedom.

Most important of all was Packer's suggestion that a theologically naïve Pietism inevitably lapsed into precisely such a Pelagianism: 'After all, Pelagianism is the natural heresy of zealous Christians who are not interested in theology.' The critical importance of theology was thus uncompromisingly asserted and defended. Packer himself described the review as a 'fiery onslaught' on the Keswick teaching, written with all the passion of a 'burned child now dreading the fire'. Packer set himself the agenda of aiming to destroy the Keswick teaching, which he regarded as 'pernicious'. In the view of many readers of that review, he succeeded in doing so.[7]

However, he also succeeded in doing something else, which seriously prejudiced his position at Tyndale, and nearly led to his dismissal. As F.F. Bruce (the editor of *The Evangelical Quarterly* at this time) remarked, it 'evoked some very unsanctified remarks from those who disagreed with it'.[8] The chairman of the Tyndale Hall Council (A.T. Houghton) was a noted representative of the Keswick viewpoint. The review could not help but be seen as an attack on Houghton himself. Houghton wrote at length to Packer, more in sadness than in anger, inviting him to come to the next Keswick Convention and see for himself how misguided his comments were.

Furthermore, the Keswick position continued to be held in high esteem by many older evangelicals, whose support Tyndale Hall might well need to count upon to maintain its work. There were those who argued that Tyndale Hall's best interests would be served by the rapid departure of Packer from its staff, and the formal dissociation of the Hall from his critique of Keswick. It was a serious crisis for Packer, and it was far from clear what would happen. The forces ranged against him seemed considerable. However, Packer's cause was championed by William Leathem, who deployed his native Irish fighting instincts to secure Packer's continued employment at the Hall.

Looking back at Packer's onslaught on Keswick teaching, several points can be seen with the benefit of hindsight. At the time, the attack was widely regarded as 'shockingly presumptuous' (in the words of one senior observer). Nevertheless, it must be pointed out that other, more senior figures within evangelicalism who were known to have similar or related misgivings held back from expressing them. Packer can now be seen to have had the courage to say publicly what others had only muttered *sotto voce.* More significantly, the theological weight of Packer's critique seemed to many to prove unanswerable. Although Geoffrey Bromiley (Packer's predecessor at Tyndale) wrote four articles in response to Packer in the weekly evangelical journal *The Life of Faith,* these failed to meet Packer's specific criticisms. There was thus no response from the Keswick faction which rebuffed the critique offered by Packer. It is widely agreed that Packer's review marked the end of the dominance of the Keswick approach among younger evangelicals.

Looking back, it can be argued that this review simultaneously established Packer as something of a hero with an emerging younger generation of evangelicals, who were dissatisfied with the uncritical Pietism of British evangelicalism at this period, and alienated an older generation within the evangelical establishment of the day. Pietists within the evangelical movement regarded Packer as too academic and intellectual, and saw the attack on Keswick as a worrying sign that a new generation of evangelicals was emerging, who were too concerned with theology and scholarship for their own good.

Packer's review appeared at a propitious moment. In July 1951, Martyn Lloyd-Jones spoke at the third Welsh Inter-Varsity Fellowship, taking as his theme 'the sovereignty of God'. In these addresses, he vigorously rebutted some of the ideas underlying the Keswick approach, and stressed the total sovereignty of God in election. The addresses had a profound impact. J.C. Ryle's *Holiness,* which had been out of print for years, was reprinted in 1952, with a commendatory preface by Lloyd-Jones. Many, including the leading evangelical layman Norman Anderson, were initially inclined to think that what separated Keswick and the 'Lloyd-Jonesites' was little more than a difference of emphasis. Gradually, however, Anderson began to realize that a profound theological difference existed between them. Inexorably, the balance began to shift. In 1957, Packer and Johnston brought out an edition of Martin

Luther's 1525 treatise *The Bondage of the Will*, which included a substantial theological introduction stressing the manner in which contemporary evangelicalism had lost sight of many insights of the Reformation, from which it ultimately traced its descent.

We shall further explore some of the implications of Packer's growing commitment to Calvinism when we consider his views on evangelism and the sovereignty of God. Our attention now focuses on the publication of Packer's first book, which established his place as a leading younger evangelical thinker.

'Fundamentalism' and the Word of God (1958)

Much of Packer's early writing is occasional, written in specific response to the pressing needs of the moment. This is in no way to suggest that it lacks longer-term relevance; it is simply to note that Packer was sensitive to the importance of issues which needed to be addressed. Packer's understanding of church history, to which we shall return presently, suggested to him that clarification of doctrinal issues proceeded by controversy; it was therefore entirely natural that he should contribute to such clarification by engaging in controversy as and when it was necessary. The stimulus to write the book arose directly from a challenge to evangelicalism which needed to be met – and met competently.

The challenge came from the 'Fundamentalism controversy', which erupted within the English church during the period 1955–7. British critics of evangelicalism had long since discovered that one of the easiest ways of discrediting the movement was to refer to it as 'fundamentalism'. By the early 1950s, the word 'fundamentalism' had come to mean something like 'unthinking, dogmatic, narrow-minded, and unscholarly'. Liberal writers encouraged the direct identification of 'fundamentalism' and 'evangelicalism'. Billy Graham, who became well known in England during the early 1950s, was widely ridiculed by the intellectual élite of the Church of England at this time as a 'fundamentalist'. Thus Canon H.K. Luce, headmaster of Durham School, complained about the fact that Billy Graham was being allowed to lead a mission to the University of Cambridge. Universities, he argued, existed for the advancement of learning; so why was such an intellectual lightweight being allowed to speak at such an academically distinguished centre as the University of Cambridge? 'Is it not time that our religious leaders made it plain that while they respect, or even admire, Dr Graham's sincerity and personal power, they cannot regard fundamentalism as likely to issue in anything but disillusionment and disaster for educated men and women in this twentieth-century world?'[9]

Luce's haughty and condescending attitude, which treated evangelicalism (here referred to as 'fundamentalism') as totally unsuited for 'educated men and women', was widely echoed at the time. Evangelicalism was seen as being suited to illiterates, not to the cultured and sophisticated clergy of the Church of England. It could cause serious brain injury to those who imbibed its simplistic and seductive elixir. This attitude was reinforced by Michael Ramsey, then Bishop of Durham, who published an article entitled 'The Menace of Fundamentalism' in 1956, which accused Billy Graham of being heretical and sectarian. It proved to be a serious error of judgment; yet it corresponded well to mainline English Anglican attitudes to the new evangelicalism which was gaining momentum in the United States.

English critics of evangelicalism argued that no serious thinking person could be an evangelical. A threatened liberal élite reacted by refusing to take evangelicalism seriously. With the benefit of hindsight, this aggressive dismissal of evangelicalism can now be seen as reflecting a deep sense of unease within the liberal theological and ecclesiastical establishment over the growing numerical strength of evangelicalism in England. But evangelicals in the 1950s felt the pain of this assault. It was clear that they were despised, rejected and dismissed out of hand, particularly on account of their high view of Scripture. Ramsey clearly had his sights set on John R.W. Stott, who was then emerging as a significant spokesman for the growing evangelical constituency. A response was needed. In 1956 Stott himself fired off a broadside in an important pamphlet, entitled *Fundamentalism and Evangelicalism,* which sought to place clear blue water between the two movements.[10] But more was needed.

The definitive evangelical response came from Packer, in the form of his first book. Packer would later describe himself as 'an accidental author' – an allusion to one of Iris Murdoch's novels, entitled *An Accidental Man.*[11] The reason for this lies in the background to that first book, eventually entitled *'Fundamentalism' and the Word of God,* which was published in 1958. 'One day I was asked to write up a talk I had just given, and like Topsy, the script "just growed" into a full-length book.'

It is often suggested that Packer's first book was written in direct response to A.G. Hebert's book *Fundamentalism and the Church of God* (1957), which was severely critical, even to the point of being dismissive, of what Hebert termed 'fundamentalism'. The truth is slightly more complex than this. Packer had written on the general theme of the inspiration and authority of Scripture earlier in his career. In 1954, he contributed an article on 'Revelation and Inspiration' to the second edition of a one-volume Bible commentary co-edited by his friend Alan Stibbs.[12] The book which would now appear went far beyond this. Its origins lay in an address which Packer was asked to give to the Graduates' Fellowship meeting at London in 1957, with the title 'Narrow Mind – or Narrow Way?'. Packer spoke for about an hour, and his remarks were transcribed into a 7,000-word manuscript. His initial intention was to write this up for publication as a pamphlet. Ronald Inchley, then publishing director of the Inter-Varsity Fellowship, had expressed an interest in the work, and invited him to publish it.

However, as Packer mulled over the possibilities, he began to form the impression that it was necessary to engage with the issues – and especially the critics of evangelicalism – in greater depth. In particular, he felt the need to engage directly with Hebert's depiction and criticisms of evangelicalism. An article on 'The Fundamentalism Controversy', which he published in the spring of 1958, provided him with the opportunity to gather his thoughts on Hebert's work, and begin to assemble the elements of an informed and articulate evangelical response. One of Packer's goals was to show the critics that their criticisms fell wide of their intended targets. The book virtually wrote itself, and ended up as 55,000 words in length. As Packer himself recalls, it seemed 'to spring full-grown from the womb'. Ronald Inchley was expecting a 6,000-word pamphlet; after eighteen months, a typescript nearly ten times that length landed on his desk.

The fact that the book was to be published by the Inter-Varsity Fellowship is significant. The IVF was seen as a mainstream evangelical organization, with a specific concern to minister to the pastoral and intellectual needs of students in British universities. Part of that programme was the production of literature for British evangelical students. As early as 1926, the Executive Committee of the IVF had laid tentative plans in place for a series of publications dealing with theological, apologetic and moral issues then confronting evangelical students. By the early 1930s, a series of 'Inter-Varsity Papers' and 'Inter-Varsity Booklets' had been produced. It was not until the publication of T.C. Hammond's *In Understanding Be Men* (1933) that the IVF really scored a publishing success. By the early 1950s, however, the publications division of the IVF was firmly established, and had scored a major success with John R.W. Stott's best-selling book *Basic Christianity*.[13]

The year 1958 would prove to be a significant one for the publishing work of the Inter-Varsity Fellowship. Up to that point, it had produced all its books in hard covers. Although evangelistic tracts and other pamphlets were prepared with soft covers, there was a prevailing conviction that serious books ought to appear with hard covers, not least because they lasted longer. However, the development of the mass paperback market by British publishers such as Penguin and Pan was causing some to reconsider this policy. In 1957, Inchley felt that the time had come for the IVF to enter the paperback market. He happened to have six titles scheduled for publication the following year, all of which seemed suitable for this new mass-market format. Two were proposals to republish existing works, including Stott's *Basic Christianity*. Four were new works, including Packer's book and Martyn Lloyd-Jones's *Authority* (based on three lectures given in Canada in 1957). This seemed to Inchley to offer a timely opportunity to enter the paperback market. So the 'IVF Pocket Book' format was devised, and launched the next year. It proved to be a major success, and placed significant titles dealing with issues of evangelism, apologetics, theology, and practical living within the reach of students (whose budgets generally prevented them from buying the more expensive hard-cover editions).

On account of the wide range of styles of evangelicalism found within university Christian Unions, the IVF had an aversion to books which were seen as 'divisive' or 'polemical'. Although Packer had been seen as an exponent of a potentially divisive style of theology (and the repercussions of his 1955 critique of the Keswick holiness teaching were still keenly felt in some IVF circles), it was clearly felt that Packer's approach in this book was one around which evangelicals in general could unite.

The title for the work was not chosen by Packer himself, but by Ronald Inchley. Packer wanted to use the title 'The Faith Once

Delivered', which seemed to him to be an excellent summary of the book's contents and approach, as well as an excellent allusion to Jude 3. Inchley, however, felt that this would not help the book to sell. In the end, the title chosen was suggested by that chosen by Hebert for his attack on evangelicalism. Packer had responded immediately with a critical review of the book,[14] some of whose themes can be discerned within the typescript on which he was working at the time. It became clear that it was necessary to undertake not merely the negative critical task of refuting Hebert, but also the positive and constructive task of setting out an articulate, informed and persuasive evangelical understanding of the authority and inspiration of Scripture. Inchley's instinct told him that Packer's book needed to be presented as a definitive evangelical response to Hebert.

He therefore suggested the title *'Fundamentalism' and the Word of God*. The use of the 'scare quotes' immediately called into question Hebert's use of the term 'Fundamentalism'; the parallel betwen 'Church of God' and 'Word of God' then flagged up one of the fundamental theological differences between the Anglo-Catholicism of Hebert and the evangelicalism of Packer. The book got noticed, as Inchley fully expected it to. The work first appeared as an 'IVF Pocketbook' in March 1958, and had to be reprinted twice that same year, selling 20,000 copies in the first year of its publication.

The success of this book immediately established Packer as an authority on the subject. Previously, he had been seen particularly as a champion of the Puritans. His vigorous campaigning on behalf of Puritan theory and practice had gained him a following within a limited section of evangelicalism. *'Fundamentalism' and the Word of God* gained him an enthusiastic and appreciative audience within every section of evangelicalism. Not only did Packer provide a clear and accessible statement of what is generally known as the 'Old Princeton' or 'Hodge-Warfield' position on the inspiration and authority of Scripture; he also demonstrated that some recent English critics of this classic evangelical position – including Gabriel Hebert, Michael Ramsey and Alan Richardson – had grossly misunderstood and misrepresented it.

The book led to a significant alteration in Packer's reputation. Whereas he was initially viewed as a powerful proponent of a sectional (and potentially divisive) viewpoint within evangelicalism, he was now increasingly seen as a spokesman for the whole movement. Packer's increasing authority in relation to this major area of evangelical thought can be seen from the lectures he was invited to deliver in the aftermath of the publication of the book. In 1960, he delivered a lecture on 'The Origin and History of Fundamentalism' to the Oxford Conference of Evangelical Churchmen, in which he analysed evangelicalism's distinctive appeal to the authority of Scripture. In 1961, he spoke at the International Conference for Reformed Faith and Action, held in Cambridge, on the subject of 'The Bible and the Authority of Reason'.

The book was published that same year in the United States by Eerdmans, and was warmly received. Once more, it was welcomed as providing a clear and credible statement of a classic evangelical understanding of the authority and inspiration of Scripture. Packer began to attract the attention which has been so characteristic of his ministry in North America in the aftermath of this work. Roger Nicole (Reformed Theological Seminary, Orlando) recalls purchasing the book on its appearance for 95¢. He sat down at ten o'clock one evening to read the work, intending to read for an hour or so, before retiring for the night. It was six hours later before he felt able to put the book down, and go to sleep.[15]

The book had a particularly significant influence in Australia, where it became a standard text in evangelical theological institutions. For example, D. Broughton Knox recommended it strongly to first-year students at Moore College, one of the leading theological institutes in Sydney. It is possible that the impact of the book in Australia may have something to do with the fact that Hebert – against whom Packer directed some penetrating criticisms – was himself resident in Australia.[16]

The book can be seen as a distillation of the approaches to biblical authority and inspiration developed at Princeton Theological Seminary, New Jersey, during the nineteenth century, and particularly through the writings of Charles Hodge (1797–1878) and Benjamin B. Warfield (1851–1921). Packer himself intended the book to be 'a constructive restatement of evangelical principles in the light of the current "Fundamentalism controversy"'. It was his intention to show that evangelicals did not hold views about Scripture which were 'new, eccentric and in reality untenable', which were a direct response to 'literary and historical criticism of the Bible, and attacks launched in the name of science against what the Bible was thought to teach about creation'. In particular, Packer was concerned to combat the view that evangelicals' views of Scripture represented 'a defiant hardening of pre-critical and pre-scientific views, a desperate attempt to bolster up obsolete traditions'.

In defending the authority of Scripture, Packer made it clear that he had no sympathy with the 'dictation theory' of biblical inspiration, which had been so severely criticized by Hebert. For Packer, God has 'adapted his inspiring activity to the cast of mind, outlook, temperament, interests, literary habits and stylistic idiosyncrasies of each writer'. This leads Packer to stress the importance of the 'biblical idea of God's concursive operation in, with and through the free working of man's own mind'. While Packer does not explain this notion in extended detail, it is clear that he wishes to draw attention to the way in which God's inspiring action does not abolish individual human characteristics, but somehow allows them to find their proper way into the biblical text without compromising the reliability of Scripture. We shall return to this point later, in looking at the 'Battle for the Bible' of the 1970s (see pp. 196–203).

It is no exaggeration to say that this work moulded the thinking of evangelical students in the late 1950s and early 1960s. The publishers, the Inter-Varsity Fellowship, worked hard to ensure that the work was noticed and read by university students, whether theologians or not. Its overall impact was to transform the general perception of Packer within evangelicalism, and to significantly extend his influence and enhance his reputation. It is regarded by many older evangelicals as Packer's most creative work. It can be seen to have drawn two things to the attention of a rising generation of evangelicals. First, that the equation of 'fundamentalism' and 'evangelicalism' was quite improper. In that this identification lay behind much of the contemporary liberal critique of evangelicalism, the credibility of this critique was thus significantly eroded. More significantly, Packer allowed this new generation of evangelicals to realize that they were in possession of a coherent and credible understanding of the inspiration and authority of Scripture.

The result was a significant growth in self-confidence within evangelicalism at this point. Anecdote after anecdote confirms this. Although it is notoriously difficult to measure such subjective notions, the oral history of British evangelicalism at this time points to this book having caused a significant increase in the 'feel-good' factor within the movement. Geoffrey Shaw recalls how he and many of his contemporaries found that the book gave them a new sense of confidence, and eased the 'siege mentality' under which they had laboured until then. Frank Entwistle, who later joined the Inter-Varsity Press, recalls that it provided 'a resurgent post-war evangelicalism with a coherent statement of the orthodox Warfield doctrine of Scripture, and related it to the "fundamentalism" controversy which was then raging'. It proved to be of foundational importance for many evangelical theological students at this critical period in the history of the movement.

One of the most interesting results of the publication of this book took place later in the year of its publication. Towards the end of the Michaelmas term 1958, the Student Christian Movement at Oxford University arranged a debate over the authority of the Bible. The two main speakers were to be Packer and Christopher Evans, dean of Packer's old Oxford college, Corpus Christi (and subsequently professor of New Testament at King's College, London). The debate was to be chaired by Katherine Ross. The debate was originally to be held at 8.00 p.m. in the church hall of the Wesley Memorial Church, in New Inn Hall Street. However, the crowd which assembled to hear the debate proved so large that it could not be accommodated in the church hall. It had to be moved to the church itself, which could hold the 800 or so who turned up for the occasion. By the time everyone had found seats in the new venue, it was past 9.00 p.m.

Packer – who had driven across to Oxford for the occasion with some colleagues, including John Wenham and Richard Coates – was asked to speak first. Evans had already decided that he would not prepare his address in advance, but would respond directly to Packer's presentation. This, he believed, would result in a more useful debate. Packer's presentation took seventy-five minutes. As Evans recalls it, the presentation was 'a classic statement of the high Calvinist position, which was superbly done'. He realized that he was 'up against heavyweight stuff'. Evans then responded, challenging Packer over issues such as the relationship of Matthew and Mark in regard to the Synoptic Problem. However, at 11.00 p.m., Katherine Ross announced that she would have to bring the meeting to an end, to allow the audience to catch their buses home. The evening had not been entirely satisfactory, as there had not been enough time to explore issues in depth. Nevertheless, certain impressions had been made on the audience.

Some in the audience felt that evangelicalism was shown to be vulnerable in the face of the kind of arguments that Evans had advocated. At least three people present decided that they could not maintain their evangelical positions in the light of the debate. However, this was distinctly a minority verdict. The audience which went home that night generally adopted one of two positions. Perhaps the more common was that the situation was not as simple as they had thought, and that the evangelical position seemed to be rather more resilient than they had anticipated. The other viewpoint was that evangelicalism had shown that it could hold its own against its critics.

Perhaps the most telling analysis of the debate was found the following morning, over the breakfast table at Wycliffe Hall. A substantial number of Wycliffe students had attended the debate, not least because Packer himself was a former Wycliffe student. At the time, Wycliffe still maintained a generally liberal Protestant ethos. The evangelical faction within the Hall were exhilarated over the outcome of the debate, and felt that it marked a turning point in the fortunes of evangelicalism. The more liberal members of the student body were not persuaded by the debate; nevertheless, it was clear that some of them were having second thoughts about their position.

Packer and his colleagues drove home to Bristol late on the night of the debate in high spirits. The evening had persuaded them that the evangelical position could be defended in Oxford. As they talked, the germs of an idea emerged, which would eventually lead to the establishment of an evangelical research institution at Oxford – but that must wait until a later stage in our narrative (see pp. 101–4).

So what is the significance of *'Fundamentalism' and the Word of God* to our understanding of Packer's own theological development? Taken together with his earlier writings on Puritanism (particularly its teaching on sanctification), the book allows us to gain an insight into the type of theology which Packer was forging. At the risk of simplification, Packer's thought at this stage can be seen as a synthesis of aspects of Reformed thought from both the Old and the New World. English Puritanism (as found in John Owen and Richard Baxter) and the Old Princeton theology (as found in Charles Hodge and Benjamin B. Warfield) were brought together in Packer's vision of an academically rigorous yet pastorally relevant theology.

It must be stressed that there are direct continuities (despite subtle differences) between the English Puritans and the Reformed theology developed at Princeton Theological Seminary during the nineteenth century (most notably through the influence of Jonathan Edwards). Packer did not bring together two quite different streams of theology, but rather two strands of the international Reformed tradition which were often allowed to go their separate ways.

For many of his followers, Packer's theological perspective seems to have become more or less firmly established by about the year 1960; subsequent writings often focused on the further exploration of these theological insights, and their application and communication to the life of the church and individual Christians. One such area of major importance was the immensely complex dynamic between the Christian responsibility to preach the gospel, and the sovereignty of God. As we shall see, Packer was able to hold these two principles together at a time when they seemed likely to lead to serious divisions within British evangelicalism. The issues in question were addressed in his second book, *Evangelism and the Sovereignty of God.*

Evangelism and the Sovereignty of God (1961)

We have seen how Packer was instrumental in reviving interest in the writings of the Puritans, and how the Banner of Truth Trust committed itself to making classic works of Puritan and Reformed theology available, often after they had been out of print for many years. One writer who was brought back into circulation in this way was the leading Puritan writer John Owen, who had had such an impact upon the young Packer during his time as a student (p. 25). In 1959, Packer contributed a foreword to the Banner of Truth's reprint of Owen's classic treatise *The Death of Death in the Death of Christ.* The treatise was not one of the works by Owen which had so influenced him as a student; it was, nevertheless, an important work, not least because it set out one of the most influential statements of the doctrine of 'limited atonement' or 'particular redemption'.

At this point, it is important to appreciate that not all Puritan writers were committed to the view that Christ died only for the elect. Packer's doctoral thesis at Oxford had dealt with the views of Richard Baxter on this issue, and brought out clearly the manner in which Baxter held that Christ died in order to make satisfaction for the sins of all. This teaching is most clearly set out in Baxter's posthumously published work *The Universal Redemption of Mankind by the Lord Jesus Christ* (1694). Packer, however, had not chosen to study Baxter because he agreed with him at every point; indeed, it was axiomatic for Packer that the Puritans were to be challenged and corrected, along with everyone else, when they seemed to be at odds with Scripture. For Packer, the theme of the sovereignty of God expressed itself both in creation and redemption; in the former case, it showed itself especially clearly in relation to God's providential guidance and government of the world; in the latter, in relation to the sovereign election of those who were to be saved, for whom alone Christ died. This view, which is clearly stated by Owen, came to be Packer's position as well.

Packer's views on predestination and election were strongly Reformed, stressing the sovereignty of God in creation and redemption. Not all students at Tyndale Hall were entirely sympathetic to Packer's views in this area, particularly in relation to predestination. One issue which emerged as particularly important in the late 1950s concerned a tension between the sovereignty of God and the need to evangelize. If God was sovereign, why bother to evangelize? It was an issue which had emerged as important at several points in church history. For example, when the Baptist missionary William Carey announced his intention to found a Mission Society, he met with the following response from one of those whose advice he asked. 'When God is pleased to convert the heathen, he will do so without your aid or mine.'

The issue became of major importance in British evangelicalism. Billy Graham's crusades – initially in London, and subsequently at Cambridge and elsewhere – had raised the profile of evangelism enormously. Many churches and student Christian organizations were beginning to see evangelism as having a central place. Often, evangelism was presented in rather human terms, as if the gospel were a commodity which merely needed to be marketed effectively to ensure its successful adoption. This often led to disillusionment, as students tried to evangelize, and found that their efforts failed to bear the fruit which they expected. It also suggested that evangelism was simply a matter of human technique, in which God's personal involvement was of no moment. Just as Packer suspected the Keswick holiness teaching of ultimately resting on a Pelagian view of human nature, he also came to share Benjamin B. Warfield's view that aggressive evangelistic campaigns were ultimately based on a Pelagian foundation.

Packer developed this point in his paper on 'Puritan Evangelism', delivered at the 1955 Puritan Studies Conference. It seemed necessary to Packer to present a theological corrective to an implicit Pelagianism lying behind the tactics and approaches which seemed to be of foundational importance to the new evangelistic campaigns. He pointed out that the origins of the modern evangelistic campaign – including some of the methods still being used in the 1950s – lay with Charles Finney in the 1820s. The renewed interest in Puritanism – which owed so much to Packer – led to a growing attachment to its teachings on grace and predestination. If God was in control, why was it necessary to evangelize at all? Some supporters of the Puritan Studies Conference began to challenge the very idea of holding missions to universities.

The new interest in Reformed theology gave rise to some difficulties, perhaps in part because those who were discovering the intellectual and spiritual riches of this theology were impatient to master it, and came to certain judgments on the basis of a lack of familiarity with its nuances. One major illustration of this difficulty can be seen in relation to evangelism. The 1950s were a remarkable period in British evangelicalism, noted both for the new appreciation of the importance of evangelism, stimulated to no small extent by the Billy Graham crusades, and the rising interest in Reformed theology, stimulated to no small extent by Packer, Johnston and Lloyd-Jones. By the end of that decade, a tension appeared to be emerging between these two increasingly important trends. Many were openly questioning whether a Reformed pastor could also be an evangelist.

Packer drew attention to this situation in his address to the 1959 Puritan Studies Conference, delivered on 15 December at Westminster Chapel. Referring to the growing influence of

Reformed theology in recent years, Packer pointed out how many had come to accept a Reformed theological position, but could not 'see on this basis how to preach evangelistically'. For example, he reported that some argued that the central Reformed doctrine that faith and repentance were gifts given only to the elect was quite incompatible with the preaching of the gospel indiscriminately to everyone. The outcome of this situation was that some were preaching the gospel as if it was in the power of their audiences to respond to Christ, without any need for the grace of God to move them, and others were 'not preaching evangelistically at all'. The tragedy of this situation was that a theology which was intended to invigorate evangelism was threatening to strangle it. Packer then turned to the Puritans, to illustrate the way in which preachers such as Richard Baxter and John Rogers were able to combine a Reformed emphasis on divine sovereignty in election with a strong sense of responsibility (or 'duty', to use a favourite Puritan term) to preach the gospel.

It was against this background of confusion and disagreement that *Evangelism and the Sovereignty of God* had its origins. The book arose from a specific need and a particular occasion. The London Inter-Faculty Christian Union (LIFCU) was planning a mission. At this stage, the Union was dominated by individuals who held that no theological justification could be offered for vigorous evangelistic activity. Tension arose within the organizing body particularly over whether evangelistic appeals should be made to the audience at the mission meetings. Some of the committee had been influenced by the Calvinism of Banner of Truth publications, which had begun to make their appearance since 1957; they held that there were serious criticisms to be made of this practice. Others felt that it was unthinkable that there should not be some form of appeal. A pre-mission meeting was therefore arranged for 24 October 1959 at Westminster Chapel, with the intention of addressing and attempting to resolve the issues involved. Packer was an obvious choice as speaker. In 1957, he had published an article on 'Puritan Evangelism', in which he had argued that Calvinism and evangelism were not mutually exclusive.[17]

Packer agreed to speak, and the resulting address was expanded into the book *Evangelism and the Sovereignty of God*. The work was again published by the Inter-Varsity Fellowship. It was unquestionably the right choice. IVF had a wide student readership, and the controversy outlined above was raging in student circles at the time. The work which resulted would be one of Packer's most influential and widely read books. It opens with an affirmation of the sovereignty of God, with particular reference to prayer. Following a line of argument developed by Augustine during his controversy with Pelagius, Packer notes that Christians acknowledge their dependence upon God by praying to him.

> The recognition of God's sovereignty is the basis of your prayers. In prayer, you ask for things and give thanks for things. Why? Because you recognize that God is the author and source of all the good that you have had already, and all the good that you hope for in the future. This is the fundamental philosophy of Christian prayer. The prayer of a Christian is not an attempt to force God's hand, but a humble acknowledgment of helplessness and dependence.

Continuing the Augustinian line of exploration, Packer notes that one of the things that Christians do – and ought to do – is pray for the conversion of others. In praying for this, Christians are implicitly acknowledging that God is sovereign in conversion. 'On our feet we may have arguments about it, but on our knees we are all agreed.'

Having established this point, Packer moves on to consider the 'antinomy' (that is, the apparent opposition) between divine sovereignty and human responsibility. Human reason is inclined to suspect that these cannot both be true at one and the same time; Scripture asserts that they are, and leaves us the task of thinking through the implications. 'To our finite minds, of course, the thing is inexplicable. It sounds like a contradiction, and our first reaction is to complain that it is absurd.' Like the great nineteenth-century Baptist preacher Charles Haddon Spurgeon, Packer argues that these two great biblical truths must be held together. There is no need to reconcile friends. 'In the Bible, divine sovereignty and human responsibility are not enemies . . . they are *friends*, and they work together.' Packer pointed out that two early Methodists, John Wesley and George Whitefield, had very different understandings of the extent of Christ's saving work, and the way in which grace worked in human lives. Nevertheless, 'both were content to preach the gospel just as it stands in Scripture: that is, to proclaim "the living Christ, with the virtue of his reconciling death in him", to offer him to sinners, and to invite the lost to come to him and so find life.'

Finally, Packer goes on to show how these two themes work together positively. The human responsibility to evangelize must be affirmed – evangelism is not an 'optional extra'. But the success of that evangelization lies not in human wisdom, power or specialized techniques, but in the power and grace of God at work in the world. Packer's emphasis on this point can be shown to have resonated with many of his readers, who had been told that, if only they preached the gospel in a certain way, or used certain evangelistic techniques, then conversions would be assured. Packer reminded those readers that this was a thoroughly human-centred way of thinking, which failed to recognize, let alone honour, the grace of God. The result was disillusionment and doubt about the wisdom of evangelism.

> Why have we these doubts? Because we have been disillusioned. How have we been disillusioned? By the repeated failure of the evangelistic techniques in which we once reposed such confidence.
>
> What is the cure of our disillusionment? First, we must admit that we were silly ever to think that any evangelistic technique, however skilful, could of itself guarantee conversions; second, we must recognize that, because man's heart is impervious to the word of God, it is no cause for surprise if at any time our evangelism fails to result in conversions; third, we must remember that the terms of our calling are that we should be faithful, not that we should be successful; fourth, we must learn to rest all our hopes of fruit in evangelism upon the omnipotent grace of God.

Packer would return to the theme of the relation between divine sovereignty and the human responsibility to evangelize at several points subsequently. In 1966, he contributed a significant article entitled 'A Calvinist – and an Evangelist!' to the 'Minister's Viewpoint' section of a British religious paper.[18] Packer conceded that some extremists (whom he described as 'hypercalvinists') did indeed teach that the gospel should not be preached or offered to the unregenerate. However, Packer insisted that this was a minority viewpoint, which was seriously out of line with the mainstream. He cited approvingly Spurgeon's comments in his lecture 'Misrepresentations of True Calvinism Cleared Away',

given at the newly opened Metropolitan Tabernacle on Thursday
11 April 1861:

> A yet further charge against us is that *we dare not preach the gospel to
> the unregenerate*, that, in fact, our theology is so narrow and cramped
> that we cannot preach to sinners. Gentlemen, if you dare to say this,
> I would take you to any library in the world where the old Puritan
> fathers are stored up, and I would let you take down any one and
> tell me if you ever read more telling exhortations and addresses to
> sinners in any of your own books.

Once more, it is important to note the way in which the Puritan
writers are being singled out as role models for Reformed theology
in action – that is, a theology which is applied to the life and ministry
of believers and the church.

Packer's article is also significant on account of his critique
of the evangelistic methods of Charles G. Finney, such as the
'altar call', which had become widely accepted within evangelistic
crusade movements in the United States. Packer's concern here,
which was echoed in the 1961 work just noted, is that the
emphasis on evangelistic technique and the personality of the
evangelist seriously obscured the fact that 'God himself is the true
evangelist'. From a Calvinist perspective, Packer was alarmed that
the approaches associated with Finney and his successors make
evangelism into a human achievement, primarily concerned with
technique, method and atmosphere, and neglect the vital role of
God in the conversion of individuals. It was an important point,
and found sympathy with many readers who felt uneasy about the
way in which evangelism was being detached from the life of the
local church, and focused on major campaigns which sometimes
seemed to depend more on the human qualities of the evangelist,
especially his power to persuade, than on the power of God.

Packer developed this point further at the 1960 Puritan and
Reformed Studies Conference. On the afternoon of 20 December
1960, Packer spoke on 'Jonathan Edwards and the Theology of
Revival'. It was an important address, in that Edwards was directly
linked with the origins of the 'Great Awakening' in New England
during the eighteenth century. Packer's point was simple: revival is
something which has its origins and instigation with God, not with
human effort or planning. The very idea of an evangelist 'planning'

a revival was therefore theologically ridiculous. Packer explored this theme further in a major address on the theme of 'revival' given to the London meeting of the Graduates' Fellowship in November 1966.[19] This address remains of major importance, and we shall summarize its main points below.

'Revival is widely thought of as a work of man, something that man can and should organize.' With these words, Packer summarized what seemed to him to be the theological misperception which lay behind so much evangelistic entrepreneurship, especially in North America. 'But the truth is exactly opposite. Revival cannot be organized or planned by man.' It is a work of God, which must be recognized to lie under his sovereign control. A failure or refusal to accept this point seemed to Packer to be typical of many major North American evangelistic campaigns, which traced their history back to Charles Finney, and especially his work *Revivals of Religion*.

> I once saw in an American journal an advertisement which began, in large letters, *DON'T PLAN A REVIVAL* – and I thought, how remarkably right-minded! But alas, the ad. went on, in smaller type – *until you have these free samples of color advertising planned especially for the church which wants something different but must operate on a conservative budget.*

Against this idea of revival as something that churches or evangelists can engineer or contrive by the use of suitable techniques, Packer argued for the recovery of a biblical understanding of revival as 'a gracious work of God, restoring spiritual vitality'. For Packer, three major principles could be discerned lying behind the biblical witness to revival within the church. First, we need to recognize the need for revival. Second, 'we must be clear that we cannot create or work up revival. We can remove hindrances to revival, but we cannot restore life.' While we can humble ourselves before God, raising us up is something which God alone can do. The corollary of this was clear: just 'as we cannot ensure revival by our preparations, so we cannot preclude it by our lack of preparation'. This, for Packer, was a particularly encouraging thought. Third, we should be praying for revival. For Packer, the theological analysis he had just presented should lead directly to prayer. If revival is a work of God, we should be crying out to God to do what he alone can do, and we cannot do – revive his church.

Where next?

Packer had come to Tyndale Hall in the firm conviction that there was a need for good academic theologians in the theological colleges. He had already established a reputation as a major theological resource for evangelicals. Marcus Loane, the evangelical Anglican Archbishop of Sydney, recalls becoming involved in a complex theological debate with other Anglican bishops over the issue of prayers for the dead at the Lambeth Conference of 1958.[20] Sensing that he was losing the argument, Loane asked a leading evangelical within the Church of England, Canon T.G. Mohan, for advice. Mohan told Loane that the best thing he could do was to ask Packer for a definitive statement of the evangelical position on this issue. Mohan offered to contact Packer on Loane's behalf. The following evening, Mohan placed into Loane's hand a single side of paper which set out the issues at stake in what Loane recalled to be a remarkably lucid manner. Loane took the document to the next committee meeting, and won the argument.

As its Senior Tutor, Packer was a significant figure in the life of Tyndale Hall. But he could not stay at Tyndale for ever, even though he had no fixed idea of how long he intended to remain there. His principal, J. Stafford Wright, seemed to have no definite views on the matter. He himself had spent a substantial part of his career in theological education; indeed, he would remain as principal of Tyndale Hall until 1969. Both Packer and his colleague John Wenham were advocates of the concept of the 'career academic' – an idea which ran counter to the prevailing notion that the teaching staff of theological colleges were simply clergy taking five years out from their parish careers.

Packer was convinced that the church needed individuals who were prepared to dedicate their entire careers to the teaching and intellectual equipping of students for ministry. For Packer, the old Keswick teaching showed what happened when good intentions were married to poor theology. Yet he was labouring under a heavy teaching load. His opportunities for research and writing were limited by his commitments at Bristol. The situation was not ideal. But was there an alternative? Initially, it seemed not.

The future, then, seemed unclear. There was no pressing reason for Packer to leave Tyndale. But a development was taking place which would open up a possibility which would offer him new horizons, and a potentially significant role in directing the evangelical movement within the national church. The idea which gave birth to this new possibility was conceived on the car journey from Oxford to Bristol after Packer's 1958 debate with Christopher Evans. We must now revisit that journey, and pick up the story from there.

«7»

Oxford: Latimer House, 1961–70

THE GREAT EIGHTEENTH-century French diplomat Talleyrand once remarked that 'without individuals, nothing happens; without institutions, nothing survives'. The 1960s was to prove to be a remarkable period of renaissance within evangelicalism in England, both within the national church and in many other Christian bodies. As we shall see, Packer would play a significant part in directing this rebirth of a theologically articulate and confident evangelicalism. His 1958 work *Fundamentalism' and the Word of God* had established his reputation as a constructive evangelical theologian and a vigorous critic of its opponents. The issue was now the fostering of a positive atmosphere of confidence and purposefulness, which would allow evangelicals to begin to engage with the issues which were facing the churches at this time.

The 1960s was also to be a period of massive cultural shifts. A process of change had been set in motion within the Church of England, as in other churches. There was a need for evangelicals to be able – if possible – to anticipate future developments, and provide theologically convincing and pastorally effective strategies for dealing with issues. Many evangelicals sensed that liberalism was poised to make substantial gains within the mainline churches, in England and beyond, making it imperative that evangelicals should be able to provide coherent and credible responses. But who was there who could do this? An environment fostering creative and responsible thinkers was needed, a platform which would allow them to project their wisdom into the church at large. In short: individual thinkers needed institutions to support and foster their work, and ensure that their ideas and strategies were made known and available as widely as possible.

Packer has always been a strategic evangelical thinker. At an early stage, he came to appreciate the importance of theology for a right understanding of and approach to the Christian life. This can be seen initially in his response to the Keswick holiness teaching, and subsequently in his careful analysis of the foundations of evangelism. It is perhaps at its most evident in the classic work *Knowing God*, which we shall consider later in this book. Packer was quite convinced that an evangelicalism which lacked any sense of theological basis would lapse into Pietism or Pelagianism. Realizing the importance of good theology, however, is one thing; allowing others to catch that vision is quite another. Individuals have their limits; they need to be allied to structures which can allow them to reach beyond their personal limits. There was a need for a platform from which this theological vision could be developed, applied and projected. In short: there was a need for an evangelical institution dedicated to this end.

There were a number of evangelical models to hand. In 1955 Francis Schaeffer established L'Abri in the tiny Swiss village of Huemoz. This blossomed into a community which sought to provide credible and convincing answers to the questions that were emerging from a young post-war generation, which had largely lost touch with the reality of God and authentic Christian life. L'Abri was the institution which allowed Schaeffer to sustain and develop his distinctive apologetic ministry. An earlier model was provided by Tyndale House, an evangelical research and study institute established by the Inter-Varsity Fellowship in the English university city of Cambridge in 1944 (see p. 50). The institution provided a home for the Tyndale Fellowship for Biblical Research, and subsequently encouraged the formation of a series of groups concerned with the formulation of evangelical approaches to other theological disciplines. We have already seen how the Puritan Studies Conference had its origins under the aegis of this body. Cambridge thus had its centre of evangelical scholarship and research; Oxford did not. It was therefore natural to suggest that any new institution should be located in Oxford.

Packer was instrumental in the formation, direction and flowering of one of the most significant evangelical research institutes in post-war Britain – Latimer House, Oxford. This institute was specifically orientated towards engaging with issues within the Church of England. This distinct denominational identity and focus set Latimer House apart from other evangelical institutions in existence at the time. Many readers of the present and following chapters will find themselves perplexed by the turn now taken in Packer's life. Why is it that an evangelical thinker, with a growing following and reputation in evangelical circles irrespective of denomination, should choose to invest so much effort in fostering the growth of evangelicalism within one specific denomination? Does not this seem to be something of a misjudgment?

Packer did not think so. Whatever responsibilities he saw himself as having towards evangelicalism as a transdenominational movement, he was quite clear that individual evangelicals are called to work within their denominations for the furtherance of the gospel cause. The Church of England was the national church of England, with considerable influence in the British Commonwealth, particularly in Australia, Canada and New Zealand. Yet it was not this pragmatic realization of the importance of the Church of England which moved Packer to become deeply involved in its affairs (even if it affected his thinking at points). Packer viewed the Reformation in England as having brought into being an authentic form of Christianity which needed to be recovered by the contemporary church. Part of his vision for the Church of England was to recall it to its theological and historical roots in the English reformers of the sixteenth century (such as Bishop John Jewel), and subsequently the Puritan writers of the seventeenth. Its future depended on the contemporary reappropriation of its past.

The 1960s were to prove of decisive importance for the consolidation of evangelicalism within English Christianity as a whole, and especially within the Church of England. Packer is of central importance to this development, as was the research institute which became so closely linked with him during this period. We must now tell the story of how this research institute came into being.

The Origins of Latimer House

We have already noted the importance of a car journey for the genesis of Latimer House. Late one night in the final days of the autumn of 1958, three members of the teaching staff of Tyndale Hall were returning to Bristol after a debate at Oxford. The debate had pitted Packer against Christopher Evans on the issue of the authority of Scripture. The success of the evening had raised some important questions. As Packer, John Wenham and Richard Coates drove home that night, Wenham began to articulate the idea of having some kind of evangelical research centre in Oxford which would permanently consolidate what Packer had achieved that evening on a temporary basis. Wenham had already been involved in bringing Tyndale House, Cambridge, into being; his new vision was for a different kind of institution with quite distinct aims and objectives. It was a good idea, and both Wenham and Packer decided to work on it.

In December 1958, Wenham produced a memorandum, setting out his vision for an Oxford Evangelical Research Centre. Noting the relative lack of evangelical scholars, and particularly the weakness of the evangelical voice within the Church of England, he argued that there was a need to establish a permanent base in Oxford, which would allow evangelical scholars time to think and write, and address issues which would be of importance to the church. There was a real danger that liberalism would increase its stranglehold on the church in the years that lay ahead, unless firm and decisive action was taken to counter it. Wenham noted Tyndale House, Cambridge, as a model for the kind of institution he had in mind. However, Tyndale was specifically dedicated to New Testament scholarship, and had no particular denominational involvement. Indeed, Tyndale House saw itself as standing above denominational concerns, in order to promote evangelical scholarship at the broadest level. Wenham's vision was of a specifically Anglican centre, which would focus on issues such as doctrine, worship and church polity. A good working library would be an essential component of such a centre.

Packer followed this up with a complementary memorandum, extending the vision still further. Packer noted that, without such a centre, 'the thinking and writing necessary to maintain the evangelical cause in the Church of England will almost certainly not be done'. For this reason, Packer argued that the creation of such a research centre was 'a strategic requirement of the very highest priority'.[1] Noting that one of the lessons of church history was that 'the best theological work has been done under pressure of controversy and urgent need', Packer stressed the need for a centre which would not be about 'ivory tower scholarship' but about directly addressing the 'actual present-day needs of Anglican evangelicalism'.[2] Packer regarded this vision as necessitating the establishment of a centre in Oxford (on account of its library facilities and other resources), yet with a ministry directed towards the Church of England in particular.

The vision was agreed to be persuasive. Packer, Wenham and Coates were, however, based in Bristol; the proposed centre was to be in Oxford, and thus needed local expertise. A committee was therefore established which brought together Coates, Packer, and Wenham with Basil C. Gough (rector of St Ebbe's church), John S. Reynolds, and Malcolm H. McQueen. It met for the first time on Monday 29 December 1958, at St Ebbe's rectory in Oxford, and agreed to pursue the project further, while inviting the rising evangelical scholar Philip E. Hughes to join the committee. The committee met again on Tuesday 10 February 1959, and took the decision to invite Coates to lead the centre 'at such time as the necessary house and money were forthcoming', and Hughes to join as a second member of staff as soon as the financial means were available. Coates and Hughes were known to be friends, thus creating a firm expectation that they would form a good working partnership within the centre. A duplicated letter was circulated, informing prominent evangelicals of the intention of the committee, and inviting pledges of support. By June, £4,784 had been pledged; by September, this had risen to £8,716. The project began to attract serious attention. A large gift of books provided the nucleus of a future library. In October, John R.W. Stott assumed the chairmanship of the newly-constituted Oxford Evangelical Research Trust. While Stott's high profile and reputation cannot be regarded as the sole cause of the subsequent success of the project, his very public endorsement of its goals was of no small significance in its advances.

The second meeting of the Council, held at Church House, Westminster, on 12 January 1960, confirmed that Coates would be invited to be the first warden of the Research Centre, and Hughes its first librarian.[3] The appointments were for three years initially. It was agreed to purchase 131 Banbury Road (a large house just north of Oxford city centre, close to both Wycliffe Hall and St Michael's House) as the site of the centre, including accommodation for both men and their families. The house was sufficiently large to divide into two separate sets of living quarters, one upstairs and one downstairs. This would permit the kind of scholarly interaction and team work which the Council hoped for. The Centre's objects were defined as:

a) to provide opportunities for study and writing for staff members;
b) to organize a select fellowship of Anglican scholars to work together on important projects;
c) to strengthen the evangelical witness in Oxford.

The financial situation of the Trust was sufficiently positive to ensure both that the house was purchased, and that the salaries of both warden and librarian could be guaranteed for at least three years.

Packer was not formally involved in the work of the centre at this stage, but given his high profile within evangelicalism, it seemed right to involve him in some way in its work. Some such thought seems to have gone through the minds of some present at the first meeting of the Council in October 1959. That meeting asked (it is not clear at whose suggestion) that Tyndale Hall (Packer's employer at this stage) should be invited to release him for two days a week (the costs of this to be covered by the Trust) in order to allow him to contribute towards the work of the centre. By January 1960, Tyndale Hall had signalled their agreement: from 1 April of that year, Packer was to be allowed to devote two days a week to the Centre.

By April, the vision had more or less become a reality. The 'Research Centre' (it seems to have had no other name at this stage)[4] was equipped with books, funding, and two members of staff. All that was necessary was for those who had brought this dream to its fulfilment to await results. But the results were not quite what had been hoped for. To gain an understanding of the circumstances which led to the opening of a new – and highly productive – chapter of Packer's life, we need to explain the flaws in the structure of the newly established Centre.

The Warden

By May of that year, it was clear that Coates and Hughes had fallen out with each other. Although a number of factors were probably involved, the issue which proved decisive was the manner in which two families were expected to live in the same house. Matters reached a crisis, and an extraordinary meeting of the Trust was called in London on 4 June 1960. At this meeting, Coates announced his withdrawal of acceptance of the post of warden, citing personal difficulties with Hughes as the basis of his decision. Hughes was distressed at the criticisms made of him, and offered to resign. The Council thus, in effect, had to choose between the two men, in that both could not live in the same building. After much thought, the Council decided that they needed Coates more than Hughes. If the work of the Centre was to focus on the needs of the Church of England, it was obviously important that someone who was clearly part of and working within that church should be at its head. Perhaps Coates was a weaker scholar than Hughes; nevertheless, he was more fully in touch with a situation which Hughes would be seen to address from a more distant and detached perspective. But the committee did not want to lose Hughes from the ministry of the Centre. They eventually managed to put together a compromise solution, in which Coates would live in the house as the warden, and Hughes, while continuing to work as the librarian of the Centre, would live in alternative accommodation elsewhere in Oxford. Hughes was not satisfied with this arrangement, which seemed to fail to resolve the difficulty. On 9 June, he resigned as librarian.

The Council accepted his decision with regret at its next meeting, held at St Michael's House, Oxford, on 2 July 1960. The Council found itself in a very difficult position. Not only had Hughes resigned within months of his appointment; the position of librarian was now vacant. At this point, the Council made what proved to be a critical decision. They invited Packer to become librarian. Packer pointed out that he was still on the staff at Tyndale Hall, and could not accept the position on a full-time basis until 1 April 1961 at the earliest. However, the Council undertook to negotiate with Tyndale Hall in order to secure his earlier release, if possible.[5] In the light of the territorial squabble which had led to Hughes' resignation, an arrangement was made by which Coates would occupy the downstairs living quarters, and Packer the upstairs accommodation. All then seemed settled. The name 'Latimer House' was agreed upon for the new Research Institute.

The Packers duly arrived in Oxford in April 1961, and settled into their accommodation. The day after their arrival, Packer and Coates met together. Coates told Packer that he intended to resign, and somehow find his way back into parish work. In his view, he would be able to undertake more significant academic work within a parish context, rather than in the isolation of a research centre such as Latimer House. It was a serious blow. The decision was announced at the Council meeting on 21 July. The price which the Council had paid to keep Coates as warden was the loss of Hughes as librarian. Now they would lose Coates as well. They had little option but to accept his resignation, and encourage him to publish any research he had managed to undertake thus far.

Coates, however, had given no date for his impending resignation. He had announced his declaration of intent, in order that the Council might not be taken unaware by the move when it came. Given the uncertainty over his precise date of departure, the Council felt it could not at this stage make any plans for his replacement. It was only on 20 September that Coates was able to announce that he would be accepting a parish appointment in Kirkheaton, near the northern city of Huddersfield, and hoped to move in January 1962. The Council agreed to employ him until such time as he moved, provided that this took place by the end of January.

Only then did the Council feel it was appropriate to consider Coates's replacement as warden. Eight names were considered, including the recently departed librarian (Philip E. Hughes), Dr Geoffrey W. Bromiley, and Alan M. Stibbs. Packer's name was not mentioned at this stage as a possible warden. The meeting ended without any agreement. A decision on this matter would be taken at the next meeting, scheduled for 13 June 1962 at Latimer House. It was at this meeting that Packer was invited to be warden. No other names were suggested. Packer was quite clear who he wanted to work with, and why. Roger T. Beckwith (whom Packer had got to know during his time at Bristol) was an excellent researcher, with interests which complemented Packer's and ensured that Latimer House would be able to contribute with competence on a broad front. During that meeting, the Council discussed inviting Beckwith to assume the position of librarian; this invitation was confirmed at its meeting of 19 September.

Packer himself may have helped to crystallize the Council's choice for the successor to Coates. Packer had been told by Coates in April 1961 that he intended to resign; a decision concerning Coates's successor was not taken until June 1962. It was entirely natural that Packer should have anxieties about the situation. What was his own future? He had left an important position in Bristol in order to work at Latimer House. He needed some indication as to whether he had a future at Latimer House, and if so, what that future would be.

So a Research Institute originally founded with one warden and one librarian had experienced a total change of staff within two years of its establishment. It was not a particularly auspicious beginning. However, the team that was now in place proved to be what was needed for what lay ahead, as we shall see. A sustained criticism of the theological ethos of the 1960s was essential, if evangelicalism was to gain the high ground within the national church. Latimer House rose to the challenge.

Packer's Critique of the Radical Theology of the 1960s

The 1960s was the period of radical theology *par excellence*. The 'death of God' controversy exploded in the United States, with certain theologians declaring that God had ceased to have any relevance to modern secular culture. In England, similar developments took place, with many academic theologians deciding to jettison traditional teachings on the grounds that they failed to match up with the modern mood. One commentator sums up the mood of the era as follows;

> English religion of the mid-sixties was being pushed rather fast in quite a number of directions – ecumenical, liturgical, world-orientated, charismatic. Proposals and pilot schemes were jostling each other on every side. In part this sprang from, and yet it was not really made easier by, the increasingly obvious absence of an agreed basic position as to belief or goal ... At times it looked as if the authority of the Bible, the church, scholastic theology and Christian spiritual experience were all alike being rejected as 'irrelevant' and outdated, to leave as the new sources of enlightenment little more than sociology, linguistic analysis, modern Marxism, or the study of other religions.[6]

This is a judgment that can be seen as entirely justified, with the benefit of hindsight. But there were few at the time who had the wisdom to see this.

The most influential work of radical theology was pitched at a popular level. On 19 March 1963, John A.T. Robinson published a book with the title *Honest to God*. It attracted particular attention on account of the fact that its author was a bishop in the Church of England. Shortly before the publication of the book, Robinson had contributed an article to the *Observer*, a leading British Sunday newspaper with the provocative title (chosen by the *Observer*, rather than Robinson himself): 'Our Image of God Must Go.' When the book appeared, it became a bestseller in Britain, and earned the nickname 'Honest John' for its author.[7] The initial print run ordered by the publishers was a mere 8,000 copies, of which 2,000 were intended for export to the United States. The print run was sold out on the first day of publication. The demand for the book took everyone by surprise. It is estimated that it sold 350,000 copies during its first seven months.

Its impact on the public impression of traditional Christian beliefs was strongly negative. They were seen as outdated, meaningless relics of a bygone era. The Archbishop of Canterbury, Michael Ramsey, denounced the book for caricaturing the ordinary Christian's view of God. 'It is utterly wrong and misleading', he stated in a television interview on Sunday 1 April 1963, 'to denounce the imagery of God held by Christian men, women and children: imagery that they have got from Jesus himself, the image of God the Father in heaven, and to say that we can't have any new thought until it is swept away.'

It is significant that the general calibre of the evangelical response was such that it failed to penetrate to the heart of the matter. A convincing evangelical rebuttal was needed as a matter of urgency. Most responses by evangelicals could be summarized as simple variations on one or both of two themes. First, a bishop should not be allowed to write books of this kind and remain in office. Second, what the bishop described is not Christian orthodoxy. One exception may be noted. It is widely agreed that by far the best evangelical critique of Robinson was Packer's *Keep Yourself From Idols*. This twenty-page pamphlet, produced in great haste in order to be available as quickly as possible, appeared in the same year as Robinson's work. Although Packer was invited to engage in various broadcast discussions relating to the *Honest to God* controversy, it is generally thought that his most effective response is found in this brief work, which represents an expanded version of an article originally published in the *Church of England Newspaper*.

The title of the pamphlet derives from John's warning to his readers to 'keep themselves from idols' (1 John 5:21). For Packer, the choice was not between two different ways of thinking about God; it was about two different Gods, two different Christs – and ultimately, about two different religions. Robinson had not 'updated' the gospel; he had 'changed the truth about God into a lie'. Packer was particularly critical of the way in which Robinson had behaved in his role as a bishop. 'No doubt the church needs its gadflies . . . But it is not to the office and work of a gadfly that a bishop is consecrated.' Robinson had, perhaps in effect rather than intention, used 'a position of trust as a vantage-point from which to torpedo the deepest convictions of those who trust him'.

In making these points, Packer can be seen to have incorporated the two themes which we noted above. But Packer's response penetrated far more deeply. He argued that Robinson's work lacked theological rigour, and rested on misunderstandings or misreadings of other writers. For Packer, Robinson's work represented a very superficial reading and application of the work of three theologians: Dietrich Bonhoeffer, Rudolf Bultmann, and Paul Tillich. Robinson applauded Bonhoeffer for his idea of a 'religionless Christianity', Bultmann for his attempt to 'demythologize' the gospel, and Tillich for his concern to relate Christianity to human 'ultimate concerns'. Indeed, Robinson felt that the time had come to abandon traditional Christian language about a God who was 'out there' or 'up there', and pick up on the insights of depth psychology, which spoke of God (if it spoke of God at all) in terms of the 'ground of our being' – a term much favoured by Tillich.

It is now widely agreed that Robinson had misunderstood or oversimplified the approaches of these writers. Packer anticipated this important future judgment when he declared that the work was little more than 'a plateful of mashed up Tillich fried in Bultmann and garnished with Bonhoeffer'. Every page, he argued, bore the unmistakable 'marks of unfinished thinking'. The fundamental flaws of the work were thus theological. While recognizing that Robinson was clearly concerned with relating Christianity to the needs of modern men and women, Packer declared that the entire project was misconceived. It was not Christianity which was being presented in a new manner, but a new religion, which made no reference to the incarnation, the atoning death of Christ, or the resurrection of Jesus. How could this legitimately be described as 'Christianity'? Far from rescuing the perishing, Robinson was merely sinking their lifeboat.

Packer relentlessly pointed out the consequences of Robinson's position. Robinson's Jesus cannot in any meaningful sense be termed 'Saviour' or 'Lord'. Robinson had eliminated anything distinctively Christian from his conception of God, ending up with a vague form of theism to which any religious person could give at least some degree of assent. Perhaps most tellingly, Packer stressed the serious tension which Robinson generated between theology and worship. On the basis of Robinson's theology, no meaningful account can be given of Christian worship. Robinson's God 'has done nothing to be praised for. He did not make us; we do not depend on him for our existence; he has not ransomed us from Hell, nor has he promised to bring us to glory.' Robinson's theology had no place for the concepts of God as creator or redeemer; what, therefore, can he be praised for? Perhaps it was no cause for surprise that Robinson redefined worship in terms of some kind of mental preparation for service of other people, rather than a response to God's being and deeds. In the end, he sets out a view of religion 'which will be either devoid of devotion to God, or filled with adoration of oneself; and one fears that in practice this either-or would become a both-and'.

It was a short book – and necessarily so, in that a rapid response was so clearly required, if maximum impact was to be achieved. By January 1964, the work had sold 20,000 copies. However, in a report to the Latimer House Council,[8] Packer noted that the *Honest to God* controversy had shown that Latimer House was 'vulnerable to unforeseen developments'. Even the demands of writing such a short book were considerable. The type of long-range planning which lay behind the strategy undergirding the institution could be derailed by the unexpected. There was a need to be sufficiently flexible in order to deal with such urgent needs; yet scholarship was, by its very nature, a slow process, making the rapid production of considered and substantial responses to controversial works very difficult.

At this point, it is important to notice how actively involved in theological journalism Packer had become. He was a regular contributor to the *Church of England Newspaper*, at a time when this was becoming a leading resource for encouraging the consolidation of evangelicalism within the national church. Several of Packer's publications at this time – including *Keep Yourself from Idols* and *The Thirty-nine Articles* had their origins as articles in this journal. Packer was fully aware of the potential of his theological journalism as a means of engaging with the issues of the day, and also discerning what might emerge as significant in the future.

Latimer House appears to have been at its most effective in engaging issues which could, at least to some degree, be predicted to be of importance in the future, in that these issues allowed a significant 'lead time' to allow evangelical scholars to undertake both the deep background reading and the reflection which were necessary for an effective response. It also allowed them to take the initiative, instead of continually being forced on to the defensive by what others had said or written. Perhaps the most effective instance of this is provided by the Anglican-Methodist scheme of union, which began to emerge as a potential issue as early as 1960, and which continued to be debated throughout that decade. It is generally thought that this issue provided Latimer House with one of its most important roles in the theological consolidation of evangelicalism, to which we may now turn.

The Theological Consolidation of Evangelicalism

In his careful study of British evangelicalism since the Second World War, the leading scholar David Bebbington singles out four types of evangelicalism which can be distinguished at this time. First, there was a form of evangelicalism, mostly within the free and independent churches, which comes close to the kind of 'fundamentalism' which was such an important feature of North American Protestantism during the 1920s and 1930s. Second, there was a form of conservative evangelicalism (mostly found within the Church of England) which was not content to remain imprisoned in any kind of ghetto, but saw itself as having a mandate to renew church and society alike. Leading representatives of this type of evangelicalism include both John R.W. Stott and Packer himself. Third, there was a group of evangelicals (again, mostly within the Church of England) who disliked any form of label, and were 'open' in their outlook. Fourth, there was a group which were happy to be described as 'liberal evangelicals', especially within the Anglican Evangelical Group Movement, which ran a journal called *The Liberal Evangelical*. We shall return to this group later in this narrative. The history of British evangelicalism since the Second World War can be described as the irresistible advance of the second form just noted.

Packer himself saw the Thirty-nine Articles as continuing to give a theological foundation and direction to evangelicalism within the Church of England. He set out his views on their importance in a series of six articles published in the *Church of England Newspaper* during October and November 1960, and issued as a booklet the following year.[9] In particular, Packer stressed the way in which the Articles 'sought to confess, preserve and mark off the deepened understanding of the biblical faith which the Reformation had brought about'. The Articles thus set out a positive vision of 'the biblical gospel and biblical Christianity'. They aimed to safeguard the gospel, and thus ensure that three central principles – the sufficiency of Scripture; the supremacy of Scripture; and the subordination of the church to Scripture – were firmly upheld within evangelicalism.[10] As evangelicalism began its long and slow consolidation within the Church of England at this time, Packer insisted that it should remain faithful to the foundational vision of that church, as it had emerged from the Reformation.

The growing strength and sophistication of evangelicalism within the Church of England can be illustrated with reference to one specific controversy, in which Packer and Latimer House played a major role. This was the debate over a proposed scheme by which the Church of England and the Methodist Church would merge. The background to this development was the growing interest in the issue of 'ecumenism' during the late 1950s and early 1960s. Gradually, the theme of ecumenism seemed to come to dominate the agendas of mainline denominations in the west. The World Council of Churches came to see itself in part as an agency for the re-establishment of Christian unity. This 'unity' was understood in institutional and visible forms; the agenda was that of, in effect, reversing the processes which had led to the emergence of the original denominations in the first place.

With the benefit of hindsight, the ecumenical movement of the 1960s can now be seen to have rested on a series of totally unrealistic presuppositions, and to have failed to realize the serious difficulties which had to be addressed before denominational division could be overcome. For example, in a typical moment of unrealistic euphoria, the First British Conference on Faith and Order, meeting on 18 September 1964, declared that it would work for the visible union of all British churches 'not later than Easter Day, 1980'.[11] In England, the most promising possibility for union was widely agreed to lie in the reconciliation of Anglicans and Methodists. In 1963, a report was published which proposed a plan for uniting the two churches.[12] The Anglican-Methodist proposals raised a number of issues for evangelicals within the Church of England, of which two may be noted here.

First, the proposals seemed to imply that Methodist ministers were not 'true ministers of God's word and sacraments' unless they were episcopally ordained. A 'Service of Reconciliation' which was proposed, in effect implied that the ministries of existing Methodist pastors were deficient in some manner, because these had not been ordained by bishops. For most evangelicals, the only criterion which could be employed to determine whether a church or a ministry was valid was whether 'the pure Word of God is preached, and the sacraments are duly ministered according to Christ's ordinance'.[13] While many evangelicals within the Church of England at the time regarded episcopal ministry as conferring important benefits, they did not see this as being essential to a true gospel ministry. The proposed scheme of unity thus seemed to them to rest on highly dubious grounds.

Perhaps more importantly, the proposals for unity seemed determined to ignore matters of theology and doctrine. At the time, the ecumenical movement seemed to have been deeply influenced by the principle that 'doctrine divides; ministry unites', which was widely cited within the World Council of Churches. The assumption seems to have been that the establishment of a common ministry between Anglicans and Methodists would overcome any lingering doctrinal disagreements. Evangelicals were severely critical of this deliberate evasion of doctrinal matters, and argued that there was a need to face up to doctrinal differences in a frank and honest manner. For Packer and others, Methodism had become deeply influenced by a theological liberalism which they had no desire to see spread in the Church of England. There was therefore a need to insist that Christian theological integrity should be considered.

True unity, Packer insisted, was not essentially an organizational issue, but reflected at least some shared theological presuppositions about the nature of the gospel. The failure to address these adequately was deeply worrying. In effect, Packer was like a gadfly, a permanent irritant to those who wanted to quietly marginalize theological differences to allow smooth institutional unity.

The real issue for Packer, which underlies the concerns just noted, was that the proposed merger scheme would create a liberal catholic denomination, in which evangelical life would be stifled or severely limited. Packer's strategic vision for the consolidation of evangelicalism within the national church therefore required that the union scheme should be sunk.

Packer was thus in the forefront of the evangelical response to (and criticism of) the proposed merger. He edited two collections of essays, each of which can be shown to have been formative in establishing evangelical attitudes to the merger. Both were published by the Marcham Manor Press, a small independent press run by Gervase Duffield from his home near Abingdon, south of Oxford. *The Church of England and the Methodist Church* appeared in September 1963; a further collection of ten essays from Anglicans, with some free church comments, was published as *All in Each Place: Towards Reunion in England* in 1965. Both are known to have been of seminal importance in crystallizing evangelical anxieties concerning the theological weaknesses of the proposed scheme. It is clear that the subject of Anglican-Methodist unity took up most of Packer's time. In the autumn of 1968, Packer spoke at twenty-one events dedicated to this subject, as well as two private consultations and a mini-conference organized by the Eclectics (a group of younger evangelicals).

Issues of the leading evangelical Anglican journal *Churchman* dating from this time prominently displayed works originating from Latimer House having a direct bearing on the union scheme. Packer was joined by Colin O. Buchanan and Gervase E. Duffield in assembling *Fellowship in the Gospel*, a substantial and critical evangelical analysis of two major Church of England reports, *Anglican-Methodist Unity* and *Intercommunion Today*. Roger Beckwith published a major biblical and historical study entitled *Priesthood and Sacraments*, which addressed a series of issues of direct relevance to the union proposals. This work, published by the Marcham Manor Press,[14] was the first Latimer Monograph; such Monographs were seen as an important means of influencing the future direction of evangelical thought within the church.[15] At the Council meeting of 25 June 1966, Packer announced plans for four further Monographs: *British Theology in the Twentieth Century* (Packer); *Principles of Prayer Book Revision* (Beckwith); *Christian Initiation* (Beckwith); and *Theology of the Thirty-nine Articles* (Packer). Packer found himself increasingly in demand as a member of various official church bodies, including the Archbishop's Doctrine Commission (chaired at this stage by Bishop Ian Ramsey), the Faith and Order Advisory Group, and the dialogue groups between Anglicanism and other churches (most notably, with the Presbyterian church and the Methodist church).

It is easy to provide a list of writings which had their origins within Latimer House, conferences which it sponsored, events at which its warden and librarian spoke, or individuals who found it a major resource for their battles within the church debates of the day. Yet Packer is clear that the significance of Latimer House is to be seen more in its whole, than in its individual component parts. Latimer House was able to project an impression or image of the nature of evangelicalism which ran counter to that which prevailed in the church at large. At a time when many senior churchmen dismissed evangelicalism with a finely calibrated condescension, Latimer House demonstrated to the church at large that evangelicalism was still 'a cock with a lot of fight left in it on the theological front'.

The constant activity of Latimer House was not achieved without cost to its staff, particularly its warden. Packer was constantly in demand to speak at all kinds of conferences on theological issues, to address Diocesan Evangelical Unions on matters of theology and church politics, and to preach at friendly churches. In accepting such invitations, he was not merely advancing the work and reputation of Latimer House; he was also ensuring its financial survival. Latimer House depended on the generosity of its supporters, and part of Packer's task was to show that they were getting results for their donations. Yet it must also be noted that this flurry of speaking activity meant that Packer had less time than he would have liked to undertake the research and thinking necessary to Latimer House's tasks. Packer's sheer busyness at this time also caused some small degree of disagreement between him and the Council over whether he should accept overseas speaking engagements (such as the invitation to speak at Fuller

Theological Seminary in 1965). Packer felt that such engagements would enhance the profile of Latimer House, and broaden his own experience; the Council was unsure as to whether such overseas work was entirely in line with the objective of influencing debate within the Church of England. In the end, a degree of compromise seems to have been achieved.

It was clear to all that Latimer House was at the cutting edge of evangelical thinking within the Church of England. Even those who were exasperated by evangelical criticisms of their proposals (and there were many!) were quite clear as to the chief source of those criticisms. Some were inclined to the view that Packer's criticisms of the proposals might reflect his hostility (as a convinced Calvinist) to the Arminianism characteristic of Methodism. Nevertheless, the theological issues identified by Packer and others refused to go away. The failure of the negotiations to resolve them to the satisfaction of many lay and ordained Anglican evangelicals would eventually result in the entire enterprise stalling.

By late 1968, Latimer House had established itself as the leading evangelical think-tank and resource centre for evangelicals within the Church of England. But our narrative has run ahead of itself. Both Packer and Latimer House would play a major role in the redefinition of evangelicalism which took place during the 1960s, and is especially associated with a convention which took place at the University of Keele in 1967. The Keele convention is now widely regarded by historians as the most important event in the history of Christianity in England during the twentieth century. In what follows, we shall explore how that convention came to be convened, the central role which Packer played, and its implications for the future of evangelicalism.

The Redefining of English Evangelicalism: The Crisis of 1966

The state of evangelicalism within the Church of England in the aftermath of the Second World War was far from healthy. In the 1940s and 1950s, evangelicals chose to distance themselves from the mainstream of church life, perceiving themselves – as they in turn were perceived – to be outsiders. A similar situation had arisen during the 1930s, in the aftermath of the 1928 Prayer

Book vote, which left evangelicals unpopular and isolated within the church. A siege mentality descended over the movement, expressed in an aggressiveness which ultimately rested upon a deep sense of insecurity and defensiveness. Their agenda in the immediate post-war period was little more than that of survival, in a period in which the movement seemed set to be overwhelmed by the continuing strength of Anglo-Catholicism, an increasingly confident liberalism, and a new commitment to an ecumenical movement which regarded a concern for 'right doctrine' as a pointless archaism. As we saw earlier, the ill-informed and totally unmerited identification of 'evangelicals' with 'fundamentalists' by Michael Ramsey (then Bishop of Durham, responding to a mission at Durham University by John R.W. Stott) caused considerable pain to evangelicals, who felt that they had been severely mispresented and misunderstood. Packer himself made no small contribution to reversing this trend through his important book *'Fundamentalism' and the Word of God*, published in 1958.

With a clearly growing evangelical presence within the churches, a change of mood was in the air in the early 1960s. The issue which became of critical importance had emerged as decisive in the United States during the 1920s and 1930s. The negative consequences of this polarization can be seen especially from the painful history of the Presbyterian church in the United States earlier this century. In 1922, an ill-tempered controversy broke out, which is widely regarded as having marked the beginning of the spiral of numerical decline within that church, laid the foundations of schism within it, and ultimately caused a radical loss of theological vision which eroded its distinctiveness within the American situation. The row centred on whether traditional doctrines should be modified in the light of modern thought.[16] On 21 May 1922, Henry Emerson Fosdick preached a polemical sermon entitled 'Shall the Fundamentalists Win?'. Some 130,000 copies of the sermon, rewritten by a skilled public relations expert and funded by John D. Rockefeller Jr, were circulated. A vigorous riposte soon followed. Clarence Edward Macartney entitled his reply 'Shall Unbelief Win?'. The situation rapidly polarized. Toleration proved impossible. There could be no compromise or way out of the situation. Presbyterians were forced to decide whether they were, to use the categories of the protagonists, 'unbelieving liberals' or 'reactionary fundamentalists'. 'Oppositionalism' led to the issue being perceived in crystal-clear terms: either an unbelieving culture would win, or victory would go to the gospel. There were no alternatives. Conservatives soon discovered that there seemed to be nothing that they could do to stop the influence of modernist thinkers such as Fosdick growing within their denominations. The slide into modernism seemed inexorable.

One of the consequences of this was a growing demand within fundamentalist circles for separation from allegedly corrupt denominations. If it proved impossible to reform denominations from within, the only course open was to break away from the denomination, and form a new yet doctrinally pure church body. The separatist approach went back to the dawn of American Protestantism: Roger Williams (*c.* 1604–84), founder of Rhode Island, was one of the leading proponents of a pure separatist church, arguing that the Church of England was apostate, and that any kind of fellowship with it was a serious sin. Christian believers were under an obligation to separate from apostate churches and from a secular state.

These attitudes re-emerged within American fundamentalism over the period 1920–40. Indeed, for some fundamentalist writers, the only way of safeguarding the 'fundamentals of faith' was to separate. George Marsden comments on this development as follows:

> By the 1930s, when it became painfully clear that reform from within could not prevent the spread of modernism in major northern denominations, more and more fundamentalists began to make separation from America's major denominations an article of faith. Although most who supported fundamentalism in the 1920s still remained in their denominations, many Baptist dispensationalists and a few influential Presbyterians were demanding separatism. Yet the question was far from settled in the 1930s and 1940s.[17]

Separatism thus seemed the only way ahead. If culture and mainline denominations could not be converted or reformed, there was no option but to become a voice in the wilderness.

It is important to note that the separationist strategy was a response to a specific set of historical circumstances, and had not been seen as an integral, necessary or implied element of 'evangelicalism' until that point in history. The evolution of the separationist strategy resulted from the perception that nothing was to be gained from remaining within the mainline denominations. The overriding criterion employed in arriving at this conclusion was the need to establish a believing orthodoxy within those denominations. In the 1920s, it seemed increasingly clear to the fundamentalists that the orthodox cause was lost beyond salvage within the northern mainline denominations; separation was the only viable option. But had historical circumstances been different, separationism would not have been advocated.

These developments led to a significant polarization within American evangelicalism. Evangelicals adopted two different strategies in this respect: some chose to leave, and founded their distinctively evangelical denominations; others chose to remain within increasingly liberal denominations, and attempted to reform them from within. As Schaeffer remarks, with obvious sadness, evangelical fought evangelical, rather than liberal:

> The periodicals of those who left tended to devote more space to attacking people who differed with them on the issue of leaving than to dealing with the liberals. Things were said that are difficult to forget even now. Those who came out refused at times to pray with those who had not come out. Many who left broke off all forms of fellowship with true brothers in Christ who had not left. Christ's command to love one another was destroyed. What was left was frequently a turning inward, a self-righteousness, a hardness.[18]

Sadly, this pattern would emerge time and time again within evangelicalism subsequently, as the at times vicious and wounding struggle within English evangelicalism over the same issue in the 1960s would demonstrate.

The controversy can be summarized in a sentence. Should evangelicals concerned with doctrinal orthodoxy withdraw from denominations which publicly fail to maintain such orthodoxy, or should they try to reform them from within? The two approaches share a common concern for theological correctness and spiritual vitality, yet stipulate radically different means of achieving that end. The origins of the controversy are usually traced back to the year 1965. Up to that point, there had been an informal 'agreement to disagree' within English evangelicalism. Specifically denominational matters were seen as being of relative unimportance, in comparison to the all-important need to remain faithful to the gospel.

Dr Martyn Lloyd-Jones had become increasingly concerned over the theological liberalism of the World Council of Churches. By 1965, he was convinced that it was impossible for an evangelical to belong to a denomination which was affiliated to the WCC. Evangelicals who were members of such churches would be contaminated by others within the denominations who openly denied or challenged key tenets of the Christian faith. Evangelicals who remained within doctrinally mixed churches – such as the Church of England – were therefore 'guilty by association', in that they failed to maintain loyalty to their evangelical convictions through their association with such people. Lloyd-Jones was especially troubled by the collection of essays, edited by Packer, entitled *All in Each Place*, which he regarded as seriously compromising Packer's evangelical credentials. At a meeting of the Westminster Fellowship on 16 June 1965, Lloyd-Jones argued that theologically orthodox Anglicans and others should consider 'coming out' of their denominations.[19] Instead of believing that they could 'infiltrate the various bodies to which they belong and win them over', evangelicals should stand together. For Lloyd-Jones, it was inevitable that 1966 would see 'a crisis on what is to me the fundamental issue, namely, do we believe in a territorial church or a gathered community of saints?'.

With these words, Lloyd-Jones outlined two models, each of which was influential among evangelicals. Each had excellent historical and biblical credentials. John Calvin had stated the case for a 'mixed body', and some Puritan writers – including the great John Owen – the case for a 'gathered community', understanding of the church. The 'mixed body' approach recognized that the visible church (that is, the church as seen in real everyday life) consisted of both the regenerate and the unregenerate, in much the same way as wheat and 'tares' (or weeds) grew together in the same field in the parable of Matthew 13. Separation would take place at the final judgment; in the meantime, the converted and the unconverted mingled in the same church. This concept of the church was typical of Protestant churches who trace their history back though the great reformers Luther and Calvin, and include Anglicans, Lutherans, and Presbyterians. The second model argued that the church was, by definition, a body of saints, not of sinners, so that only those who were publicly recognized as regenerate could be considered to be church members. This 'pure body' approach became especially influential within the more radical wing of the sixteenth-century Reformation, and became established in England in various separatist groups, including Baptists and Puritans.

One largely disinterested observer of Lloyd-Jones's total commitment at this stage to the separatist approach was Professor Basil Hall, a Presbyterian church historian with a particular interest in Calvin. Initially professor of church history at the University of Manchester, Hall subsequently settled in Cambridge, as dean of St John's College. The reason for this change of position was that he had become an Anglican, believing that Calvin's doctrine of the church corresponded rather more closely to Anglican than to Presbyterian views. This viewpoint is, of course, contestable. However, Hall relates how one evening he found himself in debate with Lloyd-Jones over the issue of the nature of the church. Lloyd-Jones set out a separatist view of the church, and argued that this was the only view possible for someone committed to the Reformation. Hall vigorously protested. Having a copy of Calvin's *Institutes* to hand, he pointed out passage after passage in which Calvin adopted the rival view. 'So *you* say', was Lloyd-Jones's frosty response. Hall's rejoinder was immediate: 'No, it is what *Calvin* says – look!' But Lloyd-Jones did not care to look. He had made up his mind on this issue.

This had up to now been an issue of friendly disagreement among evangelicals, but had not been seen as a 'gospel issue'. In Packer's view, George Whitefield offered a role model for collaboration across evangelical bodies, in which differences of this nature could be set to one side in order to get on with the serious business of preaching the gospel. For Whitefield, it was not necessary for an Anglican to renounce his Anglicanism (with all its faults) if he was to preach the gospel to non-Anglicans. In a letter of 7 July 1742 to a Scottish Presbyterian who held that Whitefield should leave a corrupt Church of England, Whitefield replied:

You seem not satisfied, unless I declare myself a Presbyterian, and openly renounce the Church of England. God knows that I have been faithful in bearing a testimony against what I think is corrupt in that church ... I find but few of a truly catholic spirit. Most are catholics until they bring persons over to their own party, and there they would fetter them. I have not so learned Christ. I shall approve and join all who are good, in every sect.[20]

Most evangelicals were prepared to argue that these different conceptions of the nature of the church were genuine differences between the denominations, which should not be seen as of central importance. This outlook was encouraged by the evangelistic campaigns of Billy Graham, which were influential at this time in England. Graham was prepared to work with members of any denomination, arguing that the preaching of the gospel overshadowed all such denominational differences.

Interestingly, Lloyd-Jones seems to have once held this opinion as well. The simple fact appears to have been that Lloyd-Jones changed his mind on this matter over a period of roughly twenty years. During his early career, he appears to have felt little difficulty in appearing on platforms with speakers who were not evangelical. Lloyd-Jones was president of the Inter-Varsity Fellowship during the period 1939–42. Oliver Barclay (who was chairman of the Universities Executive Committee of the IVF for the period 1942–5) vividly recalls a confrontation between himself and Lloyd-Jones over an address that Lloyd-Jones had given for the Student Christian Movement in Oxford in 1940. Given the long history of antagonism between the SCM and the OICCU,[21] Barclay protested vigorously to Lloyd-Jones over his action at the following IVF Conference at Trinity College, Cambridge. Barclay argued that Lloyd-Jones had made it very difficult for the IVF by preaching for the SCM. Lloyd-Jones defended his action, suggesting that he ought to be free to preach to audiences which he might not otherwise reach.[22]

Much the same pattern can be seen in 1948. In November of that year, Lloyd-Jones agreed to speak at a mission to the University of Edinburgh along with Alec Vidler, a noted Anglican liberal theologian. The mission was organized by the IVF and other Christian groups in the University. Once more, the same principle appears to have been adopted as in 1940. Lloyd-Jones gradually moved away from this position during the 1950s, eventually to adopt the more trenchant position associated with him in the 1960s. On the basis of the documentary evidence available, it seems that the growing power and liberal tendencies of the World Council of Churches was a major factor in Lloyd-Jones's thinking on this issue.

It would not be correct to speak of 'evangelical unity' during the 1950s and early 1960s; the term 'peaceful coexistence' is probably a more accurate way of depicting the situation. Differences on certain issues, while remaining real, were not regarded as standing in the way of collaboration and shared fellowship. This peaceful coexistence within evangelicalism was now shattered by Lloyd-Jones, who seems to have been determined to make a 'pure body' doctrine of the church a litmus test as to whether someone was a true evangelical or not. Lloyd-Jones was now in open disagreement with Billy Graham over this issue, and refused to become involved with him during the 1966 Crusade at Earls Court, London. For Lloyd-Jones, fellowship was impossible unless there was fundamental agreement in the essentials of the gospel – and those 'essentials' seemed now to include acceptance of a 'pure body' conception of the church. The blurring of evangelical distinctives (which Lloyd-Jones regarded as beginning with Billy Graham's Harringay crusade of 1954) had to be arrested somehow. It appeared to some of Lloyd-Jones's more critical readers that he was making membership of the Fellowship of Independent Evangelical Churches a necessary condition of evangelical identity.[23] It seemed a sure-fire recipe for civil war within the evangelical movement.

The Puritan Studies Conference of 14–15 December 1965 presaged the tensions. Six addresses were given on the theme 'Approaches to Reformation'. Six papers were presented, of which five dealt with the sixteenth century. Packer spoke on 'Martin Luther'. The final address, by tradition, was give by Lloyd-Jones, who chose to speak on the theme of '*ecclesiola in ecclesia*' (the Latin term, which literally means 'a little church inside a church', is widely used to refer to reforming movements or groups within a larger church). Lloyd-Jones declared that all such attempts to reform a church from within had failed to take the New Testament doctrine of the church seriously, putting expediency ahead of principles. The same themes would recur in the famous clash between Lloyd-Jones and Stott in October 1966, to which we now turn.

The looming crisis finally reached its very public head at the Second National Assembly of Evangelicals meeting, held at Central Hall, Westminster, on the evening of 18 October 1966. The organizing body for this meeting was the Evangelical Alliance, a body which was formed in 1846 to ensure that evangelicalism remained a vital presence in Britain. At that stage, evangelicals found themselves in disagreements about denominational issues,[24] and engaged in often ill-tempered debates over the nature of the inspiration of Scripture, the doctrine of election, and millenarian issues. There was a clear need for evangelicals to be able to unite, in the face of these disagreements. In addition to drawing up a 'Basis of Faith', the first Assembly of 1846 therefore set out eight 'Practical Resolutions', intended to govern the manner in which evangelicals should behave towards each other when they found themselves in disagreement. The Second Assembly was intended to further this cause within evangelicalism, in pursuit of the 'unity of the Spirit' (Ephesians 4:3) which the 'Practical Resolutions' had identified as their goal.[25] The 1966 assembly would be the first major gathering of British evangelicals since 1846 to be organized by the Alliance. Its aim was to foster evangelical unity; it ended up by splitting and damaging the movement more effectively than any of its opponents dared hope. The cause of the split was a public confrontation between Lloyd-Jones and Stott.

Lloyd-Jones had been asked to give the opening address to the Assembly, in which he argued that evangelicals had failed to face up to the issues raised by the biblical doctrine of the church: 'Ecumenical people put fellowship before doctrine. We, as evangelicals, put doctrine before fellowship.' Those who were agreed on matters of doctrine should come together, rather than hold on to their inherited positions. True Christian believers who insisted on remaining in their denominations were, in effect, guilty of schism. He then issued what was widely understood to be a passionate call for evangelicals within the mainstream churches to 'come out' and, in effect, form a denomination of their own. Maybe, he argued, the ecumenical movement might one day be seen as a good thing, in that it had brought evangelicals together 'as a fellowship or an association of evangelical churches'.

Many of those present at the meeting have spoken of the 'electric' atmosphere which this address created. It seemed to Stott, who was chairing the session, that it was possible that many younger evangelicals would have walked out of their denominations there and then, unless the situation was defused. Stott intervened to suggest that the rightful and proper place of evangelicals was *within* those mainstream denominations, which they could renew from within. It is entirely possible that Stott's intervention was improper; he himself apologized to Lloyd-Jones subsequently. But Stott was convinced that his intervention was necessary to avoid an immediate crisis. His intervention prompted a crisis in itself, in that it exposed a major division within evangelicalism on the opening day of a conference which was intended to foster evangelical unity; nevertheless, Stott reckoned that it had to be done.

We shall never know what Lloyd-Jones intended his address to achieve, and it is entirely possible that the substance of his address was misunderstood by at least some of his audience. There were certainly some present on that evening who gained the impression that Lloyd-Jones's main concern was simply to stress the importance of evangelical unity. However, an analysis of the press coverage of the meeting, together with conversations with those present at the event, indicates that most believed that Lloyd-Jones was asking evangelicals to leave mainline churches; and that some further believed that he was also specifically arguing that they should join the Fellowship of Independent Evangelical Churches.[26] Some felt that Lloyd-Jones was appealing specifically to evangelicals within the Church of England; however, his address clearly invited evangelicals from denominations in general to form a united evangelical fellowship.[27] Free church evangelicals present at the meeting were generally supportive of Lloyd-Jones's approach; Baptists and Anglicans were strongly critical.

The *Baptist Times* reported that Lloyd-Jones 'seemed to be encouraging evangelicals to secede from their denominations'. *The Christian* summarized Lloyd-Jones's speech under a banner headline 'Evangelicals – Leave your Denominations', printed above a photograph of the platform party.[28] A week later, the same journal published a protest note, complaining that all save one of the platform party were opposed to Lloyd-Jones's policy; the journal's headline, it was alleged, implied that they all supported it. There were indeed those who heeded Lloyd-Jones's call, and left their denominations. But they were few in comparison with those who chose to stay.

Whatever Lloyd-Jones intended to achieve, and whatever he actually said (or meant to say) – and these remain controverted matters – a broad division opened up within English evangelicalism over the specific issue of whether evangelicals within mainline denominations should stay inside or leave. A bitter dispute arose, where there had hitherto been friendly disagreement. Rightly or wrongly, Lloyd-Jones was criticized for wrecking evangelical unity. It is no exaggeration to say that the 'shadow of 1966' has lingered over English evangelicalism ever since. It may be felt with particular force in some sections of the movement rather than in others; nevertheless, the events of that period often form the unspoken agenda of evangelical conversations since then, and constitute the background against which Packer's career in England must be viewed. To understand Packer, it is necessary to appreciate the tensions which intensified within English evangelicalism from this time onwards.

The confrontation led to a very difficult period in the history of the Evangelical Alliance. It was seriously weakened by the aftermath. Both independent evangelicals and evangelicals within the mainline denominations felt that they were entitled to support by the Alliance. It was not until the 1980s that the wounds began to be healed, and a significant level of co-operation began to be re-established between different evangelical groupings in the United Kingdom.[29]

The months following this clash with Stott were also difficult for Lloyd-Jones. At an open discussion at the next meeting of the Westminster Fellowship, held on 28 November, it became clear that the same diversity of views over the issue of secession existed within that body. This posed serious difficulties for his commitment to the 'pure church' model of evangelicalism. With great sadness, Lloyd-Jones declared that he believed the Fellowship had served its purpose, and would be disbanded.[30] (As it turned out, the Fellowship was subsequently reconstituted in such terms that those who believed that the mainline denominations could be reformed from within were excluded.)[31] More significantly, Lloyd-Jones was now subject to serious criticism from within evangelical circles, on the grounds that he had made denominational affiliation of decisive importance to evangelical identity. He was accused of needlessly dividing evangelicalism over secondary issues. The same disputes which had divided and seriously weakened American evangelicalism in the 1920s and 1930s now seemed about to be replayed with equal acrimony – in England.

The evidence, however, suggests that most evangelicals did not criticize Lloyd-Jones, or get involved in the dispute over whether to secede or remain within denominations; they just ignored him. He was seen as being personally antagonistic towards the

Church of England, and was not taken with seriousness by the new generation of evangelicals within that church. Sadly, there is good reason to suggest that the evaluation of Lloyd-Jones's theology was coloured by increasingly negative perceptions of his personality within Anglican circles – perceptions, it must be said, which often owed far more to the rather harsh and strident circle of supporters and advisers which gathered round him than to 'the Doctor' himself.

It must be stressed that Lloyd-Jones continued to be regarded with the greatest respect as a preacher and expositor, even by those who disagreed with him on other matters within the Church of England and other mainline churches. Lloyd-Jones retained wide respect as a spiritual guide, but was no longer seen as an evangelical statesman who could speak for the movement as a whole. Rightly or wrongly, he gained the reputation as a strong advocate of sectional views within evangelicalism, rather than a representative of the entire movement. He became increasingly a voice in the wilderness, as the move to regain the high ground within the mainline denominations gathered momentum. The results of this would be felt most keenly within the Church of England.

The long-standing friendship between Lloyd-Jones and Packer was now seriously strained, in that the two men were publicly seen to have taken diametrically opposed positions on a question which Lloyd-Jones had made of critical importance. Packer would become one of the most vigorous and influential defenders of the view that evangelicals within the Church of England must be free 'to pursue their historic bilateral policy of fellowship with evangelicals in other denominations, and full involvement in their own church'. While some have argued that Packer was a bold reformer who somehow lost his nerve over the period 1966–71 (a view especially associated with the circle around Lloyd-Jones), it is quite clear that Packer was following his own consistent reforming agenda, using writers such as George Whitefield, Charles Simeon and J.C. Ryle as models. This approach pointed to a bilateral agenda, rather than the unilateral agenda which was increasingly associated with the Lloyd-Jones faction. On the one hand, Packer would thus work with evangelicals across denominational divides, believing that the nature of their fellowship transcended those denominational loyalties. Packer regularly spoke at interdenominational preaching meetings throughout the nation, in pursuance of this goal. On the other hand, he would work for the establishment of orthodoxy and renewal within his own church, on the basis of what Packer would later refer to as 'an ideology of a constructive reforming agenda'. We shall document this development in what follows.

The National Evangelical Anglican Congress, 1967

We have already seen the new sense of intellectual confidence which began to sweep through evangelicalism in the late 1950s and early 1960s. Packer's *Fundamentalism' and the Word of God* and *Evangelism and the Sovereignty of God*, linked with the work which began to emanate from Latimer House in the early 1960s, helped forge a new sense of purpose and awareness of new possibilities within evangelicalism as a whole, and particularly within the Church of England. Yet theology must be married with strategy, even if that strategy ultimately rests on theological foundations for things to happen. If a theological renewal was emerging in the southern English centres of Bristol and Oxford, some significant strategic thinking was happening in the north of England, particularly in the diocese of Ripon, which includes the large industrial city of Leeds.

In 1956, Raymond Turvey began a long period of ministry at the city-centre church of St George's, Leeds. On arriving in Leeds, Turvey began to be aware of a sense of isolation, frustration, marginalization and powerlessness among local evangelical clergy. He began to convene small meetings, with a view to deepening fellowship and confidence among evangelical clergy in the region. The groups were initially small; nevertheless, they grew steadily. In 1960, Turvey convened a Northern Evangelical Conference, to be held at York. Two hundred and fifty clergy attended. The success of the event led to a laypersons' conference being arranged for 1964, and a second Northern Evangelical Conference in 1965. Major speakers, many from the south of England, were involved in these conferences. The effect on evangelical morale was significant. After the success of the first, the minds of its organizers turned towards the future. Clearly, more such conferences needed to be arranged for the north. But why not be more ambitious? Why not arrange for a *national* evangelical congress?

It was with thoughts such as these in mind that a group was

convened in May 1964, bringing together representatives of the Northern Evangelical Conference with national evangelical figures, including John R.W. Stott. Stott agreed to chair the organizing committee, and Turvey to be its secretary. The committee was clear that their intention was to mobilize ordinary church people, as well as clergy, in the parishes of the Church of England, and give them a new sense of confidence and direction. The theme chosen was the Lordship of Christ, which was expressed in the title 'Christ over All'. The congress – now named as the National Evangelical Anglican Congress – was fixed for 4–7 April 1967, at the University of Keele.

From this brief account of the origins of NEAC, it will be clear that it had been planned long before the serious polarization which developed within evangelicalism after October 1966, as a consequence of the open tension between Martyn Lloyd-Jones and John Stott. Nevertheless, that polarization lent a new urgency and relevance to the event.

'Keele', in Packer's view, 'was the child of Latimer House.' It was clear to many that Latimer House was strategically placed to organize and resource the proposed congress; this proved to be the case. *Guidelines*, the collection of essays which would provide the backbone of the Keele agenda, was planned and drafted at a series of meetings of the writers at Latimer House. At this time, Packer had stressed that the purpose of Latimer House was to:

> re-assert and re-apply evangelical principles in the context of current Anglican discussion. This programme prescribes contributions in the following areas: (a) church discipline; (b) church and state; (c) Prayer Book revision; (d) eucharistic sacrifice; (e) episcopacy in doctrine and practice; (f) church government.[32]

As evangelicals within the Church of England moved to reassert their presence within that church (over and against Anglicans who wished to exclude them) and justify that presence (over and against some free church evangelicals, loyal to Lloyd-Jones, who argued that they had no business being within that church in the first place), Latimer House proved to have already inauguarated a programme which anticipated many of the issues which needed to be addressed.

A major boost to the prestige of Latimer House resulted from a conference of 200 younger evangelical clergy of the Church of England, held at Swanwick from 28 February to 2 March 1966. This conference, which had as its theme 'Facing the Future', affirmed the importance of Latimer House, called for a significant increase in its funding, and asked that it should continue its work of identifying the issues which would face the Church of England in the future. Perhaps most importantly, the conference asked Latimer House to convene study groups, focusing on these issues.[33] By January 1967, Packer and Beckwith had set in place plans for thirteen such study groups. The Revd Philip A. Crowe was appointed as 'Study Groups Secretary', charged with the co-ordination, administration and development of this new enterprise. The active and enthusiastic involvement of younger evangelicals in the mission of Latimer House must be seen as being of major importance at this stage. By November 1967, in the aftermath of NEAC, the number of study groups had risen to fourteen, with 142 active members.[34]

As preparations for NEAC developed, it became clear that the preparation and publication of suitable study material was a top priority. The committee wanted people to have done some serious thinking before they attended the conference. It was inevitable that the task of producing 'study-course kits' should be given to Latimer House. Given the importance of the material, it was decided to entrust their publication and distribution to the publishing wing of the Church Pastoral Aid Society. Most importantly, it was decided that the conference addresses would be published in advance, in order to allow them to be studied in preparation for the congress.[35]

This was not the original intention, which was for the delegates to listen dutifully and appreciatively to the conference papers being read out to them. Discontent at this proposed approach surfaced at the October 1966 meeting of the Eclectics, a group of younger evangelicals within the church, who felt that something much more participative was required. One of those who pressed this point with particular force was Michael Saward, who felt that the resulting conference statement would not really belong to the delegates unless they had a chance to discuss it. Others, including Colin Buchanan, concurred. At a meeting of the preparation committee in December 1966, Gavid Reid put forward the case for a modification to the planned format. *Guidelines* would be available in advance of the congress, so that the papers would be read by delegates before their arrival. Instead of reading out their papers, the speakers would be able to give an informal presentation based upon their contributions (which they could assume had been read and digested by those present). The committee accepted these changes. It is possible to read too much into this change in format; nevertheless, it can be seen as a shift within Anglican evangelicalism from an essentially élitist understanding of leadership (in which keynote speakers told their followers what to think) towards a more mature and dispersed form of leadership which trusted rank and file church members to think for themselves.

The nine speakers included leading evangelical luminaries, such as Stott and the rising star of the London College of Divinity, Michael Green (who was the youngest speaker at the congress). Significantly, most of the speakers had direct links with either Bristol or Latimer House, demonstrating the remarkable influence that these centres were coming to have. A.T. Houghton had been chairman of the Tyndale Hall Council. Philip E. Hughes had been vice-principal of Tyndale Hall, and had served (briefly) as libarian of Latimer House. William Leathem had taught at Tyndale Hall, and was closely involved in its government through his links with the Bible Churchmen's Missionary Society. Alec Motyer had been vice-principal of Clifton Theological College. And Packer, who edited (and organized) these addresses was, of course, linked with both centres.[36]

In the event, exactly 1,000 people attended the congress – 519 clergy and 481 laypeople.[37] The nine conference addresses were designed to stimulate and unite, and appear to have achieved their goals. In effect, NEAC can be seen as endorsing and consolidating Stott's opposition to the strategy commended by Lloyd-Jones. Keele was determinative, not merely for evangelicals staying within the national church; it also opened up the social aspects of the gospel, to which English evangelicalism had become blind (despite its heavy commitment to this area in the period 1780–1830. NEAC signalled the final determination of evangelicals within the national church to emerge from the ghetto in which they had previously confined themselves, and prepare to exercise a considerably greater influence than before. Less than a month after the congress had ended, a study guide to the congress and its resolutions was published for the use of churches up and down the country.[38]

What was the impact of NEAC? Packer himself dealt with this issue at length in an interview in April 1967, less than a month after the convention.[39] Packer affirmed that NEAC had aimed to bring evangelicals closer together, both intellectually and spiritually. It also acted as a showcase, in that conservative evangelicalism within the Church of England was able to impress outsiders with its vitality, energy and intellectual vigour. For Packer, Keele was a platform for an 'ideology of a constructive reforming agenda', which went far beyond the idea of 'evangelicals making a contribution'.

Packer's point here is important. It is arguable that the significance of NEAC is to be seen more in the image which it projected than in its positive achievements. Looking back, many aspects of the congress statement were destined to remain hopes, rather than achieved goals. NEAC helped dispel old and predominantly negative stereotypes of evangelicalism. The large number of younger clergy who attended the congress (many of whom had also attended the 'Facing the Future' conference in 1966) clearly signalled the presence of a significant force within the church of the future. No longer would evangelicals simply make contributions to the Church of England; they would aim to change it from within.

NEAC was a powerful stimulant to evangelicalism within the Church of England. Its success could not but be noticed by other groups. The Anglican Evangelical Group Movement, whose journal was entitled *The Liberal Evangelical*, is an excellent example of a liberal evangelical organization (more liberal than evangelical, by this stage) which had found itself profoundly threatened by the dramatic renaissance of more conservative forms of evangelicalism. NEAC was the last straw. In July 1967, the AEGM held its annual conference at Lady Margaret Hall, Oxford. The main business was the Annual General Meeting, which took the decision that the AEGM should 'be dissolved as soon as conveniently practicable'. A continuation committee was established to consider 'all means of promoting the liberal outlook and objectives'; this fizzled out shortly afterwards.[40] Liberal evangelicalism had ceased to be a meaningful organized presence within the church. Conservative evangelicalism had, quite simply, eclipsed it.

The impact of these changes can also be seen from developments at a major Oxford evangelical institution, not far from Latimer House. Wycliffe Hall, which Packer attended during the years

1949–52, had gradually become associated with the third and fourth types of evangelicalism, noted above (see pp. 111–12). By 1969, the college was in a serious position. Only thirty-one students were enrolled; future recruitment seemed distinctly problematic. The Hall Council were now seriously concerned about the future. They were not attracting enough students. It was clear that there was a major resurgence in the evangelical constituency of the Church of England, with many young ordinands coming forward to fill places in the theological colleges; however, they were generally not interested in coming to Wycliffe. The simple fact was that Wycliffe Hall was widely seen as being out of sympathy with the forms of conservative evangelicalism which were now gaining the ascendency. Some of its teaching staff were not evangelical; the college as a whole was seen as 'liberal' in its ethos. Indeed, one of the reasons for establishing Latimer House was the strong perception that Wycliffe Hall could not be relied upon to provide a strong and committed evangelical lead in the future.

It was decided to appoint a new principal. The Chairman of the Hall Council, the Rt Revd Stuart Blanch (later Archbishop of York) invited the Revd James P. Hickinbotham to the position. Hickinbotham was known for his evangelical convictions, and had taught Packer during his time as a student at Wycliffe. On 1 October 1969, Blanch wrote to Hickinbotham declaring that: 'The Council, I am quite convinced, is ready for any reorientation of the Hall which you think is necessary if we are to attract the right kind of ordinands ... It seems not only desirable but essential that Wycliffe should be able to command the approval of clergy and ordinands in the Conservative Evangelical school.'[41]

Hickinbotham moved quickly to encourage the members of the Hall staff who were not evangelicals to move on to other positions, and appointed committed evangelicals (such as Arthur Moore and Peter Southwell) in their place. More conservative evangelicals were appointed to the Hall Council. Student numbers began to rise in direct proportion to the confidence in which the Hall was held. By 1977, there were seventy-nine students at the Hall.

Other illustrations of the growing strength of evangelicalism could easily be given. There was now no doubt that a major evangelical revival was under way within the national church, and that Packer was seen as one of its leading figures.

The Decision to Leave Oxford

Important though his work at Latimer House had been, Packer had no intention of remaining there for the remainder of his career. It had been a strategically important appointment; however, there was a sense in which Packer felt that he had done all that he could in this position, and needed to move on to fresh challenges. He felt that he was going dry, and hence that Latimer House was going dry as well. He needed more in the way of stimulus, such as that he had gained through interacting with students earlier during his time at Tyndale Hall. By 1968, Latimer House seemed to Packer to have assumed a function primarily of co-ordinating evangelical scholars, writers and activists around the country.[42] This was an important role, and would continue to be necessary in the foreseeable future. Latimer House could provide a forum in which evangelical scholars in the theological colleges, and able clergy developing their specialisms in a parish context, could be kept in touch with each other, help each other, and work towards common goals within the church. Many felt that this could be done by a competent administrator, allowing Packer to develop his own personal gifts to greater effect. Latimer House was firmly established, and Packer need not feel that its survival or well-being was totally his responsibility. But what could Packer go on to? Four general possibilities would have been open to him at this stage in his career.

First, he could have returned to parish ministry in the Church of England. He was an ordained minister in that church, and would have been able to find a position which would have allowed him at least some time for writing and research. However, although this was a real possibility, it would not have appeared particularly attractive or realistic, given Packer's particular gifts and concerns.

A second possibility was to enter the British academic world, perhaps exploring the possibility of a lectureship or professorship at a leading university. For example, the Lady Margaret Chair of Divinity at Oxford became vacant in 1969. Some of Packer's colleagues wrote to him, suggesting that this was an appropriate position for him to consider. Packer, however, saw this as leading him away from his own understanding of his appropriate role. 'I really am called, if I know anything at all, to make ministers and establish consciences, rather than to advance learning as an

Oxbridge professor should.'[43] Packer's own involvement in the ministry of St Andrew's, a large evangelical parish church close to Latimer House, was an important expression of his deep commitment to the ministerial aspects of theology. Involvement in the ministry of a local parish church was essential to Packer, who felt uncomfortable in its absence. The pattern of local parochial involvement which he established in Oxford would later be repeated in Bristol and Vancouver.

Third, Packer could leave England, and take up a position in North America. He was increasingly well known as a speaker and writer in that region. He had delivered the prestigious Payton Lectures in May 1965 at Fuller Theological Seminary in Pasadena, California.[44] This was the first time that Packer had been invited to speak abroad, and it proved to be the first of many such invitations.

Trinity Evangelical Divinity School in Deerfield, Illinois, was known to be interested in Packer as a possible professor of the history of Christian thought. At that stage, Trinity was in the process of making the transition from a small denominational school of theology of the Evangelical Free Church to a major evangelical divinity school; Packer's presence would undoubtedly have assisted this transition. During his visits to the United States, Packer had been particularly impressed by Westminster Theological Seminary near Philadelphia, at which he had served briefly as visiting professor in 1966; it was possible that an invitation from such an establishment might lure him away from England. Yet Packer was unsure that it was right to leave England at this stage. There was much that still needed to be done.

One factor which was influencing Packer at this stage was a conflict which was developing in Bristol over the relation of Tyndale Hall (at which Packer had recently been a member of staff) to Clifton Theological College – a matter to which we shall return presently. The tension between the Councils of the two colleges, which became especially acute in 1968–9, caused anxieties to many influential English evangelicals. It seemed to raise serious questions concerning the future of English evangelicalism, not least because it seemed to imply that the movement had some kind of death wish. John Wenham, who served as the Secretary to the Council of Latimer House, had no doubts about the seriousness of the issue. On 30 October 1968, he wrote:

This [i.e., the Bristol controversy], linked as it is with Jim Packer's probable departure to America, seemed to me perhaps the greatest disaster that has ever overtaken the Evangelical cause in the Church of England . . . [I have had to live with] the realization that the action of Evangelical Councils was making more and more likely the loss of Jim Packer from the country. Jim is head and shoulders above all other Evangelicals in his influence in the Church of England, and to lose him at this time scarcely bears contemplation.[45]

A fourth possibility was to return to theological education in an English theological college. Packer was convinced that he was called to educate ministers; a theological college provided precisely that opportunity. He had already served on the staff of Tyndale Hall, and his experience from that situation would be an important factor in allowing him to return to such a teaching position. Furthermore, Packer's work at Latimer House had firmly established him as a leading evangelical thinker, not simply in England as a whole, but within the Church of England in particular. It would thus have been unthinkable for him to return to a theological college in a junior position. His experience and ability pointed to him being a potential principal. In terms of influencing events and thinking within the Church of England, there were few more significant positions. To become the principal of a major evangelical theological college was to assume a strategic position, from which considerable influence could be exercised, both in the short term (for example, through being able to influence various church committees) and the longer term (most notably, through personal influence over those being trained for ministry, who would subsequently go on to positions of influence within the church).

Furthermore, Packer had given considerable thought to issues of theological education, especially in relation to the present structure of theological colleges.[46] Having spent some time in 1966 as a visiting professor at Westminster Theological Seminary, and visited other seminaries in the Chicago area, Packer had noted the way in which the ethos of American seminaries seemed to be determined more by the tone of their faculties than by their presidents.[47] The faculty were all treated as equals, and were specialists in their fields. In a subsequent article of 1968, Packer had noted that the existing understanding of the relationship between a theological college principal and his teaching staff was based on a series of models dating from the distant past – for example, a vicar and his curates (a parish model), or a headmaster and his junior masters (a school model). Packer argued that this model was outdated, and quite inappropriate to the emerging needs of the colleges. What was needed was a break with both this system and the habit of mind which it presupposed and sustained. In its place, Packer proposed 'some sort of parity pattern', in which the principal related to the staff after the manner of 'a faculty chairman in a university, or the leader of a team ministry of specialists'. In particular, he stressed the need to involve the teaching staff in the government of colleges, through direct staff representation on college governing bodies. Failure to do this would inevitably generate friction within the staff bodies. (The wisdom of Packer's analysis – which dates from 1968 – would become clear from events which would take place at Bristol in 1969, and to which we shall return in the following chapter).

In the end, Packer was drawn by the fourth of these options. All were open to him; this was his choice. But which college principalship should he apply for?

Packer informed the Council meeting on 5 June 1968 that he was interested in pursuing the possibility of becoming the next principal of the London College of Divinity, an evangelical theological college of the Church of England. Although the college was then located at premises in Northwood, a suburb of London, the decision had been taken to relocate the entire college to Nottingham, a city in the east Midlands, in the summer of 1970. A suitable site had been identified in the Nottingham suburb of Bramcote, and a major building programme was to be set in place in readiness for the move. The governors were looking for a dynamic and farsighted principal to lead the college in this new period of its existence. Unusually for those days, it was decided to advertise the position. (It may be noted here that the normal pattern was for college councils to seek suitable candidates through various networks and personal contacts. LCD broke this pattern, and can be seen as setting a pattern which would increasingly become the norm for the future.)

It was an attractive possibility for Packer; and Packer was an attractive possibility to the governors. The governors of the London College of Divinity agreed to short-list five candidates for interview in London on 29 July. Packer, who had arranged to spend the period 12 July to 12 September in the United States with his family, would not be available for this, and the governors therefore arranged to meet him separately at their regular meeting on 1 July. The appointment procedure was complicated by the intervention of Anthony Hanson, professor of theology at the University of Nottingham, who insisted that the university should be represented in its choice of a new principal. The Bishop of London, in his role as college visitor, supported this demand, placing the governors in a difficult position. In the event, on 29 July the governors thus found themselves having to consider an extra candidate for the principalship, imposed by Professor Hanson. Bishop Russell White, the chairman of the governors, duly arranged to meet informally with Hanson to clarify the relation of college and university.

The governors did not reach a decision directly as a result of their interviews, although they at least managed to reduce the field to three candidates. The decision was finally made to appoint Michael Green, a present member of the college staff, to the position. Green attached a series of conditions to his acceptance. First and foremost was his request that a new senior position should be established within the college, to be known as 'Director of Studies', and that the first occupant of this senior position should be Packer. The governors agreed unanimously to this proposal, and a formal press release was issued to this effect on 14 November 1968:

> The Council of the London College of Divinity announces the appointment of the Rev. E.M.B. Green to succeed Prebendary H. Jordan as Principal with effect from July 1969. It is the desire of the Principal-designate that, when the college moves to Nottingham in 1970, a new office of the Director of Studies should be established, and, with the unanimous goodwill of the Council, he has invited the Rev. Dr J.I. Packer to undertake this office.

Packer duly reported this development, including his acceptance of the offer, to the Council of Latimer House at its meeting on 5 December.

The proposed staffing arrangement brought together two of the most significant evangelicals in the Church of England within a single organization. Nevertheless, it gradually became clear that the arrangement would not work. The role of the 'Director of Studies' seemed unclear, and Packer finally came to the conclusion that he would find it difficult to work in this new environment. Early in 1969, he wrote to Green, indicating his misgivings, and the course of action which this suggested. At its meeting on 26 February 1969, the Council accepted Packer's withdrawal of acceptance, and issued a statement to this effect:

> The London College of Divinity and the Rev. Dr J.I. Packer jointly announce that Dr Packer has decided to withdraw his acceptance of the post of Director of Studies at the College following its move to Nottingham in the Summer of 1970. The College accepts this with very great regret.

(Green and Packer would, however, serve together in a single institution in the future; both were members of the faculty at Regent College, Vancouver, in the 1980s.)

So a door had been closed. Where next? Packer was not sure, and shared his anxieties and uncertainties over the matter with the Latimer House Council at its meeting on 2 July. He expressed the view that he ought to leave Latimer House at some point in 1970, even though at present there was no prospect of a new position elsewhere. It seemed to him that he might well have to leave England in order to find suitable employment. The Council was supportive of him, and assured him of their prayers. In the meantime, they began to consider potential replacements for him.[48]

But elsewhere, events were in motion which would lead to Packer securing a position as principal of the thelogical college at which he had taught with such distinction 1954–61: Tyndale Hall, Bristol. The events were so complex that they need to be explained in more detail. Packer was about to enter a situation which would turn out to be one of the most stressful in his entire career. In what follows, we shall tell the story of events in Bristol 1968–71, which proved to be one of the most turbulent incidents in the normally placid world of British theological education. The story cannot – and, in any case, need not – be told in full. But it must be told in part to allow an understanding of the next period in Packer's life. And so our narrative shifts to Bristol geographically, and back to 1968 chronologically, as we set the scene for the next chapter in Packer's life.

«8»

Bristol: Tyndale Hall, 1970–2

PACKER HAD ALREADY spent five years as a resident lecturer at Tyndale Hall before moving to Oxford to begin his ministry at Latimer House. His time in Bristol had been happy and productive, and given him a clear idea of the potential importance of Tyndale as a centre of theological education within the church at large. We have already explored the attraction of a principalship for Packer. To be principal of an evangelical theological college would be a good thing; far better, however, to be principal of such a college which he already knew and loved. However, the road by which Packer became principal of Tyndale Hall in 1970 was remarkably tortuous and convoluted, mainly on account of a series of events which took place at Bristol after Packer had left for Oxford. Those events are essential background to an understanding both of how Packer came to return to Bristol, and the remarkably difficult situation which he faced on that return.

Tyndale and Clifton: The Failed Merger of 1968–9

As we have already seen, Bristol had two evangelical theological colleges – Clifton Theological College and Tyndale Hall. Clifton traced its origins back to 1931, when a disagreement had led to the resignation of the entire staff body of the the Bible Churchmen's Missionary and Training College (later to become Tyndale Hall), who went on to establish a new college at Clifton in 1932. Since then, the two colleges had, so to speak, glared at each other across a mile of the Downs, the area of parkland adjacent to both institutions. It was never a particularly easy situation, although the rivalry between the two was often of a very friendly nature.

But why should there be two evangelical theological colleges so close together in Bristol? During the 1960s, when the painful memories which had led to the original split during the 1930s had ceased to have their original potency, the two colleges found themselves under pressure to consider some form of merger – not necessarily with each other, however. In February 1968, the Church of England published a report entitled *Theological Colleges for Tomorrow*, which acted as a catalyst for such discussions, not least through its suggestion that the two colleges should unite.[1] The report was authored by Sir Bernard de Bunsen (principal, Chester College of Education), Professor Henry Chadwick (Regius Professor of Divinity at Oxford University), and Dean Haworth (Salisbury Cathedral, and previously principal of Wells Theological College). The most striking recommendation of the report was that theological colleges should have an optimum size of 120 students, and a mininum of eighty. This could only be achieved in most cases by mergers.

This was a time of upheaval, and mergers were seen as one possible way of reducing operating costs and achieving greater efficiency. The London College of Divinity planned to move to Nottingham in the summer of 1970; early in 1968, they began to sound out other colleges to see if they might be interested in joining them in this move. Tyndale Hall was one college approached, along with Dalton House, a BCMS college concerned with the training of women missionaries. A joint meeting of the councils of all three colleges was arranged for 22 March 1968; in the event, this did not lead to a positive proposal for a merger or move.

So why did the two Bristol colleges not merge? John Wenham (Tyndale) and Alec Motyer (Clifton) had seen the case for a merger from 1960. Indeed, both were actively working towards creating an increasingly positive relationship between the two colleges. So what was the problem? Did the lingering memories of the 1930s continue to exercise a controlling influence? The evidence suggests that they did not; the problem lay in much more recent events, which created an atmosphere of distrust and considerable unease. The 'events of 1965' (as they are often referred to in discussions within Bristol) cast their shadow over the events of Packer's second period at Bristol. It must be stressed that Packer was not in any way involved in the events, directly or indirectly. Yet everyone involved in theological education at Bristol thereafter had to come to terms with these events and their aftermath, making at least some degree of explanation necessary.

At 11.00 p.m. on the evening of 11 February 1965, three of the five members of the teaching staff of Clifton Theological College were summoned before the college Council, and told that they were dismissed. No reason was given. Two other staff members resigned in sympathy shortly afterwards. To outside observers, Clifton seemed to have some kind of death wish; the staff members who had been most instrumental in attracting students to the college had been fired. The action caused consternation and distress far beyond Clifton. Many within evangelical circles were rumoured to have been critical of the dismissals. Among them was Packer, who was dismayed at this unforeseen turn of events.

There was concern particularly within the staff body at Tyndale Hall. Many Tyndale staff were on close terms with their colleagues at Clifton, and were shocked at the dismissals. Colin Brown, a member of the Tyndale staff, criticized events at Clifton in a paper set before the Church of England Evangelical Council. An atmosphere of distrust began to emerge between the two colleges, but above all between the staff of Tyndale Hall on the one hand, and the principal and Council of Tyndale Hall on the other. It is very difficult – and, for our purposes, not of any great relevance – to explore precisely how this mistrust developed and the ways in which it made itself evident. The point which needs to be stressed is that a merger was being proposed between two institutions at a time when feelings were running high.

There had been some preliminary discussion about a possible merger between the two colleges following the publication of the de Bunsen report. It was not clear whether this would meet with approval within the colleges. In any case, de Bunsen seemed to have assumed that, as Clifton and Tyndale were both evangelical colleges in the same part of Bristol, a merger was both natural and easy. He failed to understand the depth of feeling which existed as a result of the 'events of 1965'. This became clear towards the end of the academic year 1967–8. As part of a process of exploring the possibility, a joint meeting was arranged between the teaching staffs of the two colleges for 18 June 1968. It was, by all accounts, a very difficult and tense meeting, at which issues and memories from the past were much in evidence. On the basis of their strongly negative reactions to this meeting, the Tyndale Hall teaching staff asked that negotiations between the two institutions should cease. A meeting of the two college councils, scheduled for 3 July, was expected to endorse this decision. In fact, the councils reversed it, and determined to proceed with a merger, without informing the Tyndale staff that this was intended. The colleges were in recess for the summer vacation, and were not due to reconvene until late September. Discussions concerning the basis of the merger had reached an advanced stage by the end of the summer vacation, without the Tyndale Hall staff being aware of what was going on.

The new academic year began badly at Tyndale. On 25 September 1968, the principal of Tyndale Hall informed his staff meeting that a merger was intended, and that two candidates would be interviewed for the position of principal of the merged college. The two names mentioned – Michael A. Baughen and John B. Taylor – were both senior and respected members of the evangelical wing of the Church of England; they were not, however, associated with the particular ethos on which Tyndale Hall had built its reputation in recent years. The staff were stunned at the news, and expressed their 'dismay and grave concern' over the names of the two prospective principals, the proposed method of appointing staff, and above all the fact that, while the Clifton Council had kept their staff fully informed about developments, the Tyndale Hall Council had deliberately withheld such information.

Other news began to filter through. The merger plan included an explicit decision not to appoint Colin Brown to the staff of the new college. Brown, it will be recalled, was the member of Tyndale Hall staff who had voiced criticisms of the actions of Clifton Council. This shocked some of the staff at Tyndale. Furthermore, it emerged that the doctrinal statement of the BCMS (which had given Tyndale its distinctive theological ethos) would not be carried over into the merged college. One matter of particular concern began to emerge. Who was to be the principal of the merged college? It soon became clear that one name was not considered; indeed, that one name appeared to have been excluded from consideration – that of Packer. The reasons for this are not entirely clear. Some argued that Packer was likely to be the new principal of the London College of Divinity, and therefore would not be in a position to accept this post. However, most observers suspected that Packer had been passed over because he was known to have been critical of the 'events of 1965', and especially on account of his support for Colin Brown.

Distrust and suspicion increased. The Tyndale Council were convinced that the merger was a good thing; the staff were increasingly uneasy. Yet their views were not taken into consideration. John Wenham described the situation as follows:

> Separation [between staff and council] was so complete that [the Council] could work away like beavers on future plans, leaving the staff to gain their information from the *Church of England Newspaper* and the Clifton prayer letter. News that seemed (to those with no access to the reasons) like incredible folly began to reach us – the dropping of the most efficient tutor the colleges have ever had (apparently because his criticisms of Clifton were unacceptable), the abandoning (with very little discussion) of the BCMS basis, the agreement not even to shortlist Dr Packer for the principalship.[2]

On Friday 18 October 1968, a 'declaration of intent' was jointly issued by the two college councils. This announced the plan to unite the two colleges, and declared their 'intention to work towards this by September 1970, and to this end have appointed Rev. Michael A. Baughen, BD, to be Principal of this College'. On the same date, the principal of Tyndale Hall wrote to Colin Brown formally confirming that, since his name 'had been connected with certain criticisms of Clifton', it was only fair to inform him that 'our Council do not at present envisage your name going forward as a member of staff of the united College in 1970'. It was the end of the road for John Wenham, who resigned in disgust from the staff on 30 October over the way in which his colleague had been treated.

Tensions within Tyndale Hall had now reached such levels that the term 'crisis' was being openly used. Senior evangelicals were expressing alarm at the damage that the situation was causing to the public image of evangelicalism in the country. The *Church Times* would use the term 'fiasco' to illustrate what it referred to as 'deep splits' among evangelicals, and particularly the extent to which paternalism was deeply embedded within evangelicalism.[3]

Tyndale Hall, however, found itself in the slightly unusual situation of being answerable (although in different ways) to two bodies. On the one hand, there was the Tyndale Hall Council, which was strongly supportive of the merger between the two institutions; on the other, there was the BCMS, who owned the property which constituted Tyndale Hall. The BCMS found itself under increasing pressure to respond to the situation at Bristol. In particular, concern was expressed over the way in which the BCMS doctrinal basis had been discarded so readily, in order to facilitate the merger between the two colleges. By March 1969, it was clear that opposition to the merger was growing. The BCMS General Committee meeting of 25 March gave vent to these misgivings, with the result that it was decided to arrange a joint meeting in April between the BCMS Committee and the Tyndale Hall Council, in order to discuss remaining misgivings.

No public document referred to the growing unease over the merger. The public statements issued on behalf of Tyndale and Clifton, either directly or through the Church of England's press office, continued to foster the expectation that the merger was on course. On 27 March, the Church of England announced formally that the name of the merged institution would be 'Trinity College'. The name had been suggested by the principal-designate, Michael Baughen. Yet despite the public pronouncements issued on behalf of both Tyndale and Clifton councils concerning the advanced state of negotiations, tensions were steadily rising within Tyndale over the issue.

Misgivings were now widely being expressed within the staff and student bodies at Tyndale. On 28 March, the Tyndale Hall teaching staff drew up a memorandum which was severely critical of the proposed merger, and the means by which it was being engineered. It was now becoming clear that the number of students applying to the college had dropped sharply since the announcement of the merger. Indeed, later documents made it clear that new student admissions had virtually ceased as a result of anxiety over the direction the college was taking. It seemed that Tyndale was in danger of alienating its traditional sources of students, as well as many former students and BCMS supporters. Malcolm Widdecombe, a local Bristol vicar, had commented on the crisis in his parish magazine.[4] After outlining what was known of the situation, Widdecombe demanded to know 'what the hell is going on'. While apologizing for his profanity, he made it clear that this was the only kind of language that might get noticed. These comments were taken up by the *Bristol Evening*

Post, in an article which suggested that a 'black list' of tutors now existed.

The whole issue was now as public as it was messy. An issue which emerged as significant was the manner in which the principal (and subsequently the director of studies) of the new college had been appointed. The position had not been advertised, and there were strong rumours that at least one suitable candidate had been passed over as a matter of policy. In a circular letter of 12 March, Harry Chapman, a member of the Tyndale Council, expressed his grave concerns that they 'were not allowed to consider Jim Packer for either post when head and shoulders he was ahead of anyone else in the field. Remember our Principal was appointed before Jim accepted the LCD post which he has since withdrawn from.'

One of the central issues concerned the lack of any relationship between the Tyndale Hall staff and Council; the former felt that the latter were deliberately and systematically ignoring their feelings. A confidential memorandum was circulated by the Tyndale staff on 28 March stressing their hostility towards a merger with Clifton, and expressing their anxiety that the Council had chosen not to note their concerns.

> We earnestly ask that they will meet the staff and attempt to re-establish a common mind with them, with a view either to re-negotiating the merger with Clifton, or, if necessary, to reconstituting Tyndale Hall in a way which will command the confidence of supporters of the College and of BCMS and of the evangelical public generally.[6]

On 28 April, thirty-five members of the student body expressed their reservations about the proposed merger, particularly as it involved the non-employment of a member of the teaching staff whom they held in high regard (Colin Brown). That same month, a petition signed by seventy-four former students was circulated, arguing that confidence in the proposed united college was already so undermined that the whole project should be reconsidered.[7]

A crisis meeting was eventually held in London on Monday 28 April, at which the staff set out, and required to have minuted, their many objections to the merger. A further meeting was arranged for 13 May, at which it became clear that one of the most serious concerns, expressed by both staff and the senior student, was the absence of a person of scholarly or theological distinction on the proposed staff of the new college. Each of the two meetings had lasted five hours; it was clear that no consensus was reached, and that serious and potentially far-reaching divisions had been exposed.

Meanwhile, the BCMS was agonizing over what to do. The joint meeting with Tyndale Hall Council on 9 April had clarified issues, but not resolved them. The General Meeting of the BCMS on 22 April 1969 had revealed what gave every indication of being mounting criticism of the merger from within the society. Drastic action could not be postponed. On 29 May, an extraordinary meeting of the General Committee of the BCMS was called in London. Three possibilities were discussed: acceptance of the merger as presently proposed; acceptance with modifications; rejection of the proposals. Roger T. Beckwith, a leading critic of the merger proposals (and also, of course, Packer's colleague on the staff of Latimer House), was invited to the meeting, at which he spoke forcefully against the form of the proposed merger. He had actively campaigned against the proposals in the past, in particular drawing attention to the negative implications for the distinctive doctrinal identity of the BCMS. As the meeting progressed, it became increasingly clear that the mood of the meeting was for rejection. Finally, a vote was taken, and the following resolution passed:

> The BCMS Committee cannot give the support asked for the proposed merger unless all present staff appointments be re-examined, with greater weight being given to the primacy of theology, and that none be excluded from consideration.

With that, the merger plans were fatally wounded. Michael Baughen was a fine pastor (as he would show in the remainder of his distinguished career, and particularly as Bishop of Chester). But he was not, and did not want to be, a theologian. If that was a sticking point, then Baughen believed that he was the wrong man. At their joint meeting on 3 June, the Councils of the two colleges reluctantly concluded that the merger could not now proceed. A press release was issued to this effect two days later.

It had been a very stressful period for all concerned. Michael Baughen had experienced what was probably the worst nine months of his career. Those who opposed his appointment, particularly on the BCMS General Committee, went out of their way to stress their high personal regard for him; their opposition was not directed towards him as a person, but concerned the style of leadership which he would bring. Despite this, Baughen could not help but feel wounded and hurt by what had been a very trying experience.

It also left Tyndale Hall in a very exposed situation. It was now very far from clear as to whether it could survive this trauma.

The New Principal of Tyndale Hall

The plans for a merged college were now in ruins. So what would happen to Tyndale? Could it survive on its own? The future seemed uncertain, and was made even more so by the principal's announcement that, following the failure of the merger negotiations, he felt he had no option other than to resign with effect from the end of December 1969. He wrote to the chairman of the Hall Council to the effect that he could not associate himself with the 'breach of faith towards the Rev. Michael Baughen and Clifton Theological College into which the Council has been forced.' He announced his decision to the staff meeting on 17 June, exactly two weeks after the decision to call off the merger had been taken. Tyndale now needed a new principal, in addition to an entire rethink over its future.

We have presented this narrative in some detail, in order to cast light on Packer's career at this important juncture. The important point to appreciate is the following. Tyndale Hall, the theological college of the Church of England which had established a distinct reputation for the priority of theology in relation to ministry, had entered into a series of discussions which, for reasons we have noted, had potentially seriously compromised its reputation at exactly this point. Not only did the college now need a new principal; it needed one who could restore its sense of purpose and direction (and above all provide *theological* leadership), offer it a new vision for its future, and restore confidence amongst the staff, students and former members. Morale had plummeted. Things could not go on like this.

There were some who felt that the Tyndale Hall Council should resign in the aftermath of the debacle. But wiser counsels prevailed.

Some members of the Oxford Inter-Collegiate Christian Union (OICCU) gathered together for a garden party in Trinity Term 1948 at St Ebbe's Rectory. Included in the photograph are James Packer (third row, seventh from right of photograph) and James M. Houston (back row, second from right of photograph). Elizabeth Lloyd-Jones (now Lady Catherwood) is sitting immediately in front of Packer.

Packer (standing centre) overlooking the production of the script for a filmstrip about Wycliffe Hall in December 1949.

Packer (right-hand corner) playing table-tennis in the Upper Common Room, Wycliffe Hall, c. 1950.

The Boy's Brigade Annual Camp, Exmouth, South Devon, 1954.
The five leaders, seated in the front row, are (from left to right):
Jim Lees, Norman Sheppey, Eric Wildman, James Packer and Les
Hyett. The two camp cooks were Mary Cossar (standing on left of
second row) and Elsie Sheppey (standing on right of second row).

The staff of Tyndale Hall, Bristol, 1956. From left to right: Denis
Tongue, John R. Wenham (Vice-Principal), James Packer, J. Stafford
Wright (Principal), Richard J. Coates (subsequently first
Warden of Latimer House), Emrys B. Davies.

Packer signing copies
of the anniversary edition of
Knowing God, 1993.

Portrait of Packer, 1990.

Packer pictured with his colleagues Eugene Peterson (left) and Gordon
Fee (right) outside Regent College Bookstore, 1993.

Had the Council resigned, Tyndale Hall would have been without any form of government or leadership, and thus been unable to put in place the reconstructive measures which were so sorely needed. The Council met on 18 June, and decided that they would immediately proceed to advertise for the principalship of the Hall. Advertisements would appear on two consecutive weeks in *The Times*, the *Church of England Newspaper*, and the *Church Times*. The first advertisements appeared on Friday 27 June. The Council were strongly aware of the urgency of the situation. It was vitally important to be able to announce the appointment of a new principal before the new academic year began, in order to reassure past and existing students, and attract new recruits for the following year. The serious decline in student applications as a result of the merger proposals had to be reversed as a matter of priority.

It was clear to many that Packer was the ideal candidate. He was regarded throughout evangelicalism as a person of theological stature, and commanded wide support within the traditional Tyndale Hall constituency. His emphasis on the 'primacy of theology' (to pick up a phrase from the BCMS resolution of 29 May) was widely known. In addition, in 1968, he had published an article which showed that he was alert to the issues facing theological colleges, and may be regarded as having predicted with alarming accuracy the disastrous consequences of an inadequate model of the relationship of principal and teaching staff in a theological college.[8] His name had been mentioned frequently in BCMS circles as a candidate for the principalship of the merged college, and some on the Tyndale Council were known to support him strongly. Tyndale students would discuss the issue frequently in the communal bathrooms, which seemed to many to be the hub of college life. Packer's name was enthusiastically canvassed by students, even though they had no say in the appointment. Richard James, who was senior student at the time, found an intriguing advertisement in a Christian magazine, and displayed it on the college noticeboard: 'WANTED: Packer for general duties in a Christian Establishment.'

In addition to whatever other gifts he might possess, Packer was unquestionably able to offer exactly the theological leadership which the staff and students of the Hall felt was required. The lobbying began immediately the decision had been made to proceed to an appointment. Packer, however, was hesitant. Beckwith, one of the leading critics of the merger proposals, was Packer's colleague as librarian at Latimer House. The suggestion had been made by some that Packer was 'at the centre of a Latimer House plot to secure this position' for himself. Packer was aware of these rumours, and their implications. What self-respect, Packer asked, could he hope to retain if he were to apply for the position under such adverse conditions?

In the light of such rumours, Packer held back. However, the Council was in no mood to waste time, or to pay much attention to what they clearly regarded as spurious rumours. Packer declined to apply for the position, but expressed interest in it, and a willingness to discuss the various issues surrounding it. On 21 July, Packer was invited to a meeting of the Council, and spent two hours in general discussion, addressing a series of specific questions put to him by Council members. Although other applications were to hand, the Council clearly felt that Packer was the right man for the job. They therefore immediately resolved to inform the BCMS General Committee of the identity of the various applicants, as well as their belief that Packer was the obvious choice. This Committee met the following day, and warmly endorsed the invitation. At a subsequent meeting in London on 31 July, Packer set out more clearly his vision for what needed to be done under his principalship, and secured the Council's consent. In particular, Packer had specified that a working party would be established to restructure the government and general policy of the college.

On 4 August, the outgoing principal of Tyndale Hall was able to write to all his students, confirming that Packer would be his successor. The letter included an explicit statement that Packer intended to retain all current full-time teaching staff, an issue which had been a serious concern to the student body.[9] Colin Brown would therefore remain on the teaching staff of Tyndale.

So Packer prepared to leave Oxford for Bristol. It was clear that Packer had contributed immensely to the consolidation of Latimer House, and used it as a vehicle for the furtherance of the evangelical cause within the Church of England and beyond. The Council were deeply appreciative of his contribution:

> The Council wish to place on record their gratitude to God, and under Him to Dr Packer, for the outstanding leadership he has been enabled to give to the cause of the gospel during his time

at Latimer House, first as Librarian for fifteen months, and then as Warden for seven and a half years. The Council believe that the books and articles he has written and the symposia he has edited, together with his membership of the Anglican/Methodist Unity Commission, the Doctrine Commission, and numerous evangelical Councils and groups, have made a significant contribution to the contemporary growth of evangelicalism within the Church of England. The Council are thankful that his appointment as Principal of Tyndale Hall, Bristol, will make it possible for him to continue to exercise his varied gifts in the service of the church.

In a bold move, the Latimer House Council subsequently appointed John Wenham to succeed Packer as warden.

The Reorganization of Theological Education

The Packer who prepared to take up his position as principal of Tyndale was, in one sense, the same man who had taught there for five years a decade earlier as a member of staff. His theology had not changed in any significant way. But in another sense, it was a new man who returned. Packer's time at Oxford had broadened his horizons, deepened his influence, and expanded his circle of supporters. The new principal had first-hand experience of theological education in North America, and had little doubt that the English system was seriously inadequate in comparison. Packer would prove to be a reforming principal. Not only was there an urgent need to restructure the government of the college, in the light of the serious flaws exposed by the merger fiasco; there was a need to give new direction to theological education itself. Those who tend to think of Packer only as a writer or speaker will need to modify this view in the light of Packer's determination to restructure and rescue Tyndale Hall.

For Tyndale Hall was in serious trouble. As the academic year 1969–70 opened, it became clear that student numbers were dangerously low. Only twenty-eight students were in residence. The financial situation was serious; a working loss of just under £7,000 was predicted for the current academic year, with a further deficit forecast for the following year. Although Packer was not due to take up his position until 1 January 1970, he had negotiated permission to begin to restructure the college with immediate effect. This was no easy matter. Packer's appointment as principal was finally agreed on 31 July; on 10 August, he set off on a major lecture tour of Australia and New Zealand, from which he would not return until late September.[10]

A working party, established to oversee the revision of the government of Tyndale Hall, had its first meeting 24–25 October 1969. At that meeting, Packer announced that he had appointed Alec Motyer as lecturer in Old Testament at Tyndale Hall. Motyer, who had been vice-principal of Clifton Theological College until the 'events of 1965', was at that time serving in parish ministry at St Luke's, Hampstead, in London. News of his return to teaching was greeted with enthusiasm by the student body.[11] The combination of Packer and Motyer was seen as further confirmation of Tyndale's growing reputation in the now-burgeoning Reformed constituency within the Church of England and beyond.

A second meeting was held 31 October–1 November.[12] The working party aimed to formulate goals for the college as it faced what gave every indication of being a difficult future; to plan internal restructuring of the Hall, particularly to ensure a sense of partnership between Council, staff and students; and to consider the relationship of the Hall with the BCMS. The outcome of the discussion was both significant and positive. In the second week of December, Packer issued a circular letter to all present and past members of the Hall, and others concerned with its future. The letter outlined the main changes proposed to the college structures.

1. A new body, the 'Tyndale Hall Association', would be formed, hopefully with effect from Easter 1970, charged with responsibility for administering the college. Its membership would be by subscription. One quarter of the College Council would be elected directly by Association members. In this way, Packer believed that the college would remain sensitive and responsive to the concerns of its supporters, and be able to resist centralizing and standardizing pressures from Church authorities. In this way, also, the distinctive identity of the Hall could be safeguarded, its particular constituency given a voice in its government, and additional income secured.

2. All teaching staff would serve on the Hall Council *ex officio*, ensuring that those who were required to implement college policy

would also be in a position to determine that policy in the first place. This proposal ensured that the serious communication breakdown between Council and staff of 1968 would not recur in the future.

3. The college syllabus and pastoral training programme would be reviewed, with the objective of ensuring that it met the known needs of the church. However, Packer stressed that Tyndale would retain its distinctive emphasis on the importance of theology, while insisting that such an emphasis in no way implied that the college was weak on the pastoral side of training.[13]

These were bold moves, and were clearly welcomed by the student body. Powerful new wine was being poured into old wineskins. Other moves followed. A registered company was established, 'Tyndale Hall Ltd', which allowed the Hall greater financial flexibility, particularly in relation to covenants. A new prospectus, 'Tyndale is People', was produced, aiming to project a positive image of the Hall as it entered the 1970s.[14] It was circulated to all past members of the Hall, with a request that it should be passed on to any who were thinking of preparing for the ordained ministry of the church.

Packer took up his position as principal on 1 January 1970. It was clear to him that a series of measures had been, or were about to be, put into place which, as far as was humanly possible, would safeguard the future of Tyndale Hall. The term got off to a good start. As Packer reported to a meeting of the working party, held at Tyndale over 30–31 January, there was a very good spirit within the college. An extraordinary meeting of the BCMS General Committee, held on 27 January, had gone well, and had quickly given its approval to the proposals to restructure the Hall. There were good reasons for hoping that, even if it was not possible to recruit many more fee-paying students for the following year, there might be the possibility of attracting some Bristol University students as lodgers for the coming year.

The faculty was outstanding. The five resident faculty were: Packer (Principal); Alec Motyer (Deputy Principal, with teaching responsibilities in Hebrew and Old Testament); Colin Brown (Dean of Studies, with teaching responsibilities in church history, historical theology, and the philosophy of religion); Anthony Thiselton (teaching responsibilities in New Testament theology, biblical interpretation, and the philosophy of religion); and John

Tiller (teaching responsibilities in the area of worship and church history). It is fair to say that no English theological college, before or after, has ever managed to pack in such a concentration of theological talent. Financially, it would require a student body of at least forty-five, and preferably fifty, to maintain a staff body of this size; Packer was clear that, unless the student body reached forty-five by the beginning of the academic year 1971–2, the Hall could be in financial difficulties. However, the structural and educational developments Packer had set in place were entirely likely to lead to the renewal of Tyndale, and the successful recruitment of at least the required number of students in the future. All that was needed was time to allow things to settle, and Tyndale's new vision to become more widely known and appreciated. But, as events would prove, time was someting Tyndale would not be allowed to have.

Packer had hardly settled in to his new position when ominous storm clouds began to gather on the horizon. Tyndale's future was in question again. As if that was not enough, the important personal relationship between Packer and Martyn Lloyd-Jones came under stress, and finally ruptured. The period 1970–72 was without doubt one of the most stressful of Packer's life. Those who wonder why Packer wrote so little over this period will find their answer in what follows. We begin by dealing with the final break with Lloyd-Jones.

The Break with Martyn Lloyd-Jones, 1970

Packer was firmly committed to a bilateral application of his commitment to evangelicalism. On the one hand, he saw himself as working within the Church of England to reform and renew it in evangelical terms (note that the term 'reform', as used in Puritan works, often has the sense 'renew'). On the other, he regarded it as important to work with evangelicals in other denominations to further the overall aims of the evangelical movement. At times, those two components of Packer's agenda were seen by some to be in tension. This was especially the case after the 1966 National Assembly of Evangelicals, in which Martyn Lloyd-Jones antagonized evangelicals within the Church of England and other mainline denominations through his separatist agenda. Such was the polarization that developed that for an evangelical to be committed to the Church of England was now seen by some free church evangelicals as an act of betrayal. Evangelicals within the Church of England generally responded by the deadliest strategy of all – ignoring their free church brethren. Packer was one of the very few evangelicals within the national church to advocate continued collaboration with free church evangelicals after the showdown of 1966.

This bilateral policy would come to an end (at least in England) in 1970, when Packer was declared *persona non grata* by his free church brethren. The precipitating cause of this public rupture in relationships was the publication of a short book, of which Packer was one of four co-authors. In view of the importance of this small book, we may consider its origin and intended purpose in more detail.

In his final report of October 1969 to the Latimer House Council, Packer mentioned a number of projects which were now coming to completion. Among them, he noted what he referred to as 'a mixed Willesden-Mascall-Buchanan-Packer grill, on unity and union in England'. By this, he intended his readers to understand a short work entitled *Growing into Union*, which was eventually published in May 1970. Its four authors were the Bishop of Willesden (Graham Leonard), E.L. Mascall, Colin O. Buchanan and Packer. The last two were evangelicals; the first two leading Anglo-catholics (that is to say, members of the catholic wing of the Church of England). It was highly unusual for evangelicals and Anglo-catholics to author a joint volume; in the event, it proved highly controversial for some. Packer himself was quite clear about what he hoped to achieve through this book, and his reasons for collaborating with two leading Anglo-catholics to achieve this end. For Packer, it was clear that there were two quite distinct groups within the Church of England who were opposed to the 1968 Anglican-Methodist proposals. One of the groups was evangelical, the other Anglo-catholic.[15]

While the grounds of opposition to the scheme within these two groups differed significantly, Packer and his three co-writers concluded that they were totally united in their belief that the theological basis for the proposed action was inadequate. The proposed course of action could in no way be regarded as an obedient and faithful response to God's revealed truth. The four felt that this needed to be said and heeded. Despite their differences on matters of importance, they were united in their defence of theological orthodoxy against what they considered to be the incipient liberalism of those who advocated the merger. In particular, they stressed the need for an adequate agreed basis of faith for the proposed united church. They had therefore come together to bear common witness to the importance of theology, and especially the need for theological *orthodoxy*, in any plans for church union. A united church must be a doctrinally orthodox church – and all those who were committed to theological orthodoxy should therefore work for the cause of its advancement.

Growing into Union therefore set out an approach to union which injected some much-needed correctives into the debates then going on within English Christianity. It was, in Packer's view, a tract rather than a treatise; to be seen as a contribution to an ongoing discussion, rather than something more pretentious and grandiose. The argument of the book focused on some practical suggestions concerning how such discussions should proceed. In the course of the book, some doctrinal issues which were the subject of disagreement between evangelicals and Anglo-catholics were addressed – such as the authority of Scripture, the doctrine of justification by faith, and the nature of the sacraments. The purpose of this was to indicate that, despite disagreement on some matters among the four writers, there was substantial agreement on these – agreement which, in conscience, they felt bound to note and report, and build on.

For Packer, the issue was thus that of exploring existing common ground between evangelicals and Anglo-catholics within the Church of England, not the artificial manufacture of such agreement by compromise or concession, where such agreement did not exist in fact. But this is not how the book was read. In a series of three articles in *The Evangelical Magazine*, David N. Samuel of the Protestant Reformation Society denounced the book in no uncertain terms. He was scathing concerning its analysis of the doctrinal issues linked with the Reformation: 'Can it be that the world has had to wait until the breakdown of the Anglican-Methodist conversations for the differences that have divided Christendom for four hundred years to be resolved by four Anglican clergymen, and that all within the space of six months?' Packer mildly replied that all that the authors were doing was setting out the extent of their personal agreement as a means of showing the merits of the practical proposals which they wished to commend.[16]

Other criticisms followed. It is far from clear how many of Packer's critics at this stage had read the 200 pages of text; many seemed to condemn their impressions of what the book said, or the very fact that evangelicals had in some way collaborated with Anglo-catholics. In the eyes of many, collaboration was presumed to amount to compromise. Packer's credentials as an evangelical were openly called into question by some.[17]

The most important criticisms were voiced by Martin Lloyd-Jones and his colleagues. For Lloyd-Jones, the book represented a compromise, brought about through a weakening of evangelical convictions.[18] Lloyd-Jones, supported by John Caiger and David Fountain (the other free church members of the Puritan Conference Committee), wrote to Packer to terminate the Puritan Conferences. In the circumstances, they believed, it was impossible for them to continue. The fact that Packer had brought the Conferences into being seemed to count for little in the new and harsh climate of denominational politics which now intruded. A meeting of the Westminster Fraternal in November 1970 requested that the Conference should be reconvened in an appropriately modified form in the following year, under the new title of the 'Westminster Conference'. Packer was conspicuously omitted from the list of speakers and organizers. The final Puritan Conference thus met in December 1969, and the first Westminster Conference in December 1971.

Through a series of such actions, Packer was, in effect, frozen out of certain evangelical circles in which he had once been a welcome participant. He was removed from the organizing committee of a monthly Bible Rally held in the Cotswold region of England. Lloyd-Jones's influence was, of course, at its greatest in the free church movement in Wales, and – despite Kit's Welsh roots – Packer now found himself being shunned by evangelical organizations in Wales which would once have counted him as a friend. One leading independent evangelical went so far as to advance the view that Packer could 'no longer be regarded as an evangelical'. Arrogant and misguided though this judgment must now seem, it appears to have reflected the hardening views now settling in within the Lloyd-Jones camp, which clearly decided to take an absolute stand over what was actually a relative issue. Once more, it is necessary to point out that it is generally agreed that it was those who advised Lloyd-Jones, rather than 'the Doctor' himself, who appear to have been responsible for this hard-line attitude.

A further exclusion order against Packer concerned *The Evangelical Magazine*. This journal had been founded in 1959, with Elizabeth Braund as its managing editor, and Packer and the Revd J. Elwyn Davies as consulting editors. Braund and Davies both had close links with Lloyd-Jones. Packer's involvement with this journal is an excellent example of the 'bilateral' policy he had consistently followed, which allowed him to work together with evangelicals across denominational lines, while at the same time affirming his commitment to and involvement in the Church of England. Following the break with Lloyd-Jones, Packer was thrown off the editorial board. The irony of this cannot be overlooked. An introductory letter, circulated in June 1959 by the three persons just noted, had stressed that the new magazine would not be 'identified with any particular groups or interests, denominational or otherwise'.[19] The clear intrusion of a denominational agenda could hardly be overlooked. Without Packer, the magazine proved to have little appeal, and folded shortly afterwards. The *Magazine* is of some interest to our narrative, in that the constituent chapters of Packer's classic work *Knowing God* originally appeared in this publication. They attracted little attention until published by a mainline publishing house (see p. 189).[20]

Nevertheless, Packer had no intention of retracting his views on the merits of collaborating with other Christians who were not evangelicals. For Packer, evangelicalism was 'Christianity at its purest'; this did not, however, preclude collaboration, dialogue or debate with 'other mutations of Christianity . . . which seem less close overall to the spirit, belief and thrust of the New Testament'. Indeed, he developed and justified his views still further in the course of the next decade. Packer's fullest statement of the approach at issue was set out in two pamphlets published by Latimer House, of which Packer had once been warden.[21] The 'Latimer Studies' series, to which Packer was consulting editor, aimed to identify issues of major importance concerning evangelicalism within the Church of England. Packer's forty-page pamphlet was the first in the series, and focused on the issue of evangelical identity within the Church of England. Packer notes the difficulties which face evangelicals in doctrinally-mixed churches, such as the Church of England. The arguments which he counters in these works are primarily those deriving from the circles around Lloyd-Jones; above all, Packer was concerned to engage with the demand that evangelicals withdraw from such mixed churches to form 'pure' denominations:

> Some have urged evangelicals in 'doctrinally mixed' churches to withdraw into a tighter fellowship where the pre-critical, pre-liberal view of Scripture is rigorously upheld and sceptical revisionism in theology is debarred. It has been said that failure to do this is as unprincipled as it is foolish. It is unprincipled, the argument runs, because by staying in churches which tolerate heretics you become constructively guilty of their heresies, by your association with them; and it is foolish because you have not the least hope of cleaning up the Augean stables while liberals remain there. Withdrawal is the conscientious man's only option.[22]

Both these arguments can be discerned within Lloyd-Jones's writings from 1965 onwards, including his address at the 1965 Puritan Studies Conference.

Packer's response involved a number of observations. First, he noted that all mainline churches are, as a matter of historical fact, founded on a set of beliefs (embodied in the Christian creeds, and sets of confessional documents) which commit those churches to theological orthodoxy. Some may depart from this; evangelicals within those churches have a duty to recall them to faithfulness. They cannot be regarded as 'guilty by association' if they protest in this way. The idea of 'guilt by association' was, for Packer, 'a nonsense notion, which has been given an unhappy airing during the last two decades'.[23] If trends towards liberalism are not resisted, a denomination will slide into heresy. And who will protest and argue against this, unless evangelicals remain within those mainline churches for as long as possible?

Packer also offered a criticism against those who argued that their own congregations or denominations were theologically correct. He noted that smaller doctrinally-pure bodies, such as the Fellowship of Independent Evangelical Churches, are open to the charge that they might 'purchase doctrinal purity at the price of theological stagnation, and are cultural backwaters out of touch with society around'. Underlying this point is Packer's conviction that cultural engagement – of such importance to effective evangelism – is not assisted by a total withdrawal from the society which is to be evangelized.

It is easy to see this episode as an incident of purely local interest, relating to a particularly difficult period in the history of English evangelicalism which has no wider relevance. But this is not so. Packer, as we have had cause to stress throughout this work, is a strategic thinker, concerned with the formulation of theologically grounded strategies which are appropriate to ensure that the long-term goals of evangelicalism are advanced. By the time Packer was preparing to leave England, he had given careful formulation to a coherent understanding of the ways in which evangelicals can and should relate to non-evangelicals within mixed denominations, and with other churches in general. Packer's understanding of evangelicalism as 'Christianity at its purest', and of non-evangelical versions of Christianity as 'mutations which seem less close overall to the spirit, belief and thrust of the New Testament' involves the recognition that evangelicalism is not the *only* form of Christianity.[24] This opens the way to dialogue and debate with other forms of Christianity over a number of issues, including collaboration against mutual opponents (a strategy usually referred to as 'co-belligerence').

Two major events of the 1990s – the Anglican Church of Canada's *Essentials '94* congress (1994; see pp. 275–7) and the celebrated document *Evangelicals and Catholics Together* (1993; see pp. 264–75) – can be seen to rest on precisely the theological foundations developed by Packer in England during the 1970s. Packer's response to these developments in North America in the 1990s was thus no pragmatic response to events, thought up on the spur of the moment; rather, it represented the application of a coherent and historically and theologically justified approach, which had been set in place twenty years earlier. But this is to look to the future; we must now return to the acrimony of 1970.

Why this bitterness? The general consensus appears to be that non-Anglican evangelicals, especially those associated with Lloyd-Jones, saw Packer's support and enthusiasm for the Puritan Studies Conference as pointing to equal support and enthusiasm for every aspect of Puritan thought – including a separatist agenda. Did not the great John Owen – whom Packer admired so much – stress the importance of a 'pure body' doctrine of the church? The

Puritans had turned their backs on the Church of England. So why not Packer also? Packer's increasing commitment to the Church of England was seen as simply inconsistent with his Puritan concerns. To these same critics, the liaison with Mascall and Leonard was nothing short of betrayal. Packer (with perhaps a more informed awareness of the history and nature of the Church of England than his critics) saw no inconsistency at this juncture, and felt that his critics perhaps knew less about Reformed theology than they led their readers to believe.

This public rejection of Packer by the Lloyd-Jones camp was painful for Packer, not least on account of the very high esteem in which he held Lloyd-Jones. It was little comfort that the strategy proved abortive. Without the cachet afforded them by Packer's reputation, many of the bodies who had frozen him out found themselves lacking figures of substance to support them. *The Evangelical Magazine* limped along for a further edition, before finally folding for good. Packer had been one of the relatively few evangelicals of influence within the Church of England who had championed links with Lloyd-Jones. With that link so publicly broken by Lloyd-Jones himself, the scene was set for the further marginalization of his views within the English national church.

Distressing though this termination of an important friendship was, Packer found that he had other things to worry about. By the end of 1970, the future of Tyndale Hall was in serious doubt. Having just emerged from one crisis, Tyndale now found itself plunged into another.

A New Crisis: The End of Tyndale Hall?

It had been known for some time that a reorganization of theological education within the Church of England was not far over the horizon. The de Bunsen report of February 1968 had led to the formation of a Joint Planning Group. In December 1969, this group produced a report which outlined two general strategies for the future:

A) a policy of *laissez-faire*, which allowed the present situation to continue, and in effect allowed student numbers to be determined by market forces;

B) a policy of consultative planning, which would carry the full authority of the church.

Tyndale Hall was an institution recognized by the Church of England for training for ordained ministry. Should the Church of England for any reason withdraw that recognition from Tyndale, or any other college, it would have no hope of survival unless it could sustain itself in another role.

The first real signs of trouble came on 4 February 1970. The Church Assembly debated the future of theological education, in the light of falling numbers of candidates for ordination, and decided in favour of option 'B'. The importance of the discussion was recognized by Tyndale staff and governors. Any proposal to merge theological colleges would affect them in some way.

At a residential meeting of the working party in March, it was noted that there appeared to be a lingering suspicion of Tyndale amongst bishops and other senior church personnel, as a result of the failed merger negotiations with Clifton. There seemed to be something of a consensus that four evangelical theological colleges would come under pressure to merge: Ridley Hall, Cambridge, might find itself being asked to merge with Wycliffe Hall, Oxford; Tyndale could expect to be asked to merge with Clifton. Both these moves had been recommended by the de Bunsen report; the proposals, though not accepted at the time, were now being studied with increasing interest by senior church figures.

A meeting of senior staff and council members of the seven evangelical theological colleges[25] was hastily arranged for 12 March. The meeting reviewed the situation. Of the 426 places which the colleges had at their disposal for students, ninety-nine were either vacant or filled with non-theological students. Four possible responses were discussed, including amalgamation with colleges of other denominations or traditions within the Church of England. These were felt to be impractical. The only viable option appeared to be considering the merger of some evangelical colleges. No decisions were reached, but the four colleges noted above – including Tyndale Hall – were singled out for particular discussion.[26]

At the next meeting of the Tyndale Hall working party in April, Packer duly reported that it was now expected that the number of theological colleges would be reduced from twenty-one to fourteen.

In other words roughly one in three colleges could expect to cease to exist in its present form. The threat to Tyndale was clear. The college was facing a deficit for the year 1969–70, and another was projected for 1970–71. If economic viability was to be of critical importance, Tyndale could face some difficult questions.

The Church of England body entrusted with this issue was the Advisory Council for the Church's Ministry (ACCM). ACCM finally decided that the best way of handling such an extremely sensitive matter was to invite a small group of senior figures to visit every theological college in the country, and gain an understanding of its strengths, weaknesses, plans and potential. The committee – which was virtually invariably referred to as the 'Three Wise Men' – consisted of Robert A.K. Runcie (Bishop of St Albans, later Archbishop of Canterbury), Kenneth Woollcombe (principal of the Episcopal Theological College, Edinburgh, and subsequently Bishop of Oxford) and Derek R. Wigram (former headmaster of Monkton Combe School). The 'Runcie Commission' (as the committee preferred to be known) set about its task with alacrity. It was decided that Woollcombe should visit every college on his own, and that the other two committee members would follow up those visits as and when necessary. The object was to produce a smaller number of economically viable colleges, and retain the balance between the different traditions within the church.

On 30 May, Kenneth Woollcombe visited Tyndale Hall. He had lunch with the Hall Council, at which he explained his brief from the Church Assembly, and heard Packer and the Council explain their plans for the future. At this meeting, the Council made it clear that they were prepared to explore once more a merger with Clifton, which they continued to regard as viable. Woollcombe had friendly memories of Packer; they had both been at Oxford around the same time, and Woollcombe had narrowly beaten Packer for the prestigious Ellerton Theological Essay Prize back in 1951. The meeting was friendly and constructive, and left the Tyndale representatives feeling that they had made a good impression, in particular in relation to the pioneering approach to theological education that was being developed under Packer. The college was able to point to a new theological syllabus for ministerial training, a strongly gifted faculty, and a new style of college government. Student numbers were increasing, and there was every expectation that they would reach the critically important number of forty-five from the opening of the next academic year.

After meeting the student executive, Woollcombe went on to meet Professor Kenneth Grayston, the professor of theology at the University of Bristol. It was at this point that Woollcombe began to realize he might have a serious problem on his hands. It became clear that there was a great gulf between the theological style and approach of the university on the one hand, and the conservative theological colleges on the other. As Woollcombe listened to Grayston (who was a personal friend from their time together at St John's College, Oxford), he was forced to the conclusion that the gap was unbridgeable. From the university side, there was no willingness to collaborate with either Clifton or Tyndale.[27] A further consideration emerged subsequently, when Woollcombe discovered that the staff of the local Methodist training college were hostile towards both Clifton and Tyndale; this, however, was secondary to the much more serious issue of the university's attitude.[28] Tyndale and Clifton, however, do not seem to have appreciated that such negative perceptions were circulating in Bristol concerning them.

It must be stressed that every one of the twenty-one theological colleges in England felt under threat. There were perhaps some obvious possibilities for closure or merger; however, the Runcie Commission had made it clear that they did not intend to exclude any courses of action in pursuit of their brief. Their report was due in October. Basil Moss, who at this stage was a senior figure in ACCM, with responsibilities for the future of the theological colleges, recalls that theological colleges across England, irrespective of their theological tradition, found themselves plunged into fierce and bitter battles for survival. It seemed to him that just about every college felt it represented something indispensable to the church at large, which it would fight to defend to the end. Moss was quite clear that the storm at Bristol was being replicated in other places throughout the land, even if the Bristol situation would achieve more public attention than others.

Aware of the coming storm, senior evangelical figures within the Church of England were determined to develop strategies which would preserve as much as possible of the existing evangelical resources in this field. At a joint meeting on 12 March, six of the seven evangelical theological college councils decided to set up a working party to explore the options.[29] The three-man group (often referred to by evangelicals as 'the three wiser men') consisted of John R.W. Stott (chairman), Hugh R.M. Craig, and Douglas Webster. In the middle of September, Packer wrote as follows:

This autumn, ACCM's 'three wise men' will produce their plan for closing, merging and restructuring the theological colleges of this country so as to reduce the total number of places available by one third. This report is being compiled in fulfilment of a mandate given by the Church Assembly last February. An unofficial working party was set up by a group of evangelical colleges to make its own report on the situation, and it too will produce its findings shortly. What will be recommended, and what reaction to the recommendations may appear right, cannot at this stage be guessed.[30]

On 25 September, Stott, Craig and Webster issued their report. Although having no official authority within the Church of England, the personal status of the three members within evangelicalism was such that their opinions would carry considerable weight. They argued that there were only two viable solutions for the situation in Bristol.[31] It was clear that two evangelical colleges could not continue to exist side by side. But what were the options? The group refused to countenance any proposal which would preserve the life of one college, while causing the death of the other. The two solutions set out were the following.

1. A merger between Clifton, Tyndale and Dalton House. In making this suggestion, the group had made informal contact with Dalton House, and explored their reaction to the possibility. It was clear to the group that this proposal integrated the training of women for ministry in a future united college, while having the potential to safeguard the traditions represented by Tyndale and Clifton. The group came to the opinion that 'an amalgamation of the strengths of the three colleges could create a united Bristol college of international reputation'.

2. A merger of Clifton with Wycliffe Hall, Oxford; and of Tyndale with Dalton House. The group saw this proposal as having merits; nevertheless, they inclined to the view that Tyndale might not be able to survive on its own, even if merged with Dalton. The removal of Clifton from Bristol would probably lead to the death

of Tyndale, and hence the ending of an evangelical theological college in Bristol.

The group therefore suggested that the most realistic option was for a merger of the three Bristol colleges. A possibility it considered was suggesting that Tyndale move to Nottingham, and merge with the London College of Divinity, which was then relocating. However, the committee saw serious weaknesses in this proposal, and did not think it was viable.

Important though this report was, it was purely unofficial, and carried no weight within ACCM circles. The Runcie Commission duly made its report to ACCM on 19 October, who passed it on to the House of Bishops for consideration the following day. As the report's recommendations were sensitive and provisional, considerable care was taken to prevent unauthorized disclosure. A college which was known to be under consideration for closure would suffer an immediate loss of morale, and find it intensely difficult to recruit students in the future. This would make it very difficult to reverse a recommendation of this nature.

The Runcie Commission recommended that theological training should cease in Bristol. Clifton was directed to move to Oxford, where it would merge with Wycliffe Hall; Tyndale was directed to move to Nottingham, where it would merge with the relocating London College of Divinity (which it was now known would be referred to as St John's College, Nottingham). The Commission made it clear that it had given careful consideration to a possible merger between Clifton and Tyndale in Bristol, but had been advised that it stood little chance of success. 'We cannot help being impressed by the Faculty which is being assembled at Tyndale Hall, and the new curriculum which is being worked out, but we believe that they would be of better service to the church if they combined with St John's to form a strong united college at Nottingham.'[32]

The proposal to end theological training in Bristol sent shock waves throughout Tyndale. Packer openly spoke of having been betrayed by Kenneth Woollcombe. But what could be done? Packer immediately wrote to the secretary of Clifton Council, asking if the question of a merger, along the lines of the Stott report, could be considered.[33] Clifton was, however, not interested. On 13 November, the Clifton Council resolved to accept the recommendation to merge with Wycliffe, and to begin negotiations towards that end.[34]

The Tyndale Council, meeting the following day, decided to write immediately to St John's College, Nottingham, to ascertain how they viewed the recommendation that they should merge, while keeping the Bishop of Bristol fully informed of developments.

Following frantic telephone conversations, representatives of Clifton, Tyndale and St John's met together on 19 November to discuss their options. Wycliffe Hall were unable to send a representative, but indicated their views by telephone. Two important conclusions resulted from this meeting.

1. That an Anglican evangelical theological college should remain in Bristol.

2. That the suggestion that Tyndale move to Nottingham was impractical.

The possibility that Wycliffe Hall might move to Bristol in order to merge with Clifton was considered, as was a more complex possibility – that Wycliffe Hall, Tyndale Hall, Clifton College and Dalton House should all merge to form a single college in Bristol. No agreement was reached, however, and a further meeting was arranged for 8 December, when John Stott would be able to be present and help them move towards a resolution of the situation.[35]

The December meeting made it clear that the proposal for a merger between Tyndale and St John's College was unacceptable. St John's was sufficiently strong to be able to survive on its own, and did not require to be merged with anyone else to survive. This was certainly the view of St John's, Nottingham.[36] It was therefore clear that the most promising possibility was to explore the feasibility of a merged college in Bristol (rather than Oxford), going beyond the Runcie Commission's recommendation to include Tyndale and Dalton House. A joint meeting of the Councils of Clifton and Tyndale was therefore arranged for 1–2 January 1971. The Tyndale Hall Council met on 18–19 December to prepare for this critical meeting. Packer declared that, after careful consideration, he did not believe that it was right that he should remain principal in a united college. His desire in accepting his present employment had been to bring about certain reforms in theological education; if these reforms could be embodied in a united college, he would be happy to step down from the principalship.

The final decision as to which colleges would be closed and which merged would not be taken by ACCM but by the House of Bishops of the Church of England. Aware of the fact that some of the Runcie Commission recommendations would be controversial and distressing, the bishops allowed time for extended comments on the proposals before reaching their decisions. The closing date for comments to be sent to the House of Bishops was 6 January. On 2 January, the Tyndale Council prepared its final submission to the Runcie proposals, arguing that the fate decreed for Tyndale was unworkable, and requesting that fresh consideration be given to the idea of a united college in Bristol. All that Tyndale could now do was to sit back and wait for the decision of the bishops, which was expected to be made on 26 January.

The decisions were duly made, and announced on 2 February.[37] The decision concerning Tyndale's future was totally unexpected. The college would not be merging with St John's, Nottingham. It would not be merging with any of the Bristol colleges. It would be closed with effect from 1 October of that year. Three other colleges would also be closed; however, in each case, a provision was made that these could be re-opened in the future, if student numbers increased. No such provision was made for Tyndale. The bishops endorsed the recommendation of the Runcie Commission that Clifton should merge with Wycliffe Hall on the Oxford site.

The decision was greeted at Tyndale with disbelief, and then mounting anger. There had been no consultation whatsoever with Tyndale over this decision. There had been no opportunity to contest the grounds of the decision.[38] Packer wrote immediately to the Archbishop of Canterbury, making the point that an enormous amount of effort had gone into the restructuring of the curriculum and government of the college. Above all, the decision could only mean the end of theological education in Bristol, in that Dalton House could not be expected to survive on its own.[39] This final point had been noted elsewhere. The Bishop of Bristol, the Rt Revd Oliver Tomkins, met with Packer and Motyer during the week in which the decision was announced, and made it clear that he was opposed to the removal of theological education from his diocese.[40]

The Tyndale Hall Council met in emergency session in London on 4 February. At stake was the future of the college, and the mood was sombre and angry. Vested interests seemed to be involved. It was decided immediately to write an open letter to the Archbishop of Canterbury, challenging the grounds of the decision, and to mobilize key members of the Tyndale Hall Association, with a view to challenging the decision in the forthcoming meeting of the General Synod. For, under the new system of church government introduced by Archbishop Michael Ramsey, the bishops' decision was not final, and had to be ratified. An open letter was produced by Canon Colin Craston (Chairman of the Council) and Packer, stressing the flaws in the recommendation, and suggesting alternatives. On 8 February, the senior students at both Clifton and Tyndale also produced an open letter, in which they affirmed that the option favoured by the majority of students in both colleges was for both colleges to remain in Bristol, and for a united college to be formed including them both.[41] This letter was produced without consultation with the Clifton Council; on learning of its existence, they requested that their senior student should no longer make any use of it. In the meantime, the Clifton Council travelled to Oxford to enter into negotiations with Wycliffe Hall on the proposed merger. At their joint meeting on 11 February, the two councils found themselves disagreeing over the site of a merged college.[42] It was far from clear that the Oxford merger would work. For Clifton, other options might need to be explored.

The critical date was 18 February 1971. The General Synod of the Church of England was in session, and the future of theological colleges was high on the agenda. At 2.00 p.m., the Archbishop of Canterbury rose to support the bishops' recommendations. He conceded that the decisions were difficult, and likely to prove unpopular in many quarters. However, they – or some such decisions very like them – had to be taken. If the General Synod were to take a decision to save one college, it would only condemn another. There simply were not enough students to justify the current number of colleges. He was followed by Runcie, who explained the questions which he and his fellow committee members had been forced to consider. In the course of his address, Runcie dealt with two institutions, recommended for closure by the bishops, which possessed certain distinctive features which would be lost if they were closed. One was Kelham, a monastic foundation of particular importance to the Anglo-catholic wing of the church; the other was the situation at Bristol, where the future of the colleges was seen to be bound up with the question of whether they could indeed amalgamate. The opening was too good to be missed. Later that afternoon, Colin Craston managed to attract the chairman's attention:

> May I refer to the possibility the Bishop of St Albans offered of a renewal of the merger negotiations. Is a merger between the Bristol colleges now possible after the abortive attempt two years ago? Certainly there is pressure from the Tyndale Association and the former students of both colleges as there was not formerly. The present students of both colleges are almost unanimous in urging it. I ask therefore that the bishops consider the possibility of these two colleges merging with the women's college at Dalton House.[43]

Perhaps, with the benefit of hindsight, that speech can be seen to have marked a turning point in the events that gave birth to Trinity College.

The Birth of Trinity College

The House of Bishops met that same evening. In response to the points made in the debate, they resolved to reprieve Kelham unconditionally. A reprieve was also offered to Tyndale – but on condition:

> In the opinion of the House of Bishops, the continuation of training for ordinands at Bristol is only possible if Tyndale Hall, Clifton and Dalton St Michael's agree to amalgamate on the Clifton site ... The House, therefore, asks that the Governing Bodies of the colleges concerned should immediately explore this possibility and submit their decisions to the House of Bishops not later than 1 May 1971.

This decision was announced to the Synod on the morning of 19 February. Oliver Tomkins, the Bishop of Bristol, immediately wrote to Packer and the principals of Clifton and Dalton, informing them that he would be prepared to chair the joint meeting which would negotiate a merger between them. One condition he insisted upon was having the resignations of all members of staff and governors, in order to allow for a new college to be formed. In other words, not all those currently involved with the three colleges could expect to serve the new college. Packer accepted these conditions, as did the other two principals.[44] After some thought, the Tyndale Council offered to put on record its sense of repentance for any faults on its part relating to the failed 1968 merger negotiations, and regretting the distress they thereby caused. It was a small yet effective demonstration of a serious intention to move forward, and not be trapped by the legacy of the past.

The first joint meeting was held at Bristol Cathedral on 3 March. The deadline set by the bishops was 1 May, a mere eight weeks distant. It is clear that a sense of urgency pervaded that meeting, perhaps allowing difficult decisions to be made with greater ease than might otherwise have been the case. Tomkins was committed to the idea of a merged college in his diocese, and was not disposed to tolerate any grandstanding or posturing by anyone. There was immediate agreement that the merged college should be named 'Trinity College' (thus reviving the name proposed for the merged college of 1968).[45] Agreement was reached concerning seven broad areas which needed to be addressed, including financial, doctrinal and administrative issues. The next meeting was agreed for 13 April, again at the cathedral. In the meantime, a working party was appointed, to consider these issues in time to allow the new college to be established by the autumn of 1971.

Tomkins formed the private opinion that there were some serious, if not openly acknowledged, differences between Clifton and Tyndale which were going to make the negotiations very trying. He noted the generally Arminian outlook of Clifton, and the tensions which this would generate when set alongside the more Calvinist world-view of Tyndale. In addition to this, Tomkins picked up that Clifton seemed to see itself as reflecting the social values and attitudes of the Public Schools Camps, and tended to look down on the more working class and northern sympathies of Tyndale.[46]

The working group met four times before the April joint meeting. The complex network of financial issues was more or less resolved, as was the question of the doctrinal basis of the merged college. The leadership was conceived as a triumvirate of three senior staff: a Dean of College, a Dean of Studies, and a Dean of Women. The working group made it clear that it had certain specific individuals in mind for each of these positions: an existing member of the Clifton staff was mentioned in connection with the first, Packer in connection with the second, and Miss Joyce Baldwin (Dalton) in connection with the third. No mention was made of a single principal, with overall charge of the institution. The working group clearly felt that the simplest means of transferring power was to ensure that each merging institution would contribute one senior staff member to the new college. For Packer, the proposed structure made evident that the merger was to take place on a basis of partnership and a pooling of resources on the basis of equality.[47] In addition to the three deans, there would be three other teaching staff members. The House of Bishops met on 11 May, and gave broad approval to the proposals.[48]

And so the preparations began for the birth of Trinity College. However, it soon became clear that this would be no easy delivery. Complications set in. The precise nature of the difficulties was complex, and focused on the senior staff positions within the new college. Tyndale and Dalton had both indicated that they would be prepared to nominate specific individuals for the 'deanships'. As we have seen, the general understanding was that Packer would be Dean of Studies, and Joyce Baldwin Dean of Women. Clifton had drawn up a list of seven people they had in mind for the position of 'Dean of College'. The first of the seven whom they approached was an existing member of the Clifton staff; he indicated that he did not wish to be considered for the position. It now remained for the Clifton Council to approach others; they decided to nominate individuals from outside their present staff team.

Their second choice for the position was a well-respected pastor. Not knowing the Bristol situation at first hand, he asked if he might be permitted to discuss the position of the Dean of College with his potential colleagues in the merger. The candidate's discussion with Packer was to prove of critical importance.

From Packer's point of view, the conversation was an exploration of the dividing lines of responsibility between the Dean of College and Dean of Studies. There was also a hypothetical discussion of who the remaining staff members of the new college might be. These had not yet been defined by the Interim Council, and it was clear that the precise job descriptions of each position were somewhat fluid, rather than being set in stone. Packer's intention was to explore what the working relationship might look like, and who would assume responsibility for what.

That was not how the conversation was seen by Clifton's candidate. He formed the impression that Packer was laying down – in effect, dictating – conditions for working with the incoming Dean of College, including the specific identity of the staff members of the new college. He wrote to the Bishop of Bristol, conveying his impressions. Packer, on being shown the letter, replied immediately, indicating that there had been a serious misunderstanding, and apologizing if he had in any way misled his colleague. The Clifton Council, however, were in no mood to accept explanations as a result of their candidate's withdrawal. On 26 July, the Clifton Council resolved to withdraw from the negotiations. The merger was off.

Tomkins was furious. It seemed that his efforts had been totally frustrated, and that the blame was to be placed on Packer's shoulders. He wrote a severe letter of rebuke to Packer, and walked the mile from his residence to Packer's home. He delivered the letter by hand to Packer at 2.00, and asked him to come round to his residence at 4.00 for a full and frank discussion of the matter. This discussion lasted two hours. By the end of it, Tomkins decided that Packer had not misled anyone; the problem was that Packer simply seemed to have difficulties in dealing with people.

That insight, however, would not be enough to save the merger negotiations. The enormous amount of effort which Tomkins had invested in the tortuous negotiations seemed to have been wasted. However, he had gone too far to turn back now. He wrote immediately to all members of the college Councils. There was an urgent need to clarify the 'three-dean' structure, and get it sorted out for once and for all.[49] Furthermore, the identity of each dean needed to be sorted out as a matter of urgency. If this could not be done, they would simply have to admit defeat, and see the end of Trinity College. He was therefore summoning as many council members as possible to a meeting in Room 302 at Church House, Westminster, on 3 August.

The meeting was arranged in some haste, and attendance was lower than might have been hoped. The haste also led to a constitutional difficulty. The gathering was described as a meeting of the Councils of the three participating institutions. However, the Clifton representatives argued that, as the meeting had not been convened according to their Standing Orders, it could not be regarded as a proper Council meeting, and hence could not take any executive decisions. The meeting was to fall into two distinct parts. First, members of the college staff were to be allowed to make any points which they considered relevant to the discussion; the staff would then withdraw, leaving the remainder of the college representatives to thrash out a possible compromise solution, which would allow the Clifton Council to see their way to reversing their decision of 26 July.

Discussion initially centred on the 'three-dean structure', using Packer's memorandum as a basis for discussion. However, it soon became clear that the issue of the future staff of the college was going to be critical and divisive. Packer argued that there was a need for an outstandingly good faculty, and saw no problem about discussing specific names. This was interpreted by some as an attempt to ensure that Tyndale faculty dominated the new college, and by others as a legitimate issue which was essential if the new college was to attract students. It was pointed out that one reason why Clifton looked as if it might have a relative shortage of staff on the new body was that they had not nominated an existing Clifton member of staff to be the Dean of College.

Eventually, the staff left the meeting, and went off to a nearby room to await the outcome of the discussion. Colin Craston, speaking on behalf of the Tyndale Council, stressed that they were sensitive to the charge of somehow engineering a 'Tyndale takeover'. This, he insisted, had never been their intention. It seemed to him reasonable to suggest that at least two members of each of the existing faculties should be appointed to the new college, even if it might prove necessary to appoint additional members subsequently. Others then argued that, if Clifton could appoint one of their own staff to the contested deanship, the difficulties would be alleviated.

As discussion proceeded, it became clear that the Clifton representatives did not want Packer to have *any* significant role in the new college administration. One Clifton Council member even suggested that Packer ought to be asked to resign, even if this caused a negative reaction within evangelicalism at large. The Tyndale representatives made it clear that this was not a serious option. Packer's reputation and his achievements in transforming Tyndale made his inclusion in a senior capacity in the new college of critical importance. Not for the first time, it was pointed out that Packer could be lost to North America if the situation was badly handled. Increasing doubts were also expressed about the 'three dean structure', with the Clifton representatives pressing the case for a principal to be appointed – either in addition to the three deans, or as one of the three deans. In the case of the former option, an external candidate could be brought in to ensure parity between the three colleges, each of which could then appoint one of the three deans.

At an early stage in the discussion, mention was made of a suggestion that Alec Motyer should be considered as the Dean of College. Bishop Russell White initially rejected this on behalf of Clifton. However, as it became clear that other solutions were unacceptable to at least one of the participating colleges, the Motyer proposal began to appear increasingly attractive. Motyer had served on the teaching staff of both Clifton and Tyndale; he had also significant parish experience at St Luke's, Hampstead. Slowly, the meeting came around to the view that a potential solution to their problems was to invite Motyer to become principal of the merged college, and act as the Dean of the College. This proposal met strong opposition from one of the Clifton representatives, who felt that it would lead to a principal in name only, without any real power or authority. However, in the end, the committee agreed to this proposal being put before the Clifton Council at its next meeting on 7 September. If that meeting rejected the proposal, the merger would end. Tomkins grimly remarked that if Clifton rejected the proposal, they would have to explain their reasons to the public. It was a cliffhanger. No firm decision had been made, and it would be necessary to wait more than a month to know the final outcome.[50] The meeting broke up having decided to meet again on 20 September in Bristol. August was a difficult month for many in Bristol that year.

The Clifton Council were asked simply to accept or reject the plans. In the event, they decided to lay down conditions which had to be met before they would accept. Tomkins was furious that Clifton Council acted in such a unilateral manner, and wrote to insist that, in future, all joint meetings should be binding on those who were present. The conditions demanded by Clifton reflected their own preference for a principal (rather than just three deans), and their determination to minimize the influence of Tyndale, and especially Packer, in the new college. Their conditions included the following requirements.

1. There would be a Principal, in fact and not merely in name.

2. There would be two Deans, who would be subordinate to the Principal, and to whom appropriate duties could be delegated.

3. There would be a 'Reader in Theology', freed from administrative responsibilities, who would be available for lecturing and consultation within the church at large, and that this specific position was to be offered to the Revd Dr J.I. Packer.

4. The position of Principal should be advertised immediately. Candidates would be interviewed by the Interim Council, whose decision would require to be approved by each of the three college councils.

The Clifton proposals thus marginalized Packer. If they were accepted, the new college would be in the hands of three people, none of whom would be Packer.

Tyndale were left stunned by this response. There would be an outcry from former Tyndale students if Packer was to be treated in this way. The new college would not command the support of the constituency which Tyndale represented if Packer did not have a significant role in Trinity.[51] At its meeting on 14 September the Tyndale Council noted with relief that Tomkins intended to stand by an earlier decision that Packer should be Dean of Studies. After an extensive discussion, lasting nearly five hours, it was decided that the college had no option but to agree to the immediate advertisement of the principalship of Trinity College. The council then formally requested Motyer to apply for the position.

The meeting of the three Councils to appoint the first principal of Trinity College was arranged for 29 September in the Chapter House of St Paul's Cathedral, London. Maurice Wood, a former principal of Oak Hill College, was to be consecrated Bishop of Norwich, and many members of the Councils would be present for the occasion. At that stage, it was still unusual for prominent evangelicals to be appointed bishops in the Church of England, and the evangelical establishment turned out in force to celebrate this event. In his letter convening the meeting, Tomkins stressed its critical importance. The bishops wanted a full report by 6 October if the scheme was to receive their approval; in addition, there was mounting disquiet within the church at large, as well as within the staff and student bodies of the three colleges, over the indecision and confusion.

Three decisions had to be taken by the meeting. First, it had to be decided whether to accept the general conditions laid down by Clifton Council on 7 September for accepting the merger. This was agreed, by a large majority of those present. There was then a discussion over the precise meaning of the terms 'Principal' and 'Reader in Theology', as used in the Clifton resolution. It was agreed that the term 'Reader in Theology' should be discarded, and that a special senior position should be created to do justice to Packer's reputation, while at the same time freeing him from as much administration as possible, to enable him to carry out research and writing. Short-listed candidates, including Motyer, for the Principalship were then interviewed. It became clear that Motyer was the front runner for the job, with 80 per cent of the Interim Council voting for him.

The Clifton proposals, however, required that each Council should individually approve of the choice of principal. By now, it was getting late, and some council members were in the process of departing. The Tyndale Hall Council members present unanimously supported the decision; the Dalton House Council members supported the decision by a large majority. The Clifton Council, however, argued that there were not sufficient of their members present to constitute a quorum, and so declined to vote on the motion. Others present at the meeting gained the impression that the Clifton representatives were generally hostile. Nevertheless, a compromise proposal was agreed, which would be put to the full Clifton Council by postal vote as a matter of urgency. The motion, proposed by the Revd Keith Weston of the Clifton Council, was that Motyer be appointed Principal, on condition that the Dean of Studies be chosen from the Clifton staff. Clifton would be given no option or room for manouevre. Either they accepted the proposal, or rejected it. If they failed to agree to the proposal, the merger would fail.

Clifton agreed, and the merger was approved. The successful proposal gave to Clifton a position (Dean of Studies) which had been intended for Packer, while giving to Tyndale a position (Dean of College, now expanded to include the position of Principal) which was originally intended for a Clifton nominee. It was therefore agreed to offer Packer the senior position of 'Associate Principal', with a brief to develop theological education and maintain links with similar institutions in England and overseas.[52]

This was intended to give him a major role in the future direction of the college, while allowing him time for writing and research. Joyce Baldwin was confirmed as Dean of Women, and a member of the Clifton staff (the Revd Gervais Angel) was appointed Dean of Studies. The 'scheme of union' was approved by the House of Bishops on 6 October.

Trinity College finally came into being on 1 January 1972. The formal announcement of the merger came in a letter to all former students and friends of the three merging colleges (signed by Motyer, Packer, Baldwin and Angel), which hinted at the enormous complexity of the negotiations:

> We are sure that you will have been following with interest the project to unite the colleges and no doubt you will be aware of some of the difficulties which have been encountered on the way.
>
> It has not been an easy road to travel and some have paid no small price in the ebb and flow of negotiations in these recent years . . . The final realization of Trinity College may properly be described as a story of death and resurrection. When it is so described, the glory is given where alone it is due: to the God of all grace who has stretched out His hand to establish what otherwise would have perished. The 'whole story', especially of 1971, is too lengthy and complex to record here, but we who have lived through its weekly and often daily unfoldings cannot but share with you our testimony to the wonder-working, gentle and sovereign hand of God, and call you to join us in worshipping, praising and loving Him.

And so Trinity College came into being. The sense of delight and celebration which resulted within the three institutions was almost tangible. A particular cause of relief was that no members of staff of any colleges would have to be made redundant as a result of the merger. Packer himself regarded the founding of Trinity as being like the exodus from Egypt – something remarkably long and protracted, with a wonderful goal in prospect, like the Promised Land. But would they ever get there? When they finally did, there was an enormous feeling of relief and joy, especially at Tyndale. The buildings which formerly made up Tyndale Hall would be converted into apartments for the use of Trinity College students. Joint teaching between the three colleges would begin in October, and would finally move to the Clifton site with effect from 1 January 1972. The combined college would have about eighty students, and hopes were high that this could eventually reach ninety or one hundred.

The final job description for the Dean of Studies points to a very demanding position.[53] The Dean was to be responsible for the supervision of the syllabuses for a variety of courses, arranging timetables and teaching, supervising tuition and examinations, liaison with Bristol and London Universities (each of which validated courses then being offered at the college), and all negotiations with ACCM concerning courses and teaching. In addition, the Dean would be required to teach in his areas of competence. Given that Trinity College expected to attract at least eighty students, the deanship had a very substantial administrative workload, which could well have prevented the holder of the position from undertaking personal research or writing.[54] Packer's responsibilities at Trinity would be real; they would also be comparatively light, allowing him the time to continue the kind of scholarly ministry he had exercised so effectively at Latimer House. The reforms which he had introduced at Tyndale would be largely carried over into Trinity College, allowing him to set a new personal agenda for the period which now lay ahead.

It will be clear from the material presented in this chapter that 1970–72 was a very difficult period in Packer's life. At times, the future seemed very uncertain. He was unquestionably wounded and saddened by some of the happenings at Bristol, and by the way in which he had been treated by his fellow evangelicals. But at least the future was settled, and he would have more time for writing. And one of the writings which would result from this new phase in Packer's career would gain him a new standing, far beyond any he had imagined in the past. We are now in a position to tell the story of the birth of one of the twentieth century's most influential and admired Christian books – *Knowing God*.

«9»

Bristol: Trinity College, 1972–9

WITH THE COMPLETION of the merger negotiations between the three Bristol colleges, a period of relative calm settled over Packer and his Bristol colleagues. While the practical preparations to merge the three colleges into a single unit were exhausting, theological education in Bristol was no longer under any threat. By the middle of 1972, a degree of normality had been restored. The new college had come into being, and was attracting students. There was no longer any need to worry about the future, at least in the short term.

Under Motyer, a significant part of the vision for theological education which had emerged at Tyndale Hall under Packer was carried over into the new college. There is no doubt that it got noticed. In the eyes of many young evangelicals, Packer and Motyer together represented a form of evangelicalism which possessed both intellectual rigour and spiritual integrity. Under their joint leadership, Trinity College began to attract more students than before from college and university Christian Unions. As one observer commented:

> A large proportion of the Christian Union members were entering the ministry. Up till then it had been almost automatic to go to either Wycliffe Hall, Oxford, or Ridley Hall, Cambridge. Now the great attraction was in the two Bristol theological colleges, Tyndale and Clifton (now combined into Trinity College) . . . Here the students sat at the feet of Jim Packer and Alec Motyer, and Bristol became the launching pad to send bright young men into the ministry of the Church of England.[1]

It is probably true to say that the 1970s represented a new

lease of life for the style of theology associated with Packer and Motyer: biblically grounded, theologically rigorous, and ministerially orientated.

Freed from much of the crippling burden of administration which is the inevitable lot of a theological college principal in England, Packer was free to begin to start writing and thinking again. As we have seen, the period 1970–2 was, at least by Packer's standards, somewhat sterile. The considerable pressure under which he found himself during that period made it difficult to undertake major research or writing projects. As Trinity settled down, Packer again found he had time and space for thinking, speaking and writing. With the position of 'associate principal'[2] came a degree of freedom which would have been impossible if he had been in a position of major administrative responsibility, such as that traditionally associated with the positions of principal and vice-principal of a theological college. In addition to his college responsibilities, Packer was able to establish a link with a local church, in which he could have a pastoral ministry. A genial Irishman by the name of George Cassidy was the vicar of St Edith Sea Mills, a local Anglican parish. Cassidy suggested to Packer that he might like to have such an association, and the deal was soon done. The close link which Packer valued between theology and ministry was thus secured.

Perhaps more significantly, Packer was able to negotiate an arrangement with the college Council, by which he would spend the autumn and spring terms teaching in Bristol, leaving the summer term free of commitments in order to allow him to spend time in North America. It was an arrangement which suited Packer well. His North American tours, which would last up to ten weeks at a time, allowed him to develop personal contacts and his theological horizons. Increasingly, Packer became a well-known figure in North America – not simply through his books, but through his personal presence at seminaries as a teacher and lecturer.

So what did Packer teach? In what follows, we shall explore the basic structure of the major course which Packer offered over two terms at Trinity College during the 1970s.

Packer as a Theological Teacher

Packer's teaching at Trinity was contained in four regular courses of lectures, each of which consisted of twenty lectures. Each lecture was accompanied by duplicated handouts, painstakingly typed out on to stencils by Packer himself, and printed out on pink foolscap paper. These 'pink sheets' became legendary at Trinity, and can easily be shown to have become incorporated into countless early sermons delivered by Trinity Graduates. In what follows, we shall explore Packer's method of teaching theology, based on 'pink sheets' dating from 1972–5, and student accounts of those lectures. Given Packer's critical role as a teacher of theology, both in England and North America, it is of considerable importance (not to mention interest) to examine his didactic approach to this enormously responsible task.

Packer's style of delivery was slow and methodical, ideally suited to those taking notes. The inevitable result of this style of lecturing has already been hinted at: Packer's lectures regularly proved to demand more time than the hard-pressed college timetable allowed. Students recall Packer regularly going over his time limit, or having to abandon his discussion of a complex point due to the pressure of time.

It must be recalled that Packer's teaching responsibilities were not simply to teach theology, but to teach theology largely to those preparing for ministry in the Church of England. For this reason, frequent reference is made to the Thirty-nine Articles, which Packer regarded as a classic statement of the basics of a Reformed faith.[3] His lectures have a distinctively Anglican flavour, which is strengthened by his determination to engage in debates by which his students might be affected. As a result, reference is made primarily to English theologians and theological debate.[4]

The first series of twenty lectures was entitled 'An Introduction to Theology'. In this course, Packer provided a survey of the tasks and tools of theology, prior to their application in the three lecture series which followed. For Packer, theology serves three critical functions:

a) it deepens our understanding of Scripture, God, human nature, the church, the world, and so forth;

b) it controls our thinking and living as Christians;

c) it assists communication of the Christian faith in mission and evangelism.

Faith is something which both needs and seeks understanding. Packer here alludes to the classic dictum of the eleventh-century writer Anselm of Canterbury, who formulated the task of theology in terms of 'faith seeking understanding' (*fides quaerens intellectum*). Although Packer frequently uses the noun 'theology' to refer to this activity, he often preferred to refer to it in the form of a verb – 'theologizing'. For Packer, this served to bring out the fact that theology is an *activity*. It is about asking and answering questions about God and his relation to created realities. 'Theologizing' could be thought of as an attempt to place together in a logical relationship what already lies together in reality. Theology is thus concerned with uncovering, explicating and communicating the reality of God as he has revealed himself in Scripture.

Packer acknowledges a significant degree of hostility towards theologizing, not least the way in which theology often seems to stifle faith or lead to acrimonious debates. Nevertheless, he insisted that it was an essential aspect of Christian discipleship. Without it, believers would not learn to be self-critical in their thinking about their faith, and would lack the understanding which is essential to the effective communication and living out of the faith. A believer who does not have a good theology has a bad theology.

Having set out the importance of theology, Packer turned to deal with the history of Christian doctrine. He argued that human understanding of the inner logic of revealed truth was clarified through pressure of controversy. Initially, that controversy centred on the doctrine of God, particularly his role as creator (as in the second-century debates which pitted Irenaeus against Gnosticism) and as Trinity (in the debates of the third and fourth centuries, especially those relating to Athanasius and the Cappadocian fathers).[5] This was followed by debates focusing on the identity of Jesus Christ, culminating in the fifth-century Council of Chalcedon. The next phase concerned the characterizing of fallen human nature (here Packer has in mind the fifth-century debate between Augustine and Pelagius). Attention then turned to the nature of Christ's atoning work (seen in Anselm of Canterbury's eleventh-century presentation of representative satisfaction and Luther's sixteenth-century analysis of penal substitution), to be followed by clarification of the application of redemption, the means of grace and the nature of the church (and here Packer notes the importance of the Reformation of the sixteenth century and the Puritans of the seventeenth). Throughout, he stressed the importance of learning from classical writings.

Packer's discussion of the achievement of the patristic period is of especial interest. He argued that three central controlling principles were hammered out during the course of the debates of this era.

a) 'The redeemer is the creator' (formulated by Irenaeus in the second century, which established the unity of Scripture);

b) 'If Christ was not divine, he could not save' (formulated by Athanasius in the fourth century, establishing the divinity of Christ);

c) 'God gives the faith and love which he requires' (formulated by Augustine in the fifth century, establishing the sovereignty of grace).

This was followed by a detailed analysis of different types of theology, and an overview of the potential sources of theology, with supreme authority being accorded to Scripture. An extract from Packer's 'pink sheets' reveals the clarity of his thought, his approach to complex issues, and his distinctive position on the points at issue. For example, consider some extracts from his handouts on 'Biblical Inspiration':

Meaning of Biblical Inspiration

Basic idea. 'My words in thy mouth' (Jer. 1:9); 'God-breathed' (2 Tim. 3:16); 'men spoke from God' (2 Pet. 1:21); 'God (or, the Holy Spirit) says' (Acts 4:25, Heb. 3:7, 10:15; Matt. 19:5); 'the Scripture says/preached' (Rom. 9:17; Gal. 3:6); dual authorship through divine superintendence – wholly human, wholly divine.

Psychological types of inspiration: distinguish (a) *dualistic* (prophets, Rev.) – 'God through me' (b) *didactic* (historians, theologians, wisdom writers) – 'I for God' (? Did they always know that they were writing Scripture? probably not); (c) *lyric* (Psalms, Song.) – responsive, 'I before God'.

Mystery of Inspiration (Mystery = incomprehensible divine reality).

i) Inspiration is one instance of the larger mystery of *free agency,* under God's control (cf., God's overruling sins, God working the Christian's faith, repentance and good works in him).

ii) The nearest analogy to inspiration is incarnation: there too divine and human become one without the humanity being necessarily faulty, and there too the scandal of particularity operates – the absolute, universal and eternally valid reality being found in a relative, particular and historically transient form.

Questions about Inspiration

i. Is inspiration *verbal?* In defence of the word – yes, it has to be, for it is the words that carry the meaning (cf. 1 Cor. 2:12). Against the word – it directs attention away from the meaning to the words themselves, as in the Koranic doctrine of inspiration; so that *plenary* might be a more useful description, if it was understood.

ii. Is the Bible *infallible* (Westminster Confession I.v) and *inerrant?* Yes, within the limit of its intended assertions. Exegesis must determine these limits; to assert biblical infallibility and inerrancy is not to decide any point of exegesis, nor any question of the contemporary application of biblical teaching. (Jehovah's Witnesses are happy with both adjectives!)

iii. How does inspiration affect *interpretation?* Only by committing us to accept what the Bible proves on inspection to teach: otherwise, the work of exegesis and synthesis of teaching is the same for all, whatever their view of the nature of Scripture. Note that (a) the word 'literal' as denoting the right way in exegesis is systematically ambiguous; (b) that the linguistic form of assertions must be distinguished from their content, and that the content is known by observing their implications (e.g., 3-decker universe, diffused-consciousness psychology, sunrise); (c) that statements in Scripture as in ordinary life can be vague and open-textured (e.g., the death in the flood story).

iv. Does inspiration attach only to *autographs,* or to *copies* and *translations* too? To the latter, so far as their meaning corresponds to that of the autographs; though no inspiration attaches to textual and translators' errors, and misprints!

It will be clear that an enormous amount of material has been packed into these synopses, allowing his listeners to reconstruct the lectures on their basis. As Packer would later put it: 'I love pregnant brevity, and some of my material is, I know, packed tight (Packer by name, packer by nature).'

This introductory course led into three substantial series dealing with the central themes of Christian theology. The first series, entitled 'God, Christ and Creation' dealt with the basic themes of the Christian doctrine of God (including the themes of creation, preservation, and the tri-unity of God) and Christology, with a lecture on human nature (as part of the created order). The second series, entitled 'Sin and Salvation', focused on the four themes of sin, atonement, grace and the application of redemption. The fourth and final series was entitled 'Church, Sacraments, Last Things'. Throughout, Packer's intention – explored in many of his published books – was to encourage his hearers to know God and to share God.

But it was one such book, published during Packer's period at Trinity College, which caused his profile and reputation to soar. The book? *Knowing God.*

Knowing God: The Origins and Anatomy of a Classic

During the 1950s, a series of individuals came to faith through the ministry of Westminster Chapel, London. One such convert was Elizabeth Braund, a journalist then working with the British Broadcasting Corporation on the history of the Bible. It seemed natural to Lloyd-Jones to encourage Miss Braund to put her considerable talents to Christian service. An obvious possibility was to develop an English equivalent to the *Evangelical Magazine of Wales*, which began to appear in 1955. The result of this was the *The Evangelical Magazine*, which initially had Miss Braund as its managing editor, and Packer and J. Elwyn Davies as consulting editors. In June 1959, a circular letter was issued on behalf of the three editors, announcing that, God willing, the new publication would appear for the first time in September 1959. The magazine, which published six editions each year, soon reached a circulation of about 3,000.

Soon after the magazine had become established, Miss Braund asked Packer if he would consider writing a series of articles on the general theme of 'God'. Knowing the importance to the authors of such pieces of defining a likely readership Braund carefully described the kind of person she hoped would read Packer's articles: people who were 'fed up with religious verbiage', who were 'prepared to do some honest and serious thinking', and who 'want reality'. It proved to be an excellent brief. Braund had noted the manner in which many religious writers hid behind words, and failed to take any trouble in communicating the reality of God to their readers. Packer, she believed, might be able to say something worthwhile to such people.

For Packer, the resulting work would thus need to be both evangelistic and nurturing. He gave considerable thought to how best this might be achieved. The opening article clearly had to ask the question of where you start talking about God to the kind of person Braund had described. Thereafter, Packer wrote each piece in succession, using each article to build on the line of thought established in the previous article. In effect, Packer wrote each article by reading the previously published one, and asking himself: 'Well, what do I say now?' He did not attempt to work out what the *next* article would be about; the important thing was to build on what had already been established. The result was a tightly argued series of articles, with a strong thread of continuity between them. Each led naturally into the following, which built on what had already been established. The overall objective was to build up a knowledge of God in the mind, heart and life of the reader. Packer's wide reading in Calvin and the Puritans had persuaded him that it was of the utmost importance to apply knowledge of God to the human heart. In true Puritan fashion, each article ended with an application of the theological principle to the life of the reader.

The Evangelical Magazine appeared six times a year, and one of those six issues was given over to other matters. As a result, Packer's articles appeared in sequences of five. After five years, the overall pattern to emerge was that of five broad themes relating to the overall theme of 'knowing God', each of which had five closely interlocked sections.

Initially, Packer had no intention of publishing the articles in book form. However, at the end of the five-year period, he felt that the resulting set of articles could indeed be strung together to produce a coherent and valuable book. Packer had already published two books with the Inter-Varsity Press, and it seemed entirely sensible to let the publishing director, Ronald Inchley, have first sight of the set of articles, with a view to publishing them as a book.

Inchley, however, had his own agenda. The charismatic movement was becoming increasingly important within British Christianity, especially within student Christian circles. Inchley suggested that Packer should turn his attention to a book on this theme.[6] Packer was reluctant. He did not feel that he knew enough about this subject. In any case, these discussions were taking place when Packer was making the move from Latimer House to Tyndale Hall during the period 1969–70, which placed Packer under such pressure that it would have been difficult for him to undertake the fresh research necessary for this kind of book. In its place, Packer offered him the collection of articles which would later become *Knowing God*. Inchley insisted on a book on the Holy Spirit, and informed Packer that he would think about this other work only when the book on the Spirit had been written.

Undaunted, Packer then made an appointment to visit Edward England at Hodder & Stoughton, one of the most important publishing houses in Britain. England had succeeded Leonard Cutts as the director of Hodder's religious publications in 1966. Although Hodder's had extensive publishing interests in the fiction and reference markets, it also had a long tradition of publishing significant Christian works. Whereas the Inter-Varsity Press had a particular association with the student Christian world, Hodder's saw its readership as being much wider. Packer had already had dealings with Hodder & Stoughton through a series entitled *Christian Foundations*, edited by John R.W. Stott. This important series began to appear in 1965, and was intended to lay the foundations for an intellectually renewed and encouraged evangelicalism within the Church of England. Packer had contributed an important volume to the series, dealing with the issue of biblical inspiration and the nature of revelation, with the title *God has Spoken: Revelation and the Bible*.

Edward England thus already knew about Packer. He had read his earlier work *'Fundamentalism' and the Word of God*, and had formed a high opinion of Packer as an author. England also had a reputation as a highly critical yet deadly accurate judge of books. In 1969, the religious publications department at Hodder's were accepting only three in every thousand submissions. However, England was quite clear that a major work by Packer could be a very significant publishing proposition. There was a keen sense of anticipation as Packer set out his proposal.[7] Even though Packer did little more than show England the articles which would be brought together as 'a string of beads', England was clear that a potentially important work was in the offing. Even as he perused the raw material which would eventually become the final book, he was convinced that he might well have a classic on his hands.

It was, however, clear to both Packer and England that some rewriting would be needed. In the first place, the articles were originally written in magazine format, and would need to be recast somewhat if they were to appear in the form of a book. England also sent the collection of articles to a non-evangelical reader whom he respected, and obtained some valuable comments concerning possible additions which he passed on to Packer. However, Packer found that he could not treat the book as having top priority; other pressures were to hand at this point in his life. At that stage, he was busy with administrative and teaching work, and coping with the pressures and tensions associated with the long-drawn-out discussions over the merger between Tyndale Hall, Clifton Theological College and Dalton House to form Trinity College (see pp. 140–79). Packer recalls casting the final chapter in its present form during a holiday spent in the family cottage in North Wales in August 1971.

The title *Knowing God* arose directly from the material itself. The brief and pithy phrase 'knowing God' implies purpose and process – in other words, the book is concerned to enable its readers to know God, and offers them advice and guidance so that this purpose might be effected.

The work was initially published in a hard-cover edition, before going into a cheap paperback edition. This involved resetting the book. It was this process which led to a major hiatus. Packer had provided an index for the hard-cover edition of the work. Resetting for the paperback edition involved alterations to the page numbers. On receiving his six complimentary copies of the paperback edition, Packer discovered that the index to the hardback edition had mistakenly been used. As England ruefully recalls, Packer was furious, and insisted that the mistake should be rectified before any copies of the paperback edition were sold. The printer was duly ordered to strip out the pages, and replace them with the correct index. Although this caused a slight delay to the production, the public were unaware of the problem that had arisen.

It was in North America that *Knowing God* would have its greatest impact. Although Packer was a known writer in the region, the book would propel him to levels of fame within the evangelical community which exceeded anything he had hitherto known. The editor at InterVarsity Press in the United States who was responsible for acquiring the North American rights to the book was James Sire, himself a distinguished writer. In May 1972, Sire travelled to Switzerland to work with Os Guinness, who was then finalizing the text of his major work *The Dust of Death* from his base at L'Abri, the community founded by Francis Schaeffer. Guinness was already established as an important InterVarsity author. Sire spent ten days with Guinness, completing the final edit of the text.

Rather than return directly to the United States, Sire decided to head home via England, and meet up with some of his editorial counterparts at the Inter-Varsity Press and at Hodder & Stoughton. Both publishers were at that time located in London, making a brief visit to both possible in a single stopover. He was introduced to Edward England, who – in the course of a short meeting lasting about fifteen minutes – showed him the text of *Knowing God*. Sire immediately asked for an option, which England granted. About a week later, the page proofs arrived in the offices of InterVarsity Press in Downers Grove, Illinois. Sire showed them to Jim Nyquist, the director of the press. After a few minutes spent perusing the proofs, Nyquist was convinced that they had a major work on their hands. 'Your fifteen minutes with Edward England', he told Sire, 'will be worth more to us than your ten days with Os Guinness.' *The Dust of Death* proved to be an important book, which sold very well; it was, however, eclipsed by *Knowing God*.

By 1992, the work had sold more than a million copies.[8] Packer had no idea that his work would be a bestseller, or that it would play such an important role in Christian nurture. Packer's expectation was that the book might find about ten thousand readers who would be prepared to look up and reflect for themselves on the texts which he dealt with. In addition, Packer felt that the work was considerably more intellectually demanding than the type of book which generally became a bestseller. In Packer's view, a book about God which was *not* demanding could not really be considered to have dealt properly with its subject. Packer's personal opinion is that the book succeeded because it allowed its readers to find and experience the *reality* of God. This can be seen to resonate with one of Packer's concerns as a young man, when the issue of the reality of God was central to his thinking.

So why was the book so successful? It makes considerable demands of its readers, and is not an easy book to read. It totally avoids the 'self-help' approach of books which aim to sell by offering their readers quick and simple (and generally superficial and simplistic) answers to complex questions. There had been no huge surge in demand for *The Evangelical Magazine* as a consequence of Packer's original articles. Packer himself had no intuition that the work would become such a strong seller; indeed, he originally had no intention of turning the articles into book form.

The simplest, and most persuasive, answer appears to be that this was the right book for the right moment. Packer's clear style of writing, his wealth of verbal illustration, linked with his determination to apply biblical theology to life and 'make it real' were all significant elements. One of the book's earliest reviewers was John R.W. Stott, who found his attempts to read the book were frustrated through being constantly moved to prayer by Packer's writing. 'The truth he handles', Stott wrote, 'fires the heart. At least, it fired mine, and compelled me to turn aside to worship and to pray.' Those who read the book commended it to their friends – and kept on commending it, as the continuing sales of the book, twenty-five years after its original publication, demonstrate. It met a real need, and met it well and faithfully.

The work combines the use of powerfully evocative language, extensive implicit citation of or allusion to biblical passages, and a thorough undergirding of spiritual insights upon solid theological foundation. Perhaps the most helpful way of bringing out the richness of Packer's work is to consider a very brief passage, and explore it in a little more detail. As an example, we shall consider ten lines from his discussion of 'Knowing and Being Known'.

What matters supremely, therefore, is not, in the last analysis, the fact that I know God, but the larger fact which underlies it – the fact that *he knows me*. I am graven on the palms of his hands. I am never out of his mind. All my knowledge of him depends on his sustained initiative in knowing me. I know him, because he first knew me, and continues to know me. He knows me as a friend, one who loves me; and there is no moment when his eye is off me, or his attention distracted from me, and no moment, therefore, when his care falters.[9]

These ten lines, which are in many ways typical of the book as a whole, illustrate the amount of thought which has gone into Packer's writing in this volume. We shall focus on the three points just mentioned in the above discussion.

1. Note the powerful imagery used: we are 'graven on the palms of his hands'. This image is itself biblical;[10] it also acts as a stimulus to the human imagination to build up a Scripture-based picture of God, governed by the biblical narrative of our redemption in Christ and its cost to the Saviour. It evokes the image of the hands of God the creator (an image used extensively in the Christian tradition – see Irenaeus of Lyons for its use) being wounded in order to save his creation. The creator and redeemer are one and the same. More specifically, it evokes the deeply moving scene of the crucifixion, in which Christ's hands were pierced by nails. Why did Christ die? Why was he wounded in this way? In order to purchase our redemption by his saving death. It also calls to mind the remarkable scene of recognition in which Thomas – the one who doubted the reality of the resurrection – was reassured of the reality of the presence of the risen Lord, by being allowed to see the wounds in the hands of Jesus (John 20:24–8). Packer's imagery is thus grounded in Scripture, and evokes the recollection of appropriate biblical passages on the part of his readers.

2. Packer's Scripture-saturated prose is rich in allusions to passages of Scripture, none of which are explicitly identified. Once more, the effect is to generate a cascade of biblically-focused reflection on the part of the reader. For example, the use of the phrase 'I am never out of his mind' will immediately evoke the memory of a whole series of biblical passages, particularly those in the prophetic literature referring to God's constant love for and attention to his wayward people. 'Can a mother forget the baby at her breast and have no compassion on the child she has borne? Though she may forget, I will not forget you!' (Isa. 49:15). The reference to God knowing us before we knew him immediately calls to mind the affirmation of the priority of God's love for us in the First Letter of John (1 John 4:19). The affirmation of the constant watch of

God over his people ('there is no moment when his eye is off me') will call to mind the great statements, particularly in the Psalter, concerning the Lord's continual watch over and care for his people: 'He who watches over Israel will neither slumber nor sleep' (Ps. 121:4).

3. Packer's spiritual insights are rigorously grounded in theology. The application of theology to life – a key theme in Puritan writings – can be seen at point after point in Packer's writings, especially in *Knowing God*. The passage noted above is a remarkably fine application of the doctrine of providence to the personal life of the Christian believer. Notice how Packer uses a series of phrases and statements to develop and explore what is substantially the same rich theme – the providential care of God for his people. In this case, Packer focuses this theological theme on the individual; elsewhere, he applies this and other themes to different contexts, such as the life of the church. Packer does not merely state a theological premise; he aims to apply it to the life of the believer – in short, he seeks *to make it real,* in response to the brief originally given to him by Elizabeth Braund (see p. 187).

Underlying *Knowing God* can be discerned a set of theological guidelines which – like the title of the book itself – can be argued to derive from the great reformer John Calvin (1509–64). Packer set out his understanding of the notion of 'knowing God' in an important lecture, originally delivered at the 1975 Philadelphia Conference on Reformed Theology, which was published shortly after the appearance of the book of that same name.[11] Packer opens his analysis by stressing the importance of the theme of 'knowing God' in Reformed theology, and chose to illustrate his theme with reference to the writing for which John Calvin is best known – the *Institutes of the Christian Religion.*[12]

Packer draws the attention of his readers to four main themes which occur in Calvin's writings.

1. In the first place, 'knowledge of God' does not refer to some natural human awareness of God, but to knowledge which arises within a covenanted relationship – 'knowledge of God as the one who has given himself to you'.

2. Knowledge of God is more than any particular experience of God. Faith is about trust in God, from which particular experiences of God have their origins.

3. Knowledge of God is 'more than knowing *about* God', although knowing about God is its foundation. Packer here draws a distinction between 'knowledge by description' and 'knowledge by acquaintance'. While it is necessary to have a correct understanding of God as the righteous, wise and merciful creator and judge, true knowledge of God must also be 'relational knowledge, knowledge that comes to us in the relation of commitment and trust, faith and reliance'.

4. To know God is also to know his relationship to us. Calvin affirmed that all human wisdom could be summed up as 'knowledge of God and of ourselves', and stressed that these two were inseparable. To know God is to know ourselves; to know ourselves truly, we must know God. 'Knowing God' is therefore 'not knowing God in isolation; it is knowing God in his relationship to us, that relationship in which he gives himself and his gifts to us for our enrichment'. To know God, we need to know his gracious gifts to us, and our need for such gifts in the first place.

On the basis of this analysis, Packer concludes by declaring that 'knowing God' consists of three components, which must be taken together:

1. Apprehension of what God is;

2. Application to ourselves of what God is and what he gives;

3. Adoration of God, as the giver of these gifts.

Packer's major work *Knowing God* can be seen as a careful exposition of these three components, which are presented in a closely interrelated manner. Packer's general strategy is to begin by allowing his readers to apprehend the reality of God; then to move on to allow them to apply these insights to their lives; and finally, to respond to God in adoration. Packer avoids a mechanical repetition of this pattern; *Knowing God* is not constructed woodenly around a rigid pattern predetermined in this way, but responds naturally to the biblical passage or theme being explored. Nevertheless, these three themes recur throughout Packer's analysis, as he aims to allow his readers to apprehend, apply and adore.

So why not provide readers with a convenient summary of the work at this point? After much thought, I felt that this would be quite inappropriate. *Knowing God* is a work that demands to be read at first hand, rather than summarized by someone else. The very act of reading the book is itself part of the exercise of wrestling with God. Nobody else can do this in our place; it is something that must be done for ourselves and by ourselves. It is like going on a long walk along a forest trail, rich in flora and fauna, nestling under the shadow of the great Rocky Mountains. It is something that cries out to be experienced, not described. Packer's approach demands that the reader accompany him, and discover with him the depths and heights of the Christian knowledge of God. The discipline of making the journey is part of the benefits which the book brings. I have felt that it is right to try to point out some of the concerns Packer had in writing the book, and describe its origins, so that readers will gain as much as they can from reading it – but there is, and can be, no substitute for reading it at first hand.

Knowing God shows Packer in a role which many regard as his best – a positive, constructive communicator of the reality and relevance of the truths of the Christian faith. The book established Packer as a leading Christian writer, transcending the divisions between denominations and the perhaps more complex divisions between different styles of evangelicals. Although Packer continued to be regarded as a heavyweight academic by those familiar with his wider spectrum of writing, many came to know him only through this one book. Like his great mentor John Calvin, Packer was to many *homo unius libri*, 'a man of a single book'[13] – not someone who wrote a single book, but someone who was known for one book in particular.

The success of *Knowing God* took Packer by surprise, and appears to have convinced him both of the importance of relating theology and spirituality (although this latter word was not used much in the 1970s by evangelical writers),[14] and of his own ability to contribute to this process. We shall return to this point in a following chapter.

On his reading of church history, Packer was convinced that controversy was an appropriate means by which clarification of Christian teaching could be achieved. No stranger to controversy in the past, Packer demonstrated his willingness to continue to contribute to this process of clarification. One particularly significant debate to break out around this point came to be known as 'the battle for the Bible', and focused on the issue of the inerrancy of Scripture. The nature of this controversy, and Packer's role within it, are important and require discussion.

The 'Battle for the Bible'

Packer's concern for the authority of Scripture is evident from his earliest writings. In general, the question of the precise nature of biblical authority did not become an issue within British evangelicalism. British evangelicals were content to affirm the inspiration and authority of Scripture, without feeling the need to stipulate the precise manner in which these were to be formulated. The Inter-Varsity Fellowship Basis of Faith referred to Scripture as 'infallible', yet made no reference to the term 'inerrancy'. For many British evangelicals, 'inerrant' was American in origin, exotic in its implications, and was associated with various obscurantist attitudes and beliefs for which British evangelicals had no enthusiasm. The leading British evangelical New Testament scholar F.F. Bruce, who had a major influence on a generation of evangelicals, avoided the term, seeing it as unhelpful.

Packer himself can be seen as having made a significant contribution to the defence of the term 'infallibility' and the acceptance of the term 'inerrancy' within British evangelicalism, not least by pointing out that the negative tone of the words nevertheless pointed to a positive affirmation concerning the 'total reliability' or 'total truth and trustworthiness' of Scripture. Packer took a much more positive attitude towards the terms, and was one of the very few English evangelicals to do so in the 1960s. Most British evangelicals were quite content to affirm that Scripture was true and trustworthy in all its statements, without using the vocabulary that was emerging in North America. Packer argued that the terms 'inerrancy' and 'infallibility' stated these positive ideas, although in a negative manner, and thus prepared the way for their increased use in British evangelical circles.

Packer found himself being called upon to defend the authority of Scripture against liberal critics at an early stage in his career. During the period 1956–8, he was especially concerned to defend a high view of Scripture against its critics, as the background to the writing of *'Fundamentalism' and the Word of God* in 1958 (see pp. 80–9) indicates. This concern continued in the next decade. For example, in 1962, the English journal *Breakthrough* arranged for a debate to take place between Hugh Montefiore (Dean of Chapel at Gonville and Caius College, Cambridge) and Packer over the doctrinal basis of the Inter-Varsity Fellowship. Montefiore argued that conservative evangelicals (who he was careful to distinguish from 'fundamentalists') held teachings concerning the infallibility and inerrancy of Scripture which many thinking people found difficult to believe. In the course of a good-natured and lively debate, Packer responded by clarifying and defending the evangelical use of these terms, and the truths which they denoted.

'Infallible' means 'not liable to be mistaken, or to mislead'; 'inerrant' means 'free from all falsehood'. Both words express negatively the positive idea that the Bible is entirely reliable and trustworthy in all that it asserts. To profess faith in the infallibility and inerrancy of Scripture is therefore to express the intention of believing all that it is found to teach, on the grounds that it is true ... The conservative evangelical differs from his liberal brother, not by committing himself to interpret the Bible in a different way, but by committing himself in advance to believe whatever the Bible turns out to be saying.[15]

Packer here spoke as an evangelical for evangelicals; the issue of biblical authority and inspiration served to distinguish evangelicals from liberals, and acted as a rallying-point around which evangelicals could unite. There were, however, rumblings of distant thunder, clouds gathering on a distant horizon, which would draw Packer into a debate of major importance in North American evangelicalism.

The debate, which at times threatened to destroy the unity of American evangelicalism, can be seen as focusing particularly on the changing stance of Fuller Theological Seminary concerning the inerrancy of Scripture.[16] Packer became involved in the debate over inerrancy, and was one of a very few delegates from outside the United States to attend a conference called to discuss the issue in June 1966.[17] The conference, which met at Wenham, Massachusetts, failed to secure agreement over the issue of inerrancy; indeed, the final statement avoided the use of the term, and spoke instead of 'the entire truthfulness' of Scripture.

It is likely that the format of the conference itself contributed to that failure, in that it tended to highlight differences rather than provide an atmosphere in which serious discussion and rapprochement could take place. Packer felt that the organizers seemed to have based the structure of the conference on the assumption that differences could be settled by merely reading papers to each other. In the event, poor chairmanship in the early stages of the conference led to the discussions becoming so polarized that agreement would be complicated by issues of personality. 'There were some very rough moments', as Packer recalls, including sessions at which Fuller faculty were accused of duplicity by some of their more combative opponents. In such a poisoned atmosphere, reconciliation or mutual understanding was impossible.

The issue was further polarized to the point of near catastrophe through the publication of Harold Lindsell's *Battle for the Bible*,[18] which appeared in April 1976. Lindsell singled out Fuller for special criticism, and took the step of making commitment to inerrancy, in the strict sense of the term, a criterion of evangelical identity. This single-issue approach to evangelical identity was widely regarded as simplistic and confusing. Lindsell's uncompromising views caused serious difficulties even for evangelicals who were inerrantists, such as Carl Henry, who felt that Lindsell's 'theological atom bombing' hurt evangelical allies as much as their enemies. In a subsequent volume, Lindsell argued that the term 'evangelical' should be abandoned in favour of 'fundamentalist' as a demonstration of (at least part of) the movement's commitment to inerrantism.[19] Inerrancy by now had ceased to be a doctrine; it was a weapon.

Packer, who has always insisted on the inerrancy of Scripture, was something of a diplomat in a conversation often dominated by power politics and institutional rivalry.[20] For example, it has been argued that the debate can be seen as an attempt by the northern evangelical establishment to impose its technical language on the entire evangelical coalition in the United States.[21] Some of those present at the earlier debates between Fuller faculty and their opponents had certainly gained the impression that Trinity Evangelical Divinity School was trying to set itself up as a rival to Fuller as the leading post-fundamentalist theological community.

As an outsider to the often claustrophobic world of North American theological institutional rivalry, Packer was able to focus on the theological issues without being dragged into the power struggles that were linked with the debate. In 1977, he became a founder member of the International Council on Biblical Inerrancy, chaired by James Boice of Tenth Presbyterian Church, Philadelphia. Indeed, it can be argued that Packer's inclusion in this council determined its title; as the only non-American member, his inclusion necessitated the term 'International' rather than 'National'. Packer was active in the three summit meetings of the Council in Chicago (1978, 1982 and 1987), and the two Congress meetings in San Diego (1982) and Washington, DC (1988), and drafted the 'Exposition' for the summits of 1978 and 1982.[22] Each of these 'Expositions' can be seen as a masterly summary of a classic evangelical approach to the issues involved, meriting further discussion at this point.

The 1978 exposition focused on the total trustworthiness of Scripture as the foundation of the Christian life. Canonical Scripture is to be interpreted on the basis of the recognition that it is infallible and inerrant – two negative terms which express and 'safeguard crucial positive truths'. Packer set out clear guidelines by which these concepts were to be understood.

> We affirm that canonical Scripture should always be interpreted on the basis that it is infallible and inerrant. However, in determining what the God-taught writer is asserting in each passage, we must pay the most careful attention to its claims and character as a human production. In inspiration, God utilized the culture and conventions of his penman's milieu, a milieu that God controls in his sovereign providence; it is misinterpretation to imagine otherwise.[23]

So history must be treated as history, poetry as poetry, hyperbole and metaphor as hyperbole and metaphor, generalization and approximation as what they are, and so forth. Differences between literary conventions in Bible times and in ours must also be observed: since, for instance, non-chronological narration and imprecise citation were conventional and acceptable and violated no expectation in those days, we must not regard these things as faults when we find them in Bible writers. When total precision of a particular kind was not expected nor aimed at, it is no error not to have achieved it. Scripture is inerrant, not in the sense of being absolutely precise by modern standards, but in the sense of making good its claims and achieving that measure of focused truth at which its authors aimed.

In his exposition on the theme of biblical interpretation, Packer developed a classic approach, along the lines set out by Reformed and Puritan writers of the sixteenth and seventeenth centuries. Three activities were identified as of central importance.

1. *Exegesis,* which is to be understood as the extracting of meaning from the text.

2. *Integration,* in which the interpreter seeks to correlate what one particular biblical passage has to say with others, to ensure that the entire weight of the biblical testimony is being conveyed.

3. *Application,* which aims to bring together thought and action.

It must be stressed that the term 'inerrancy' meant different things to different people. Indeed, at times one gains the impression that the 'Battle for the Bible' was waged on the basis of a wide range of understandings of what that battle concerned, and the identity of both allies and enemies. Some North American evangelicals were adamant that all forms of the theory of biological evolution were contrary to Scripture, and therefore were explicitly off-limits to evangelicals. Packer expressed reservations concerning this point:

> I believe in the inerrancy of Scripture, and maintain it in print, but exegetically I cannot see that anything Scripture says, in the first chapters of Genesis or elsewhere, bears on the biological theory of evolution one way or the other. On that theory itself, as a non-scientist, watching from a distance the disputes of the experts, I suspend judgment, but I recall that B.B. Warfield was a theistic evolutionist. If on this count I am not an evangelical, then neither was he.[24]

More generally, Packer can be seen as developing Calvin's understanding of the way in which biblical interpretation and scientific analysis may interact.

> It should be remembered, however, that Scripture was given to reveal God, not to address scientific issues in scientific terms, and that, as it does not use the language of modern science, so it does not require scientific knowledge about the internal processes of God's creation for the understanding of its essential message about God and ourselves. Scripture interprets scientific knowledge by relating it to the revealed purpose and work of God, thus establishing an ultimate context for the study and reform of scientific ideas. It is not for scientific theories to dictate what Scripture may and may not say, although extra-biblical information will sometimes helpfully expose a misinterpretation of Scripture.
>
> In fact, interrogating biblical statements concerning nature in

the light of scientific knowledge about their subject matter may help toward attaining a more precise exegesis of them. For though exegesis must be controlled by the text itself, not shaped by extraneous considerations, the exegetical process is constantly stimulated by questioning the text as to whether it means this or that.[25]

In his 1978 exposition, Packer commented that Scripture 'is sometimes culturally conditioned by the customs and conventional views of a particular period, so that the application of its principles today may call for a different sort of action'.[26] At a conference organized by the Fellowship of Evangelical Baptist Churches in Canada, held over the period 11–14 February 1985, Packer amplified these comments. He stressed the importance of the truthfulness of Scripture, and noted how this was to be applied to the issue of the cultural difference between the world of Scripture and our own situation:

> The fact that certain cultural and dispensational changes have changed the application of certain biblical passages to our time, as compared with the time when they were first written, must not be confused with the trustworthiness – that is, the inerrancy – of the passages themselves, as expressions of the truth and will of God for those to whom they were first addressed, and as applications of those unchanging truths about God and man which we also must apply, as God's wisdom leads us, to our own different situation.[27]

The situation to which biblical truths must be applied may have changed; that truth itself has not.

Packer's views about biblical inerrancy can be studied to advantage from his approach to the subject in the course of his regular teaching at Regent College. In these lectures, Packer was free to develop his ideas in a non-controversial and constructive context. We shall explore them from the lecture course 'Systematic Theology I: Knowledge of God', delivered in the fall term of 1987.[28] Packer noted that the terms 'inerrant' and 'infallible' tended to mean different things to different people. However, the definition of inerrancy which 'expresses most accurately and persuasively what those who use the term and defend it' are essentially concerned about seems to be 'total trustworthiness as a consequence of entire truthfulness'. This neat aphorism stands out as a superb summary of a debate which was often characterized by verbal turgidity. Turning to deal with the question of the meaning of the older term 'infallibility', Packer argues for its core meaning as being 'complete reliability, neither misled nor misleading'.

What, then, is the difference between these two terms? Do we have a distinction without a difference, as some more puzzled readers of the Chicago Statement certainly felt was the case? Packer's summary of the situation once more seems admirable: 'Inerrancy and infallibility thus become synonyms, differing only in nuance and tone (the former accenting trustworthiness as a *source*, the latter accenting trustworthiness as a *guide*). Neither word need be used; both may be used to advantage.'

Although a vigorous defender of both notions, Packer identified four reasons why the term 'inerrancy' in particular was disliked by some evangelicals. For Packer, the term 'conjured up fear' of a number of things:

1. Bad apologetics. Here, Packer is concerned that rationalist claims that the truth of the Bible can in some way be proved may turn out to be flawed, with serious implications for biblical authority.

2. Bad harmonizing. Harold Lindsell had argued that one good way of solving the problem of apparent differences over the exact timing of Peter's three denials of Christ was to suggest that there were actually six denials, of which only three were mentioned in any one gospel.[29] Although Packer mentions no names, he argues that 'intellectually disreputable expedients must be avoided', and cites the 'claim that Peter denied Jesus six times' as an example of such an expedient.

3. Bad interpretation. Here, Packer notes the problems which emerge when the defence of inerrancy leads to a preoccupation with what are actually the minor aspects of the Bible, and a failure to focus on its central message. It can lead to a 'majoring in minors and minutiae, e.g. genealogies, rather than in central gospel truths'.

4. Bad theology. The danger here is that the human character of Scripture can easily be overlooked, or that Scripture can be treated simply as a source of information, thus missing its Christocentric dimension.

But all of these are dangers – and dangers can be avoided. Packer had no doubt that the concept of inerrancy – if properly understood – affirms biblical inspiration, determines interpretative method, and safeguards biblical authority. It was a theme which was essential to evangelical biblical interpretation and application.

Packer has always been a peacemaker in terms of the controversies into which he has been drawn, and concerned to ensure that controversy does not blind evangelicalism to truths which it needed to hear. Although a vigorous defender of inerrancy, he felt that there was a danger that evangelicalism might fail to engage with some critically important issues through its preoccupation with this matter.

> It will be sad if zeal for inerrancy entrenches a wholly backward-looking bibliology. Fruitful questions thrown up in the liberal camp – questions about revelation as communication, about hermeneutics as the theory of understanding, about the use of Scripture in preaching and theology, about the way in which the historically relative may have absoluteness and finality for all time, about the epistemological status and quality of the knowledge Scripture gives us and so on (I could extend the list, couldn't you?) – await evangelical exploration, which as yet they have hardly had. The battle for the Bible must continue as long as unbelieving babble about the Bible continues, but as Archbishop Michael Ramsey once said, the best defence of any doctrine is the creative exposition of it, and the creative exposition of the doctrine of Scripture requires work on these questions which still waits to be taken in hand.[30]

It could be said that Packer's entire theology is founded on 'the trustworthiness – that is, the inerrancy' of Scripture. It is a debatable point as to whether Packer understood the term 'inerrancy' in quite the same terms as others who were participants to the debates of the 1970s and early 1980s. But that is a matter which can be left to future historians to discuss; it is questionable whether it is of real significance. What is unquestionably of enduring importance is Packer's affirmation, defence and application of the trustworthiness of Scripture to Christian thought and life – or, to use the terms which have now become widely used, to systematic theology and to spirituality.

In exploring the 'Battle for the Bible', we have allowed our account to run ahead of itself. We may now bring the narrative back to the 1970s, as we turn to another major theme of classic evangelical theology which appeared to be coming under threat – the notion of penal substitution.

The Tyndale Lecture: Packer on the Atonement

We have already noted the importance of the Tyndale Fellowship for Biblical Literature, and the significance of Tyndale House as an evangelical research and study centre. Packer was involved with the work of the Fellowship from an early stage. The Tyndale Fellowship was concerned to promote the advancing of evangelical scholarship across a broader front than biblical studies in the strictest sense of the term. It will be recalled that the Puritan Studies Conference, founded in 1950 by Packer and O.R. Johnston, was originally con-stituted as a study of the Tyndale Fellowship, and was known simply as the 'Puritan Studies Group'. Packer subsequently remained a contributing member of the Tyndale Fellowship, and chaired the Biblical Theology Group for several years. He was invited to deliver the Tyndale Biblical Theology Lecture for 1973. This lecture, which was delivered at Tyndale House on 17 July 1973, dealt with the theme of penal substitution – a specific way of understanding the meaning of the death of Christ on the cross.

Why penal substitution? Evangelicalism once regarded the doc-trine of penal substitution as the only valid means of interpreting the cross of Christ. However, the doctrine came under mounting criticism during the later nineteenth century, and subsequently during the twentieth. Works such as John McLeod Campbell's *Nature of the Atonement* (1856) and R.C. Moberly's *Atonement and Personality* (1901) placed an emphasis on the recreative impact of Christ's sufferings on all of humanity, rather than adopting a penal or substitutionary approach. A particularly severe criticism of the concept of penal substitution was launched in 1962 by Geoffrey W.H. Lampe, who argued that it should be discarded as outdated and offensive.[31] It is clear that by 1970, many evangelicals had concluded that the traditional (and closely related) concepts of 'substitutionary atonement' and 'penal substitution' were being seen as one approach to the cross, among others. The cumulative impact of such criticisms on evangelicals was significant.[32] The sec-ond National Evangelical Anglican Congress, held at Nottingham in April 1977 (see pp. 213–17), can be seen as witnessing to this increasing reluctance on the part of many evangelicals to commit themselves exclusively to this understanding of the atonement. The final statement of the congress made reference to this diversity amongst evangelicals in the following terms:

Regarding the Atonement, we all gladly affirm that the death and resurrection of Jesus is the heart of the gospel of salvation: 'Christ died for our sins in accordance with the Scriptures, and was raised on the third day.' Nevertheless, we give different emphasis to the various biblical expressions of the Atonement. Some see the truth that Christ died in our place as the central explanation of the cross, while others, who also give this truth a position of great importance, lay greater stress on the relative significance of the other biblical pictures.[33]

Packer's lecture, entitled 'What did the Cross Achieve? The Logic of Penal Substitution', should be seen as a vigorous defence of the centrality of the concept of 'penal substitution' against some of the criticisms offered against it. The lecture is a remarkable piece of constructive theology, showing a deep awareness of the development of Christian theology, along with a shrewd and critical awareness of the theological trends of the 1960s. Many regard it as one of Packer's finest essays. In view of the importance of the issue for evangelism, apologetics and systematic theology, we shall explore it in some detail.[34]

Packer opens his lecture by noting the importance of his theme. 'The task which I have set myself in this lecture is to focus and explicate a belief which, by and large, is a distinguishing mark of the worldwide evangelical fraternity; namely, the belief that Christ's death on the cross had the character of *penal substitution*, and that it was in virtue of this fact that it brought salvation to mankind.' In affirming its importance, Packer noted the need to defend it against both misunderstandings and criticisms.

One such misunderstanding concerns the status of the approach. Many loosely refer to it as the 'doctrine of penal substitution'. As Packer points out, this is not strictly correct; the approach is better defined as a model, or way of picturing, what God achieved on the cross, showing some parallels with the ideas developed by the Swedish writer Gustav Aulén in the 1930s:

It is a Christian theological model, based on biblical exegesis, formed to focus a particular awareness of what Jesus did at Calvary to bring us to God. If we wish to speak of the 'doctrine' of penal substitution, we should remember that this model is a dramatic, kerygmatic picturing of divine action, much more like Aulén's 'classic idea' of divine victory (though Aulén never saw this) than it is like the defensive formula-models which we call the Nicene 'doctrine' of the Trinity and the Chalcedonian 'doctrine' of the person of Christ.

Having clarified the status of this approach, or way of picturing God's action on the cross, Packer moved to clarify the precise meaning of the term 'substitution', arguing that many of the criticisms directed against the approach rest on misunderstandings at this point.

> Substitution is, in fact, a broad idea that applies whenever one person acts to supply another's need, or to discharge his obligation, so that the other no longer has to carry the load himself . . . In this broad sense, nobody who wishes to say with Paul that there is a true sense in which 'Christ died for us' (once, on our behalf, for our benefit), and 'Christ redeemed us from the curse of the law, having become a curse for us' . . . and who accepts Christ's assurance that he came 'to give his life a ransom for many' . . . should hesitate to say that Christ's death was substitutionary.

Packer then proceeded to show how the notion of substitution was of fundamental importance to responsible Christian approaches to an understanding of the meaning of the death of Christ. Packer sets out three broad approaches to the atonement, along the following lines:[35]

> 1. A subjective approach, which identifies the locus of the effect of the cross in terms of the effects of Christ upon us, particularly in engendering a response of human love to the divine love made known in the death of Christ.
>
> 2. An objective approach, which sees the impact of the cross in terms of the defeat of satanic or demonic forces, which hold humanity in captivity.
>
> 3. A substitutionary approach, which affirms that Christ's death on the cross is to be understood as a satisfaction for human sins, by which their guilt may be expunged and we may be accepted by God.

Packer's view is that the third approach combines all the authentic elements of the first two.

The third type of account denies nothing asserted by the other two views save their assumption that they are complete. It agrees that there is biblical support for all they say, but it goes further. It grounds man's plight as a victim of sin and Satan in the fact that, for all God's daily goodness to him, as a sinner he stands under divine judgment, and his bondage to evil is the start of his sentence, and unless God's rejection of him is turned into acceptance he is lost for ever. On this view, Christ's death had its effect first on God, who was hereby *propitiated* (or, better, who hereby propitiated himself), and only because it had this effect did it become an overthrowing of the powers of darkness and a revealing of God's seeking and saving love. The thought here is that by dying Christ offered to God what the West has called *satisfaction* for sins, satisfaction which God's own character dictated as the only means whereby his 'no' to us could become a 'yes'. Whether this Godward satisfaction is understood as the homage of death itself, or death as the perfecting of holy obedience, or an undergoing of the God-forsakenness of hell, which is God's final judgment on sin, or a perfect confession of man's sins combined with entry into their bitterness by sympathetic identification, or all these things together (and nothing stops us combining them together), the shape of this view remains the same – that by undergoing the cross Jesus expiated our sins, propitiated our Maker, turned God's 'no' to us into a 'yes', and so saved us. All forms of this view see Jesus as our representative substitute in fact, whether or not they call him that, but only certain versions of it represent his substitution as penal.

Packer also pointed out how the second approach implicitly assumes that Christ is our substitute, even though this is not brought out explicitly in most treatments of the matter.

[The second type of account] sees Christ's death as having its effect primarily on hostile spiritual forces external to us which are held to be imprisoning us in a captivity of which our inveterate moral twistedness is one sign and symptom . . . The assumption here is that man's plight is created entirely by hostile cosmic forces distinct from God; yet, seeing Jesus as our champion, exponents of this view could still properly call him our substitute . . . What this type of account of the cross affirms (though it is not usually put in these terms) is that the conquering Christ, whose victory secured our release, was our representative substitute.

On the basis of this analysis, Packer points out how the theme of 'substitution' can be seen as being fundamental to all proper Christian thinking concerning the atonement.

> It should be noted that though the [first two views noted above] regularly set themselves in antithesis to the third, the third takes up into itself all the positive assertions that they make; which raises the question whether any more is at issue here than the impropriety of treating half-truths as the whole truth, and of rejecting a more comprehensive account on the basis of speculative negations about what God's holiness requires as a basis for forgiving sins. Were it allowed that the first two views might be misunderstanding and distorting themselves in this way, the much-disputed claim that a broadly substitutionary view of the cross has always been the mainstream Christian opinion might be seen to have substance in it after all. It is a pity that books on the atonement so often take it for granted that accounts of the cross which have appeared as rivals in historical debate must be treated as intrinsically exclusive. This is always arbitrary, and sometimes quite perverse.

Having explored the development of Christian thinking on the atonement, Packer concludes that the theme of substitution is of foundational importance, whether this is explicitly recognized or not. This then raises the question of how this can be understood in 'penal' terms.

'Penal substitution', according to Packer, 'presupposes a penalty (*poena*) due to us from God the judge for wrong done and failure to meet his claims.' Noting that the *locus classicus* for this view is Romans 1:18–3:20, Packer argues that four central biblical insights may be distilled into this approach.

> 1. God, in his holiness, justice and goodness, has announced a rightful sentence against sinful humanity. This verdict includes death, both spiritual and physical.

> 2. Sinful humanity lacks the ability to undo the past or break free from sin in the present. In consequence, we are unable to avert the righteous judgment of God.

> 3. Jesus Christ, as God-man, took our place under judgment, and 'received in his own personal experience all the dimensions of the death that was our sentence', thus laying the foundation for our pardon and immunity.

4. Faith recognizes that God's righteous demands remain as they were, and that God's retributive justice does not and will not cease to operate. Nevertheless, those demands have been met in Christ. 'All our sins, past, present and even future, have been covered by Calvary ... Our sins have already been judged and punished, however strange the statement may sound, in the person and death of another.'

To talk about 'penal substitution' is thus not to become involved in muddled argument about the propriety of the transference of guilt (which Packer argues to rest on rationalist assumptions, typical of sixteenth-century humanistic Socinian rationalism, and, later, the Enlightenment), but to articulate the insights of believers who recognize that Jesus bore whatever punishment, penalty and judgment was due to us. For Packer, this is the essential meaning of Paul's declaration that Christ 'loved me, and gave himself for me' (Gal. 2:20).

Packer's defence of this doctrine confirmed his reputation as a competent and vigorous defender of classic evangelical orthodoxy. There were many, particularly among former students at Tyndale Hall and subsequently at Trinity College, who hoped that he might expand the lecture into a book, given the growing misgivings within evangelicalism over the traditional teaching. Curiously, however, Packer soon found himself being lambasted for having *failed* to defend evangelicalism adequately. The occasion of these criticisms was a report published by the Church of England Doctrine Commission, of which Packer was a member, to which we now turn.

Renewed Controversy: Christian Believing

Packer had been a member of the Doctrine Commission of the Church of England for some time. The Doctrine Commission was a body appointed to consider issues of doctrine which might, from time to time, be seen as being of relevance to the Church of England. In practice, the Commission tended to act as little more than an indicator of the prevailing theological mood. The comments of the Doctrine Commission are best seen as reflecting the ethos of the dominant party or constituency in the church, rather than as a statement of what Anglicans believe. During the late 1960s, theological liberalism began to gain the ascendancy in English universities and some of its theological colleges. By the early 1970s, it seemed invincible. A series of works published around this period point to the dominance of this ethos. James Barr's aggressively anti-evangelical *Fundamentalism* and John Hick's edited collection of essays entitled *The Myth of God Incarnate* were both published in 1977; taken together, they constituted a formidable broadside against evangelicalism. The publication of the Doctrine Commission report *Christian Believing* the previous year also caused considerable concern to evangelicals, but for slightly different reasons. It was not simply that the report seemed dismissive of evangelicalism; it was that a leading evangelical seemed to have had a hand in its drafting.

The Doctrine Commission was originally chaired by Ian Ramsey, Bishop of Durham. Ramsey was a fine theologian, who had previously held the Nolloth chair of the philosophy of religion at Oxford University. His sudden death in 1972 was widely attributed to over-work. It robbed the Church of England of a promising bishop, and the Doctrine Commission of an eirenic chairman. His successor as chairman of the commission was Maurice Wiles, Regius Professor of Divinity at Oxford University. In 1974, Wiles published a work entitled *The Remaking of Christian Doctrine*, which reflected a strongly sceptical stance towards traditional Christian teaching, particularly in regard to the person and work of Christ. Dennis Nineham argued that there was no point in trying to ground Christianity in anything that was specifically linked to the person of Jesus. Geoffrey Lampe affirmed such criticisms, and argued strongly against traditional views of the atonement (see p. 204). For writers such as Wiles, Nineham and Lampe, the central dogmas of the Christian faith required radical restatements in the light of their increasingly sceptical attitude towards them.

Nineham and Lampe were members of the Doctrine Commission; Wiles became its chairman, in succession to Ian Ramsey. Evangelicals on the commission – including Packer and Michael Green – now found themselves in a difficult situation. They sensed that the dice were loaded against them. Hopelessly outnumbered on the Committee, they could at best hope to ensure that some evangelical concerns were represented. In the end, the Commission found itself so divided that it could not reach a common mind, except on the most elementary issues. The report consisted of a fairly short 'joint report', to which were appended a series of individual statements by eight of the Commission's members. Neither Packer nor Green was included in this section.

Even the tone of the joint report was sceptical. The opening sentence described the Christian life in terms of 'an adventure, a voyage of discovery, a journey, sustained by faith and hope, towards a final and complete communion with the Love at the heart of all things'.[36] The choice of such words is enormously significant, as it calls into question such ideas as an authoritative revelation which must be accepted. This idea, the report noted, was encountered in earlier generations of Christians. However, what was accepted by Christians in the past need not be accepted now. A major chapter entitled 'The Pastness of the Past' drew attention to a series of difficulties concerning the authority of the past in the present, and raised the kind of issues which Wiles, Lampe and Nineham had stressed in their works. Nineham argued, along lines established by Rudolf Bultmann, that it was difficult for modern people to accept the stories about Jesus exorcising demons and other supernatural events. There was a need for a radical overhaul of belief. Lampe argued that traditional credal statements, though correct in their own day, were now misleading and should be set to one side; taken at face value, they were now untrue. The radical theological agenda of the 1960s had clearly had its impact.

It was a deeply disappointing work, and critics on all sides were not slow to express their frustration. Packer was singled out for particular criticism by some evangelicals, who felt that he had failed to ensure that evangelical distinctives were clearly defended and enunciated. For Packer, there was little that he could have done. He was convinced that it was right to represent evangelicalism on the Commission. But he was hopelessly outnumbered, so what could he do? He had tried to be an evangelical voice in a conversation which was not leading to a conclusion, but merely to a statement of differences. The document was thus a work of phenomenological rather than kerygmatic or dogmatic theology. Once the decision had been taken to use the report to describe what its members believed (rather than prescribe what ought to be believed), the outcome was inevitable. The resulting report had some use and value as a guide 'to what different folk do and do not believe, and why'.[37] Given the fact that there was a strong liberal contingent on the Commission, and a very small evangelical representation, the outcome could not have been averted. Packer was distressed at the manner in which many of his fellow evangelicals assumed that this was intended to be a statement in 'critical normative theology', and had not appreciated that it was really little more than a phenomenological analysis of the views of its members.

It was, however, a controversy which soon passed into history, and is remembered by few. It was soon eclipsed by others. The publication of *The Myth of God Incarnate* the next year caused considerable anger within the Church of England. The reaction to *The Myth* – whose launch was accompanied by a major publicity campaign by its publisher, SCM Press – neatly illustrates the dead end into which the prevailing theological trends, illustrated by the writings of Nineham and Wiles, had led. The book delighted non-Christians, perplexed an increasingly irritated Christian public, and convinced many that the dominant religious liberalism had nothing to offer the church or the world. As the historian Adrian Hastings observes:

> If *The Myth* produced excitement, it was principally the smirking excitement of an agnostic world amused to witness the white flag hoisted so enthusiastically above the long-beleaguered citadel of Christian belief, the stunned excitement of the rank and file of weary defenders on learning that their staff officers had so light-heartedly ratted on them. It was hardly surprising that more than one of the contributors soon after ceased, even in a nominal sense, to be Christian believers, or that Don Cupitt, one of the most forceful and publicity minded of the group, published only two years later his commitment to objective atheism.[38]

Three of the contributors to this volume – Lampe, Nineham and Wiles – were members of the Doctrine Commission. Ordinary Anglicans were furious. How could such people, who did not believe in some central doctrines of the Christian faith, exercise such influence on its Doctrine Commission? It was not long before the Commission was disbanded, and a new one reconstituted.

Looking back, the year 1977 may be seen as representing the high water mark of theological liberalism in England. Thereafter, it passed into irreversible decline. Much of the liberal theology of the 1960s appears to have been based on the mistaken assumption that the new cultural trends actually represented permanent changes in western culture.

In retrospect the dominant theological mood of that time in its hasty, slack rather collective sweep reminds one a little painfully of a flight of lemmings ... A good deal of the more publicized theological writing in the sixties gives the impression of a sheer surge of feeling that in the modern world God, religion, the transcendent, any reliability in the gospels, anything which had formed part of the old 'supernaturalist' system, had suddenly become absurd. There were plenty of fresh insights but too little stringent analysis of the new positions. Everything was to be enthusiastically 'demythologized' in a euphoria of secularization which was often fairly soft on scholarly rigour.[39]

If liberalism was now in decline, evangelicalism seemed to be coasting along on an upward spiral. It continued to be under-represented on church committees (as the domination of the Doctrine Commission by liberals illustrated); nevertheless, the movement was now a force to be reckoned with in terms of its numerical strength, as well as its theological integrity. As it happened, an evangelical congress held in Nottingham in April 1977 served to highlight the contrast between a declining liberalism and a growing evangelicalism. The event is of importance in relation to English evangelicalism; it also marks an important point in the development of Packer's career.

The Nottingham Event: NEAC 2

In 1975, John Stott convened a meeting to take forward the work of the National Evangelical Anglican Congress (NEAC) of 1967. The Keele congress of 1967 was now recognized as a landmark, representing a decisive change in the mood of evangelicalism within the Church of England. Stott felt that it would be appropriate to hold a follow-up conference to this event, to be held ten years afterwards in 1977. Among those whom he invited to discuss the event was Packer. At the initial meeting to discuss the proposal, it became clear that Packer had misgivings concerning the idea. He felt that the proposed conference would be a distraction, which would get in the way of carrying forward the work of NEAC in local churches. The meeting concluded, however, that such a conference would be appropriate, and arranged a further meeting to discuss its details.

At the second meeting, disagreements again emerged. Packer was clear that, if a conference was needed, it ought to focus on a specific theme of importance, such as ethics. The resurgence of evangelical scholarship, both biblical and theological, meant that evangelicalism was now much more secure in its doctrinal convictions than before. A study conference, at which evangelicalism sought to educate itself on matters on which it was deficient, would be an appropriate way of ensuring that the new ethical issues which were opening up would be fully addressed by evangelicals. Stott, however, felt that a conference could only have significant appeal if it addressed as wide a range of issues as was reasonably possible. In the end, this view prevailed, leaving Packer feeling increasingly isolated.

Packer then expressed the view that there was little point in such a conference producing a report. Given that the conference was intending to cover such a wide range of issues, a report based on its wide-ranging discussion would be rather thin, and might create a negative impression of evangelicalism to its more critical readers. In the end, it was decided to produce three books as 'study guides' for the proposed conference. These books were given the titles *The Lord Christ*, *The Changing World* and *The People of God*, each indicating the broad area they explored.

The Nottingham Congress, held at the Sports Hall of the University of Nottingham over the period Thursday 14 April to Monday 18 April 1977, was well attended. A crowd of 1,000 had gathered at Keele; double that number came to Nottingham. The Congress can be regarded as three full days, back- and front-ended with short sessions on Thursday and Monday. Friday was devoted to studying the first conference book, *The Lord Christ*; Saturday to *The Changing World*; and Sunday to *The People of God*. Each of the books had contained six chapters, and presentations were arranged for each. In effect, delegates had to choose which two to attend, in that scheduling considerations made it impossible to attend all. In the event, the most significant presentation (as judged by the responses of those present at the Congress) would be that offered by Anthony Thiselton on the Saturday.

The congress witnessed a number of developments which Packer regarded with anxiety. One such trend was what appeared to be an increasingly critical approach to the Reformation on the part of a younger generation of evangelicals. For example, David

Watson, noted for his important evangelistic ministry in the city of York and in the student world, declared his view that 'the Reformation was one of the greatest tragedies that ever happened to the church.'[40] The traditional evangelical approach of relating theology to practical issues was also called into question. Bruce Kaye set out the new approach in one of the study guides published prior to the congress:

> Traditionally, evangelicals have done their theology by trying to work out the basic principles from the Scriptures and then by either applying these principles to the question under discussion or seeking to discover their practical implications. We might call this a deductive approach to doing theology. The method which has been adopted ... [at this congress] ... runs in the opposite direction, without, however, denying the propriety of the older method. Here an issue in the present situation has been taken, and then analysed in depth to see what is at stake in it and how Christian truth can be related to it. We might call this an inductive approach to doing theology.[41]

It need hardly be added that the 'older method' was that adopted and defended by Packer.

It is, however, generally agreed that the most significant achievement of the congress was to highlight the importance of hermeneutics to the church. Initially, the subject was treated with amusement. For example, David Watson opened his address on Friday with what was clearly intended to be a joke: 'I heard of one delegate who thought that Hermann Neutics was a German professor of theology.' However, by the end of the congress, it was clear that hermeneutical questions were now seen as intensely significant by many. It is widely held that the long-term achievement of the Nottingham congress, which was attended by a large number of lay persons, was to establish the importance of hermeneutics. The leading figure linked with this development was Anthony Thiselton, formerly on the staff of Tyndale Hall while Packer was principal. One observer commented:

> Tony Thiselton's lecture on hermeneutics had become the standing joke of the Congress, especially for those who were impatient with the heavyweight academic theology of the study session. But many who were there would reckon this the most important part of the

whole Congress. For the first time in a major gathering of evangelicals, Thiselton had opened up the possibility of critical studies, form criticism, etc., as being acceptable subjects for evangelicals. Of course, this had been recognized for some time in the theological colleges, but it came as something of a shock for many people.[42]

One of the major points to emerge from Thiselton's presentation was the danger of attempting to force the Bible to answer distinctively modern questions to which the text itself does not specifically refer. The result was that evangelicals went away from the congress aware that they had a lot of thinking to do. As Colin Craston commented, 'the significance of the Congress was in the beginning of a debate on such issues as hermeneutics'.

The congress left Packer feeling isolated and low. It seemed to have set to one side his own concerns and agenda in favour of approaches and issues which he felt were not important strategically. Where Packer had hoped for a study conference, which would send evangelicals home with answers to relevant questions, Nottingham seemed to send them home with questions to which there were no real answers at present to be had. John Tiller, also on the teaching staff at Tyndale during Packer's period as principal, commented that the congress had 'revealed widespread ignorance on many issues', and pointed to the evangelical mind as being 'obviously divided, uncertain or uninformed'.

So what was the significance of Nottingham 77? Many answers have been given. Some see it as a further landmark which demonstrated the growing strength and sophistication of evangelicalism. There is no doubt that the congress raised the profile of evangelicalism still further within both the Church of England and the English media. It remains, however, something of a matter of debate within English evangelicalism as to whether the congress achieved anything of long-term significance. It may have gained a tactical success; with the benefit of hindsight, however, it can be seen to have lacked the strategic significance which was so evident in the case of the earlier Keele congress.

In opening the congress, John R.W. Stott pointed out that the main purpose of the congress was 'not to produce a statement, but to meet each other and above all to meet the Lord Christ'. Nevertheless, a Statement was produced, which generally avoided giving clear and unequivocal conclusions on contentious matters, such as the ministry of women. For Packer, the resulting report was much as he had feared it would be – 'a series of virtuous statements, amounting to nothing in particular'. Keele was a landmark; Nottingham was, in Packer's view, something of a dud.[43] For the purposes of our study, we must note one achievement of the congress which has not been noted in any official account of that meeting. It persuaded Packer that the time had come to leave England.

The Decision to Leave England

Packer was by now regarded in North America as the best-known and most highly respected British evangelical theological writer. He had been a significant presence at a number of major evangelical institutions in North America, most notably at Westminster Theological Seminary (Philadelphia), Fuller Theological Seminary (Pasadena, California), Trinity Evangelical Divinity School (Deerfield, Illinois), Regent College (Vancouver, British Columbia) and Gordon-Conwell Theological Seminary (South Hamilton, Massachusetts). His book *Knowing God* had firmly established him as one of the most important writers in the area of spirituality (although that term was not being used extensively in evangelical circles during the 1970s). He had been a major force in a number of North American discussions, most notably the celebrated 'Battle for the Bible', and the Philadelphia Conference on Reformed Theology. On 27 May 1978, Gordon-Conwell Theological Seminary awarded him an honorary Doctor of Divinity, in recognition of his major contribution to the Christian public in North America, especially through his writings. In short, Packer was being lionized in North America.

In England, however, he was being marginalized. The reasons for this are complex, and require a little explanation. In the first place, the type of Puritan theology which Packer had worked hard to foster and encourage seemed to be falling out of favour. The Nottingham conference of 1977 seemed to leave little place for a continuing interest in the Puritans. This was already clear to Packer by the opening months of 1975, as the planning for the congress proceeded. In an interesting analysis of the state of evangelicalism within the Church of England in late 1977, David F. Wells comments:

By 1977 the revival in Puritan spirituality that had been borne aloft on the wings of Banner of Truth's inexpensive paperbacks that first appeared in 1954 had more or less run its course. Perhaps the task of translating Puritan concepts into modern terms in the end proved too daunting, but the thirst for Puritan spirituality had also abated. What had once seemed so invigorating, now looked stilted and disagreeable, and the Calvinism that had lent such substance to the evangelical confession seemed to vanish overnight.[44]

Perhaps there is a degree of overstatement here; nevertheless, it is clear that after (and perhaps on account of) the 1977 National Evangelical Anglican Congress, many of Packer's theological concerns and emphases seemed to have been discounted by an emerging generation within the Church of England. The main stream of evangelicalism within the Church of England appeared to have headed off in a direction which seemed something of a dead end to Packer. His relationship with many free church evangelicals was still somewhat chilly in the aftermath of Martyn Lloyd-Jones's decision to freeze him out of those circles following the publication of *Growing into Union*. If Packer was not needed or welcomed in free church or national church circles, what was the point in remaining in England?

New theological issues were emerging, particularly in relation to hermeneutics. Packer's former colleague at Tyndale Hall, Anthony Thiselton, had stressed the importance of hermeneutics at Nottingham; his address had been well received, and hermeneutical issues now seemed to dominate the evangelical discussion of the authority of Scripture. How could the two horizons – the horizon of Scripture itself, and the horizon of the modern world – be bridged? How could Scripture be allowed to speak into the modern situation? George Carey, now Archbishop of Canterbury, recalls how something of a generation gap seemed to be opening up between older evangelicals, such as Packer, and younger evangelicals (including himself) who felt that hermeneutical issues could not be ignored, and had to be confronted. It would be wrong to suggest that Packer dismissed such concerns; nevertheless, he clearly felt that the Nottingham conference (which was unnecessary in any case) had sent evangelicals off in pursuit of inappropriate issues and goals. Packer never discounted the importance of hermeneutical questions;[45] however, he felt that the approach adopted by Thiselton risked generating a relativistic mindset, which could pervade every aspect of theology. Having 'battled for the Bible' for twenty years, Packer felt that this new turn threatened to undo his work in this critically important area.

A further matter had to do with the charismatic movement, which was now a major presence in England. During the 1950s, Packer had vigorously opposed an approach to personal holiness (the 'Keswick sanctification teaching'), which he regarded as unacceptable. In its place, he set views on sanctification which had their roots in the Reformed and Puritan tradition. With the rise of the charismatic movement, a new understanding of the nature and basis of sanctification had arisen, which offered a response to the issue rather different from that associated with Puritanism. Alongside this was a perceptibly growing disinterest in the Puritan approach to a major issue of Christian thought and life, which Packer had done much to revive and popularize. Indeed, the charismatic movement, with its strong emphasis on experience, seemed to run counter to Packer's emphasis on the importance of beginning with the mind grasping truth. As one observer commented in 1977, Packer's influence (and that of the Puritans)

> . . . seems to have diminished considerably over the past few years . . . This Puritan period passed fairly quickly. Although giving a solid theological basis, it was not really relevant to the contemporary needs of a fast changing Church of England. It can be sensed that the passing of this era has left its leader, Jim Packer, sitting a trifle uneasily amongst the wreckage, as the main course of evangelicalism has gone off in another direction.[46]

It could be argued that this depicts the situation in too negative a manner. But these comments are none the less important, in that they reflect the way in which the perception of Packer within evangelicalism had altered over the twenty-year period 1958–77.

During his time as warden of Latimer House, Packer had found that he had become a leader of the evangelical wing of the Church of England. Although Packer and Latimer House, as the individual and the institution, were closely linked, the way in which Latimer House had been established was such as to identify the house itself, along with its warden and librarian, as exercising leadership, both intellectual and political. When Packer left Latimer House, he found that his influence within evangelical groups (such as the Church of England Evangelical Council [CEEC]) diminished. The turmoil of his period as principal of Tyndale House diminished his ability to become involved to any great extent in the direction of the evangelical movement. However, once the situation at Trinity College had stabilized, Packer found himself without any significant *institutional* role within evangelical circles within the Church of England. Leadership now rested firmly in the hands of John R.W. Stott and his colleagues. This became especially clear to Packer in relation to the planning of NEAC 2, which he regarded as unnecessary.

Packer had a clear understanding of what issues needed to be addressed within the English situation. In particular, he was concerned to foster local leadership initiatives within churches. The issue of leadership within the local church was becoming of increasing importance, with the old model of clergy domination proving itself to be inadequate to meet new situations. Packer had earlier pursued a model of theological education which moved decisively away from the idea of the principal of a theological college being in personal charge of every aspect of its life, in favour of a North American model, which stressed the role of principal (or president) as an enabler and encourager, a *primus inter decanos*. He now wished to apply such insights to local churches, exploring the potential relevance of existing presbyterian models. In particular, Packer wanted to develop structures for local leadership which were self-governing, self-supporting and self-propagating. But his efforts to get 'leadership groups' on the evangelical agenda met with no enthusiasm. It seemed to Packer that things were being increasingly centralized in certain evangelical figures (such as Stott) and organizations (such as CEEC), which did not seem to have much place for Packer. Increasingly, Packer felt he was a 'pelican in the wilderness'. Nobody seemed to want him very much.

But the decision to leave one position merely begged the question of which position to assume. So where could he go next? There was no point in moving to another theological college within England. A senior position within the church – for example, as bishop, or as dean of a cathedral – was improbable, given the perceptions concerning Packer which existed in senior church circles. A move into a university context might also have been difficult; despite his enormous success as a popular writer, Packer had not produced the kind of academic books which would have been needed to secure academic advancement in an English university. In any case, this was not what he wanted; he was adamant that theology should not be detached from worship, prayer and evangelism. An English theological college offered something approaching a suitable environment in which to teach, as would a North American seminary. But a university department of theology or religion would lack the commitment and link with the local church which Packer valued so highly.

A further point concerns the way in which Trinity College, Bristol, was regarded by senior figures within the Church of England. By about 1975, Trinity was being seen as a theological college of the Church of England which seemed to have an increasingly tenuous connection with that church. Clearly, the possibility that this perception was misjudged or overstated must be conceded. Nevertheless, it existed. As a senior figure within the leadership of the college, this placed Packer in a difficult position. It suggested that he might have difficulty in obtaining a senior position within that church, when the time came for him to move on from Trinity.

For that move could not be delayed indefinitely. Packer had a great regard for Alec Motyer, the first principal of Trinity College and a much admired member of the teaching faculty of Tyndale Hall prior to its merger to form the united college. Motyer did not wish to spend the remainder of his ministry as principal of a theological college, and had indicated his interest in returning to a pastoral ministry at some point. Packer was clear that he could not see himself continuing at Trinity if Motyer were to leave. He had worked hard to build up his working relationship with Motyer, and would find it difficult to establish such a relationship with a future principal. Packer did not particularly want to succeed Motyer as principal. He disliked administration, and had noted how Motyer had been swamped at times with paperwork. He also knew that he would face some continuing hostility from council members, in the aftermath of the merger negotiations. This would either mean that he would not be offered the job in the first place, or that if it were offered to him, it would be against the wishes of a significant number of council members. That would hardly bode well for the critical working relationship between principal and council. No; it was better in his view that he thought in terms of leaving. Either he could move at his own convenience to a job which he liked the look of; or he could move at someone else's convenience, possibly to a job which he might not care for, but would have to accept for lack of something better available at that time. By late 1975, he was minded to leave, even if he had not publicly declared his slowly crystallizing views on this matter.

Many factors suggested that Packer's future might lie in North America, where he was highly respected and well known. This possibility had emerged as significant back in the mid-1960s, when it seemed for a while that, once Packer's first five years as warden of Latimer House expired, he would emigrate to North America for want of a suitable position in Britain. He was now a more senior figure, and could expect to receive offers from a number of institutions. But where should he settle in North America? The decision to move would not be easy, and had to be right.

Around this time, far away on the other side of the world, a former Oxford don was wondering who he should ask to fill a soon-to-be-vacant chair of theology. His mind had wandered back to the days when a young Oxford student attended his local Brethren church in east Oxford. He had made quite a name for himself since those days. But would he be interested? Finally, he made his decision. It was just after three o'clock in the morning local time. He lifted his phone, and placed an international call.

«10»

Vancouver, BC: Regent College, 1979–96

IN THE PREVIOUS chapter, we documented a series of concerns which led Packer to conclude that his future lay in North America. Our story now focuses on a gifted young Scottish student, who came to know Packer during his time as an undergraduate at Oxford. James M. Houston was carrying out research in geography at the time, which would eventually involve field work in Spain, and the publication of a series of works which led to him becoming recognized as a leading expert in this field. Had Houston pursued his career in geography, many of his former Oxford colleagues believe that he would have become one of Oxford's professors in this field. But Houston had other ideas; in fact, he had a vision for Christian education which had emerged during his time at Oxford, yet seemed incapable of realization in an Oxford context. It was in the Canadian city of Vancouver that the vision began to become reality, in the form of Regent College.

The Origins of Regent College

The full story of the origins and development of Regent College is likely to feature prominently in any future history of evangelicalism. Regent is now firmly established as one of the most significant institutions of theological education, with a remarkable ability to attract senior distinguished faculty. As evangelicalism becomes of increasing importance in the Pacific Rim, Regent – with its strong links with Asian communities in the greater Vancouver area, as well as in south-east Asia itself – is poised to make a still greater contribution in future.

The story of the origins of Regent College can best be understood as the happy convergence of a group of people with a need and a man with a vision which met that need. The origins of Regent College lie within the Christian Brethren, a group of Christians who traced their beginnings to a group of young men associated with Trinity College, Dublin, who pioneered the movement back in 1825. The movement soon spread, and became known in England as the 'Plymouth Brethren', on account of the establishment of a Brethren assembly in that town in 1831. The Brethren were noted for their concern for intense study of the Bible, and for the mature quality of their Christian discipleship. The influence of the movement in England can be judged from the fact that many senior members of the Oxford Inter-Collegiate Christian Union – such as Donald Wiseman and James Houston – in the immediate post-war period were members of the denomination. The leading British New Testament scholar of the post-war period, F.F. Bruce, was also a prominent member. The denomination was active in North America, where it had a significant presence in many major cities, including Vancouver.[1]

The issue of leadership of Brethren congregations (known as 'assemblies' within the denomination) became of increasing importance within the movement in North America during the 1950s and early 1960s. How were tomorrow's leaders to be educated and trained? In 1964, E. Marshall Sheppard, a prominent member of the Brethren in Vancouver, began to explore the possibility of establishing something locally in Vancouver. Although the proposals were perhaps not especially sharply focused at this stage, it is clear that Sheppard was moving towards the idea of a Brethren graduate school of theology. This idea was given further encouragement, and a certain degree of clarification, at the December 1964 convention of the Inter-Varsity Christian Fellowship, meeting at Urbana, Illinois.

Informal discussions now began to proceed apace, focusing on the specific needs of the denomination, the resources available in Vancouver, and the best model for any resulting institution of theological education. A 'School of Theology Committee' was formed early in 1965, chaired by Sheppard, exploring possibilities. By the late summer of 1965, they were ready to go public with an analysis of the needs and possibilities – and a specific proposal, which could, if accepted and implemented, be up and running by September 1969.[2]

Noting the increased number of students now entering higher education, the committee argued that the future leaders of their denomination would inevitably be drawn from among this constituency. It was therefore necessary to plan ahead, in order to provide suitable theological education for such leaders. The committee therefore proposed a graduate school of theology, to be located in the Vancouver area, on account of the strength of the denomination in this area. It was clear that this school of theology would, at least in part, be modelled on existing institutions, such as Fuller Seminary in California. Fuller had a high profile on the western seaboard of North America, including Vancouver; in addition, two student members of the committee – W. Ward Gasque and Donald Tinder – had studied at Fuller, and knew it well. However, the school would differ from Fuller in that it would reflect specifically Brethren needs and structures. The phrase 'a Brethren-orientated seminary for lay people' was often used to articulate this vision.

The Christian Brethren did not accept traditional church structures focused on the distinction between 'clergy' and 'laity'. The 'elders' of an assembly are generally not professional or full-time church workers, but retain employment in the secular world in addition to their pastoral and ministerial roles within the assembly. The Brethren have no ordained ministry, set apart for functions which other members of the assembly cannot carry out. The traditional role of a school of theology, however, was to train clergy. From the outset, the committee laid down a fundamental principle, reflecting the rejection of the 'layperson-clergy' distinction. Existing models of theological education would 'probably be modified to emphasize the training of laymen rather than the development of clergymen'.[3] The vision was therefore of a graduate school of theology, along the lines of an American seminary. Although students from other denominations would be welcomed to the proposed school of theology, it was clear from the outset that the teaching faculty and the board of trustees would be Brethren.

This analysis and proposal was thus firmly established by September 1965. Four years had been allowed for all necessary measures to be taken to put the proposal into practice. It was, however, only an idea. And ideas need to be backed up by the right people if they are to be implemented. So who was to be put in charge of the vision, which at this stage was nothing but a tender shoot which needed careful nurturing if it was to grow? It is necessary to focus our narrative on James Houston to make sense of the next development in this narrative.

James Mackintosh Houston was born as the first of three children to James and Ethel May Houston on 21 November 1922. Houston's parents, who had close links with the Plymouth Brethren, were missionaries in Spain who subsequently returned to Scotland to settle in Edinburgh. Houston entered the University of Edinburgh at the age of seventeen, and formed friendships with a number of Scottish evangelicals who would subsequently rise to theological prominence, including Thomas F. Torrance and James Torrance. He received an MA with first class honours in 1944, and was elected a gold medallist of the Royal Scottish Geographical Society. In 1945, he was awarded a research fellowship which allowed him to begin research at Hertford College, Oxford. In 1947, he was appointed to a lectureship at the School of Geography. He obtained his DPhil from Oxford in 1949. In 1964, he was elected a fellow of Hertford College. He would remain as a lecturer in geography and fellow of Hertford until he left Oxford in 1970.

Although he was professionally a geographer, Houston's heart was in theological education and above all spiritual formation. His friendship with C.S. Lewis had brought home to him the importance of mentorship in the Christian life,[4] and further reinforced his awareness of the need for a new vision for theological education, directed at the laity, aimed at deepening faith rather than just imparting theological knowledge. Maybe as early as 1961, and certainly by 1962, Houston had come to a series of conclusions as to what was needed in the world of Christian education. As a member of the Brethren, he felt a special concern for this area, and his experience at Oxford had convinced him of the need for some kind of institute for Christian studies on the campus of a major university. But which? Oxford was not a realistic possibility. No doors seemed to be opening. The vision was real and exciting, but it was far from clear if it would ever come to pass. History, after all, is littered with visions which came to nothing. It was then that Houston read the article in *Calling* which set out the vision of a graduate school of theology in Vancouver. Someone somewhere seemed to have convergent thoughts.

Houston was not, however, sure how to proceed from this point. It seemed improper to draw attention to his interest in the proposals. As a prominent member of the Brethren, with extensive educational experience at Oxford, he might well have been an obvious person to become involved with this visionary project. But it would have seemed presumptuous to write in response to the article. In the end, he chose to wait and see what happened.

In October 1969, news of the proposal reached England. Ward Gasque was by then undertaking doctoral research at the University of Manchester into the Acts of the Apostles under the direction of Professor F.F. Bruce, himself a distinguished member of the Christian Brethen. At the meeting of the Christian Brethren Research Fellowship, Gasque spoke of the proposals and their potential. Although Houston was not present on that occasion, others who knew him – and his vision for Christian education – were. It was not long before Houston and Gasque met, and discussed the proposal. Gasque gained the impression that Houston could well be the right person to head up the new school.

There are, however, reasons for thinking that some on the committee – including Marshall Sheppard – felt that the obvious choice was none other than F.F. Bruce himself. Bruce and his wife spent the months of July and August 1966 in New Zealand. They returned to England via Canada, to spend two weeks with their son Iain and his family in Newfoundland. They interrupted their journey in order to spend two or three days in Vancouver as guests of Marshall Sheppard. In addition to preaching at Granville Chapel, Bruce spent some time with the 'School of Theology Committee'.[5] No records of this meeting exist; it seems, however, that Bruce indicated that he would not be available to direct the project, and recommended Houston as a potential alternative.

Houston, who was in North America for a semester in 1967 as a visiting professor at the University of Texas, was invited to Vancouver to discuss the possibility with the committee. Houston outlined his vision for the new college, which differed at points from that originally envisaged by the committee. Houston recalls arguing for a school with three defining characteristics:

1. The school should be located on a university campus, and have some formal affiliation with that university;

2. The new institution should be a graduate school of theology, rather than a 'Bible school';[6]

3. The new school should be transdenominational and evangelical in character, rather than specifically Brethren in its outlook.

The second of these points posed no difficulties; it was already an integral part of the vision of the committee. The first, although not explicitly suggested by the committee, was clearly consistent with what they intended for the new school. It caused no difficulties, although it seems that few on the committee really understood Houston's belief that it was important to make a statement to the world about where and how theology should be done. Most saw the location of the school on the campus of the University of British Columbia as convenient and appropriate – but nothing more.

But it was the third point that caused some problems. It ran counter to the original proposal altogether, and caused controversy. However, Houston's vision for the school prevailed. Those who felt that his vision was flawed resigned from the committee; those who remained felt that Houston brought a significant degree of academic respectability to their project, and could see the merit of his transdenominational conception of the school. They were eventually able to shake hands on the deal.[7]

Nevertheless, this shift in emphasis would have major importance to the reputation in which Regent College was held in North American Brethren circles. Regent is probably the most important contribution made to North American evangelicalism by the Brethren in this region. However, from about 1975 Regent was increasingly marginalized within North American Brethren circles, which came to reflect attitudes more typical of fundamentalism. Houston's shift in emphasis can be argued to have led directly to this marginalization and the subsequent lionization of the college within evangelicalism as a whole.

By 1968, all the necessary work had been done to ensure that a charter would be granted by the provincial government for the new school. At this stage, the school was given a name. One of the committee members, who subsequently became a trustee of the school, was in the insurance business, and used the word 'regent' in the name of his insurance firm. It seemed an appropriate name for the new college. A 'regent' was a 'steward' or 'custodian'. What better name could there be for a college which hoped to stress the responsibilities of Christians to their Lord?

One issue concerning the origins of Regent College remains slightly unclear. Houston's three distinctives, as set out above, make no explicit reference to Regent College placing an emphasis, let alone defining its mission solely or explicitly, in terms of *lay* Christian education. In part, this rests on a series of assumptions, inherited from the Brethren constituency which was of foundational importance in relation to the college, concerning the nature of ministry: all ministry, in some sense, is lay, in that there is no formal 'ordination' or professional group of 'clergy' to be educated in some distinctive manner. As it became clear that Regent would exercise a significant ministry to people from outside Brethren circles, it became increasingly important to articulate the school's vision in terms which would be understood by others. The increasing use of the term 'lay' can be seen as an attempt to convey a Brethren understanding of ministry in language familiar to non-Brethren, for whom the clergy-laity distinction was routine.

Despite this emphasis on lay ministry, it seems to be clear that some form of professional Christian training for ministry was in the minds of the committee which formulated the original vision for Regent College. If this were the case, it would be inevitable that, sooner or later, Regent would wish to offer the degree of Master of Divinity (MDiv), widely seen as the standard qualification for those who wished to proceed to ordination in North American churches. This issue was debated within Regent in the period leading up to the introduction of this degree in 1979 and the associated decision to collaborate with a local Baptist institution (Carey Hall), which had the necessary resources to provide seminary training, especially in the areas of pastoral studies. All this, however, lay in the future; we must return to the granting of the 1968 charter to Regent College, and explore what happened subsequently.

It was decided that the best way of preparing the ground for the opening of the new school was to inaugurate a series of summer schools in Vancouver.[8] Regent College was scheduled to open its doors in September 1970 (a year later than the original committee had intended), with preparatory summer schools in 1968 and 1969. The numbers attending were encouraging.[9] At this stage, Regent

College did not possess any buildings of its own, and rented space in the basement of the Presbyterian school (Union Theological College) on the University of British Columbia (UBC) campus. The enrolment for the first year was less than ten. Tragically, nearly half of these incoming students were killed in a car accident on the first day of term. As a result, a mere four students finally registered for the first one-year 'Diploma in Christian Studies'.

From then on, the new school never looked back. Its relentless growth forced it to reconsider its accommodation arrangements. The basement of Union Theological College (which subsequently became part of the 'Vancouver School of Theology' following the merger of three denominational schools in 1971) soon became too small to cope with the large numbers of students now attending classes. By 1973, there were sixty-three full-time students. It was clearly time to make other arrangements. Houston got wind of a significant possibility the following year. UBC, like most North American universities, operated a fraternity system. A series of fraternity houses had been built along Wesbrook Mall, on the eastern perimeter of the UBC campus. Houston heard that two of these had become vacant, and moved to secure them for the fledgling college. The premises were small and cramped – but they were adequate, and they were on the UBC campus, a matter of no small importance to Houston. Regent College would remain on this site until a purpose-built and more spacious building was opened in 1989.

Houston was convinced that Regent College needed to be affiliated to UBC in order to secure its academic reputation and attract suitable students.[10] He made this a priority of his first period as principal.[11] In 1972, Regent was affiliated with the Vancouver School of Theology (VST), which had close links with UBC. There are reasons for thinking that this affiliation may have rested on verbal assurances from Houston to Jim Martin (principal of VST) that Regent would not enter into competition with VST (for example, by offering the MDiv). Houston's growing emphasis on the importance of lay education may thus, at this stage, have partly been intended to assure VST that Regent did not intend to become a seminary, and thus attract students for the ordained ministry of mainline churches in western Canada away from the merged school.

Houston, however, wanted something more than this – direct

affiliation with UBC for Regent as an institution in its own right. The UBC Senate was suspicious. They had already granted affiliation to VST; why should they recognize another religious institution? In addition, Regent was a recent newcomer to the scene, whereas the various constituent elements of the VST had been around for some time. Houston, who had argued for the distinctive identity of Regent, recalls his sense that the Senate vote would go against him. He therefore decided to argue for conditional recognition – that the UBC Senate should have the right to withdraw recognition from Regent after one year if it was in any way dissatisfied with its new affiliate. The Senate was thus not being asked to take some irreversible step, and had a way out if it needed it. It was enough to swing the vote Houston's way. When the matter came up for review a year later, the motion to renew affiliation for a further four years was passed without serious objections. Finally, in 1977 the Senate voted to recognize Regent without imposing any time limit.

So Houston finally secured a core component of his vision – academic recognition of a Christian graduate school of theology on a major university campus. Two of the founding faculty – Houston and Bill Martin – both taught part-time at UBC for a while. Yet it must be noted that, despite its close proximity to UBC and its affiliate status, Regent never really entered into the life of the university. Houston gradually shifted his interests from the university to the business community, reflecting a growing conviction that the best interests of Regent would be served by stressing the links between theology and everyday life.

The Background to Packer's Appointment

Regent was now well on its way to becoming a theological school, in line with its founders' vision. A theological school, however, requires a theological faculty. One of Houston's most immediate concerns was to build up a faculty which would be of sufficient quality to attract graduate students in sufficient numbers to sustain the school's vision. The first two major appointments were in biblical studies. Ward Gasque, who had now completed his doctoral studies at Manchester, was appointed assistant professor of New Testament; Carl E. Armerding was appointed assistant professor of Old Testament. Given anticipated student numbers in those early days, it was impossible to make other full-time appointments.[12] Houston himself taught in the area of 'interdisciplinary and environmental studies'. By 1974, student numbers were buoyant; it proved possible to make Regent's first full-time appointment in theology – Clark H. Pinnock.

Pinnock was an excellent choice. He was a Canadian, who had studied under F.F. Bruce at Manchester, and subsequently served as professor of New Testament and systematic theology at New Orleans Baptist Theological Seminary. He thus had the international experience which Houston wished to foster within Regent College. Pinnock had established himself as a leading younger theologian within North American evangelicalism through major writings in the areas of revelation and apologetics, including *A Defense of Biblical Infallibility* (1967), *Set Forth Your Case* (1967), *Evangelism and Truth* (1969), and *Biblical Revelation: The Foundation of Christian Theology* (1971).[13] Pinnock's growing reputation is known to have been a significant factor in attracting students to the college. But he was not to be a permanent presence.

In 1977, Pinnock departed from Regent to take up a position in McMaster Divinity School, Ontario. The move did not come as a surprise; Pinnock had indicated his intention to leave the previous year. A huge gap loomed, not simply in Regent's teaching faculty, but also in its reputation and potential ability to attract students. There was an urgent need to find a major international theologian, of sufficient personal stature to ensure Regent's continued excellence in this area. The search began in 1976.

Houston had no doubt about who he wanted to attract to this position, and set about the business of approaching him. It was at this point that he made the telephone call mentioned at the close of the previous chapter. Packer remembers receiving that call; it was to prove a turning point, although he did not realize it at the time. He was working in his study at Trinity College Bristol one morning in 1976, when the telephone rang. It was 11.10. The caller turned out to be Houston, who asked Packer whether he would be interested in a chair of theology which Clark Pinnock was in the process of vacating.

Packer knew about Regent; he had visited the institution, and was thoroughly in favour of what he found, especially its implicit emphasis on breaking down the barriers between clergy and laity. He saw this as paralleling the kind of ethos which he and Alec

Motyer were attempting to create at Trinity. It was not the first invitation he had received to relocate on the other side of the Atlantic, and he had become quite used to turning such approaches down with gentle firmness. He asked Houston if he would be kind enough to write his ideas down, and he would give it careful thought. However, it was his expectation that he would not be able to accept the invitation.

The letter arrived a week later. Packer studied it, initially with the intention of being able to tell Houston, with integrity, that he had given the proposal his full consideration, but did not think that it would be appropriate. However, as he read Houston's letter, he began to realize that the proposal had a lot going for it. Negatively, he was frustrated with his situation in England, on the basis of the considerations noted earlier, and could see no hope of things improving in the next few years. Positively, he was attracted to Regent College. He knew and respected Houston from their time together in Oxford in the late 1940s, and the prospect of working along with him was attractive. Houston was committed to the idea of peer-parity within the faculty of Regent College, an idea which Packer had tried to ensure was incorporated into the structure of Trinity College at the time of the merger. *And there would be no administration!* In addition, Packer liked Vancouver, and he liked Canada, which seemed to him to be culturally half-way between Britain and the United States. If he had to move to North America, it would be to Canada, rather than the United States.

Going to Regent would also fit in well with his bilateral strategy, which led him to focus both on Anglicanism and on transdenominational evangelicalism. In England, he was employed at an Anglican theological school, and used this as a base for his transdenominational ministry. At Regent, he would be employed at a transdenominational school, which he could use as a base for his ministry within Anglicanism. This would be much more difficult if he were to be employed by a North American theological school with a specific denominational commitment.

Houston's letter thus acted as a stimulus to Packer's thoughts concerning the future. It helped him focus his frustrations concerning the ecclesiastical and educational weaknesses of English Christianity. And it seemed to open the door to a very satisfying future prospect. Packer's mother had died in 1965, and his father in 1972. He thus had no further family responsibilities in England. His children's education could be arranged.

However, Packer felt that he could not leave England at that stage. Uppermost in his mind was NEAC 2, the congress which had been summoned to Nottingham in April 1977. Packer's misgivings about this venture were well known. He felt that leaving England immediately before the congress would be interpreted in unhelpful ways by some. It could lead to him being portrayed as walking out of the Church of England. He was also concerned about his relationship with evangelicals in the free churches. After his 1970 split with Martyn Lloyd-Jones, Packer found himself in a somewhat ambivalent relationship with his free church brethren. His relations with many remained warm and friendly; he had, however, been frozen out of the Lloyd-Jones circles. To leave so soon after the split might be seen as indicating that Packer was fed up with free church evangelicals. It was not a message that he wished to convey.

Another consideration which influenced Packer's decision was the clear need for an increased evangelical presence in Canada, especially its great cities. When John Stott was considering what future shape his ministry might take after twenty-five years of ministry at All Souls, Langham Place, he consulted a number of colleagues, including Packer, over where he might best be used. Packer replied that Stott should consider emigrating to Canada, settling in Toronto, and 'doing the All Souls thing' in that great city. There was a need for someone of Stott's calibre in that country. Packer's advice given to Stott in the early 1970s was clearly based on considerations which would subsequently influence his own judgment: Canadian Christianity needed evangelicals in positions of leadership.

And finally, Packer could not overlook the fact that Regent College would give him more time to write than Trinity ever could. It was an important consideration, for Packer was clear that an integral part of his vocation was to write books which would encourage, sustain and inform the church.

After much thought, in which all the issues noted above played a significant part, Packer wrote his reply to Houston. He would probably say 'yes' – but he would not be in a position to move before 1979. One of the reasons for suggesting this timeframe related to NEAC 2. Packer felt he needed to wait sufficiently long after this congress before announcing his move. He did not wish a decision to leave England to be interpreted as personal pique. NEAC was only one of a number of considerations which were conclusively pointing towards accepting the Regent offer. Packer thus indicated his positive feelings towards the possibility, without any firm commitment.

That reply, however, was enough to allow Houston to put the faculty recruitment procedure at Regent into operation. During one of his tours of North America, Packer inconspicuously spent a period of twenty-four hours at Regent. He later discovered that Klaus Bockmuehl (then teaching at St Chrischona Bible Seminary, in Switzerland) was also being interviewed for a faculty position at the college, Houston having approached him in much the same way as he had Packer. To begin with, the Regent Council felt that they would have to choose between Packer and Bockmuehl; by the end of their discussions, however, the decision had swung to employing them both. Bockmuehl was able to move to Vancouver with relative ease later in 1977; Packer had to insist on a 'waiting period', not on account of any reluctance on his part, but due to his need to serve out his time in England. No announcement of any kind would be made. Packer had not yet finally said 'yes'; but he was morally certain that he would accept.

A further development which seemed to confirm the rightness of the move to Vancouver took place in 1978, when Packer learned that Harry S.D. Robinson, a noted evangelical, had moved to Vancouver to become rector of St John's Shaughnessy. Robinson offered Packer an honorary assistantship in his parish. Packer, who had always regarded active involvement in a local Anglican church as central to his ministry, had been unaware that this move was in the offing. Indeed, one of the considerations which weighed against a move to Vancouver was the apparent absence of a suitable church with which to get involved. Robinson's move appeared to the Packers to be a sign of an especially welcoming providence. Things seemed to be falling into place.

Packer came to his final decision during the Regent College Summer School of 1978. He and Kit had been invited to spend three weeks in Vancouver, allowing Packer to teach a basic course in systematic theology. Packer was clear that he could not make a final commitment without allowing Kit to experience Vancouver at first hand, and decide whether she felt she could settle there. This period of immersion proved to be the final stage in the process of acceptance. Kit liked Vancouver; Packer then agreed firmly to accept the offer which had been made to him. The announcement was then made, at the end of Packer's contribution to the summer school, that Packer would return in September 1979 to take up a full-time faculty position at Regent College. On returning from Regent to Bristol, Packer told Motyer of his decision, which subsequently filtered through to staff and students alike. No formal announcement needed to be made.

The news that Packer was to leave England for Canada surprised and distressed many back home. It came like a bolt from the blue. Many were saddened that the English church was to lose Packer's gifts and talents. Some, perhaps with inflated views of the importance of England, felt that his move was to the general loss of Christianity, apparently unaware of the new opportunities for ministry which his new position would bring. Packer himself never felt that he was leaving the centre of the world to move to its circumference, being aware of the strategic importance of Vancouver for the Pacific Rim.

And so the preparations began for the move. The Packers were able to spend some time looking around Vancouver during the summer school, and get an idea of what kind of property there was in the area, and what its likely cost would be. Ward Gasque advised the Packers to rent property for their first year in Vancouver, to allow them time to look around and find somewhere suitable. However, the price of real estate in Vancouver began to surge at this time, and the Packers felt that there was no point in postponing buying a house if they could find somewhere suitable immediately.

So in May 1979, Kit travelled to Vancouver, with the object of finding and buying suitable property. Harry Robinson, the newly-appointed rector of St John's Shaughnessy, was an old friend of Packer, and was able to help Kit with the practicalities of choosing a house. About half-way through her stay, Kit found a house that seemed to her to be ideal – 2398 West 34th Street.[14] The asking price was $140,000. Kit was able to negotiate the price down by $1,000. By realizing all their assets, the Packers were able to buy it. It seemed to both Packer and Kit that the remarkable ease with which they had been able to find a suitable house was God's confirmation that the proposed move to Vancouver would have his blessing.

The move was not without its problems. Three contractors were approached for quotations for moving the Packer family effects to Vancouver. The most economical was a firm based in Somerset. So their personal possessions were duly loaded into a container for the long sea journey to the west coast of Canada. The routine for exporting goods in this way was well established, and involved sending on by airmail in advance of the container a 'manifest' (that is, a document setting out the full contents of the container) for the Canadian customs to examine at the point of entry, and thus authorize the unloading of the container and its contents. It was a routine matter, and Packer gave it no further thought. Until they arrived in Vancouver, that is, and found that there was no sign of their belongings. The container turned out to have been impounded by the customs, who would not release it without the proper and necessary documents.

It did not take long to find out what had happened. The firm had mailed the manifest to Vancouver; the secretary entrusted with this task, however, had failed to realize that Vancouver was in Canada, and had used a postage stamp sufficient for domestic postage only. As a result, the manifest had been sent by surface mail, and had failed to arrive in time. As it happened, it duly turned up – four months later. The Packers had to go through a complex process of arranging for a customs broker to take charge of proceedings. Packer was angry and frustrated. However, eventually the container was cleared through customs, and delivered to 2398 West 34th Street. It seemed that all was now well. Until, that is, the container was opened. It was estimated that the damage to the contents came to over $1,000.

Eventually, repairs were made and the removers' insurance paid up – but it added considerably to the stress of the move.

Professor of Theology at Regent College

Packer began his teaching at Regent in September 1979. One hundred and forty students were registered for that year. Packer found his first year at Regent immensely stimulating. Many of his students were able and enthusiastic, and a joy to teach. The Regent to which Packer returned was not quite the same as that he had visited back in 1977. There had been significant personnel changes.

Houston had been appointed by the board to the newly-created position of Chancellor, and had been succeeded as principal by Carl Armerding. It was a difficult, and somewhat painful, time for Houston. Armerding had brought in a series of measures designed to enhance the appeal and profile of the college, most notably setting up an MDiv course.

This development caused some friction with the Vancouver School of Theology, who saw it as a move into their own territory – ordination training – and necessitated the ending of the affiliation of Regent with the VST. The principal of VST clearly regarded this step as a betrayal of an assurance that Regent would not offer competition to academic activities already offered by VST. Further tensions between Regent and VST arose over other issues, including theological differences between the schools, squabbling over library rights, and increasing alarm within VST over Regent's rapid growth at a time of stagnation within the traditional school. It was clear that VST could no longer be a partner with Regent. Regent responded to this development the following year by entering into a working relationship with Carey Hall, a theological college of the Baptist Union of Western Canada.

One of Packer's administrative responsibilities related to the provision of library facilities. Up to this point, Regent had supposed that it could survive by allowing its students to make use of other people's libraries – specifically, those of the VST and the University of British Columbia. By 1980, VST were charging Regent something in the region of $50,000 per annum for the use of their library. Economics clearly pointed towards Regent investing in its own working library, and Klaus Bockmuehl was particularly concerned, as a matter of principle, that Regent should have its own independent library resources and acquisitions policies. It was not long before the second of the two fraternity houses was converted into library facilities, with the two floors of the building eventually being entirely devoted to books. The expansion of library facilities, though necessary, caused increase pressure on the space available for administrative, faculty and teaching resources. The lessons which were learned about the use of space at this stage found their application in the design of the new building, which was eventually opened in 1989.

Packer's presence at Regent College considerably increased its profile in North America and beyond, and acted as a powerful draw for student recruitment. In the mid-1970s, Regent was a tiny institution, using borrowed rooms; by the end of the 1980s, Regent was the largest graduate institution of theological education in the region, with a new purpose-built home on a high-profile site on the university campus. There is no doubt that Packer played a major role in ensuring the continuing rise in fame of the school. The year 1985 marked a landmark for Regent, in that it then secured accreditation from the Association of Theological Schools in the face of intense opposition from other Canadian schools (including VST) who clearly regarded Regent as a major competitor.

As numbers increased, the old buildings came increasingly under strain. In 1985, the year in which accreditation was achieved, the college was attracting nearly 450 students. Two converted fraternity houses were simply not able to cope with the large numbers of students the college was now drawing. It was clear that new premises were required. After careful negotiations with the University of British Columbia, a building site (consisting of the old fraternity house site and the adjacent vacant corner lot at the intersection of Wesbrook Mall and University Boulevard) was secured, and funds raised. The new building was opened in 1989, a tangible symbol of the new strength of the college and the ethos which it represented. The imposing building, fronted by a small park, occupies a prime site on the eastern perimeter of the UBC campus, directly opposite Gate 1.

Packer's main teaching commitment was in historical and systematic theology. He offered four main lecture courses,[15] each of which is directly based on teaching which he had carefully developed and perfected during his time at Trinity College, Bristol (see pp. 182–6).

Systematic Theology I: Knowledge of God
This course seeks to explicate in the context of modern discussion the historic Christian belief that the sole source of reliable knowledge of God our Creator and Saviour is Holy Scripture. Different elements in this conviction and different interpretations of it will be explored, and the course as a whole will constitute a full-scale introduction to systematic theology from the standpoint of its method.

Systematic Theology II: Doctrine of God, Creation and Man
This course deals with God – his existence, nature, character and triune unity; Creation and providence – God as maker and upholder;

and Humanity – our nature, dependence, destiny and fallenness. To think and talk about these matters with biblical correctness and logical clarity is the hardest task that adult minds ever face; reviewing rival options in reliance on the written Word, we shall try to plot paths through the jungle.

Systematic Theology III: Christology and Soteriology

Themes explored include God's plan of salvation, the person and place of Jesus Christ, grace, faith and salvation, calling, conversion, regeneration, repentance, union with Christ, justification, adoption, freedom, universalism, the place of the Holy Spirit, concepts of sanctification, ethics and spirituality, healing, the corporate dimension of Christian life, and Calvinism and Arminianism: sovereignty, preservation, apostasy. The aim throughout is to provide theological resources for personal life and pastoral ministry. Rival options, past and present, will be compared.

Systematic Theology IV: Ecclesiology and Eschatology

In this century the church has become a focus of Christian concern, partly because its outward divisions (Roman Catholic, Orthodox, and the many Protestant national churches and denominations) are felt to be a scandal and an obstruction to evangelism and growth, partly because its inward divisions (evangelical, liberal, catholic, neo-orthodox, charismatic) are chronically painful to live with. The Bible is and always was the book of the church, reflecting as well as directing its life. This course reviews the biblical materials and the different ways of understanding them.

The certainty that one's life in this world will end; the agony of losing loved ones; the threat of ecological doomsday for our planet; the pastoral demands of Christian ministry to the bereaved and frightened; the spectacle of the church apparently losing ground, and of millions leaving this world without even having encountered the Christian gospel: all compel careful study of things to come. This course seeks to clarify and explore all aspects of the Christian hope.

In addition to this demanding teaching programme, Packer and Kit were involved in the pastoral care of students. A college 'Community Group' would meet weekly at their home, and Kit was active in the college wives' group.

Packer's initial appointment was as professor of historical and systematic theology. However, in 1989 his position was upgraded; he became the holder of the first endowed chair at Regent College. On 11 December 1989, Packer was formally installed as the first Sangwoo Youtong Chee Professor of Theology. This chair (which was almost invariably referred to the 'Chee Chair' in internal Regent discussions) had been endowed by two sons, one a prominent member of Vancouver's increasingly significant Chinese community, the other a businessman in Hong Kong, in memory of their father, who had been a distinguished lay leader there. The endowment was an important confirmation of the growing importance of the Cantonese Christian community, which was also reflected in other developments at Regent around this time, including the initiation of a Chinese Studies Programme in 1985.

Vancouver proved to be a base from which Packer could develop his ministry to the United States. As has often been pointed out,[16] Packer's enormous influence in the States has come about without his ever residing in that country. Until 1979, he lived in England; from 1979, in Canada. Packer's substantial base of influence rests partly upon his publications, and partly upon his extensive speaking ministry in the United States. Residing in Vancouver gave him easy access to the United States, allowing him to undertake a number of major speaking engagements from 1979 onwards.

After allowing himself the fall of 1979 and all of 1980 to settle in at Regent, Packer resumed a brutal speaking schedule. Major lecture series included the Ryan Lectures at Asbury Theological Seminary in Wilmore, Kentucky (1982); the Staley Lectures at the Lutheran Bible Institute in Seattle (1982); the Day-Higginbotham Lectures at Southwestern Seminary in Fort Worth, Texas (1985); and the Reformation Heritage Lectures at Beeson Divinity School in Birmingham, Alabama (1994). In addition, he undertook visits to a large number of divinity schools, including Canadian Theological Seminary in Regina, Saskatoon (1981), Conservative Baptist Seminary in Denver, Colorado (1982), and the Bible Institute of Hawaii (1983). He also served as visiting professor (generally involving extended or repeat visits) to Reformed Theological Seminary in Jackson, Mississippi (from 1985); New College, Berkeley (from 1985) and Westminster Theological Seminary, Escondido, California (from 1982).

Packer's teaching ministry at Regent led to him becoming involved in many of the debates which were widespread within evangelicalism at that time. It is widely accepted that two of the most important debates within evangelicalism during the period 1970–95 centred on the ministry of women and the role of the

Holy Spirit. Packer was actively involved in both these debates. In February 1991, he contributed an article to *Christianity Today* entitled 'Let's Stop Making Women Presbyters'.[17] In this article, Packer argued that five factors could be discerned as underlying the widespread trend within many Protestant denominations to ordain women to ministry.

1. The feminist movement has heightened the demands for equal opportunities for women within the churches.

2. Since the Second World War, women have been moving towards positions of equality with men throughout society.

3. The present-day application of biblical passages which debar women from certain areas of ministry is seen to be problematical. Was Paul prohibiting women's ministry only in his own local situation, or issuing a permanent prohibition? The former view was gaining sway.

4. God appears to have blessed the ministry of women.

5. Christian professionals who are denied this status are lacking full job satisfaction.

Packer's concern was that secular, pragmatic and social factors were dominating the debate, with authentically biblical considerations being marginalized. For Packer, 'the creation pattern, as biblically set forth, is: man to lead, woman to support; man to initiate, woman to enable; man to take responsibility for the well-being of woman, woman to take responsibility for helping man'. Presbyters are set apart for a role of authoritative pastoral leadership, which is reserved for 'manly men rather than womanly women, according to the creation pattern which redemption restores'.

The article created a stir at Regent, which had a large number of women students by this stage. Ward Gasque, a senior member of the Regent community, was publicly identified with the group 'Christians for Biblical Equality'. The general (but not the only) reaction of women students at Regent was that they were pleased that Packer felt able to set out his views in this way, but they disagreed with him profoundly on the point at issue. Reaction was not slow in coming from other quarters. *Christianity Today* received a large number of responses to Packer's article. Some were laudatory; most were not. Cornelius Plantinga, a professor of theology at Calvin Theological Seminary, took issue with Packer's theology, arguing that Jesus's maleness was not fundamental to his role as Saviour: 'One might as well argue that because God incarnate was Jewish, single and an inhabitant of a pastoral setting, that Jewishness, bachelorhood and thorough knowledge of sheep are all basic to Jesus's saving us.' A student at Fuller Theological Seminary wrote to complain that Packer failed to take into account the idea of a call from God. If God called women to preach or lead, what could they do but preach or lead?[18] Packer began to sense that he was *persona non grata* at the Pasadena seminary from the appearance of that article.

The second major area of debate concerned the charismatic movement, which first became a major force in western Christianity during the 1970s. Packer was a close observer of this development, and an acute analyst of its significance for evangelicalism. The rediscovery of spiritual gifts is linked with the movement known as Pentecostalism, generally regarded as the first modern movement to demonstrate clearly charismatic inclinations. Although this movement can be argued to have long historical roots, its twentieth-century development is generally traced back to the ministry of Charles Fox Parham (1873–1929), and events at the Azusa Street Mission, Los Angeles, in 1906–8.[19] The full impact of the charismatic movement within evangelicalism, however, dates from the 1960s. The incident which brought it to public attention took place in Van Nuys, California. The rector of the local Episcopalian church, Dennis Bennett, told his congregation that he had been filled with the Holy Spirit and had spoken in tongues. Reaction varied from bewilderment to outrage; the local Episcopalian bishop promptly banned speaking in tongues from his churches.

However, it soon became clear that others had shared Bennett's experience. Philip E. Hughes, a noted evangelical theologian, witnessed the phenomenon at first hand, and wrote up his experiences for both the North American *Christianity Today* and the September 1962 edition of the British evangelical journal *The Churchman*.[20] Hughes reported that he was convinced that 'the Breath of the Living God is stirring among the dry bones of the major, respectable, old-fashioned denominations, and particularly within the Episcopal Church'. From that moment, the Holy Spirit was firmly on the agenda of evangelicalism.[21]

In Britain, there was initially some confusion over what was happening. To some, the new experiences being reported seemed to be capable of being explained on the basis of the Keswick approach (see pp. 23–4), which interpreted the experience in terms of an intensification of an existing spirituality. Martyn Lloyd-Jones introduced the subject for discussion at a meeting of the Westminster Fellowship on 8 October 1962, reading from Dennis Bennett's testimony in doing so. It is widely thought that the issue began to become of major importance in Britain early the following year, when it became clear that a number of younger Anglican clergy had experienced some form of charismatic renewal, with St Mark's, Gillingham, becoming especially significant. Having great respect for Lloyd-Jones's judgment, four Anglican clergy (three of whom served at St Mark's, Gillingham) arranged to meet him in London on 9 April 1963. The four were John Collins, Michael Harper, David MacInnes and David Watson – each of whom would become a major figure in the English charismatic movement as it subsequently developed.[22] Lloyd-Jones listened to the four describing their experiences, before telling them of something similar which had happened to him during the summer of 1949, during a visit to the Hebrides. Lloyd-Jones concluded that they had 'been baptized in the Holy Spirit'.

Although the movement in Britain initially had its greatest impact within the evangelical wing of the Church of England, it soon came to spread far beyond, particularly through the rise of the 'house church' movement. Controversy focused on a number of issues, particularly the question of the nature and value of 'baptism in the Holy Spirit', and the value of speaking in tongues, especially in relation to public worship. There is little doubt that the charismatic movement has brought fresh life to the church through its rediscovery of the role of the Holy Spirit in Christian life and experience. Many of those who had regarded Christianity as simply 'right believing' have discovered the power and delight of an immediate and direct experience of God in their lives, often accompanied by such outward manifestations of the presence of the Spirit as speaking in tongues. Yet this new emphasis upon the role of the Holy Spirit has also brought with it tensions and controversy, most notably over the issue of the importance of experience of the Spirit in the normal Christian life, and the relation between word and Spirit.

Packer has been a significant voice – indeed, at times, it has to be said, a lonely voice – in this important discussion since the late 1960s.[23] We have already noted Packer's strategy, evident in his involvement in the book *Growing into Union* (pp. 155–6), of collaborating where possible with others who were committed to basic Christian orthodoxy. By the early 1970s, it was clear to Packer that the charismatic movement was coming of age, and needed to be taken seriously and viewed positively by evangelicals. The growing strength of the charismatic movement gave new relevance to Packer's concern and ability to bridge the theological and experiential divide between classic evangelicalism and the charismatic movement. Packer's concern for spirituality and evangelical collaboration naturally led to his taking this new movement seriously, where other senior evangelical figures tended to dismiss it. Indeed, Packer was one of the few actively working during the 1970s to forge bridges in this way, at a time when many senior evangelicals within the Church of England were inclined to view the movement with hostility, especially over the issue of 'baptism in the Spirit'.

The issue emerged as of particular importance in 1974. The Senior Eclectic Conference of that year brought together a number of significant evangelicals, including John Stott, to discuss the progress made since the National Evangelical Anglican Congress of 1967 (see pp. 128–33). The conference met at Swanwick, a conference centre in the east Midlands much used by evangelical organizations. Packer concluded his survey of developments since Keele by turning to address some of the issues which arose from the growing strength of the charismatic movement. Surely, Packer argued, the time had come for non-charismatic evangelicals to appreciate that there was sufficient 'essential evangelicalism' within the charismatic movement to allow the former to begin to relate to the latter in strongly positive terms, and begin working with them on matters of importance.

It was the final point in Packer's address, and it proved to be the most important. After the ensuing discussion, John Stott caused a small group to meet together with a view of exploring ways of strengthening links between evangelicals and charismatics, and invited Packer and John Baker (a noted Calvinist who trained at Tyndale Hall, Bristol) to draft a statement. Michael Harper, by then firmly established as a charismatic leader, wrote an article for the *Church of England Newspaper* around that time in which he drew attention to the 'charismatic divide' within Anglican evangelicalism. For Harper, there was an urgent need for dialogue, with a view to reconciling differences and overcoming misunderstandings and estrangements. Packer's address was to prove vitally important in establishing such a dialogue.

The 'Gospel and Spirit' group (as it came to be known) drew together leading evangelicals from the Church of England Evangelical Council (including both Stott and Packer) and charismatics (including Michael Harper and David Watson) from the Fountain Trust (founded in 1966 to strengthen the charismatic presence within English Christianity). The group met together for four day conferences over a period of eighteen months, and was finally able to issue a joint statement. It is widely agreed that this statement was of fundamental importance in ensuring that the charismatic issue was not a cause of division at the Second National Anglican Evangelical Congress of 1977 (see pp. 213–17). The group issued a statement which went some considerable way towards creating a much more positive relationship between the two groups.

The 'Gospel and Spirit' statement opened by noting that the failure to establish dialogue between charismatics and others may have 'helped to prolong unnecessary misunderstandings and polarizations'. While recognizing that they did 'not all see eye to eye on every point', they affirmed that 'what unites us is far greater than the matters on which some of us still disagree'. The statement affirmed that the two groups 'share the same evangelical faith', and declared the intention of the two groups to work together more closely in the future. Perhaps the most helpful sections of the statement dealt with the controversial issues of 'baptism in the Spirit' and 'speaking in tongues'. A common concern for renewal allowed these differences in emphasis to be seen in their proper perspective. The statement ended by setting out a vision not merely of 'renewed individuals but a renewed and revived church, alive with the life of Christ, subject to the word of Christ, filled with the Spirit of Christ, fulfilling the ministry of Christ, constrained by the love of Christ, preaching the good news of Christ, and thrilled in its worship by the glory of Christ'. It was a powerful and moving vision, and went some considerable way towards healing old wounds and divisions, and creating a new environment of trust and mutual respect.

This development clearly shows Packer's interest in the Holy

Spirit, and illustrates both the nature and the vital importance of his strategic vision of encouraging collaboration between ortho- dox Christians. The 'Gospel and Spirit' document represented a milestone within the evangelical revival in England, and laid the foundations for further growth and development, both within the church at large and especially within student circles (where charismatic issues were hotly debated). Ronald Inchley's insistence that Packer should write a book for the Inter-Varsity Fellowship on the Holy Spirit (which eventually led to Packer offering *Knowing God* to Hodder & Stoughton: see p. 188) rested on the entirely accurate perception that the Holy Spirit was becoming a significant issue in student Christianity, and that Packer was well placed to address the issues arising. The constructive yet critical theology set out in Packer's *Keep in Step with the Spirit* can be seen as a 'coming-of-age gift' offered to the charismatic movement, both as a mark of appreciation and a guideline for future reflection. The work is notable for both its strongly biblical and Reformed framework for approaching the charismatic movement and for its equally strong affirmation of the divine authenticity of characteristic charismatic experiences, despite what Packer saw as the theologically improper way in which these were often explained. He distances himself both from the 'orthodoxism' (if we might use this word) that will not recognize a work of God when the accompanying theology is deficient, and from the 'experientialism' that treats ambiguous experiences as unambiguously self-authenticating without overall biblical assessment. He recalls his readers to the God who according to Scripture revives his work by renewing his people in repentance, the God whose power in this regard the West has not yet fully seen. The book earned a Gold Medallion award from the Evangelical Christian Publishers' Association, and is unquestionably one of Packer's more significant works, repaying close reading.

Yet Packer did not wish to write such a book until he had researched it thoroughly. He had already explored the Keswick view of the role of the Holy Spirit while on the teaching staff of Tyndale Hall, Bristol, in the 1950s. In 1967, he addressed the Puritan and Reformed Studies Conference on the theme of 'The Puritans and Spiritual Gifts', in which he touched on the relation of the classical Puritan witness to the growing interest (and controversy!) over this issue.[24] Later, while serving at Trinity College, he researched the theme in greater depth, publishing his findings as a substantial two-part article in the English evangelical journal *The Churchman*.[25] He was also able to develop his thinking on John Wesley's views on the role of the Holy Spirit when he gave the 1982 Ryan Lectures at Asbury Theological Seminary in Kentucky. Packer's most careful statements on the person and work of the Spirit can be seen in his 1984 work *Keep in Step with the Spirit*, which incorporates much of this research.[26]

For Packer, the most reliable way of understanding the work of the Holy Spirit was to affirm that 'the Spirit makes known the personal presence in and with the Christian and the church of the risen, reigning Saviour, the Jesus of history who is the Christ of faith'. This comprehensive statement aims to avoid getting sidelined into debates about the place of speaking in tongues and the like, and instead to discern the general divine strategy lying behind the work of the Spirit. The Spirit 'empowers, enables, purges and leads generation after generation of sinners to face the reality of God . . . in order that Christ may be known, loved, trusted, honoured and praised'. Packer stresses the connection between the Holy Spirit and Jesus Christ, refusing to see the Spirit simply as a 'heightener of religious consciousness' or a 'communicator by inner urges'.

Packer's understanding of the work of the Spirit is strongly biblical, based on a comprehensive analysis of all biblical texts having a bearing on the matter.

Inevitably, Packer's discussion of the work of the Spirit leads him into controversy. In affirming one view of the matter, he is obliged to correct others where he regards them as deficient. Yet the tone of the work is strongly pacific. Even in his criticism of the Keswick holiness teaching (which he subjected to a devastating critique in 1955 – see pp. 76–80), we find a measured assessment of the teaching in question, with a studied determination to affirm the positive intentions of those who held to this position.

The Importance of Tradition for Evangelicals

One of Packer's most important contributions to the development of modern evangelicalism is his insistence on the importance of tradition. Noting the individualism and shallowness of much American evangelicalism, Packer stressed the importance of learning from the wisdom of the past. His studies of the Puritans often caused him to reflect that the past produced theological and spiritual giants, in contrast to the generally weak and shallow theology and spirituality of the present. One of a number of antidotes for this situation was immersion in the study of tradition, to gain access to the rich resources which it could offer. In many ways, the Puritan and Reformed Studies Conferences (see pp. 49–54) illustrate this general approach: we can learn and benefit from the past, even though we must feel free to criticize it and disagree with it where this is appropriate.

To speak of 'tradition' is, however, immediately to run into potential misunderstandings. For some writers, particularly within Roman Catholicism and Eastern Orthodoxy, 'tradition' has considerable authority. Tradition would here be understood to designate a traditional doctrine or belief, which has binding force on account of its antiquity. Yet this can easily degenerate into an uncritical sentimentality. 'We've always believed this' can simply mean 'we've always been wrong'. As the third-century writer Cyprian of Carthage pointed out, 'an ancient tradition can just be an old mistake'. Tradition is to be honoured where it can be shown to be justified, and rejected where it cannot. This critical appraisal of tradition was an integral element of the Reformation, and was based on the foundational belief that tradition was ultimately about the interpretation of Scripture – an interpretation which had to be justified with reference to precisely that same authoritative source.

The word 'tradition' is best defined primarily as 'the process of passing on and handing down'. It can be seen at work in the New Testament, particularly in Paul's handing on to the Corinthian believers the beliefs which were of foundational importance to him.

> Now, brothers, I want to remind you of the gospel I preached to you, which you received and on which you have taken your stand. By this gospel you are saved, if you hold firmly to the word I preached to you. Otherwise, you have believed in vain. For what I received I passed on to you as of first importance: that Christ died for our sins according to the Scriptures, that he was buried, that he was raised on the third day according to the Scriptures, and that he appeared to Peter, and then to the Twelve (1 Cor. 15:1–5).

Here, Paul speaks of 'passing on' what was of first importance to him. In a sense, evangelicals have been doing the same ever since: passing down from one generation to another the gospel of Christ, and the ways in which they understood and applied it to their situations.

Packer is clear that 'tradition' is of particular importance to modern evangelicalism. Evangelicals have always been prone to read Scripture as if they were the first to do so. We need to be reminded that other believers have been there and have read it before us. This process of receiving the scriptural revelation is 'tradition' – not a source of revelation in addition to Scripture, but a particular way of understanding Scripture which the Christian church has recognized as responsible and reliable. Scripture cannot be read as if it had never been read before. The hymnodies and liturgies of the churches constantly remind us that Scripture has been read, valued and interpreted in the past.

Evangelicalism, steeped in the heritage of the Reformation, has always been resolutely opposed to the introduction of any 'human traditions' into matters of Christian doctrine. Yet this does not mean that the labours of previous generations of faithful Christians to understand and apply Scripture are to be ignored. 'Tradition' is understood by Reformers such as Luther and Calvin as a history of discipleship – of reading, interpreting and wrestling with Scripture. Tradition is a willingness to read Scripture, taking into account the ways in which it has been read in the past. It is an awareness of the communal dimension of Christian faith, over an extended period of time, which calls the shallow individualism of many evangelicals into question. There is more to the interpretation of Scripture than any one individual can discern. It is a willingness to give full weight to the views of those who have gone before us in the faith, providing forceful reminders of the *corporate* nature of the Christian faith, including the interpretation of Scripture.

As Packer pointed out in his earliest major writing, the Christian past provides a resource for the Christian present. As we seek to interpret Scripture and unfold its many treasures, we can learn from the wisdom of the past.

The Spirit has been active in the Church from the first, doing the work he was sent to do – guiding God's people into an understanding of revealed truth. The history of the Church's labour to understand the Bible forms a commentary on the Bible which we cannot despise or ignore without dishonouring the Holy

Spirit. To treat the principle of biblical authority as a prohibition against reading and learning from the book of church history is not an evangelical, but an anabaptist mistake.[27]

Packer can therefore be regarded as stressing the importance of being aware of the historic and corporate nature of the Christian faith. Here he offers a critique of the 'widely prevailing but intellectually suicidal American tendency to act as if exegesis, hermeneutics and dogmatizing on the doctrine of Scripture take place in a vacuum'.[28] This point is developed further in his 1992 essay 'The Comfort of Conservatism', which points out the dangers of refusing 'to affirm the positive role of history and community in shaping one's understanding'. Everyone has 'traditions', whether they recognize them or not; the key question is 'whether our traditions conflict with the only absolute standard in these matters: Holy Scripture'.

Clearly, the danger of accepting the importance of the past must be acknowledged. There is a real danger that we may treat 'as divine absolutes patterns of beliefs and behaviour that should be seen as human, provisional, and relative'. The way in which Christians have behaved or thought in the past can easily become normative for future generations, even though these have no absolute divine sanction whatsoever. Up to this point, we have focused on doctrines; let us explore this point by considering a traditional evangelical practice. Many evangelicals would regard it as quite unthinkable to have an evangelistic meeting without a final 'altar call'. Yet this tradition only goes back to the middle of the nineteenth century, when it was introduced by Charles Finney (1792–1875).[29] Yet the fact that many evangelicals have accepted the tradition of 'altar calls' neither makes those calls sacrosanct nor godless. Tradition, in one sense, is neutral. As Packer points out,

All Christians are at once beneficiaries and victims of tradition – beneficiaries, who receive nurturing truth and wisdom from God's faithfulness in past generations; victims, who now take for granted things that need to be questioned ... We are all beneficiaries of good, wise, and sound tradition, and victims of poor, unwise and unsound traditions. This is where the absolute 'last word' of Scripture must sort out the wheat from the chaff. Hence the apostle Paul's counsel: 'Test everything. Hold on to the good' (1 Thess. 5:21).

This approach has implications at every level, especially in relation to the interpretation of Scripture.

For Packer, every traditional way of reading Scripture must, in principle, be open to challenge. As the study of church history makes clear, the church may sometimes get Scripture wrong. Thus the sixteenth-century Reformers believed that Scripture had been misunderstood at a series of critical junctures by the medieval church, and undertook to reform its practices and doctrines at those points. This, however, is a case of a tradition being criticized and renewed from within, in the light of the biblical foundations upon which it ultimately rests. The Reformers did not regard themselves as founding a new tradition; their concern was to reform a tradition which already existed, but which appeared to have become detached from its scriptural foundations. Affirming the authority of Scripture ultimately entails recognizing that even its most prestigious interpreters can be mistaken on occasion, and need to be challenged and corrected in its light. As Packer states this point, 'Scripture must have the last word on all human attempts to state its meaning, and tradition, viewed as a series of such human attempts, has a ministerial rather than a magisterial role.'

Evangelicalism has, at least in principle, accepted this emphasis on Scripture as the absolute authority in all matters of doctrine. Yet during the course of its history, evangelicalism has developed certain habitual or set ways of interpreting Scripture. These need to be checked out, rather than accepted uncritically. Furthermore, in more recent times charismatic individuals have arisen, demanding that we interpret critical passages *their* way, thus interposing themselves between evangelicals and Scripture. Packer's demand is that we constantly return to Scripture, rather than rely upon what some sage of yesteryear happened to say about Scripture. It may indeed turn out that we have much to learn from that sage of the past; yet this cannot be presupposed. In all things, we must 'test everything and hold on to the good'.

Packer's approach is thus an antidote to traditionalism – that is to say, a nostalgic and backward-looking approach to the Christian faith which 'can quench the Holy Spirit and cause paralysis and impotence in the church' by demanding that we blindly and uncritically repeat exactly what evangelicals did and said back in the 1950s, the 1920s, the 1820s or the 1730s – or whatever period in evangelical history happens to be regarded as a 'golden age' by its supporters. Elsewhere, Packer pointed out that the mechanical repetition of the verbal formulae of yesteryear could become a serious obstacle to faithfulness to the gospel. 'The formalist idea of orthodoxy as a matter merely of keeping yesterday's dogmatic formulae intact seems inadequate to evangelicals, vigorously as they often defend those formulae; the orthodoxy that evangelicals seek is one which, while wholly faithful to the substance of the biblical message, will be fully contemporary in orientation and expression.'[30] The wooden repetition of ancient theological terms and formulae is no guarantee of a living and orthodox faith, even if those terms and formulae are totally defensible in themselves.

Yet at the same time, Packer lays the foundation for *the critical affirmation and reappropriation of the past.* In other words, he sets out an approach by which what is wise, good and true from the past can be discerned, and gladly and joyfully reappropriated by today's church. Rediscovering the historic and corporate dimensions of our faith makes the great treasures and resources of the Christian past accessible and available to the present, thus enriching the life and witness of modern evangelicalism. We are enabled, as Packer puts it, to 'receive nurturing truth and wisdom from God's faithfulness in past generations'.

So why is this emphasis on tradition so significant? Why does Packer need to be heard on this point? The answer to this question is complex. Packer himself points to four major reasons why a recovery of tradition is important to evangelicalism. It allows us to discover our historical *roots*, introduces a sense of *realism* concerning our own situation, provides *resources* for the modern church, and acts as a *reminder* of yesterday's successes and failures, so that the church may learn from them.

Packer's intimate knowledge and experience of North American evangelicalism led him to appreciate the dangers of individualism, which seemed to him to engender a dangerously superficial and ephemeral form of Christianity. For Packer, tradition is an antidote against precisely such an individualism. North American evangelicalism, steeped in individualism, often seems to have no real sense of historical 'belonging' or rootedness. As such, it is radically prone to destabilization. Too often, as Packer comments, the North American evangelical has been 'a spiritual lone ranger who has proudly or impatiently turned his back on the church and his heritage' – a development which, for Packer, is 'a surefire recipe for weirdness without end!' Rediscovering the corporate and historic nature of the Christian faith reduces the danger of entire communities of faith being misled by charismatic individuals, and affirms the ongoing importance of the Christian past as a stabilizing influence in potentially turbulent times.

The importance of Packer's point can be seen in many ways. For example, in terms of the cultural history of North America, it is no accident that the most bizarre recent religious cults, as well as innovative approaches to Christianity, generally have their origins in California, where a deep sense of rootlessness prevails. In his important study entitled *The Evolution of Human Consciousness*, John H. Crook comments on the rise of the 'hippie' movement in California around the time of the Vietman War: 'It is no accident that the impetus came largely from the immigrant state of California where traditional cultural values are perhaps most fragmented and a need for new roots is most pronounced.'[31]

This deep sense of rootlessness is directly related to many of the destablilizing developments especially associated with Christian churches in this fragmented and unstable region. The rediscovery of tradition is an important means by which balance can be restored to churches which are lurching from one new teaching to another, and longing for some stability and security. Tradition thus acts as a safeguard against maverick lone rangers, who try to drag evangelicalism down their idiosyncratic doctrinal routes. It has been well said that heresy is as much about demanding additional beliefs as it is about denying central beliefs.

Tradition is like a filter, which allows us to identify suspect teachings immediately. To protest that 'We have never believed this before!' is not necessarily to deny the correctness of the teaching in question. But it is to raise a fundamental question: *why* have Christians not believed this before? And, on further investigation, it usually turns out that there are often very good reasons for not accepting that belief. The past here acts as both a resource and a safeguard, checking unhelpful and unorthodox doctrinal developments by demanding that their supporters explain their historical and theological credentials.

Packer's approach thus points towards the need for evangelicals to be aware of the great defining moments in the development of Christian doctrine.[32] Why did the church renounce Arianism? Why did the church fight against those who rejected the full divinity of the Holy Spirit? Why did Augustine repudiate Pelagius' doctrine of total human freedom, or the Donatist view of the church? Why did Luther reject works-righteousness? These controversies are landmarks in church history, in that they brought to a sharp focus some central issues of biblical interpretation. And they remain relevant today, as modern evangelicalism struggles to gain a sense of stability and responsibility. Church history is no irrelevance; it is a means by which today's Christians can learn of the ways in which God's people have served him in the past, whether that service ended in success or failure. It is no accident that evangelicalism seems prone to replay the great doctrinal debates of the patristic or Reformation periods; too many evangelicals know nothing of the past, and are unaware of these past debates and their momentous implications.

One of Packer's major contributions to modern evangelicalism lies in his emphasis on the importance of the Puritan heritage. It should be noted here that Packer's approach at this point represents a specific application of a more general truth – namely, that there are periods of great creativity and vitality in Christian history, which can nourish and sustain those who live in less happy times. 'No age shows equal insight into all spiritual truths and all facets of godliness, but the explorer of tradition finds the wisdom of every age opening up for him to draw on.' Packer himself exemplifies this style of theologizing; his approach encourages others to do the same. Perhaps his greatest contribution lies in his exploration of the relation of theology and 'spiritual truths', to which we may now turn.

Theology and Spirituality

Packer's characteristic emphasis has been on the primacy of theology. Bad theology hurts people, as he himself had discovered during his early days as a Christian, wrestling with his difficulties with sanctification in the light of the Keswick teaching on this matter. For Packer, theology was fundamental to everything – and for that reason, could never be restricted to mere thinking about ideas. The Christian vision of God, nourished and governed by theologizing, impacted on every aspect of Christian life. He often cited with approval the famous words of advice given by

Charles Haddon Spurgeon to his students: 'Brethren, if in your pastorates you are not theologians, you are just nothing at all.'[33] Packer's bestseller *Knowing God* represented a classic statement and justification of the intimate relationship between knowing correct ideas about God and the relational activity of knowing God. It was a theme to which he would return extensively during the 1980s and 1990s.

During his teaching at Regent College, Packer often stressed the close link between theology and doxology, a point he affirmed in a dramatic and powerful way by beginning his theological lectures by inviting all his students to join him in singing the doxology:

Praise God, from whom all blessings flow,
Praise him, all creatures here below.
Praise him above, ye heavenly host,
Praise Father, Son and Holy Ghost.

A traditional concern which was frequently addressed by Packer along such lines was the relationship between theology and preaching. Packer's great heroes as preachers – George Whitefield, Charles Haddon Spurgeon, Jonathan Edwards and Martin Lloyd-Jones – were all thoroughly grounded in Reformed theology.[34] For Packer, such a theology was a powerful motivation to preach, on account of its dramatic, thrilling and large-scale vision of the gospel. 'We have a giant-size gospel. It ought to produce giant-size preachers.'

During the 1950s, Packer was concerned that evangelism had come to be seen as a human achievement which focused on issues of technique, rather than as something which was rigorously grounded in theology. Bad theology led to bad evangelism, all too often resulting in unrealistic expectations and consequent disillusionment and disappointment. That same concern extended to preaching. Packer was able to explore these issues in two important lectures given at Ashland Theological Seminary, Ohio, in the fall of 1989. Although these lectures were particularly concerned with the use of Scripture in preaching, Packer took the opportunity to stress the importance of a theological definition of preaching as 'the event of God bringing to an audience a Bible-based, Christ-related, life-impacting message of instruction and direction from himself through the words of a spokesperson'.[35] Preaching was thus defined, not in terms of human performance or activity, but in terms of divine communication. The test of whether a 'performance from the preacher's podium' is preaching or not is whether it conforms to such a definition. ·

Yet it was the relationship between theology and spirituality which became an increasingly important theme in Packer's later ministry, especially during his period at Regent College. On 9 March 1987, Packer delivered the commencement address at the Tokyo Christian Institute.[36] In this address, he noted a problem which he had encountered extensively in his educational ministry – how theology can serve faith. All too often, theology and Christian living seem to go their separate ways. Packer noted the tendency of many seminary students to declare that God was less real to them after their theological studies than he had been prior to them. So what had gone wrong? For Packer, one of the most significant failings of seminaries was that they failed to make any real connection between Christian theology and Christian living. College courses were too often one-sided, dealing with academic issues rather than questions of Christian living. The books of the New Testament were written to make disciples, not simply to convey Christian concepts.

The whole issue of the relation between theology and spirituality was one to which Packer had given considerable thought. Although he was prepared to use the term 'spirituality', it is clear that he did not regard it as quite the *mot juste*. In his lectures at Trinity College, Bristol, during the 1970s, he had used the term 'spiritual theology' to refer to the general Christian discipline of 'conceiving and living the life of communion with God'. Although he glossed this with the term 'spirituality', his fundamental position was that it was quite improper to treat 'spirituality' as something distinct from theology. 'Spiritual theology' concerned the proper application of systematic theology, and was not an independent discipline in its own right.

Perhaps Packer's finest statement of his views on spiritual theology are to be found in his inaugural lecture as the first Sangwoo Yountong Chee Professor of Theology at Regent College. The lecture, delivered in the college chapel on 11 December 1989, was entitled 'An Introduction to Systematic Spirituality'.[37] The title itself is of significance, in that it immediately suggests a close connection between 'systematic theology' and 'spirituality' – a connection which the lecture proceeded to explore and explain.

Packer offered his audience a definition of spirituality as 'enquiry into the whole Christian enterprise of pursuing, achieving, and cultivating communion with God, which includes both public worship and private devotion, and the results of these in actual Christian life'.[38] The definition included an emphasis on the application of truth to life, which Packer had long regarded as of vital importance. 'I have always conceived theology, ethics and apologetics as truth for people, and have never felt free to leave unapplied any truth that I taught ... To speak of the application of truth to life is to look at life as itself a relationship to God; and when one does that, one is talking spirituality.'

For Packer, spirituality was an integral part of theological education, especially for those who were called to pastor. 'We cannot function well as counsellors, spiritual directors and guides to birth, growth and maturity in Christ, unless we are clear as to what constitutes spiritual well-being as opposed to spiritual lassitude and exhaustion, and to stunted and deformed spiritual development.' But where do these norms come from? For Packer, the answer was clear – from systematic theology. But immediately, Packer qualified what he understood by that term, and specifically criticized as inadequate two influential understandings of the nature of that discipline, as practised in North America. For Packer, 'the proper subject-matter of systematic theology is God actively relating in and through all created things to human beings.' This leads to theology being seen as 'a devotional discipline, a verifying in experience of Aquinas' beautiful remark that theology is taught by God, teaches God, and takes us to God'.

The two models which Packer criticizes lack this distinguishing mark. In the first place, there is the view that the proper subject-matter of systematic theology is 'Christian feelings and ideas about God'. The New Testament is thus treated as the earliest example of Christians and feelings. Packer here delineates the general trajectory of liberal theology, from F.D.E. Schleiermacher through to Rudolf Bultmann and process thought, that God's revelation has no cognitive content. For Packer, this was quite false and unacceptable. As it would almost certainly have been regarded as such by his audience, Packer felt no pressing need to continue his analysis of its weaknesses, and passed on to deal with the second approach.

According to this second view, the proper subject-matter of

systematic theology is 'revealed truth about the works, ways and will of God'. This view places considerable emphasis on the authority of Scripture, which is seen as God's own didactic witness to himself. Packer had no difficulties with this view up to this point. His anxieties concerned the next stage in this process of doing theology – the argument that 'all the data about God that exegesis has established must be brought together in a single coherent scheme'. This was the common task of medieval writers prior to the Reformation, Protestant scholastic writers of the seventeenth century, and most of the theological writers of the evangelical theological renaissance since the Second World War.

Packer's difficulties with this view did not relate to the need to ensure that the didactic content of Scripture should be brought together into a coherent whole, lacking contradiction. His anxiety had more to do with the possible consequences of such an approach.

> I question the adequacy of conceptualizing the subject-matter of systematic theology as simply revealed truths about God, and I challenge the assumption that has usually accompanied this form of statement, that the material, like other scientific data, is best studied in cool and clinical detachment. Detachment from what, you ask? Why, from the relational activity of trusting, loving, worshipping, obeying, serving and glorifying God: the activity that results from realizing that one is actually in God's presence, actually being addressed by him, every time one opens the Bible or reflects on any divine truth whatsoever. This ... proceeds as if doctrinal study would only be muddled by introducing devotional concerns; it drives a wedge between ... knowing true notions about God and knowing the true God himself.

There was therefore a need to bring systematic theology and spirituality together. 'I want to see spirituality studied within an evaluative theological frame ... I want to arrange a marriage, with explicit exchange of vows and mutual commitments, between spirituality and theology.'

That marriage can be seen in Packer's *Knowing God* and other writings. It can be argued to be a distinctive aspect of the Puritan tradition, so that Packer is urging a recovery of older insights at this point. But this is not the issue. Packer's concern is to ensure that 'knowing true notions about God' and 'knowing the true

God himself' go hand in hand, with the one reinforcing the other. Theological students should not find that knowing more about theology impoverishes their spiritual development, or that deepening their love for God and personal relationship with him allows them to dispense with the need for critical theological reflection. The two could and should go together, as inseparable companions and friends. It is a powerful vision, which has, to an extent, been institutionalized at Regent College. But can, or will, others learn from this?

The Debate over Universalism and Conditional Immortality

Issues concerning universalism had always been important for Packer. In 1959, he had contributed an essay on 'Christianity and Non-Christian Religions' to the leading American evangelical journal *Christianity Today*. In this article, he identified a number of cultural pressures which led to the rise of universalism in the west. In particular, he drew attention to the liberal belief (which had its origins in the philosophical writings of G.W.F. Hegel and the religious works of F.D.E. Schleiermacher) that 'the essence of religion is the same everywhere'. In other words, Christianity might seem different, in terms of its structures and beliefs, from Hinduism; nevertheless, both religions were to be seen as 'climbing the same mountain to the seat of the same transcendent Being. The most that can be said of their differences is that they are going up by different routes.' Packer vigorously opposed this trend, rightly discerning that, taken to its conclusion, it led to indifference in matters of religion. If accepted and absorbed at the popular level, it would lead to the end of Christian mission.

Packer then argues that the 'theology of religions' found in the Bible could be summarized as follows: 'Christianity is a religion of revelation received; all other faiths are religions of revelation denied.' In other words, Christianity is a 'religion of faith in a special revelation, given through specific historical events, of salvation for sinners', which is 'authoritatively reported and interpreted in the God-inspired pages of Scripture'. In contrast, non-Christian religions arise from the suppression or distortion of a general revelation, even though such truths keep breaking through human attempts to smother them. The line of argument developed here by Packer has an impressive historical pedigree, being found in one form in the writings of Calvin, and in a more developed form in the works of the great apologist of Westminster Theological Seminary, Cornelius van Til.

Packer's interest in this subject continued. In 1965, he delivered the Payton Lectures at Fuller Theological Seminary on the general theme of 'The Problem of Universalism Today'.[39] Although these lectures were never published, the thought which went into them can be discerned in a number of publications from after this date. In an article entitled 'All Men will not be Saved', Packer drew attention to two theological arguments which were advocated by universalists. In the first place, it is argued that a loving God could not contemplate anyone existing in a state of everlasting punishment. God's love in redemption must be such that all rational creatures can be saved. For Packer, this represented nothing other than purely speculative inference, without any solid biblical foundation. In the second, it is argued that, since the cross of Christ secured the salvation of all people, faith is nothing other than the recognition that you have already been saved, rather than a condition or means of appropriating that salvation. This, Packer declared, was clearly at variance with the biblical witness. 'Scripture seems to make it clear that the victory of Calvary brings salvation to no one until he believes.'

Similar arguments were developed in greater detail in a paper titled 'The Problem of Universalism Today', based on the Payton Lectures, and published in the Australian journal of the Theological Students Fellowship.[40] Packer here drew a sharp distinction between two senses of the the term 'universalism': the 'universal Christian claim' on humanity, grounded in Jesus Christ as the one and only Saviour, and the universal need for redemption; and the universal restoration of humanity 'to the fellowship with God for which Adam was made, and from which he fell'. Packer notes that it is the first form of universalism which establishes the credentials of Christianity as a world religion, and establishes its missionary credentials; the second, however, threatens to erode the distinctiveness, authenticity and integrity of the Christian faith, and rob it of its evangelistic thrust. In a later discussion of the same issues, dating from 1986,[41] Packer notes the growing importance of the challenge both of other religions and of an increasingly secular western culture, which resent Christianity's claims to represent the final and definitive revelation of God. However, he also pointed out that it is, in some ways, rather pointless to speculate over what happens to those who do not hear the gospel:

> Our job, after all, is to spread the gospel, not to guess what might happen to those to whom it never comes. Dealing with them is God's business: he is just, and also merciful, and when we learn, as one day we shall, how he has treated them we shall have no cause to complain. Meantime, let us keep before our minds mankind's universal need of forgiveness and new birth, and the graciousness of the 'whosoever will' invitations of the gospel. And let us redouble our efforts to make known the Christ who saves to the uttermost all who come to God by him.

Although forms of universalism appear to have gained increasing support within evangelicalism since 1985,[42] most evangelicals continue to hold (for reasons such as those outlined by Packer) that the doctrine is unbiblical. However, a related debate developed, in which some of the arguments associated with universalism appear to have found at least a degree of acceptance in some evangelical circles. How, universalists demanded, could a God of love consign anyone to eternal torment? Was not the traditional doctrine of hell inconsistent with the idea of a loving God?

For some evangelicals, this question had merit. The idea that no one will be damned has gradually emerged as a significant viewpoint within evangelicalism since 1988, when two leading evangelical writers committed themselves in print to the idea of 'conditional immortality'. This idea can be defined as the belief that God created humanity with the potential to be immortal. Immortality is a gift conveyed by grace through faith when the believer receives eternal life and becomes a partaker of the divine nature. The distinctive feature of the teaching is that it sees no continuing place for human beings to exist in continuous torment, unreconciled to God.[43] The traditional view held that humanity was immortal, and was therefore subject to eternal life or eternal punishment. The 'conditionalist' approach argued that immortality was only bestowed on those who were to be saved, so that none would endure the torment of eternal punishment in hell.

In 1988, two leading conservative evangelicals published their doubts concerning the traditional understanding of the nature of hell and eternal punishment, and tentatively advocated annihilationism as a serious option for evangelicals. Philip E. Hughes, a former librarian of Latimer House (see p. 103), and subsequently a member of the faculty of Westminster Theological Seminary, published his views in *The True Image*; John R.W. Stott contributed to a dialogue with David L. Edwards, in which he affirmed (although very tentatively) his inclination to believe in the final annihilation of the wicked, rather than their eternal punishment. Stott stressed that he stated this view with some hesitation, partly on account of his 'great respect for long-standing tradition which claims to be a true interpretation of Scripture' and partly because of his high regard and concern for 'the unity of the worldwide evangelical constituency'.[44] Additional support for such views also came from John Wenham, the veteran English conservative evangelical, who indicated that he had come round to this way of thinking as early as 1934, partly through the influence of Basil Atkinson, widely regarded as a bastion of orthodoxy in evangelical student circles.[45]

All of these writers were colleagues of Packer, with whom he had worked closely in the past, especially in connection with Latimer House. It was not an easy situation for him, in that his personal regard for the people concerned had to be set against his fundamental belief that their ideas were misguided and misleading. Another noted proponent of conditional immortality was Clark Pinnock, whom Packer had succeeded as professor of systematic and historical theology at Regent College.[46]

Packer responded to these developments in the annual Leon Morris Lecture, delivered to the Evangelical Alliance in the Australian city of Melbourne on 31 August 1990. He chose as his topic 'The Problem of Eternal Punishment', and indicated that he wished his lecture to be seen as 'a dissuasive from universalism and conditionalism, and particularly from conditionalism'.

Packer argued that the doctrine of eternal punishment was an integral aspect of 'the Christianity taught by the Lord Jesus Christ and his apostles', pointing out that it was also found in the writings of Christian theologians as diverse as Tertullian, Thomas Aquinas and Jonathan Edwards. The teaching is also found in the Westminster Confession, which affirmed that 'the souls of the wicked are cast into Hell, where they remain in torments and utter darkness'. Packer appealed to W.G.T. Shedd's famous work *The Doctrine of Endless Punishment,* first published in 1885, and reprinted by the Banner of Truth Trust in 1986. Shedd pointed to the teaching of Christ himself as the strongest warrant for the doctrine of endless punishment. Packer concurred, and pointed particularly to the parable of the Sheep and the Goats, in which Christ speaks explicitly of the goats being sent away to 'eternal fire' and 'eternal punishment' (Matt 25:41,46). Eternal punishment is thus, according to Jesus, departure into eternal fire.

The debate is complex, and involves a number of issues. The interpretation of a substantial number of biblical passages is clearly of importance, although other questions also emerge as significant. Perhaps the most important of these is the question of whether God creates human souls in a state of immortality (the traditional view) or with the potential for immortality (the conditionalist view). Packer was quite clear that conditionalism missed out on 'the awesome dignity of our having been made to last for eternity'. However, it is clear that one of Packer's major concerns was the impact of conditionalist teaching on evangelism. Conditionalism seriously detracted from the motivation for evangelism, in that if there is no everlasting punishment from which a sinner is to be delivered, there is correspondingly little reason to preach a gospel of deliverance. There can be no doubt that one of Packer's major concerns here – shared by others defending this position – is that missionary activity is seriously endangered by the belief, which removes a fundamental motivation for preaching the gospel. Packer's strong commitment to the importance of mission was also a significant consideration in a further controversy in which he became involved during the 1990s – the complex question of the nature and extent of collaboration between evangelicals and Catholics.

Evangelicals and Catholics Together

One of the most contentious debates to have overtaken North American evangelicalism in the past decade has concerned the way in which evangelicals should relate to Roman Catholicism.[47] In view of the enormous religious, moral, political and social implications of increased collaboration between evangelicals and Roman Catholics, it is necessary to consider this matter in detail.

To understand the background to Packer's involvement in, and distinctive contribution to, this discussion, we shall set the scene for the debate in some depth.

The relation between evangelicalism and Roman Catholicism was discussed with an unprecedented level of interest in the 1990s. There is every reason to think that there has been a lessening of suspicion on both sides, and a growing awareness both of the possibilities for working together, as well as the dangers of not doing so. Evangelicalism and Roman Catholicism are both major presences in the modern Christian world. (In fact, a leading German theologian, Wolfhart Pannenberg, is reported as predicting that the next century will have room for only three major Christian groups – Roman Catholicism, Eastern Orthodoxy, and evangelicalism.) Both evangelicalism and Roman Catholicism are alarmed at the growth in secularism and materialism in western society, and the dangers posed to Christians throughout the world by the rise of Islamic fundamentalism. Both are concerned about what seems to come close to growing moral chaos in the west, at both the individual and social levels. And both are aware of the growing tensions in Latin America, as evangelicalism continues to make deep inroads into areas traditionally dominated by Roman Catholicism. Theological disagreements can too easily explode into violence.

The issues at stake can best be appreciated by exploring the *Catechism of the Catholic Church,* a definitive statement of Catholic teaching published in 1994. The Catechism is unequivocal in its endorsement of the leading themes of traditional orthodox Christian doctrine. Indeed, there are excellent reasons for thinking that this Catechism reflects the public defeat of more liberal trends within Roman Catholicism. For example, Holy Scripture is unequivocally recognized as the inspired Word of God:

> In Sacred Scripture, the Church constantly finds her nourishment and her strength, for she welcomes it not as a human word, but as what it really is, the word of God. In the sacred books, the Father who is in heaven comes lovingly to meet his children, and talks with them . . . The divine revealed realities, which are contained and presented in the text of Sacred Scripture, have been written down under the inspiration of the Holy Spirit. For Holy Mother Church, relying on the faith of the apostolic age, accepts as sacred and canonical the books of the Old and the New Testaments, whole and entire, with all their parts, on the grounds that, written under the inspiration

of the Holy Spirit, they have God as their author and have been handed on as such to the Church herself.

Evangelicals clearly have an ally here in the defence of the unique nature of Scripture, in the face of liberal and rationalist reductionism. The extensive use of Scripture, especially in the sections of the Catechism dealing with the 'Profession of Baptismal Faith', reinforces this impression of a church which takes Scripture seriously.

Similarly, the Catechism vigorously defends the divinity of Jesus Christ, the uniqueness of his person, and the reality of his resurrection and future judgment. Salvation is only possible through the cross of Christ. The doctrine of the Trinity is forcefully defended against its Unitarian critics. The Pelagian heresy (that is, the view that we are justified on the basis of our works, rather than by the grace of God) is dismissed: 'Our justification comes from the grace of God. Grace is favour, the free and undeserved help that God gives us to respond to his call to become children of God, adoptive sons, partakers of the divine nature and of eternal life.' This is a particularly important point, in view of the persistent tendency of some Protestant critics of the Roman Catholic church, who charge it with teaching justification by works. Roman Catholicism, from the Council of Trent (1547) onwards, has unequivocally rejected this doctrine.

This vigorous and committed defence of some central Christian teachings is a major consideration for evangelicals, as they reconsider their attitude to Roman Catholicism. It indicates that an important ally could be to hand in the struggle for the restoration of doctrinal orthodoxy to the mainline denominations. The Catechism's insistence on the importance of the missionary role of the church also suggests that evangelicals and Roman Catholics will find a degree of convergence on the vital role of evangelism in the modern world, in the face of criticisms from the vociferous fundamentalists of the left who dismiss evangelism as 'cultural genocide' or 'destruction of personal integrity'. The Catechism here reflects the broad commitment to evangelism which has been typical of Roman Catholicism of late, and distinguishes it from the outdated and limpid liberalism of mainline Protestantism.

It is no accident that some evangelicals have chosen to become

Roman Catholics, sensing that there is an institutionalized orthodoxy over a series of vital issues which the mainline Protestant
churches have betrayed. Maybe, they reason, it is easier to be
an evangelical inside the Roman Catholic church, which defends
all the vital Christian doctrines yet adds on a few more, than
to remain inside some mainline Protestant denomination, which
seems bent on denying or deforming the basic tenets of Christianity
itself. Roman Catholics and evangelicals certainly do not agree on
everything; nevertheless, they agree on a lot of things that are of
critical importance.

Yet the Catechism also brings out clearly the simple fact of life
that the agenda of the Reformation remains a living reality for
modern Christian living. Time and time again, the controversies
of the sixteenth century come to mind as a result of reading
this document. Examples of areas in which evangelicals will find
themselves wishing to enter into Reformation-type debates will
include the following:

1. The canon of Scripture. The Roman Catholic canon continues to
include documents which evangelicals regard as deutero-canonical
or 'apocryphal'. It was at the Council of Trent that the Roman
Catholic church first declared its acceptance of seventy-eight biblical
books as canonical; the Catechism endorses this decision. This also
reopens the much-debated question of whether Scripture is 'recognized' as inherently authoritative (Protestantism), or 'received'
by an authoritative council (Roman Catholicism), thus making
its authority derivative and dependent on the authority of the
church.

2. Justification by faith. The Council of Trent specifically condemned Protestant views on the imputation of Christ's righteousness to believers in justification. Although Trent explicitly
condemned the doctrine of justification by works, its understanding
of justification is generally thought to be seriously at odds with
Protestant views.

3. The role of an unwritten or oral tradition in addition to Scripture
in matters of doctrine and practice is affirmed by the Catechism:

In keeping with the Lord's command, the Gospel was handed
on in two ways:
– *orally*, by the apostles who handed on, by the spoken word of
their preaching, by the example they gave, by the institutions they

established, what they themselves had received – whether from the lips of Christ, from his way of life and his works, or whether they had learned it at the prompting of the Holy Spirit.
– *in writing*, by those apostles and other men associated with the apostles who, under the inspiration of the same Holy Spirit, committed the message of salvation to writing.

The Reformers regarded this notion of oral tradition as the basis of a number of unacceptable beliefs and practices in the medieval church, and saw it as undermining the authority of Scripture. Even today, many observers feel that Catholics continue to give oral tradition priority over Scripture. Ongoing debate on this point is clearly necessary.

4. The role of Mary, especially the doctrine of the immaculate conception, which declares that Mary was redeemed from the moment of her conception, and was thus an exception to the universal human condition of sin. Evangelicals regard this as speculative and unbiblical, and as potentially undermining the uniqueness of Christ as God incarnate and the sole redeemer of humanity.

5. The number and role of the sacraments. Evangelicalism generally tends to follow the Reformers, and acknowledge only two sacraments (baptism and the Lord's Supper), regarding the remaining five as medieval additions to the beliefs and practices of the early church.

These five points of difference are to be regarded as illustrative, not exhaustive. Evangelicals therefore find that, on the one hand, Roman Catholicism is committed to a number of doctrines with which evangelicals will enthusiastically agree; and on the other, to a number of doctrines with which evangelicals will wish to disagree strongly. It will be clear that the extent of the disagreement will vary from one evangelical to another; that, however, is not the central issue. The clear outcome of any informed reading of this important document is that evangelicals will find clear statements of support for the foundational doctrines of the Christian faith, alongside others which they will find questionable in the light of their Reformation heritage.

This clearly raises the question of how evangelicalism should respond to Roman Catholicism. Two broad strategies are possibilities.

1. Refuse to have anything to do with Roman Catholics, on account of the continuing doctrinal disagreements associated with the agenda of the Reformation. This approach has the merit of the total maintenance of doctrinal integrity. But the threats to Christian orthodoxy from the fundamentalists of the left, secularism and Islam remain. The question which needs to be addressed is this: can feuds between Christians be allowed to help non-Christians win? A divided Christianity is simply a weakened Christianity.

2. Collaborate with Roman Catholics on a limited range of issues, while acknowledging that differences remain on others. This approach maintains doctrinal integrity by means of an explicit acknowledgment that disagreements remain, while at the same time permitting collaboration on a series of moral, social and political issues, and the mutual defence of Christian orthodoxy against secularism, liberalism and non-Christian religions. Yet it leaves unresolved the question of how doctrinal disagreements are to be handled. Are they just going to be ignored? Or understated for pragmatic reasons?

These kinds of considerations constitute the background against which the document 'Evangelicals and Catholics Together: The Christian Mission in the Third Millennium' (ECT) must be seen. From an evangelical perspective, the document clearly opts for the second of the two approaches just outlined. The document was issued in March 1994, and built on the work of two significant individuals, one an evangelical, the other a Catholic. Richard John Neuhaus's *Naked Public Square* (1984) was widely acclaimed as a study which demonstrated the way in which religion was being systematically eliminated from the public life of the United States. Neuhaus, a Lutheran who had become a Catholic, stressed the need for a Christian witness in this 'naked public square' of American public life. The book was widely welcomed by committed Christians across a range of denominations. The debate was taken further by Charles Colson's *Kingdoms in Conflict* (1987). Colson, a Reagan White House staffer who was converted in the aftermath of the Watergate scandal, sounded a similar note, which was developed still further in his *The Body: Being Light in Darkness* (1992). By this stage, it was clear that Colson and Neuhaus were urging similar strategies on their respective constituencies for similar reasons.

Aware that evangelicals and Catholics could easily end up fighting each other (physically as well as theologically, as the tensions in Latin America and Northern Ireland made painfully clear), Colson and Neuhaus began to build up a network of individual evangelicals and Catholics sympathetic to the idea of collaborative witness in the public arena. The group was never intended to represent denominations or denominational concerns, but was envisaged as a working group exploring the ways in which individual Christians might work together in the face of what appeared to be an increasingly hostile public arena. The election of Bill Clinton as president of the United States in November 1992 was seen at that time as potentially auguring a new phase of secularism in public life, making some such collaboration essential.

A core working group began exploring possibilities in September 1992.[48] It became clear that the group had little patience with the ambiguities of many ecumenical statements, which seemed to duck engaging with important doctrinal differences in order to ensure some kind of agreement. There was a determination to acknowledge differences honestly and openly, while at the same time to rejoice at what could be held in common. A drafting group was convened, and after seven attempts, an acceptable statement was agreed, and publicly released in New York on 29 March 1994. It was published in full in the May 1994 edition of the journal *First Things,* edited by Neuhaus.

A number of leading evangelicals publicly endorsed the ECT statement, including William Abraham (Perkins School of Theology), Os Guinness (Trinity Forum), Richard Mouw (Fuller Theological Seminary), Mark Noll (Wheaton College), Thomas Oden (Drew University), Pat Robertson (Regent University) – and Packer himself. In many ways, Packer here adopted the same set of principles in relation to dealing with Catholicism in 1994 as he had in his earlier dealings with Anglo-catholicism within the Church of England around 1970 (see p. 156). This is not a new development in Packer's thinking, but the extension of an existing understanding of the manner in which evangelicals should relate to other Christians. It represents an excellent example of 'grassroots co-belligerence'. As Packer would put it, the document 'identifies common enemies (unbelief, sin, cultural apostasy) and pleads that the Christian counter-attack on these things be co-operative up to the limit of what divergent convictions allow'.[49]

From Packer's perspective, the statement built a platform on which evangelicals and Catholics who shared a common faith in the Trinity, the incarnation, the atonement and new birth could unite and work together in reaching out to an increasingly secular society. In this context, Packer reaffirmed words once written by C. S. Lewis: 'When all is said (and truly said) about the divisions of Christendom, there remains, by God's mercy, an enormous common ground.'[50] For Packer, it was a priority task to labour to occupy that common ground by seeking substantive convergence together, without forfeiting or fudging any specific truth. It came as a surprise to him to learn that the document was being read as some kind of mandate for the convergence of churches. Some observers gained the impression that Richard John Neuhaus was perhaps presenting the document in this light, seeing it as one further step towards bringing Protestants back into the Catholic fold. But this was certainly not how other signatories to the document understood it.

For Packer, it seemed quite clear that *Evangelicals and Catholics Together* was a parachurch document in which individual evangelicals and Catholics were invited to ally themselves for the work of Christian mission.[51] Although the Protestant and Catholic church systems are opposed to each other on, for example, major aspects of the doctrine of salvation, Packer argued that those who trust and love the Lord Jesus Christ on both sides of the Reformation know that they are united in him, making some kind of collaboration entirely proper. Packer had always argued that the most fundamental level of ecumenical activity is to be involved in Christian mission, and saw the document as an important statement of the need to bear witness to Jesus Christ as Saviour to an apostate world.[52]

In Packer's view, the present needs of both church and community in the western world called out for some such collaboration across denominational divides. Two main considerations prompted this conclusion. First, that the 'slide into secularism and paganism that is so much a mark of current culture' demands that there should be some kind of 'alliance of all who love the Bible and its Christ'. A united Christian witness is necessary in the face of an increasingly secular cultural situation. Packer stresses that he is not advocating official collaboration between denominations, but individual alliances across denominational divides, along the lines of the parachurch coalitions already existing within evangelicalism itself.

Second, the historic division between 'relatively homogeneous Protestant churches and a relatively homogeneous Church of Rome' reflects a situation which no longer pertains. A new division has emerged within Christianity, which is of considerably greater importance – the division between theological conservatives (whom Packer prefers to term 'conservationists') who 'honour the Christ of the Bible and historic creeds and confessions' on the one hand, and 'theological liberals and radicals' on the other. This division can be seen within both the Protestant and Catholic churches. Why should not conservatives form an alliance across the denominations, to fight liberalism and radicalism? 'Domestic differences about salvation and the Church should not hinder us from joint action in seeking to re-Christianize the North American milieu.' Underlying Packer's stance at this point is substantially the same understanding of 'co-belligerence' as that which he thrashed out in the English context back in the 1960s.

The document (and Packer's endorsement) gave rise to angry criticisms. One typical response was that Catholics and Protestants were antithetically opposed, with the result that neither could legitimately regard the other as being Christian with any integrity or honesty. Protestants should therefore treat Catholics as non-Christian or anti-Christian (and vice versa). It was a single-shot response, in that once this point had been made, no further discussion was possible. The result was that those who believed that such dialogue was dishonest refused to have anything to do with it, leaving those who disagreed with them to get on with the dialogue. The dialogue thus continued, without those who objected to it.

In the spring of 1995, Packer took this approach a stage further. He was invited to attend the Aiken Conference, organized by Orthodox Christians, which had been called to 'test whether an "ecumenical orthodoxy", solidly based upon the classic Christian faith, can become the foundation for a unified and transformative vision to the age we live in'. Packer's response to this question was strongly affirmative, and developed further his policy of 'collaboration' within and across 'great-tradition Christianity', in the face of opposition from fundamentalists within Protestantism, Eastern Orthodoxy and Roman Catholicism.[53] Packer offered his readers a vision of a 'transcendent new togetherness resulting both within and across denominational lines'. It was a powerful vision; it was also a controversial vision.

Packer has been subjected to severe criticism, particularly in relation to ECT, occasionally verging on personal abuse, on account of his high profile and status within evangelicalism. Indeed, there are remarkable parallels between the opprobrium heaped on Packer by some evangelicals and that dispensed by Martyn Lloyd-Jones and his supporters in England back in 1970.[54] But for Packer, the same principles were at stake, and he saw no inconsistency in his position. In his important 1995 article 'Crosscurrents among Evangelicals', Packer set out some of the objections raised against ECT, and his responses to them. One of the most important was the perception that the document represented a 'rapprochement with the Church of Rome as such'. Packer made it clear that this was not the case, whatever the secular media (with its tendency to theological misunderstanding and simplification) might have suggested.

A perhaps significant criticism concerned the failure of the statement to address a number of doctrinal issues which were matters of division between evangelicals and Catholics. The original ECT Statement did not address, for example, a series of doctrines which were debated at the time of the sixteenth-century Reformation, including the doctrine of justification by faith alone (or, more accurately, justification by grace alone through faith alone) and the concept of 'papal infallibility', as defined by the First Vatican Council. Along with two other signatories of ECT (Richard Land and John White), Packer signed a further clarificatory statement entitled 'Resolutions for Roman Catholic and Evangelical Dialogue' in March 1994, identifying a number of representative doctrinal issues which remained unresolved. It was Packer's hope that this would remove any lingering suggestion that he had somehow allowed it to be understood either that Catholics and evangelicals already were in doctrinal agreement, or that the areas in which disagreements remained were of no significance.

Nevertheless, Packer insisted that it is not 'any theory about faith and justification' which brings salvation to people, but 'trusting Jesus himself as Lord, Master and divine Saviour'. Packer drew attention to a trend which he saw as 'near to being a cultic heresy' – a doctrine of 'justification, not by works, but by words – words, that is, of notional soundness and precision'.[55] Packer pointed out how 'it is the way of fundamentalists to follow the path of contentious orthodoxy, as if the mercy of God in Christ automatically rests on persons who are notionally correct and is just as automatically withheld from those who fall short of notional correctness on any point of substance.'

For Packer, it was clear that many Catholics who would not agree with the Reformation teaching concerning justification by imputed righteousness nevertheless love and trust Jesus Christ. Surely this is what matters? Packer argued that the teaching of both the Council of Trent and the *Catechism of the Catholic Church* was basically that of Augustine. Were the critics of ECT suggesting that Augustine was not a Christian, or that he had no gospel? ECT's statement that we 'are justified by grace through faith because of Christ' seemed to be perfectly adequate as a starting point. Not everyone agreed; some argued that this meant different things to the different parties who signed ECT, and therefore had no value as a statement of agreement. Others argued that the omission of the word 'alone' represented an abandonment of the historic teachings of the Reformation on this matter.[56]

On 19 January 1995, further discussions took place concerning such points. Charles Colson convened a meeting in Fort Lauderdale, Florida, which was attended by Packer and William Bright (all of them had signed or endorsed ECT) and those who had registered criticisms or anxieties to varying degrees.[57] Packer drafted a statement indicating that the 'evangelical signatories to ECT acted in this way ... to advance Christian fellowship, co-operation and mutual trust among true Christians in the North American cultural crisis and in the worldwide task of evangelism ... Our parachurch co-operation with evangelically committed Roman Catholics for the pursuit of agreed objectives does not imply acceptance of Roman Catholic doctrinal distinctives or endorsement of the Roman Catholic church system.'

Packer insisted that he could never become a Roman Catholic on account of a number of that church's distinctive beliefs, including its views on the papacy and the infallibility of the church's teaching. However, the course of joint action which ECT advocated was, according to Packer, 'not churchly but parachurchly' – in other words, collaboration among Christians who unite for specific purposes across traditional denominational divides, such as mission agencies, student ministry organizations, and transdenominational educational units. Such bodies are not 'churches', but nevertheless exercise important ministerial roles. For evangelicals and Catholics to work together in such agencies is not to make any statements concerning the nature and identity of the true church, but to affirm the importance of collaboration among believers in relation to specified goals.

It is possible that Packer's strong advocacy of the importance of parachurch organizations, along with the potential for collaboration and mission which they offer, may prove to be one of the more significant contributions that he has made to the future direction of evangelicalism. While some older evangelicals, particularly those having their origins in fundamentalist contexts, continue to regard Catholicism as anti-Christian, there is clear evidence that many in a younger generation of evangelicals regard increased collaboration with individual Catholics as proper and necessary, both as a pragmatic response to secularism and paganism, and as an expression of a shared Christian fellowship. The co-operative mode of evangelism adopted by Billy Graham, which brings together all Christian churches in a given area, is one clear example of this phenomenon. The growing importance of the charismatic movement, in which 'the distinction between Protestant and Catholic vanishes in a Christ-centred unity of worship, fellowship and joy' is another indicator of future developments.

That same policy of collaboration also lies behind Packer's deep involvement in the struggle for theological orthodoxy within the Anglican Church of Canada. Just as Packer advocated collaboration with Anglo-catholics in 1970 in order to head off a liberal-inspired church union scheme between Anglicans and Methodists (pp. 155–6), he adopted the same strategy in the 1990s to establish a coalition for orthodoxy against the prevailing liberalism of the Anglican Church in his adopted homeland of Canada. This development, which is widely regarded as one of the most significant developments in modern Canadian church history, merits further discussion in its own right.

Canadian Anglicanism: *Essentials 94*

The Anglican Church of Canada (ACC), in common with most North American mainline churches, went through a period of expansion in the aftermath of the Second World War, followed by a period of decline in the 1960s. Liberalism gained the ascendancy within the church (particularly its bureaucracy, which was substantially expanded following the adoption and implementation of a series of recommendations from Price Waterhouse in the later 1960s). Theological education within Canadian Anglicanism increasingly came to be devolved to ecumenical schools of theology (such as the Atlantic School of Theology in Halifax, Nova Scotia, and the Vancouver School of Theology), which were dominated by a liberal theological agenda.

However, during the 1980s, the conservative evangelical wing of the Anglican Church of Canada began to experience numerical growth and theological renewal. Barnabas Anglican Ministries became a focus for evangelicalism within the ACC. Perhaps most importantly, Wycliffe College, Toronto, began to emerge as the single most important institute of Anglican theological education in Canada, gradually eclipsing its liberal rival (Trinity College) across Hoskin Avenue. Wycliffe's growing stature during the 1970s and 1980s is widely agreed to rest on the achievements of the principals of the period, Reginald Stackhouse (sixth principal, 1975–84) and Dr Peter Mason (seventh principal, 1985–92). Wycliffe, originally founded in 1877, rose to become the third largest provider of theological education in Canada by the early 1990s. The two largest providers – Regent College, Vancouver and Ontario Theological Seminary – were evangelical (but not Anglican) in orientation. Whereas evangelicalism was once regarded as a quaint minority within Canadian church life, it had now emerged as the dominant force in Canadian theological education.[58]

Although many vested interests within the ACC were threatened and challenged by the growing strength of evangelicalism, those who were committed to the restoration of theological orthodoxy within the church were fragmented, and thus unable to mount a united witness. Packer was convinced that it was necessary to form a strategic alliance from groups within the ACC. The Prayer Book Society of Canada was formed in 1986 as a defender of classic liturgy and traditional statements of faith, particularly around the period of liturgical experimentation and revision leading to the production of the *Book of Alternative Services* (1985). Initially, the society was seen as reflecting Anglo-catholic concerns, with the result that evangelicals would have little to do with it. However, as time went on, evangelicals began to feel able to do business with it. Packer himself became an active member (and a vice-president) of the Society. As events proved, this placed him in an ideal position to become involved in coalition-forming negotiations with the Anglican Renewal Ministries of Canada (a largely charismatic group) and Barnabas Anglican Ministries. These negotiations eventually extended to involve Anglo-catholics who were strongly committed to the fundamentals of Christian orthodoxy. Packer himself tended to refer to such individuals as 'Liddonite high-churchmen', after H.P. Liddon, the nineteenth-century Anglo-catholic theologian who was noted for his vigorous and influential defence of the divinity of Christ in the face of increasing criticisms of this position.

The culmination of several years of planning took place at the 'Essentials 94' conference of 16–21 June 1994 at Montreal. It brought together on the same platform catholics, charismatics and evangelicals, all united in their advocacy of theological orthodoxy and spiritual renewal. Well over 700 delegates turned up – more than twice the number anticipated, including a remarkably high number of younger Anglicans. The Archbishop of Canterbury flew in to speak at the conference, stressing both the challenges and opportunities of the moment. The conference issued a fifteen-point statement of belief, which reaffirmed the necessity and relevance of the orthodox Christian faith, and especially the historic Anglican position.[59]

It is too early to assess the importance of this event. Will it be like the Keele Convention of 1967, which formed the basis of a new evangelical phase in the history of the Church of England? Certainly, two of the original Keele keynote speakers – Packer and Michael Green – were both prominent in the *Essentials '94* conference. However, it is clear that the conference highlights an important aspect of Packer's personal agenda – the renewal and regeneration of Anglicanism. Many have commented on the way in which Packer, although based in Canada, seemed to concentrate his efforts on transdenominational evangelicalism in the United States.[60] *Essentials '94* is an important illustration of the continuing importance to Packer of a 'bilateral' agenda (see pp. 154–5) – that is, commitment to transdenominational evangelicalism on the one hand, and to his own denomination on the other.

Conclusion

On 22 July 1996, Packer celebrated his seventieth birthday. It was an occasion for celebration, especially at Regent College, where the faculty marked the event with a formal dinner, and an official announcement of the founding of the 'J.I. Packer chair of theology'. There were tributes and festivities at other gatherings around that time, including the Christian Booksellers Association, at which the Evangelical Christian Publishers Association awarded Packer a Gold Medallion Lifetime Achievement Award in recognition of his outstanding contribution to evangelical Christian thinking, and the life of the church at large. Although entitled to retire at sixty-five, Packer continued to teach his four courses in systematic theology until the age of seventy, and intends to teach as much as possible for as long as possible, while continuing to speak at home and overseas.

The story which we have told is that of a man who made it his aim to know God, and to help others to know him better. At times, that quest focused on the great issues of theology and spirituality, as Packer wrestled with the massive themes of the Christian gospel, and their application to life. (We shall consider the long-term significance of Packer's reflections in the following chapter.) At other moments, the issues were much more personal, as Packer struggled with the personal issue of where God wanted him to be, and what he wanted him to do. At several points of major importance, the critical question which Packer found himself facing was quite simply this: what do I do next? At such moments, he felt he had no option but to trust in God's good providence, and step out in faith. At times, the results were perplexing and distressing; at others, they were enormously fulfilling and rewarding. At times, he found himself at the centre of controversy, sometimes experiencing the pain of arguing with those who were close friends and colleagues. As a public representative of both evangelicalism and 'great-tradition Christianity', Packer has experienced the pain, sadness and bitterness which are so often the lot of those who maintain 'theological watchfulness for the sake of the gospel'.[61]

Surely there is something to be learned here from two of Packer's favourite biblical passages – Ecclesiastes 12:13–14, and 1 Corinthians 15:58.[62] These texts, in their different ways, affirm

God's steadfastness in the midst of what often seems to be a bewildering and random world. Ecclesiastes speaks of 'the pain of brainwork (the more you know, the more it hurts), about the boredom of the supposedly interesting and the hollowness of achievement (all pointless! Like trying to grasp the wind!), about the crazy-quilt character of life, about our ignorance of what God is up to, and about death as life's solitary certainty'. For Packer, Ecclesiastes affirms, with the gravity and low tones of a bassoon, what Paul declares with trumpet and drums – 'be steadfast, immovable, always abounding in the work of the Lord, knowing that your toil is not in vain'. Maybe we cannot fully understand what is happening in life, or what God purposes for us – but the important thing is to keep going in the Christian life. 'With these twin texts echoing in my ears, I go on my way rejoicing.'

« 11 »

James I. Packer: An Assessment

SOME WOULD SAY Packer is a great theologian; it would probably be more accurate to say that he is a great 'theologizer' – someone who knows, loves and thinks about God, and is able to communicate that passion in his books. Those books will be part of his legacy to evangelicalism. Packer has tended to say what evangelicalism needed to hear, rather than what it wanted to hear. There will always be those within the movement who will try to dismiss him as a rigid Calvinist or a compromising collaborator. The truth is rather more complex, and considerably more challenging. Perhaps Packer may remind evangelicalism that there is more to the gospel than any of us have grasped, and that we must always be alert to the need to express faithfulness to the gospel in terms of responses to new challenges and opportunities.

It will be clear that Packer has had an enormous – possibly incalculable – influence on the emergence and consolidation of evangelicalism in the last forty years. An entirely appropriate subtitle for this work might have been 'James I. Packer and the Shaping of Modern Evangelicalism'. Evangelicalism today is very different from the hesitant, numerically weak and theologically illiterate movement that emerged in the aftermath of the Second World War. In the view of many, Packer was of critical importance in bringing about this transformation. To study the life of Packer is thus to explore the story of the emergence and consolidation of the post-war evangelical movement, seen from a particular angle.

A biography of Packer is therefore far more than the story of one of modern Christianity's most significant and accessible writers. It is about the rapid growth and development of evangelicalism throughout the western world since the Second World War. Packer is an integral and formative part of that history, one of perhaps half a dozen people who can be said to have shaped it definitively,[1] and certainly its best-known and most widely respected theologian. Packer proved to be a man of ideas at a critical moment in the history of evangelicalism – a moment at which ideas mattered profoundly. In part, this biography therefore deals with a series of defining moments in the history of modern evangelicalism, in which Packer was, alone or with others, responsible for the shaping or directing of the movement. To understand the history and shape of modern evangelicalism, it is necessary to understand the role which Packer played in its formation.

Yet it would be quite wrong to see Packer as being of purely *historical* importance, as one who has merely influenced the movement in the past. Packer's ideas and approaches are of considerable importance to evangelicalism *in the future*, as it continues to expand and consolidate its influence. This work is not the documentation of the past history of a distinguished person – though it is that, in part. Rather, it is also about a highly significant and influential understanding of the nature of the Christian gospel, and the means by which its relevance and integrity may be maintained. Above all, Packer has shown the importance of rigorous theological thinking to every aspect of modern evangelicalism, as well as exemplifying this process himself. Packer's methods and insights have already served the church well; their relevance is far from spent.

If North American evangelicalism has been distinguished by its biblical activism, Packer has sought to strengthen it through his emphasis on the practical and spiritual importance of historical and theological reflection. Packer offers a judicious counterbalance to the anti-intellectual and unhistorical trends in evangelicalism, affirming the importance of theology, tradition and historical scholarship as tools for the consolidation and stimulation of the evangelical vision. While committed to the importance of evangelism, Packer insisted that evangelicals think about what they were doing – and why – while evangelizing. While deeply concerned to ensure that theology never became detached from worship and prayer, Packer affirmed that true worship and prayer – and above all, spirituality – were grounded on and nourished by theological wellsprings. Rarely has such a coherent, persuasive and attractive apologia been offered by an evangelical for the continuing importance of 'theologizing' (Packer prefers this verbal form) to the goals of evangelicalism.

Packer's strategic importance to evangelicalism is largely grounded in his being a man of ideas. To grasp Packer's crucial role in the past and present development, and his promise as a future resource to the movement, it is therefore necessary to attempt to understand and appreciate the ideas. Packer's actions – including signing the 'Evangelicals and Catholics Together' document – have always been informed by a rigorous theology. To do justice to Packer, his biography cannot be a mere chronological listing of things he did and wrote. It must aim to explore the ideas that mattered so much to him, and which he attempted to apply in his ministry, and above all his books.

This may convey the impression that Packer is – like one of his great theological heroes, John Calvin – a man of books. But on closer inspection, like Calvin, Packer proves to be far more than an author and thinker. Without doubt, he has been one of the 'movers and shapers' of the modern church. As this biography will have made clear, Packer's career has involved him in the triumphs and failings, the joys and the woes, of modern evangelical Christianity. Many readers will find themselves able to identify with the issues with which he was confronted during his career, and perhaps learn from the ways in which he dealt with them. The man who wrote the phenomenally successful *Knowing God* was also a man who sought to know God, and discern God's will for his own life, and that of the church at large.

This biography will remind its readers that Packer was a man who was affected by much the same issues and questions as ordinary Christians. In what way could he most effectively serve God? What did God want him to do with his life? Where could he be used most effectively? Those wrestling with such questions find encouragement in discovering how others have handled them first.

Packer is widely known as a mover and shaper of modern transdenominational and international evangelicalism. Yet Packer also saw himself as having a special interest in and concern for one specific denomination – Anglicanism. He is an ordained minister of the Church of England, whose first twenty-seven years of professional ministry were spent working in institutions specifically linked to that church. He was deeply involved in the conception, planning and execution of what is now widely regarded as the most important event in twentieth-century English church history – the 1967 Keele Convention. That involvement has continued since his move to North America in 1979, although not to the same extent as in his native England. Throughout his entire period at Regent College, Vancouver, Packer served as an honorary assistant at his local Anglican church, and was the chief architect of 'Essentials 94', a major development in Canadian Anglicanism.

Some readers of this biography, particularly in North America, will find themselves surprised by what they learn of Packer's commitment to Anglicanism, having tended to think of him primarily as someone committed to transdenominational evangelicalism. Yet Packer's strategic conception of his ministry has always been bilateral, involving commitment to the consolidation of transdenominational evangelicalism on the one hand, and the reform and renewal of Anglicanism on the other. Both movements are very different today from what they were in the immediate aftermath of the Second World War. When the full story of both is told, the importance of Packer to each will be seen. More recently (since about 1990), Packer has come to see himself as representing Anglicanism as an example of 'great-tradition Christianity' stemming from the mainstream Reformation, developing strategies for collaboration within the various strands of this great tradition which may well be of considerable influence in the future. This biography begins to track that influence, even if its full impact may not be appreciated for another generation.

To assess Packer is thus no easy task. A proper evaluation will need to wait for at least two decades, and will take into account the long-term significance of the various trends he initiated. It has often been said that an integral part of the complex history of evangelicalism is the lengthening shadows of great individuals. Packer himself has become one of those few defining individuals. He emerged as the disciple of Martyn Lloyd-Jones, eventually to eclipse his master. Yet Packer has shown no inclination towards the self-aggrandizement typical of so many modern evangelicals. There is no 'J.I. Packer Inc.', no 'Packer Ministries', no organization dedicated to his name or his teachings. Packer has no doubt about how he would like to be remembered: as a voice.

Perhaps that voice on occasion cried in the wilderness, after the manner of a distinguished precedent in Scripture. Nevertheless, Packer is clear that his distinctive role and calling is *to be heard.*

At times, he may be an unpopular voice; at others, what he has to say will come as refreshment. Packer's conviction that bad theology hurts people inevitably leads him into controversy. As has often been pointed out, he has always sought to be a peacemaker in the controversies into which he has been drawn in his long career.

In what specific areas, then, will Packer remain a voice? We have already documented the manner in which he *has been* a voice; but what of his future influence? This is, in one sense, a difficult question to answer, in that it involves attempting to project what the situation faced by evangelicalism globally might be like in the next generation. However, on the basis of the likely evolution of the movement, it can be suggested that Packer's distinctive approach to the Christian faith is likely to be a significant resource and challenge to evangelicalism in four areas.

1. The Importance of History

Packer tends to see himself as standing in the main Christian stream – the 'great tradition', from a Christian point of view – which starts with the fathers, which was partly (though not totally) derailed during the Middle Ages, which recovered its balance and identity through the work of the Reformers (especially Calvin) and subsequently continued through the Puritans (especially Jonathan Edwards).[2] As a representative of what he styles 'great-tradition Christianity', Packer is able to affirm the importance of patristic and medieval writers – such as Athanasius, Augustine, Anselm and Aquinas, to limit ourselves merely to those whose names conveniently begin with the first letter of the alphabet – while at the same time recognizing the importance of the Reformation. For Packer, the Reformation corrected 'skewed western understandings of the church, the sacraments, justification, faith, prayer and ministry'; nevertheless, that correction 'took place within the frame of the great tradition, and did not break it'.

Packer's is a broad and bold view of theology, which seeks to challenge the present by exposing it to the riches of the past, and to demand that evangelicalism think about what it says and does in the company of the great saints of bygone eras. Perhaps it is Packer's Oxford theological education, possibly linked with his Anglican heritage, which has made him so appreciative of the theological resources of the grand tradition; whatever the explanation may be, there can be no doubt that he believes that the enthusiasm of modern American evangelicalism needs to be tempered with the experience and wisdom of past generations, for whom the Christian life was much more demanding, and ultimately much more rewarding. Engaging with the tradition of Christian theologizing allows today's Christians to 'receive nurturing truth and wisdom from God's faithfulness in past generations'.

Packer embodies the distilled wisdom of the theological ages, offering this heady and powerful cup to an evangelicalism which has generally yet to progress beyond the instant fixes of soda machines, in which theology is dispensed as a pre-packed, aggressively marketed product aiming at making its users feel good in the short term. This classic vision of 'theologizing' (once more, we note Packer's distinctive preference to think of theology as a dynamic activity, rather than a static subject) is quite distinct from that of many North American evangelicals, especially those who continue to operate in a fundamentalist environment, where theology is just reading the Bible, and nobody got saved between Paul and Luther (due to their failure to articulate the Reformation doctrine of justification by grace alone by faith alone).

2. The Primacy of Theology

There are many who would prefer to ignore Packer's voice, and get on with forging more effective techniques for evangelism, maximizing the number of attendees at their churches, making themselves and their congregations feel better, and developing a good rhetorical style in their pulpits – a point stressed in a number of recent criticisms of the current state of American evangelicalism, including important works by David F. Wells and Mark A. Noll.[3] Packer's point, however, is that all these activities rest on theological foundations, whether this is recognized or not – and that bad theological foundations hurt people.

Packer's detailed discussion of evangelism (pp. 89–96), revival within the church (pp. 95–6), spirituality (pp. 255–60), prayer and preaching (pp. 93–6) reaffirms his fundamental belief that all are grounded in theology, and all must be justified by theology. Those who prefer to stress techniques will find themselves puzzled and perhaps angered by Packer's insistence that they become more self-critical. Yet Packer's demand for reflection is not a recipe for inactivity or quietism; rather, it offers an opportunity for the formulation of strategies and approaches which are sensitive to the theological realities which they ultimately reflect.

3. The Coherence of Theology

Much recent writing in the area of theological education has stressed the fragmentation which it appears to have undergone. Perhaps the most widely read assessment of this development is due to Edward Farley. In his *Theologia: The Fragmentation and Unity of Theological Education*, Farley points to a series of developments in theological education which have led to the loss of a defining theological vision characterized by the coinherence of piety and intellect. Farley argues that the term *theologia* has lost its original meaning, which he defines – a little lugubriously, one feels – as 'sapiential and personal knowledge of divine self-disclosure', which leads to 'wisdom or discerning judgment indispensable for human living'. More helpfully, he elsewhere lapses into plain English, and refers to the original vision of theology as 'not just objective science, but a personal knowledge of God and the things of God'.[4]

According to Farley, theology – in the classic sense of the term – is a 'heartfelt knowledge of divine things', something which affects both the heart and the mind. It relates to both *fides quae creditur* and *fides qua creditur*, the objective content of faith, and the subjective act of trusting. But all this has changed, not on account of any fundamental difficulties with this classic conception of theology, but on account of the increasing professionalization and specialization of theological educators. The study of theology has become little more than the mastery of discrete bodies of data. It has become something you just know about – whereas it should be something that shapes your life, provides a reason to live, and gives direction to ministry. It is thus perhaps no cause for surprise that so many seminaries report a burgeoning interest in spirituality on the part of their students, when they have been starved of the experiential and reflective dimensions of theology by the unwarranted intrusion of the academic attitude towards the subject just noted. Yet when the Perkins School of Theology (a United Methodist school in Dallas, Texas) introduced spiritual formation as a curriculum requirement, some faculty and students expressed misgivings about the presence of such a course within an academic community.[5] The idea of theology as a purely academic subject forces issues of personal spiritual formation and Christian living – originally part of the idea of 'theology' – out on a limb. All too often, seminaries now see spirituality as a way of bringing back to life a faith which has been deadened by academic theology. But does it have to be like this?

Packer certainly believes that it need not – and, indeed, should not – be like this. The increasing recognition of the importance of spiritual formation as an aspect of a rounded theological education[6] is to be welcomed – but not if it is seen as a discipline which is somehow independent of theology. As we have seen, Packer is adamant that a faulty theology (including faulty approaches to theology, or faulty understanding of what theology is) will have disastrous results. The divide which has opened up between theology and spirituality is simply one illustration of the way in which theology has fragmented and lost its true understanding of its identity and role.

For Packer, Christian theology cannot remain faithful to its subject matter if it regards itself as purely propositional or cognitive in nature. The Christian encounter with God is relational and transformative. As John Calvin pointed out, to know God is to be changed by God; true knowledge of God leads to worship, as the believer is caught up in a transforming and renewing encounter with the living God. To know God is to be changed by God.[7] This theme, pursued with clarity and vigour in Packer's writings (especially the classic *Knowing God*), is essential to a recovery of the proper role of theologizing in the Christian life. The study of theology is thus recognized to be transformative, in that one is recognized not merely to be wrestling with *texts*, nor yet with *ideas*, but with the *living God*. Theology can so easily become the study of theologians; for Packer, 'the proper subject-matter of systematic theology is God actively relating in and through all created things to human beings'.

Packer's vision is strongly integrative, in that he sees theology as offering both a foundation and coherence to Christian thinking and living. As those who have immersed themselves in Packer's writings will know, he considers that the Puritan vision of the Christian life offers exactly such an integrated vision. Writing of the theological vision of the Puritans, he comments: 'If theology does not quicken the conscience and soften the heart, it actually hardens both.' Packer's distinction between different aspects of theology – such as 'historical theology, 'systematic theology' and 'spiritual theology' – reflects his unitary vision of theology as a coherent whole, which has many facets. His strong sense of theology constituting a coherent discipline contrasts sharply with the prevailing trend, nourished by factors such as the rise of professionalism and the increasing sociological distance between church and academy, to treat theology as a fragmented discipline, a series of independent and unrelated subjects which can be studied or ignored at will. Packer's vision offers a powerful challenge to evangelicalism in particular, and the world of academic theology in general. Preaching, praying and pastoring are thus all examples of 'theologizing'.

4. Co-Belligerence: Collaboration without Compromise

What does the future hold for evangelicalism? The general consensus is that the future holds some very exciting possibilities for the movement.[8] Yet the political realities with which evangelicalism is obliged to wrestle in areas in which it is expanding – such as South-East Asia, Latin America and sub-Saharan Africa – are such that it may prove necessary to coexist or collaborate with other Christian groups in those regions. This clearly raises the very sensitive and potentially divisive issue of the extent and manner in which such collaboration is possible. Potentially, this is one of the areas in which Packer will make one of his most significant long-term contributions to evangelicalism, in that he is widely regarded as the theoretical architect of 'collaboration without compromise' in the face of those who assert that *any* form of collaboration amounts to compromise.

There is no doubt that evangelicals in the past regarded collaboration with individual Roman Catholics as unacceptable, and that some today urge that same policy on the movement. Yet Packer's point is that evangelicalism cannot equate faithfulness to the gospel with the wooden repetition of past evangelical attitudes in the present. As he wrote in response to the divisions which arose within English evangelicalism during the 1970s:

> Critics sometimes say that today's evangelicals are utterly different
> from their fathers, but judging them by those evangelical essentials

which we spelt out [earlier] one is struck most forcibly by the depth of continuity. That today's evangelicals understand themselves and their faith in essentially the same terms as did their fathers, and have essentially the same goals in life and ministry, seems too plain to be denied. But, just as a ship can only stay on course as the steering is adjusted to meet wind, tide, currents and other hazards, so evangelicals can only stay on course – that is, steadily pursue the defined goal of spreading pure Christianity, by God's power and for God's praise – by responding with appropriate adaptations to what goes on in the church and the community around. This is the truth embedded in Newman's dictum (so objectionable, in the form in which he developed it) that to remain the same a thing must change often.[9]

As evangelicalism prepares to advance into the next millennium, it must face that question – how can it adapt to new contexts, without losing its identity? The issue of collaboration with others, vigorously contested by evangelicals in the past, is a case in point.

Packer's approach to this issue can be seen as having begun to crystallize through his close study of George Whitefield a few months after his conversion in 1944. The issue can be seen as being of major importance at four points in his career – the 1966–7 debate over evangelical unity in England, arising out of Martyn Lloyd-Jones's call for evangelicals to withdraw from mainstream churches and continuing into the Keele Congress of 1967 (see pp. 154–61); the 1970 publication *Growing into Union*, in which Packer entered into an alliance with two leading Anglo-catholic writers to ensure the defeat of a union scheme which he felt would inevitably lead to the creation of a liberal-catholic denomination (pp. 155–6); his endorsement of the document *Evangelicals and Catholics Together* in 1994 (pp. 264–75); and his major role in the creation of a coalition for orthodoxy within the Anglican Church of Canada, leading to the *Essentials 94* congress of 1994 (pp. 275–7). In every case, with slight differences, the same basic principles can be seen in action.

Collaboration between individual Christians in parachurch organizations does not imply any judgments concerning the denominations of which they are members, but only the personal faith of those individual collaborators. Genuine doctrinal disagreements need to be set alongside the common concern to preach the gospel, combat liberalism within the church, and address a series of moral issues which are of major importance in society as a whole. Packer offers a theoretical justification of what seems likely to become a practical necessity for evangelicalism in the new millennium. Will this be seen by a future generation as one of his most significant strategic contributions to evangelicalism in particular, and to 'great-tradition Christianity' in general? We shall have to wait and see.

Conclusion

'Packer by name, packer by nature.' Our subject often quipped that he enjoyed packing his material tightly. There are few who could manage to pack nearly three hundred major pieces of writing, including more than thirty books, into a single career. Packer's remarkable ability to deal with complex issues in crisp and concise sentences has often been noted. Yet perhaps it is fair to suggest that he is also an *un*packer, in the sense that he has consistently shown himself able and willing to explain, unfold and apply the riches of the Christian gospel for his readers. Packer found great solace and inspiration in reading the works of the theological and spiritual giants of the past. He has ended up becoming such a giant himself. It is to be hoped that evangelicalism can learn from him, just as it is to be hoped that it will prove able to give rise to more like him. For it is not merely evangelicals, but any who seek to theologize within great-tradition Christianity, who will find in Packer a congenial travelling companion who will encourage, nourish and challenge us as we prepare to enter the new millennium.

Recordings of Lectures by
James I. Packer

No book can ever hope to convey Packer's distinctive teaching style, or give an adequate account of his ideas and approaches. Those interested are strongly recommended to get hold of video and audio tapes, and listen to Packer himself. What follows is a list of such tapes, all of which can be ordered from: Regent College Bookstore, 5800 University Boulevard, Vancouver, BC, Canada, V6T 2E4. Check with Regent College for price and availability.

Audio Tapes of Packer's Systematic Theology Lectures at Regent College (see pp. 239–40).

I. Knowledge of God. Revelation, Reason, Scripture, Theological Method, 22 tapes.
II. Doctrine of God, Creation and Man, 23 tapes.
III. Christology and Soteriology, 24 tapes.
IV. Ecclesiology and Eschatology, 22 tapes.

Biblical Expositions

Christ Supreme: The Theology of the Letter to the Colossians, 10 tapes.
All You're Called to Be: Expounding Ephesians for a Generation of Seekers, 6 tapes.
The Letter to the Romans, 25 tapes.

Major Lecture Series

The Holy Spirit and Ourselves, 5 tapes, 1304s.
Puritan Theology for Today, 10 tapes, 2212S.

Christianity: True Humanism, 3 tapes.
The Theology of Renewal, 5 tapes.
The Lord of Glory, 5 tapes.
Thinking Straight about God, 4 tapes.
Systematic Theology Overview, 23 tapes.

Single Lectures

Evangelicals and Roman Catholics: Problems and Prospects.
Focus on Jesus Christ.
Forum on the Doctrine of Election (with Clark Pinnock).
George Whitefield: Reformational Revivalist.
Inerrancy Forum (with Clark Pinnock and Anthony Thiselton).
Romans and Sanctification.
The Problem of Eternal Punishment.
Theological Education: Why Bother?
The Puritans and Ourselves.
What the Bible says about Reconciliation.

A Select Bibliography of
J. I. Packer's Works

I. Books (sole author; including pamphlets [P])

1 *'Fundamentalism' and the Word of God* (London: Inter-Varsity Fellowship and Grand Rapids, Mich.: Eerdmans, 1958).

2 *Evangelism and the Sovereignty of God* (London: Inter-Varsity Press and Chicago: InterVarsity Press, 1961).

3 *The Thirty-nine Articles* (London: Falcon, 1961). (P)

4 *The Plan of God* (London: Evangelical Press, 1962). (P)

5 *Our Lord's Understanding of the Law of God* (Glasgow: Pickering & Inglis, 1962). (P)

6 *Keep Yourselves from Idols* (London: Church Book Room Press and Grand Rapids, Mich.: Eerdmans, 1963). (P)

7 *God Has Spoken* (London: Hodder & Stoughton, 1964). Also published as *God Speaks to Man* (Philadelphia: Westminster Press, 1964); new enlarged edition (London: Hodder & Stoughton and Downers Grove, Ill.: InterVarsity Press, 1979).

8 *Tomorrow's Worship* (London: Church Book Room Press, 1966). (P)

9 *The Gospel in the Prayer Book* (Abingdon, England: Marcham Manor Press, 1966). (P)

10 *The Thirty-nine Articles Today* (London: Church Book Room Press, 1968). (P)

11 *We Believe* (London: Nurses' Christian Fellowship, 1972). (P)

12 *Knowing God* (London: Hodder & Stoughton and Chicago: InterVarsity Press, 1973).

13 *I Want to Be a Christian* (Wheaton, Ill.: Tyndale House and London: Kingsway, 1977); reissued as *Growing in Christ* (Wheaton, Ill.: Crossway, 1994).

14 *For Man's Sake* (London: Paternoster Press, 1977).

15 *The Evangelical Anglican Identity Problem* (Oxford: Latimer House, 1978). (P)

16 *Knowing Man* (Westchester, Ill.: Cornerstone, 1979).
17 *Beyond the Battle For the Bible* (Westchester, Ill.: Cornerstone, 1980). Also published as *Under God's Word* (London: Marshall, Morgan and Scott, 1980).
18 *God's Words* (London: Inter-Varsity Press and Downers Grove, Ill.: Inter-Varsity Press, 1981).
19 *A Kind of Noah's Ark? The Anglican Commitment to Comprehensiveness* (Oxford: Latimer House, 1981). (P)
20 *Freedom and Authority* (Oakland, Calif.: International Council on Biblical Inerrancy, 1981). Also published as *Freedom, Authority and Scripture* (Leicester: Inter-Varsity Press, 1982).
21 *Keep in Step with the Spirit* (Old Tappan, NJ: Revell, 1984).
22 *The Thirty-nine Articles: Their Place and Use Today*, with additions by R. T. Beckwith (Oxford: Latimer House, 1984).
23 *Your Father Loves You* (Wheaton, Ill.: Harold Shaw, 1986).
24 *Meeting God* (LifeGuide Bible Study) (Downers Grove, Ill.: InterVarsity Press, 1986).
25 *God in Our Midst* (Ann Arbor, Mich.: Servant, 1987). (P)
26 *Hot Tub Religion* (Wheaton, Ill.: Tyndale House, 1987).
27 *A Quest for Godliness* (Westchester Ill.: Crossway, 1991). Also published as *Among God's Giants* (Eastbourne, England: Kingsway, 1991).
28 *A Man for All Ministries* (Richard Baxter), St Antholin's Charity Lectureship (London: Needham's, 1991). (P)
29 *Rediscovering Holiness* (Ann Arbor, Mich.: Servant, 1992). Also published as *A Passion for Holiness* (Cambridge: Crossway, 1992).
30 *Concise Theology* (Wheaton, Ill.: Tyndale House, and Leicester: Inter-Varsity Press, 1993).
31 *A Passion For Faithfulness* (Wheaton, Ill.: Crossway, 1995).
32 *Knowing and Doing the Will of God* (Ann Arbor, Mich.: Servant, 1995).
33 *Knowing Christianity* (Wheaton, Ill.: Harold Shaw, 1995).
34 *Life in the Spirit* (London: Hodder & Stoughton and Wheaton, Ill.; Crossway, 1996).
35 *An Anglican to Remember* (William Perkins), St Antholin's Charity Lectureship (London: Needham's, 1996). (P)
36 *Truth and Power* (Wheaton, Ill.: Harold Shaw, 1996).
37 *Great Grace* (Ann Arbor, Mich: Servant, 1997).
38 *A Grief Sanctified* (Ann Arbor, Mich.: Servant, 1997).

II. Books (joint author)

ed. and trans. with O.R. Johnston, *Luther's Bondage of the Will* (London: James Clarke and Old Tappan, NJ: Fleming H. Revell, 1957).

with J. A. Motyer, *Reservation* (London: Church Book Room Press, 1960). (P)

with A.M. Stibbs, *The Spirit Within You* (London: Hodder & Stoughton, 1966); reissued (Glasgow: Pickering & Inglis and Grand Rapids, Mich.: Baker, 1980).

with C.O. Buchanan, E.L. Mascall, G. Leonard, *Growing into Union: Proposals for Forming a United Church in England* (London: SPCK, 1970).

with Thomas Howard, *Christianity the True Humanism* (Waco, Tex.: Word, 1985).

III. Books (contributor)

'Revelation and Inspiration', in E.F. Kevan, A.M. Stibbs, F. Davidson (eds), *The New Bible Commentary*, 2nd edn. Also published as D. Guthrie, J. A. Motyer, A.M. Stibbs, D.J. Wiseman (eds), *The New Bible Commentary Revised*, pp. 24–30; and in *Eerdmans' Bible Commentary* (London: Inter-Varsity Press and Grand Rapids, Mich.: Eerdmans, 1954, 1970), pp. 12–18.

'Modern Theories of Revelation', in C.F.H. Henry (ed.) *Revelation and the Bible* (Grand Rapids, Mich.: Baker, 1959 and London: Inter-Varsity Press, 1960), pp. 87–104.

'Call', 'Faith', 'Freedom', 'Ignorance', 'Justification', 'Orthodoxy', 'Puritan', 'Regeneration', in C.F.H. Henry. (ed.), *Baker's Dictionary of Theology* (Grand Rapids, Mich.: Baker, 1959).

Introductory Essay in John Owen, *The Death of Death in the Death of Christ* (London: Banner of Truth, 1959), pp. 1–25; also published separately. (P)

'The Origin and History of Fundamentalism', in T. Hewitt, (ed.), *The Word of God and Fundamentalism* (London: Church Book Room Press, 1960), pp. 100–27.

'Assurance', 'Authority', 'Conversion', 'Earnest', 'Election', 'Good', 'Incarnation', 'Inner Man', 'Inspiration', 'Justification', 'Liberty', 'Obedience', 'Perfection', 'Piety', 'Predestination', 'Providence', 'Revelation', 'Temptation', in J.D. Douglas (ed.), *The New Bible Dictionary* (London: Inter-Varsity Press and Grand Rapids, Mich.: Eerdmans, 1961). Also published as N. Hillyer et al., (eds.), *The New Bible Dictionary*, 2nd edn (Leicester: Inter-Varsity Press and Wheaton, Ill.: Tyndale House, 1982); and published in *The Illustrated Bible Dictionary* (same publishers).

Introductory Essay in J. Buchanan, *The Doctrine of Justification* (London: Banner of Truth, 1961), pp. 1–9.

'Lambeth 1958', in J. I. Packer (ed.), *Eucharistic Sacrifice* (London: Church Book Room Press, 1962), pp. 1–21.

'The Nature of the Church', in C.F.H. Henry (ed.), *Basic Christian Doctrines* (New York: Holt, Rinehart & Winston, 1962), pp. 241–7.

'Episcopacy', and two other essays, in J.I. Packer (ed.), *The Church of England and the Methodist Church* (Abingdon, England: Marcham Manor Press, 1963).

'Thomas Cranmer's Catholic Theology', in G.E. Duffield (ed.), *Thomas Cranmer* (Abingdon, England: Sutton Courtenay Press, 1963), pp. 10–37.

'What Is Revival?' in D. Winter (ed.), *The Best of Crusade* (London: Victory Press, 1963), pp. 89–93.

'British Theology in the Twentieth Century', in C. F. H. Henry (ed.), *Christian Faith and Modern Theology* (New York: Channel Press, 1964), pp. 23–41.

'The Status of the Articles', in H. E. W. Turner (ed.), *The Thirty-nine Articles of the Church of England* (London: Mowbrays, 1964), pp. 25–57.

'The Wretched Man in Romans 7', in F.L. Cross (ed.), *Studia Evangelica* (Berlin: Akademie-Verlag, 1964); reprinted as an appendix to *Keep in Step with the Spirit* (21), pp. 621–7.

'Wanted: A Pattern for Union', and (with C. O. Buchanan) 'Unification and Ordination', in J.I. Packer (ed.), *All in Each Place* (Abingdon, England: Marcham Manor Press, 1965), pp. 17–40.

'Calvin the Theologian', in G. E. Duffield (ed.), *John Calvin* (Abingdon, England: Sutton Courtenay Press, 1966), pp. 149–75.

'Expository Preaching: Charles Simeon and Ourselves' and 'The Revised Catechism', in *Churchmen Speak*, selected essays from *Churchman* (Abingdon, England: Marcham Manor Press, 1966), pp. 64–70, 88–99.

'Gain and Loss', in R. T. Beckwith (ed.), *Towards a Modern Prayer Book* (Abingdon, England: Marcham Manor Press, 1966).

'Isn't One Religion as Good as Another?' in F. Colquhoun (ed.), *Hard Questions* (London: Falcon, 1967), pp. 16–19.

'The Good Confession', in J. I. Packer (ed.), *Guidelines* (London: Falcon, 1967), pp. 11–38.

'The Necessity of the Revealed Word', in M. C. Tenney (ed.), *The Bible: The Living Word of Revelation* (Grand Rapids, Mich.: Zondervan, 1968), pp. 31–52.

'Anglican-Methodist Unity: Which Way Now?' in J.I. Packer (ed.), *Fellowship in the Gospel* (Abingdon, England: Marcham Manor Press, 1968).

'Training for the Ministry', in C. Porthouse (ed.), *Ministry in the Seventies* (London: Falcon, 1970).

'Biblical Authority, Hermeneutics and Inerrancy', in E. R. Geehan (ed.), *Jerusalem and Athens* (Philadelphia: Presbyterian and Reformed, 1971), pp. 141–53.

'Towards a Corporate Presbyterate', in R.P.P. Johnson (ed.), *Ministry in the Local Church: Problems and Pathways* (Bramcote. Grove Books, 1972). (P)

'Reservation: Theological Issues', in C.O. Buchanan (ed.), *Reservation and Communion of the Sick* (Bramcote: Grove Books, 1972). (P)

'Representative Priesthood?' and 'Postscript: I Believe in Women's Ministry', in G.E. Duffield and M. Bruce (eds.), *Why Not?* (Abingdon, England: Marcham Manor Press, 1972; 2nd edn 1976), pp. 78–80, 164–74.

'Taking Stock in Theology', in J. C. King (ed.), *Evangelicals Today* (London: Lutterworth Press, 1973), pp. 15–30.

'Thoughts on the Role and Function of Women in the Church', in R. C. Craston (ed.), *Evangelicals and the Ordination of Women* (Bramcote: Grove Books, 1973). (P)

'Revelation', 'Myth', 'Puritan Ethics', in C.F.H. Henry (ed.), *Baker's Dictionary of Christian Ethics* (Grand Rapids, Mich.: Baker, 1973).

Introductory Essay in Richard Baxter, *The Reformed Pastor* (London: Banner of Truth, 1974), pp. 9–19.

'*Sola Scriptura*' in History and Today', and 'Calvin's Doctrine of Scripture', in J.W. Montgomery (ed.), *God's Inerrant Word* (Minneapolis: Bethany, 1974), pp. 43–63, 95–114.

'Life in Christ' (95 Bible studies), in *Bible Characters and Doctrines*, vol. II (London: Scripture Union, 1974).

'Abolish', 'Accuse', 'Carpenter', 'Defile', 'Despise', 'Dirt', 'Firm', 'Present', 'Ruin', in C. Brown (ed.), *New International Dictionary of New Testament Theology*, vol. I (Exeter: Paternoster Press and Grand Rapids, Mich.: Zondervan, 1975).

Introductory Essay in E. Hindson, *Introduction to Puritan Theology* (Grand Rapids, Mich.: Baker, 1976), pp. 9–12.

'What Is Evangelism?' in H. Conn (ed.), *Theological Perspectives on Church Growth* (Nutley, NJ.: Presbyterian and Reformed, 1976), pp. 91–105.

'The Reformed Doctrine of Justification', in R.C. Sproul (ed.), *Soli Deo Gloria, Festschrift* for John Gerstner (Philadelphia: Presbyterian and Reformed, 1976), pp. 11–25.

'Jesus Christ the Lord: The New Testament Doctrine of the Incarnation', in J.R.W. Stott (ed.), *Obeying Christ in a Changing World, Vol. I: The Lord Christ* (London: Collins, 1977), pp. 32–60.

'Theology of the Reformation' and 'Ignatius Loyola', in T. Dowley (ed.), *Lion Handbook of Church History* (Berkhamsted, England: Lion, 1977).

'Are Pain and Suffering Direct Results of Evil?' in F. Colquhoun (ed.), *Moral Questions* (London: Falcon, 1977), pp. 26–9.

'On Knowing God', in J.M. Boice (ed.), *Our Sovereign God* (Grand Rapids, Mich.: Baker, 1977), pp. 61–76.

Foreword to R.C. Sproul, *Knowing Scripture* (Downers Grove, Ill.: Inter-Varsity Press, 1977), pp. 9–10.

'Oxford Evangelicals in Theology', in John Reynolds, *The Evangelicals at Oxford*, 2nd edn. (Abingdon, England: Marcham Manor Press, 1977), pp. 82–94.

Preface to 1977 reprint of W.H. Griffith Thomas, *The Principles of Theology* (London: Vine Books and Grand Rapids, Mich.: Baker, 1978), pp. 5–14.

'An Evangelical View of Progressive Revelation', in K. Kantzer (ed.), *Evangelical Roots* (Nashville: Nelson, 1978), pp. 143–58.

'Situations and Principles' and 'Conscience, Character and Choice', in G.J. Wenham and B. Kaye (eds), *Law, Morality and the Bible* (Downers Grove, Ill., InterVarsity Press, 1978), pp. 151–92.

'Encountering Present-Day Views of Scripture', in J.M. Boice (ed.), *Foundation of Biblical Authority* (Grand Rapids, Mich.: Zondervan, 1978), pp. 61–84.

'A Lamp in a Dark Place: II Peter 1:19–21', in E. Radmacher (ed.), *Can We Trust the Bible?* (Wheaton, Ill.: Tyndale House, 1979), pp. 15–32.

Preface to centenary edition of J.C. Ryle, *Holiness* (Welwyn Garden City: Evangelical Press, 1979).

'The Gospel: Its Content and Communication', in J. R. W. Stott and R. Coote (eds), *Gospel and Culture* (Pasadena, Calif.: William Carey Press, 1979); shorter version, *Down to Earth*, same eds (Grand Rapids, Mich.: Eerdmans, 1980), pp. 97–114.

'Preaching as Biblical Interpretation', in J. R. Michaels and R. Nicole (eds), *Inerrancy and Common Sense* (Grand Rapids, Mich.: Baker, 1980), pp. 187–203.

'The Adequacy of Language', in N. Geisler (ed.), *Inerrancy* (Grand Rapids, Mich.: Zondervan, 1980), pp. 197–228.

Editor's Preface in J. I. Packer, M.E. Tenney and W. White Jr.(eds), *The Bible Almanac* (Nashville, Tenn.: Nelson, 1980), pp. 11–12.

'My Path to Prayer', in D. Hanes (ed), *My Path of Prayer* (Brighton: Henry E. Walter, 1981), pp. 55–66.

'Sacrifice and Satisfaction' and 'To All Who Will Come', in J.M. Boice (ed.), *Our Saviour God* (Grand Rapids, Mich.: Baker, 1981).

'Is Christianity Credible?' in D. Stacey (ed.), *Is Christianity Credible?* (London: Epworth, 1981), pp. 64–72.

'Response to Stephen Clark', in P. Williamson and K. Perrotta (eds), *Christianity Confronts Modernity* (Ann Arbor, Mich.: Servant, 1981), pp. 187–93.

Preface to Elisabeth Elliot, *No Graven Image*, new edn (London: Hodder & Stoughton, 1981).

Preface to Sinclair B. Ferguson, *The Christian Life* (London: Hodder & Stoughton, 1981), pp. ix-x.

Preface to Michael Baughen, *Breaking the Prayer Barrier* (Wheaton, Ill.: Harold Shaw, 1981).

'God: From the Fathers to the Moderns' and 'The Puritans', in R. Keeley (ed.), *Lion Handbook to Christian Belief* (Berkhamsted: Lion, 1982). Also published as *Eerdmans' Handbook to Christian Belief* (Grand Rapids, Mich.: Eerdmans, 1982).

Preface to A. Wetherell Johnson, *Created for Commitment* (Wheaton, Ill.: Tyndale House, 1982).

Foreword to Bruce Milne, *Know the Truth* (Leicester: Inter-Varsity Press, 1982), pp. 5–6.

'Infallible Scripture and the Role of Hermeneutics', in D. A. Carson and J.B. Woodbridge (eds), *Scripture and Truth* (Grand Rapids, Mich.: Zondervan and Leicester; Inter-Varsity Press, 1983), pp. 325–56.

Introductory Essay in John Owen, *Sin and Temptation*, ed. and rewritten by James M. Houston (Portland, Oreg.: Multnomah, 1983), pp. xvii-xix.

'Steps to the Renewal of the Christian People' and 'Agenda for Theology', in P. Williamson and K. Perrotta (eds), *Summons to Faith and Renewal* (Ann Arbor, Mich.: Servant, 1983), pp. 107–27.

'Response to Henry Krabbendam: The New Hermeneutic', in N. Geisler and E. Radmacher, (eds), *Hermeneutics, Inerrancy and the Bible* (Grand Rapids, Mich: Zondervan, 1984), pp. 559–71.

'A Christian View of Man', in Lynne Morris (ed.), *The Christian Vision: Man in Society* (Hillsdale, Mich.: Hillsdale College Press, 1984), pp. 101–19.

'John Calvin and the Inerrancy of Holy Scripture', in J. Hannah (ed.), *Inerrancy and the Church* (Chicago: Moody Press, 1984), pp. 143–68.

'How to Recognize a Christian Citizen', in *The Christian as Citizen* (Wheaton, Ill.: Christianity Today Institute; bound into *Christianity Today*, 19 April 1985), pp. 4–8.

'Divisions in the Church' and 'Reformation in the Church', in *The Church: God's New Society* (Philadelphia: Philadelphia Conference on Reformed Theology, 1985).

'Arminianisms', in R. Godfrey and T. Boyd (eds), *Through Christ's Word* (Phillipsburg, NJ.: Presbyterian and Reformed, 1985), pp. 121–48.

'In Quest of Canonical Interpretation'. in R. K. Johnston (ed.), *The Use of the Bible in Theology: Evangelical Options* (Atlanta, Ga.: John Knox Press, 1985), pp. 35–55.

'David Martyn Lloyd-Jones', in C. Turner (ed.), *Chosen Vessels* (Ann Arbor, Mich.: Servant, 1985). Also published as *Heroes* (Servant, 1991), pp. 109–23.

'Justification in Protestant Theology', in J.I. Packer and others, *Here We Stand: Justification by Faith Today* (London: Hodder & Stoughton, 1986), pp. 84–102.

'A Kind of Puritan', in C. Catherwood (ed.), *Martyn Lloyd-Jones: Chosen by God* (Crowborough; Highland Books, 1986), pp. 33–57.

'Why Preach?' in S. Logan (ed.), *The Preacher and Preaching* (Phillipsburg, NJ: Presbyterian & Reformed, 1986), pp. 1–29.

'Theism for Our Time', in P.T. O'Brien and D. G. Peterson (eds), *God Who Is Rich in Mercy* (Homebush West, NSW.: Lancer Books, 1986), pp. 1–23.

'Foreword: No Little Person', in R. W. Ruegsegger, *Reflections on Francis Schaeffer* (Grand Rapids, Mich.: Zondervan, 1986), pp. 7–17.

'The Holy Spirit and His Work', in K. Kantzer (ed.), *Applying the Scriptures* (Grand Rapids, Mich.: Zondervan, 1987), pp. 51–76. Also published in *Crux* 23, no. 2 (June 1987): 2–17.

'Foreword: Why We Need the Puritans', in Leland Ryken, *Worldly Saints* (Grand Rapids, Mich.: Zondervan, 1987), pp. ix-xvi.

Introduction to P. Fromer and J.I. Packer (eds.), *The Best in Theology* (Carol Stream, Ill.: Christianity Today, 1987), 1:13–23.

'Introduction: On Being Serious About the Holy Spirit', in David Wells, *God the Evangelist: How the Holy Spirit Works to Bring Men and Women to Faith* (Grand Rapids, Mich.: Eerdmans, 1987), pp. xi-xvi.

'The Trinity and the Gospel', in R.A. Bodey, *Good News for All Seasons* (Grand Rapids, Mich.: Baker, 1987), pp. 91–8.

'Inerrancy and the Divinity and Humanity of the Bible', 'Problem Areas Related to Biblical Inerrancy', 'Implications of Biblical Inerrancy for the Christian Mission', in *Proceedings of the Conference of Biblical Inerrancy 1987* (Nashville, Tenn.: Broadman, 1987), pp. 135–42, 205–13, and 245–50.

Introduction to P. Fromer and J.I. Packer (eds.), *The Best in Theology* (Carol Stream, Ill.: Christianity Today, 1988), 2:13–22.

'The Christian and God's World', in J. M. Boice (ed.), *Transforming Our World* (Portland, Oreg.: Multnomah, 1988), pp. 81–97.

'God the Image-Maker', in M. Noll and D. Wells (eds.), *Christian Faith and Practice in the Modern World* (Grand Rapids, Mich.: Eerdmans, 1988), pp. 27–50.

'John Calvin and Reformed Europe', in J. Woodbridge (ed.), *Great Leaders of the Christian Church* (Chicago: Moody Press, 1988), pp. 208–15.

'Baptism in the Spirit', 'Baxter', 'Farrer', 'Glory of God', 'God', 'Holiness Movement', 'Holy Spirit', 'Infallibility and Inerrancy', 'Method', 'Paradox', 'Revival', 'Scripture', in D. Wright, S. Ferguson and J. I. Packer (eds.), *New Dictionary of Theology* (Leicester: Inter-Varsity Press and Downers Grove, Ill.: InterVarsity Press, 1988).

'The Challenge of Biblical Interpretation: Creation', 'The Challenge of Biblical Interpretation: Women', 'The Challenge of Biblical Interpretation: Eschatology', in *The Proceedings of the Conference on Biblical*

Interpretation (Nashville, Tenn.: Broadman, 1988), pp. 21–33, 103–15, and 191–204.

Introduction to H. Smith and J. I. Packer (eds.), *The Best in Theology* (Carol Stream, Ill.: Christianity Today, 1988), 3: vii-xiv.

'Is the Charismatic Movement . . . from God?' in *Tough Questions Christian Ask* and *Pentecostals* (both Carol Stream, Ill.: Christianity Today /Wheaton, Ill.: Victor, 1989), pp. 49–60. Also published as 'Piety on Fire', *Christianity Today*, 12 May 1989, pp. 18–23, and *Renewal*, July 1990, pp. 28–32.

'Christian Morality Adrift', in K. Perrotta and J. Blattner (eds), *A Society in Peril* (Ann Arbor, Mich.: Servant, 1989), pp. 57–76.

Introduction to J.I. Yamamoto and J.I. Packer (eds.), *The Best in Theology* (Carol Stream, Ill.: Christianity Today, 1989), 4: vii-xiv.

Introduction to Jeremiah Burroughs, *Hosea*, reprint (Beaver Falls, Penn.: Soli Deo Gloria, 1989).

Introduction to Richard Baxter, *Christian Directory*, reprint (Beaver Falls, Penn.: Soli Deo Gloria, 1990).

Introduction to H. Witsius, *On the Covenants*, reprint (Phillipsburg, NJ.: Presbyterian and Reformed, 1990).

Introduction (biographical) to John Gwyn-Thomas, *Rejoice Always* (Edinburgh: Banner of Truth, 1990), pp. ix-xv.

Introduction to J. Tolhurst (ed.), *Men, Women and Priesthood* (Leominster: Gracewing, 1990), pp. vii-xvi.

'The Christian's Purpose in Business', in R. C. Chewning (ed.), *Biblical Principles and Business: The Practice* (Colorado Springs: NavPress, 1990).

'Evangelicals and the Way of Salvation: New Challenges to the Gospel – Universalism and Justification by Faith', in C. F. H. Henry and K. Kantzer (eds), *Evangelical Affirmations* (Grand Rapids, Mich.: Zondervan, 1990), pp. 107–36.

'Understanding the Bible: Evangelical Hermeneutics', in M. Tinker (ed.), *Restoring the Vision* (Eastbourne; MARC, 1990), pp. 39–58.

Foreword, 'The Means of Conversion' and 'Godliness in Ephesians,' in D. M. Lewis (ed.), *With Heart, Mind and Strength: The Best of Crux, 1979-1989* (Langley, BC.: Credo, 1990), pp. 7–8, 63–79, and 129–43. 'The Means of Conversion' originally published in *Crux*, 25, no. 4 (December 1989): pp. 14–22; 'Godliness in Ephesians' originally published in *Crux*, 25, no. 1 (March 1989). pp 8–16.

'Babel', in R. A. Bodey (ed.), *Inside the Sermon* (Grand Rapids, Mich.: Baker, 1990), pp. 185–200.

'Thirty Years' War: The Doctrine of Holy Scripture', in H. Conn (ed.), *Practical Theology and the Ministry of the Church, Festschrift* for E.P. Clowney (Phillipsburg, NJ.: Presbyterian and Reformed, 1990), pp. 25–44.

Aspects of Authority (Disley.: Orthos, 1990).

The Problem of Eternal Punishment, Leon Morris Lecture, 1990 (Victoria, Australia: Evangelical Alliance Publishing, 1990). Also published in *Crux*, 26, no. 3 (September 1990): pp. 18–25.

Introduction to Richard Baxter, *Practical Works IV*, reprint (Ligonier, Penn.: Soli Deo Gloria, 1991).

'Evangelical Foundations for Spirituality', in M. Bockmuehl and K. Burkhardt (eds), *Gott Lieben und Seine Gebote Halten* (Giessen, Germany/ Basel, Switzerland: Brunnen Verlag, 1991), pp. 149–62.

'Authority in Preaching', in M. Eden and D. Wells (eds), *The Gospel in the Modern World* (Leicester: Inter-Varsity Press, 1991), pp. 198–212.

'Richard Baxter on Heaven, Hope, and Holiness', in J. I. Packer and L. Wilkinson (eds), *Alive to God, Festschrift* for James M. Houston (Downers Grove, Ill.: InterVarsity Press, 1992), pp. 161–75.

'The Comfort of Conservatism', in M. Horton (ed.), *Power Religion* (Chicago: Moody Press, 1992), pp. 283–99.

'The Holy Spirit in the Book of Common Prayer', in S. Harris (ed.), *The Holy Spirit* (Charlottesville, Va.: St Peter Publications, 1993).

'Election', 'Predestination', in D. Jeffrey (ed.), *Dictionary of Biblical Tradition in English Literature* (Grand Rapids, Mich.: Eerdmans, 1993).

'The Empowered Christian Life', in G. Grieg and K. Springer (eds), *The Kingdom and the Power* (Ventura, Calif.: Regal, 1994), pp. 207–15.

'Anglicanism Today: The Path to Renewal' and 'Jesus Christ the Only Saviour', with A. McGrath, G. LeMarquand and J.P. Westin, in G. Egerton (ed.), *Anglican Essentials* (Toronto: Anglican Book Centre, 1995), pp. 53–63, 98–110.

'The Spirit with the Word: The Reformational Revivalism of George Whitefield', in W.P. Stephens (ed.), *The Bible, the Reformation and the Church, Festschrift* for James Atkinson (Sheffield; Sheffield Academic Press, 1995), pp. 166–89.

'Atonement', 'Richard Baxter', 'Godliness', 'Holy Spirit', 'D. M. Lloyd-Jones', in David Atkinson and David Field (eds), *New Dictionary of Christian Ethics and Pastoral Theology* (Leicester: Inter-Varsity Press and Downers Grove, Ill.: InterVarsity Press, 1995).

'The Preacher as Theologian', in C. Green (ed.), *When God's Voice Is Heard*, Festschrift for Dick Lucas (Leicester; Inter-Varsity Press, 1995), pp. 79–95.

'Crosscurrents Among Evangelicals', in C. Colson and R. J. Neuhaus (eds), *Evangelicals and Catholics Together: Toward a Common Mission* (Dallas, Tex.: Word, 1995), pp. 147–74.

'Robert Aitken', in D. M. Lewis (ed.), *The Blackwell Dictionary of Evangelical Biography: 1730–1860* (Oxford: Basil Blackwell, 1995).

Introduction to Henry Scougal, *The Life of God in the Soul of Man* (Tain: Christian Focus, 1995).

Introduction to John Owen, *The Mortification of Sin* (Tain: Christian Focus, 1995).

'The Love of God' in T. Schreiner and Bruce Ware (eds), *The Grace of God; the Bondage of the Will* (Grand Rapids, Mich.: Baker, 1996) II. 413–27.

'Theology and Bible Reading' in Elmer Dyck (ed.), *The Act of Bible Reading* (Downers Grove, Ill.: InterVarsity Press, 1996), pp. 65–87.

'Faith, Covenant and Medical Practice' in Edwin Hui (ed.), *Christian Character, Virtue and Bioethics* (Vancouver: Regent College Bookstore, 1996), pp. 11–24.

IV. Articles in *Puritan and Reformed Studies Conference Reports*

'The Witness of the Spirit: The Puritan Teaching', in *The Wisdom of Our Fathers: Puritan and Reformed Studies Conference Reports, 1956* (privately printed, 1957), pp. 14–25 (reprint edn Clonmel, Ireland: Clonmel Evangelical Bookroom, 1993).*

'The Puritans and the Lord's Day', in *Servants of the Word: Puritan and Reformed Studies Conference Reports, 1957* (London: Banner of Truth Trust, 1958), pp. 1–24.*

'The Puritans as Interpreters of Scripture', in *A Goodly Heritage: Puritan and Reformed Studies Conference Reports, 1958* (London: Banner of Truth Trust, 1959), pp. 2–7, 18–26.*

'The Puritan View of Preaching the Gospel', in *How Shall They Hear? Puritan and Reformed Studies Conference Reports, 1959* (privately printed, 1960; reprint edn Clonmel, Ireland: Clonmel Evangelical Bookroom, 1993).*

'Jonathan Edwards and the Theology of Revival', in *Increasing in the Knowledge of God: Puritan and Reformed Studies Conference Reports, 1960* (privately printed, 1961; reprint edn Clonmel, Ireland: Clonmel Evangelical Bookroom, 1992).*

'The Puritan Idea of Communion with God', in *Press Toward the Mark: Puritan and Reformed Studies Conference Reports, 1961* (privately printed, 1962; reprint edn Clonmel, Ireland: Clonmel Evangelical Bookroom, 1992).

'The Puritan Conscience', in *Faith and a Good Conscience: Puritan and Reformed Studies Conference Reports, 1962* (privately printed, 1963; reprint ed Clonmel, Ireland: Clonmel Evangelical Bookroom, 1992).*

'The Puritans and Worship', in *Diversity in Unity: Puritan and Reformed Studies Conference Reports, 1963* (London: *Evangelical Magazine*, 1964), pp. 3–14.*

'Calvin: A Servant of the Word', in *Able Ministers of the New Testament: Puritan and Reformed Studies Conference Reports, 1964* (London: *Evangelical Magazine*, 1965), pp. 36–55.

'Luther', in *Approaches to the Reformation of the Church: Puritan and Reformed Studies Conference Reports, 1965* (London: *Evangelical Magazine*, 1966), pp. 25–33.

'John Owen on Communication from God', in *One Steadfast High Intent: Puritan and Reformed Studies Conference Reports, 1966* (London: *Evangelical Magazine*, 1967), pp. 17–30.*

'The Puritans and Spiritual Gifts', in *Profitable for Doctrine and Reproof: Puritan and Reformed Studies Conference Reports, 1967* (privately printed, 1968; reprint edn Clonmel, Ireland: Clonmel Evangelical Bookroom, 1992), pp. 15–27.*

'Arminianisms', in *The Manifold Grace of God: Puritan and Reformed Studies Conference Reports, 1968* (London: *Evangelical Magazine*, 1969), pp. 22–34.

'The Doctrine of Justification in Development and Decline Among the Puritans', in *By Schisms Rent Asunder: Puritan and Reformed Studies Conference Reports, 1969* (London: *Evangelical Magazine*, 1970), pp. 18–30.*

* These articles are incorporated in *A Quest for Godliness*, published in the United Kingdom as *Among God's Giants*. See pp. 19–20 of that work for details.

V. Other articles (a selection of the more significant)

'The Puritan Treatment of Justification by Faith', *Evangelical Quarterly* 24, no. 3 (July 1952): pp. 131–43.

'Sanctification – Puritan Teaching', *The Christian Graduate* 5, no. 4 (December 1952): pp. 125–8.

'Richard Baxter', *Theology* 55 (May 1953): pp. 174–8.

'Blind Spots', *Discipulus*, Advent 1954: pp. 5–8.

'"Keswick" and the Reformed Doctrine of Sanctification', *Evangelical Quarterly* 27, no. 3 (July 1955): pp. 153–67.

'Baptism: Sacrament of the Covenant of Grace', *Churchman* 69, no. 2 (June 1955).

'Some Thoughts on General Revelation', *Christian Graduate* 9, no. 3 (September 1956): pp. 114–21.

'Puritan Evangelism', *Banner of Truth* 4 (1957).

'With All Thy Mind', *Inter-Varsity*, Autumn 1957: pp. 4–8.

'Seventeenth Century Teaching on the Christian Life', *Churchman* 71, no. 4 (December 1957); 72, no. 1 (March 1958).

'The Fundamentalism Controversy: Retrospect and Prospect', *Faith and Thought* 90, no. 1 (Spring 1958): pp. 35–45.

'Fundamentalism: The British Scene', *Christianity Today*, 29 September 1958: pp. 3–6.

'The Inspiration and Infallibility of Holy Scripture', *Symposium of Articles from Theological Students Fellowship Bulletin* (no date): pp. 16–18.

'Calvinism in Britain', *Torch and Trumpet* (1959).

'Christianity and Non-Christian Religions', *Christianity Today*, 21 December 1959: pp. 3–5.

'The Bible in Modern Theology', *Bible League Quarterly* no. 240 (January-March 1960): pp. 129–32.

'Puritan Preaching', *The Evangelical Christian*, October 1960: pp. 18–21.

The Theological Challenge to Evangelicalism Today, Fellowship of Evangelical Churchmen (1961).

'Training for Christian Service', *The Evangelical Christian*, September 1961: pp. 10–15.

'The Bible and the Authority of Reason', *Churchman* 75, no. 4 (December 1961): pp. 207–19.

'The Holy Spirit – and Authority', *The Almond Branch*, 1962: pp. 9–12.

'Questions About Inter-Varsity Fellowship', *Break Through* no. 11 (May 1962): pp. 13–19.

'Our Lord and the Old Testament', *Bible League Quarterly* no. 252 (January-March 1963): pp. 70–4.

'Fellowship: The Theological Basis', *Christian Graduate* 16, no. 3 (September 1963): pp. 7–11.

'Episcopal Idol – A Consideration of *Honest to God*', *The Evangelical Christian*, October 1963: pp. 4–5, 32–5.

'The Bible Yesterday, Today and Tomorrow', *The Gospel Magazine*, March 1964: pp. 104–13.

'Atheism', *Inter-Varsity*, special introductory issue (1964): pp. 4–6.

'The Holy Spirit and the Local Congregation', *Churchman* 78, no. 2 (June 1964): pp. 98–108.

'A Broad Church Reformation?' *London Quarterly and Holborn Review* 189 (October 1964): pp. 270–5.

'All Men Won't Be Saved', *Banner of Truth* 41 (March 1965).

'Death: Life's One and Only Certainty', *Eternity* 16, no. 3 (March 1965): pp. 22–6.

'Ministry of the Word Today', *The Presbyterian Guardian* 34, no. 6 (July-August. 1965): pp. 87–90.

'One Body in Christ: The Doctrine and Expression of Christian Unity', *Churchman* 80, no. 1 (March 1966): pp. 16–26.

'Luther Against Erasmus', *Concordia Theological Monthly* 37, no. 4 (April 1966): pp. 207–21.

'Led by the Spirit of God', *The Life of Faith*, 26 May 1966: pp. 499–500.

'A Calvinist – and an Evangelist!' *The Hour International* no. 31 (August 1966): pp. 25–7.

'Must We Demythologize?' *Theological Students Fellowship Bulletin* no. 50 (Spring 1968): pp. 1–5.

'Letter to a Leader', *CFYA Leaders' Newspaper* 1, no. 3.

'Re-tooling the Clergy Factories', *Churchman* 82, no. 2 (Summer 1968): pp. 120–4.

'The Church of South India and Reunion in England', *Churchman* 82, no. 4 (Winter. 1968): pp. 249–61.

'Revival', *Christian Graduate* 24, no. 4 (December 1971): pp. 97–100.

'The Way of Salvation: I. What Is Salvation? II. What Is Faith? III. The Problems of Universalism. IV. Are Non-Christian Faiths Ways of Salvation?' *Bibliotheca Sacra* 129, no. 515 (1972): pp. 105–25; 129, no. 516 (1972): pp. 291–306; 130, no. 517 (1973): pp. 3–10; 130, no. 518 (1973): pp. 110–16.

'Acquitted!' *Span* no. 1 (1973): pp. 10–11.

'What Did the Cross Achieve?' (Tyndale Lecture) *Tyndale Bulletin* 25 (1974): pp. 3–45.

'Revival and Renewal', *Renewal* 62 (April 1976): pp. 14–17.

'A Secular Way to Go', *Third Way* 1, no. 7 (7 April 1977): pp. 3–5.

'Why Is Authority a Dirty Word?' *Spectrum* 9, no. 3 (May 1977): pp. 4–6.

'Who Is God?' in *Simple Faith?* (Berkhamsted: Lion, 1978).

'People Matter More Than Structures', *Crusade* 23, no. 11 (April 1978): pp. 24–5.

'The Uniqueness of Jesus Christ', *Churchman* 92, no. 2 (1978): pp. 101–11.

'Battling for the Bible', *Regent College Bulletin* 9, no. 4 (Fall 1979).

'Puritanism as a Movement of Revival', *Evangelical Quarterly* 52 (January 1980): pp. 2–16.

'Theological Reflections on the Charismatic Movement', *Churchman* 94, nos. 1–2 (1980): pp. 7–25, 108–25.

'George Whitefield: Man Alive'. *Crux* 16, no. 4 (December 1980): pp. 23–6.

'The Means of Growth' and 'Body Life', *Tenth*, July 1981: pp. 2–11.

'Walking to Emmaus with the Great Physician', *Christianity Today*, 10 April 1981: pp. 20–3.

'A View from a Jacuzzi', *Regent College Bulletin* 11, no. 4 (Fall 1981).

'Poor Health May Be the Best Remedy', *Christianity Today*, 21 May 1982: pp. 14–16.

'Knowing Notions or Knowing God?' *Pastoral Renewal* 6, no. 9 (March 1982): pp. 65–8.

'The Message Is Unchanged', *Alliance Witness*, 23 June 1982: pp. 11–14.

'The Reconstitution of Authority', *Crux* 18, no. 4 (December 1982): pp. 2–12.

'Upholding the Unity of Scripture Today', *Journal of the Evangelical Theological Society* 25, no. 4 (December 1982): pp. 409–14.

'Predestination in Christian History' and 'Predestination and Sanctification', *Tenth*, July 1983; pp. 2–16.

'Lord, Send Revival', *The Bulletin*, Winter 1983: pp. 4–5.

'Feet in the Clouds', *Regent College Bulletin* 14, no. 1 (Spring 1984).

'Renewal and Revival', *Channels*, Spring 1984: pp. 7–9.

'Meeting God', *Spiritual Counterfeits Project: Special Collections Journal* 6, no. 1 (Winter 1984).

'"Good Pagans" and God's Kingdom', *Christianity Today*, 17 January 1986; pp. 27–31.

Three articles on guidance, *Eternity*, April-May-June 1986; pp. 19–23, 32–7, and 36–9.

'What Do You Mean When You Say "God"?' *Christianity Today*, 19 September 1986; pp. 22–5.

'Does It Really Matter?' *Eternity*, January 1987; p. 30.

'Dying Well Is Final Test', *Eternity*, January 1987.

'How Christians Should Understand Themselves', *Eternity*, July 1987; p. 36.

'The Way of the Weak Is the Only Healthy Way', *Eternity*, November 1987; p. 28.

'Keeping Your Balance: A Christian's Challenge', *Eternity*, January 1988: p. 18.

'Soldier, Son, Pilgrim: Christian Know Thyself', *Eternity*, April 1988, p. 33.

'Christian *Gravitas* in a Narcissistic Age', *Eternity*, July 1988, p. 46.

'Bringing the Double Mind to Singleness of Faith', *Eternity*, November 1988, p. 59.

'Bringing the Bible to Your Life', *Charisma*, January 1987, pp. 43–4.

'A Modern View of Jesus', *Faith Today*, January 1987, pp. 28–30, 32–3.

'Packer on Preaching', *New Horizons*, January 1987.

'Shy Sovereign', *Tabletalk*, June 1988.

'Jewish Evangelism and the Word of God', *Christian Witness to Israel*, Herald, June 1988.

'Is Hell out of Vogue in This Modern Era?', *United Evangelical Action*, September 1989.

'Westminster and the Roller-Coaster Ride', *Tabletalk* 14, no. 3 (March 1990): pp. 6–10.

'An Introduction to Systematic Spirituality', *Crux* 26, no. 1 (March 1990): pp. 2–8.

'The Gospel and the Lord's Supper', *Mission and Ministry* 8 (Summer 1990): pp. 18–24.

'Shepherds After God's Own Heart', *Pastoral Renewal*, November 1990.

'From the Scriptures to the Sermon: I. Some Perspectives on Preaching; II. The Problem of Paradigms', *Ashland Theological Journal* 22 (1990): pp. 42–64.

'Let's Stop Making Women Presbyters', *Christianity Today*, 11 February 1991: pp. 18–21.

'Understanding the Lordship Controversy', *Tabletalk*, May 1991.

'The Reformed Faith in the Modern World: I. Bible; II. Gospel; III. Church', *Evangelical Presbyterian* (NZ), December 1990/March 1991/June 1991.

with T. Beougher, 'Go Fetch Baxter', *Christianity Today*, 16 December 1991: pp. 26–8.

'Scripture, Inerrancy, and the Church', *Touchstone* 4 (Fall 1991): pp. 3–4.

'The Empowered Christian Life', *Faith and Renewal* 16, no. 4 (January 1992): pp. 3–9.

'The Word of Life', *The Evangelical Catholic* 4, no. 4 (July-August 1992): pp. 1–8.

'Holiness', *Faith and Renewal* 17, no. 5 (March 1993): pp. 3–11.

'George Whitefield: The Startling Puritan', *Christian History* 12, no. 2 (May 1993): pp. 38–40.

'A Reasonable Faith', *Decision*, December 1993.

'Why I Signed It', *Christianity Today*, 12 December 1994: pp. 34–7.

Forewords to books in Crossway Classic Commentary Series, Calvin (*Acts, John*), J.C. Ryle (*Matthew, Mark*), C.H. Spurgeon (*Psalms*), C. Hodge (*Romans, 1 Corinthians, 2 Corinthians, Ephesians*), T. Manton (*James*) (Wheaton, Ill.: Crossway, 1993–5).

'Higher Criticism' in *New Geneva Study Bible* (Nashville, Tenn.: Nelson, 1995), pp. 2044f.

'On from Orr: Cultural Crisis, Rational Realism and Incarnational Ontology', *Crux* 32, No. 3 (September 1996): pp. 12–26.

Acknowledgments

Assembling the material for this biography began in 1991, and took five years. The idea was born on a bus journey between Oxford and Cambridge on a cold and misty morning on Friday 22 February 1991. Jim Packer and I had met up at the London offices of Hodder & Stoughton two days earlier to plan the NIV Thematic Study Bible. He had travelled to Oxford to visit a colleague, and was now travelling on to Cambridge to give a lecture; I was due to speak to a different audience in Cambridge that same day. At 9.40 that morning, we both turned up to travel by the coach service which links the two university cities.

It is a coach journey which normally takes three hours, meandering through Aylesbury and Luton. Jim began to tell me something of his time in England during the 1960s and 1970s. As we talked, I began to realize that I was listening to the story of modern evangelicalism in the making. What I was being told was the raw material of history – and it was as fascinating as it was important. As we bade each other farewell at Cambridge, I knew that Packer's biography had to be written. Three weeks later, I approached Hodder & Stoughton with a definite proposal; together, we approached its subject, who agreed to give us every assistance. It has proved to be one of the most rewarding and fulfilling writing assignments I have ever undertaken.

Writing this book has been made all the more rewarding through the help so generously given by others. My main debt is to Packer himself. He has endured my questioning, on occasion for periods of more than three hours at a time, with enormous patience and kindness. He has gone out of his way to draw my attention to sources and people who could cast light on some of the ideas and events described in this work, insisting that his critics as well as his allies be consulted. Few biographers can have been as fortunate. I also owe thanks to just under three hundred other people, who gave me free access to their diaries, memories, filing cabinets, tape libraries and correspondence. Some of these have allowed me to thank them in this 'Acknowledgments' section; others have insisted that their contributions remain unacknowledged in any public manner. I hope that those latter will allow me to thank them in this indirect way.

I gladly acknowledge the assistance given by the following:

Professor Clifford V. Anderson; Professor Ray S. Anderson; Peter A. Andrew; the Revd Tony Baker; the Ven. David Atkinson; Dr Allan Bapty; Dr Oliver O. Barclay; the Revd Nicholas J.W. Barker; the Rt Revd Michael A. Baughen; Dr David Bebbington; the Rt Revd Wallace Benn; Birmingham City Archives; Lord Stuart Blanch; Bodleian Library, Oxford; James M. Boice; Dr John Bowden; Preb. Dr D.L.E. Bronnert; Professor Colin Brown; the Rt Revd Colin O. Buchanan; Branse Burbridge; the Revd Jack Burton; the Revd Dr Joyce Caine (née Baldwin); the Most Revd George Carey; the Ven. F.C. Carpenter; Christopher Catherwood; Lady Elizabeth Catherwood (née Lloyd-Jones); the Revd Julian Charley; *Christianity Today*, Inc.; Lord Donald Coggan; Dr Alan Cole; the Revd Alec Colson; Corpus Christi College, Oxford; Canon R. Colin Craston; Mrs Jill Dann; Dr Gaius Davies; the Revd Stephen Davis; the Rt Revd Peter Dawes; Diocese of Birmingham; W. Ormond B. Doherty; the Revd Martin Dowland; the Revd David A. Edwards; the Revd Frank R. Entwistle; Professor Millard J. Erickson; The Evangelical Alliance; the Revd Professor Chrisopher Evans; Professor Gabriel Fackre; Canon Michael Farrer; the Revd Ronald Freeman; the Revd Peter Gains; the Revd David H. Garner; the Revd Michael R. Gee; Canon David Gillett; the Rt Revd Jonathan Gledhill; Canon R.W. Grayson; Canon Professor E.M.B. Green; the Rt Revd Mark Green; Val Grieve; Dr A. Howard Gretton; John D. Griffiths; the Revd Richard Hannah; Professor Bruce F. Harris; the Ven. Ronald G. Herniman; Dr Bruce Hindmarsh; Hodder & Stoughton; Professor James M. Houston; the Revd H.H. Huxham; Leslie C. Hyett; the Revd James M. Innes; Inter-Varsity Press (United Kingdom); InterVarsity Press (United States); the Revd Richard James; the Revd Dr Peter F. Jensen; Canon W.M. Kendrick; W.J. Kilpatrick; Canon Philip King; Gordon Landreth; Mrs Enid W.

Leathem; Canon Raymond J. Lee; the Revd David Littlefair; the Rt Revd Marcus Loane; Professor Samuel T. Logan; Preb. Richard C. Lucas; Canon John D. Lytle; the Revd Gordon J.J. McDonald; Karl McIlwaine; Professor Philip N.J. McNair; Professor George Marsden; Professor Martin E. Marty; Michael G. Maudlin; the Revd Dr David M. Moore; the Rt Revd Harry W. Moore; Dr Leon Morris; the Very Rev. Basil S. Moss; Duncan C. Munro; the Revd Dr Robert Murray, SJ; Professor Mark A. Noll; Canon Alan G. Page; K.C. Parkhurst; Canon David M.M. Paton; the Most Revd Michael G. Peers; Arthur W. Penn; the Revd Martin Perris; Dr Stuart Piggin; Professor Clark H. Pinnock; J. Brian Pointon; Canon Kenneth F.W. Prior; Regent College, Vancouver; the Rt Revd Gavin Reid; the Rt Revd John R. Reid; Dr Ian Rennie; the Revd Paul Rimmer; the Rt Revd Donald Robinson; the Rt Revd Lord Runcie; Canon Michael Sadgrove; St John's College, Nottingham; Canon Michael Saward; the Revd Derek L. Sears; the Revd Dr Charles Sherlock; James W. Sire; Roy A. Stillman; Professor John G. Stackhouse, Jr; the Revd Dr John R.W. Stott; Canon Ernest A. Strickland; Professor Robert B. Strimple; the Rt Revd John B. Taylor; Ralph Thomas; Canon Professor Anthony C. Thiselton; Dafydd Owen Thomas; the Rt Revd Oliver Tomkins; Trinity College, Bristol; A.S.P. Tugman; the Revd Sumner Walters; Professor Robert Webber; Professor Jonathan Webster; Professor David F. Wells; the Revd John Wenham; Canon Malcolm Widdecombe; the Revd Dr Peter Williams; Professor Donald R. Wiseman; the Revd Dobert D. Wismer; the Rt Revd Kenneth J. Woollcombe; Robyn Wrigley; Wycliffe College, Toronto; Wycliffe Hall, Oxford.

Notes

Introduction

1 Mark A. Noll, 'The Last Puritan', *Christianity Today*, 16 September 1996, p. 51.

Chapter 1: The Schoolboy: 1926–44

1 See Geoffrey Boyd, *Railways of the Gloucester Region* (Wellingborough: Patrick Stephens, 1989).
2 The railings and gates would be removed in 1940, so that they could be melted down for munitions as part of the British war effort.
3 Packer's middle name was chosen by his father at the request of a female relative who bore that name as the last in a family line. The relative (a spinster) was a second cousin of Packer's father, who had no children.
4 Years later, Packer would use this childhood memory as a sermon illustration for his expositions of Matthew 6:9–11. See also his article 'My Path of Prayer' in D. Hames (ed.), *My Path of Prayer* (Brighton: Henry E. Walter, 1981), p. 63.
5 Packer, 'What Lewis Was and Wasn't', *Christianity Today*, 15 January 1988, p. 11.
6 *Oxford University Gazette*, March 1943, p. 355.
7 *Oxford University Gazette*, 7 October 1943, p. 21.

Chapter 2: Oxford: Corpus Christi College, 1944–8

1 At that stage, Oxford had two railway stations: the GWR station, and the LMS terminal station. By the end of the Second World War, the LMS depot was only used for coal.
2 For a useful memoir, with occasional inaccuracies, see John Reynolds,

Born Anew: Historical Outlines of the Oxford Inter-Collegiate Christian Union,
1879-1979 (Oxford: Centenary, Executive and Standing Committees
of the OICCU, 1979).

3 The speaker was Basil Atkinson, a well-known figure in Inter-Varsity
circles at this stage. Packer believes he spoke on Revelation chapter
12.

4 Packer is uneasy about this phrase, feeling that it suggests some kind
of 'personal communication'; what Calvin intended to convey was the
manner in which the Spirit makes believers conscious of the unique
divine authority and power of Scripture. See 'Bringing the Bible to
Your Life', *Charisma*, January 1987, pp. 43-4.

5 North American readers should note that the British term 'public
school' should be translated 'private school'.

6 'The Unspectacular Packers', *Christianity Today*, 16 May 1986, p. 12.

7 For his later views on his renunciation of jazz, see 'All that Jazz',
Christianity Today, 12 December 1986, p. 15.

8 See 'George Whitefield: The Startling Puritan', *Christian History*, 12/2
(May 1993), pp. 38-40.

9 Packer describes these struggles in more detail in his Preface to
the centenary edition of J.C. Ryle, *Holiness* (Welwyn Garden City:
Evangelical Press, 1979), pp. vii-xii.

10 See Packer's Introduction to John Owen, *Sin and Temptation*, edited
by James M. Houston (Portland, Oreg:, Multnomah, 1983), pp.
xxv-xxix.

Chapter 3: London: Oak Hill College, 1948-9

1 The British term 'theological college' should be regarded, for
most purposes, as directly equivalent to the North American terms
'seminary' or 'theological seminary'.

2 Packer also attended a CMS Summer Camp at Monkton Combe
School, near Bath, during the summer of 1945, cycling to and from
the conference from his parents' home in Gloucester. The speaker at
that conference was Bishop Stephen Neill, who had recently returned
home after a long period of ministry in India.

3 British theological colleges tend to use the term 'member of staff'
or 'teaching staff', where North Americans use the term 'member of
faculty' or 'academic faculty'.

4 Some Oak Hill students were entered for the General Bachelor
of Arts of the University of London, others for the Bachelor of
Divinity.

5 On Johnston, see the obituary notice in *The Times*, 25 October
1985, p. 16.

Chapter 4: Oxford: Wycliffe Hall, 1949–52

1 A reference to the practice in which the president at a service of Holy Communion stands at the north side of the communion table, rather than facing east. By the 1930s, this practice had become defining for the evangelical party within the Church of England.

2 The episode is described in *God's Words*, p. 180. See also Packer's Introduction to John Gwyn-Thomas, *Rejoice Always* (Edinburgh: Banner of Truth, 1990), pp. ix-xv.

3 Jim Hickinbotham subsequently returned to Wycliffe Hall as its principal, and was later succeeded in that position by Geoffrey Shaw.

4 Although American writers commonly talk about Packer 'receiving his PhD from Oxford University', it must be pointed out that this is not accurate. Oxford University, for reasons which have never been entirely clear, refused to follow the common custom of using the abbreviation of 'PhD' for the degree of 'Doctor of Philosophy', and insisted on using 'DPhil' instead.

5 Readers wishing to explore this type of Calvinism are referred to Brian G. Armstrong, *Calvinism and the Amyraut Heresy: Protestant Scholasticism and Humanism in Seventeenth-Century France* (Madison, Wis. University of Wisconsin Press, 1969).

6 See *Oxford University Gazette*, 18 November 1954, p. 238.

7 The thesis is on deposit at the Bodleian Library, Oxford, as MS DPhil c. 308. In November 1981, a microfilm copy was authorized for use at the Center for Research Libraries, Chicago, Illinois.

8 Foreword to *A Goodly Heritage: Puritan and Reformed Studies Conference Reports, 1958* (London: Banner of Truth Trust, 1959), pp. 2–7.

9 'Looking Forward', *Tyndale Hall Topic* (1970), pp. 15–17. By the time this article was published, the Puritan Conferences had been terminated for reasons we shall explore later: see p. 157.

10 See Mark Noll, 'The Last Puritan', *Christianity Today*, 16 September 1996, pp. 51–3.

11 See his Introduction to *A Quest for Holiness*, published in the United Kingdom as *Among God's Giants*.

12 See his Introductory Essay in John Owen, *The Death of Death in the Death of Christ* (London: Banner of Truth, 1959), pp. 1–25.

Chapter 5: Birmingham: St John's, Harborne, 1952–4

1 A 'curate' is a term now used in the Church of England to refer to an assistant minister.

2 It may be noted here that Packer had led a mission to York during his final term at Wycliffe Hall. During the period 20–29 September 1952,

Packer and several other students undertook evangelistic work at St Wulfstan's church, which was then a daughter church of the parish of Heworth, York.

3 For details of this and similar campaigns at the time, see Geraint D. Fielder, *'Excuse me, Mr Davies – Hallelujah!': Evangelical Student Witness in Wales, 1923–1983* (Leicester: Inter-Varsity Press, 1983).

Chapter 6: Bristol: Tyndale Hall, 1955–61

1 The Church of England, it may be noted, was not alone in neglecting this important city. Despite the close association of Bristol with early Methodism, there was no Methodist institute of theological education in the city until after the Second World War, when Didsbury College (originally founded in Manchester in 1842), moved to the city. The present Methodist theological college, Wesley College, was founded in 1967, through a merger of Didsbury College with Headingley College, Leeds, on the Bristol site.

2 *Bible Churchmen's Missionary Society Messenger,* vol. 1, no. 1 (January 1923), pp. 1, 3. It should be noted that the BCMS archives for this critical period were destroyed during a Second World War bombing raid, making full documentation of some aspects of these developments problematical.

3 It may be noted, however, that the subject of Bromiley's doctoral thesis was partly theological, in that the thesis focused on the German writings of some nineteenth-century theologians. It could therefore be argued that Bromiley's doctoral thesis was basically theological in character, making Packer the second theological college tutor to have a doctorate in theology.

4 After a brief period in Scotland, Bromiley moved to Fuller Theological Seminary in 1958.

5 The University of Bristol did not have a salaried faculty of theology at this stage. The five theological colleges in Bristol were held responsible by the university for the teaching of theology. The first salaried professor of theology at Bristol was Kenneth Grayston, a Methodist.

6 The work was co-published with Eerdmans, and sold 130,000 copies. Packer contributed articles on: 'Assurance', 'Authority', 'Conversion', 'Earnest', 'Election', 'Good', 'Incarnation', 'Inner Man', 'Inspiration', 'Justification', 'Liberty', 'Obedience', 'Perfection', 'Piety', 'Predestination', 'Providence', 'Revelation' and 'Temptation'.

7 In his later work *Keep in Step with the Spirit,* Packer offers a more eirenical and appreciative evaluation of Keswick, which corrects it on several points, while remaining appreciative of its intentions. The noticeably more friendly tone of this evaluation reflects Packer's belief

that, by this later stage (1984), the Keswick teaching no longer posed the threat which it once did.

8 F.F. Bruce, *In Retrospect: Remembrance of Things Past* (Glasgow: Pickering & Inglis, 1980), p. 188.

9 Letter to *The Times*, dated 15 August 1955.

10 John R.W. Stott, *Fundamentalism and Evangelicalism* (London: Crusade Booklets, 1956). North American edition published by Eerdmans in 1959.

11 Packer, 'An Accidental Author', *Christianity Today*, 15 May 1987, p. 11.

12 This replaced the article in the first edition on the same theme by Professor Daniel Lamont of Edinburgh. The first edition of the *New Bible Commentary*, which was published in 1953, was edited by Francis Davidson, principal of the Glasgow Bible Training Institute, who died on the eve of its publication. A new edition of the work, edited by Donald Guthrie, Alec Motyer, Alan Stibbs and Donald Wiseman, appeared the following year; a number of the less satisfactory articles of the original edition were replaced for this new version.

13 For an overview of the publishing history of the IVF, see Ronald Inchley, 'The Inter-Varsity Press', in Douglas Johnston, *Contending for the Faith: A History of the Evangelical Movement in the Universities and Colleges* (Leicester: Inter-Varsity Press, 1979), pp. 314–32.

14 See *The Christian Newsletter* 4, No 3 (July 1957), pp. 37–40.

15 See Roger Nicole, 'James I. Packer's Contribution to the Doctrine of the Inerrancy of Scripture', in D. Lewis and A. McGrath (eds), *Doing Theology for the People of God* (Downers Grove: InterVarsity Press, 1996), pp. 176–7.

16 See Robert Banks, 'Fifty Years of Theology in Australia, 1915–1965', *Colloquium* 9/2 (October 1977), pp. 7–16, especially p. 15. Hebert was based at St Michael's House at Mount Lofty, outside Adelaide, South Australia.

17 He had also spoken on the theme of 'The Puritan View of Preaching the Gospel' at the 1959 Puritan Conference.

18 Packer, 'A Calvinist – and an Evangelist!', *The Hour International*, August 1966, pp. 25–7.

19 Published in a slightly shortened form as 'Revival', *Christian Graduate*, 24/4 (December 1971), pp. 97–100.

20 The Lambeth Conference is a gathering of Anglican bishops in England every ten years, which discusses matters of mutual interest.

Chapter 7: Latimer House: 1961–70

1 J.I. Packer, unpublished memorandum 'A Strategic Priority', December 1958, p. 1.

2 The insight that each major area of Christian teaching has, through

God's providence, its own time for being crystallized through conflict is particularly associated with James Orr's book, *The Progress of Dogma* (London: James Clarke, 1901), a work for which Packer has considerable respect. See Packer's further comments in *Regent College Bulletin* 9/4 (Fall 1979), and especially the major study of 1995 'On from Orr: Cultural Crisis, Rational Realism and Incarnational Ontology', with its appeal for a rediscovery of Orr's relevance to the postmodern situation.

3 The term 'warden' had a well-established usage in British institutions, especially in universities and colleges; the near-equivalent American term 'director' may be more meaningful to some readers.

4 At its meeting of 27 February 1960, the Executive Committee of the Oxford Evangelical Research Trust agreed that the house should be called 'Bishop Jewel House', after the noted sixteenth-century English bishop. However, this name was never used in any minutes of the Trust, and does not seem to have been made public.

5 Tyndale Hall were not enthusiastic about losing Packer. However, they bowed to the inevitable. At their meeting of 18 October 1960, the College Council agreed to appoint Colin Brown as Packer's successor, with effect from 1 April 1961.

6 Adrian Hastings, *A History of English Christianity 1920–1985* (London: Collins, 1986), p. 545.

7 For background, see Eric James, *A Life of Bishop John A.T. Robinson* (London: Collins, 1987). For an analysis of the reaction, see David L. Edwards, *The Honest to God Debate* (London: SCM Press, 1963).

8 The Council should probably be referred to by its original title at this stage: 'Council of the Oxford Evangelical Research Trust'.

9 Packer, *The Thirty-nine Articles* (London: Church Pastoral Aid Society, 1961).

10 Packer also saw the Articles as an important weapon in the continuing struggle against liberalism within the Church of England.

11 For an eyewitness account, see John Wenham, *The Renewal and Unity of the Church* (London: SPCK, 1972), pp. 10–12.

12 *Conversations between the Church of England and the Methodist Church* (London: Church Information Office, 1963).

13 I have here followed the wording of Article XIX of the Thirty-nine Articles of the Church of England; other ways of stating the same point can easily be brought forward.

14 The importance of Gervase Duffield to the profile of Latimer House needs to be noted here. Duffield, who was active in the House of Laity of the governing body of the Church of England, had a vision of a renewed Reformation within the church, and actively promoted this agenda. Always something of an entrepreneur, Duffield established

his own publishing house, the Marcham Manor Press, based at his home near Abingdon, south of Oxford, which carried some of Latimer House's publications. Duffield subsequently published a series of works under the imprint 'Courtenay Library of Reformation Classics', which aimed to make significant Reformation works available to a new readership.

15 The print run for this work was 2,000, which was high for a specialist work of this nature. In the event, around 500 were finally sold. More realistic print runs would be planned in the future.

16 For what follows, see Bradley J. Longfield, *The Presbyterian Controversy: Fundamentalists, Modernists and Moderates* (New York: Oxford University Press, 1991).

17 George Marsden, *Reforming Fundamentalism: Fuller Seminary and the New Evangelicalism* (Grand Rapids: Eerdmans, 1987), p. 7.

18 Francis Schaeffer, *The Great Evangelical Disaster* (Westchester, Ill: Crossway, 1984), p. 75.

19 For an account, see Iain H. Murray, *D. Martyn Lloyd-Jones: The Fight of Faith, 1939-1981* (Edinburgh: Banner of Truth, 1990), pp. 501-6. Lloyd-Jones invited Packer to put the case for the involvement of evangelicals within the Church of England at a subsequent meeting of the Westminster Fellowship, held on 21 March 1966.

20 L. Tyerman, *The Life of the Rev. George Whitefield*, 2 vols (London: Hodder & Stoughton, 2nd edn, 1890), vol. 2, p. 21. See also Whitefield's letter of 20 August 1743, Tyerman, pp. 70-1. For the influence of Whitefield on Packer, see pp. 22, 121.

21 In 1925, the evangelical student organization at Oxford University was absorbed into the SCM, and lost its distinctive identity, becoming little more than a 'Devotional Union' within the SCM. In March 1928, evangelicals broke away from the SCM, and re-established the OICCU. Relations between the OICCU and SCM remained very tense during the 1930s. See John Reynolds, *Born Anew: Historical Outlines of the Oxford Inter-Collegiate Christian Union, 1879-1979* (Oxford: Centenary, Executive and Standing Committees, 1979), pp. 12-19.

22 There is no mention made of this meeting or its aftermath in the official biography of Lloyd-Jones.

23 See Packer's own assessment, cited in C. Catherwood (ed.), *Martyn Lloyd-Jones: Chosen by God* (Crowborough: Highland Books, 1988), p. 49.

24 Evangelicals found themselves gaining increasing acceptance within the Church of England around this time, and thus tended to distance themselves from their free church brethren. See D.W. Bebbington, *Evangelicalism in Modern Britain* (London: Unwin Hyman, 1989), pp. 97-9.

25 See John Wolffe, 'The Evangelical Alliance in the 1840s: An Attempt to Institutionalise Christian Unity', in W.J. Sheils and D. Wood (eds), *Voluntary Religion*, Studies in Church History 23 (Oxford: Blackwell, 1986).

26 This impression may have resulted in part from Lloyd-Jones's concluding reference to evangelicals becoming 'a fellowship or an association of evangelical churches', which could easily have been mis-heard as a reference to the 'Fellowship of Independent Evangelical Churches'.

27 With the benefit of hindsight, it is possible to suggest that Lloyd-Jones may have been unknowingly influenced by the World Council of Churches' constant emphasis on the need for visible unity. The ecumenical movement had argued for the need for a visibly united church; evangelicals had argued that unity lay at the level of doctrine, rather than organization or church polity. The demand for a visibly united evangelical fellowship thus appears to be an evangelical reflection of the original ecumenical vision.

28 *The Christian*, 21 October 1966.

29 The 1966 split loomed large over the Third National Assembly of Evangelicals held at Bournemouth in 1996, attended by some 4,000 people. The Evangelical Alliance made it clear that they regarded the 1966 National Assembly as having gone 'tragically wrong' over the secession issue, and worked to achieve unity on a broad range of fronts. The Lloyd-Jones agenda had no place in 1996. See *Shaping the Future Together* (National Assembly of Evangelicals 1996 Programme), pp. 6–7.

30 Details with primary sources in Murray, *Lloyd-Jones*, pp. 528–32.

31 The 'Statement of Principles' is reprinted in Murray, *Lloyd-Jones*, pp. 536–7. Note especially the fifth principle ('Those who are at present in denominations linked with the World Council of Churches are agreed that separation from such denominations is inevitable').

32 'Memorandum on the Development of the Work of Latimer House', June 1965.

33 A report on this conference was presented at the Latimer House Council meeting on 31 March 1966.

34 'Latimer House Study Groups General Report No. 1', November 1967.

35 The initial plan was to publish the addresses as a record of what had happened at the congress. However, a group of younger evangelicals, including Colin Buchanan and Michael Saward, pressed the case for advance publication.

36 For the addresses, see J.I. Packer (ed.), *Guidelines: Anglican Evangelicals Face the Future* (London: Falcon Books, 1967). Falcon Books was the

publishing division of the Church Pastoral Aid Society, so called from the location of the Society in Falcon Court, London.

37 See the *Official List of Delegates, Observers and Other Participants*, published on the eve of the congress.

38 *Keele '67: The National Evangelical Anglican Congress Statement, with Study Material* (London: Falcon Books, 1967). I am grateful to Latimer House for permission to consult the archives concerning NEAC, which includes early drafts of the final declaration.

39 'Face to Face with Dr J.I. Packer', *Tyndale Hall Topic* 1967, pp. 1–4.

40 For an account of the end of this organization, see A. Eric Smith, *Another Anglican Angle: The History of the Anglican Evangelical Group Movement* (Oxford: Amate Press, 1991), pp. 58–73.

41 Blanch to Hickinbotham, 1 October 1969.

42 'Face to Face with Dr J.I. Packer', *Tyndale Hall Topic* 1967, pp. 1–4; relevant material at p. 4.

43 Packer to Colin Brown, 12 February 1969.

44 This lecture series was founded in 1949, and named in honour of Grace Fuller's parents. Packer was only the second Englishman to give these lectures; the 1961 Payton Lecturer was John R.W. Stott. See *Fuller Theological Seminary Catalog 1995–1996*, p. 20. Packer's theme in 1965 was 'The Problem of Universalism Today'. The four lectures delivered by Packer were never published. See further p. 135.

45 Letter to J. Stafford Wright, 30 October 1968.

46 See his important analysis in 'Re-tooling the Clergy Factories', *Churchman* 82 (1968), pp. 120–24.

47 'Face to Face with Dr J.I. Packer', *Tyndale Hall Topic* 1967, pp. 1–4; relevant material especially at p. 4.

48 Three names were suggested by Council members, and it was agreed that they would be invited to the next meeting, to be held at All Souls Church, Langham Place, London on 22 October. In December, the position was finally offered to John Wenham.

Chapter 8: Bristol: Tyndale Hall, 1970–2

1 *Theological Colleges for Tomorrow* (London: Church Information Office, 1968) section 52, p. 31. The document is often referred to as the 'de Bunsen report', after its chief author.

2 'A Private Memorandum on the Relationship between Councils, Principals and Staffs of Theological Colleges'. The document dates from 1 December 1968, and analyses the events at Tyndale throughout that year.

3 John King, 'The Bristol Fiasco', *Church Times*, 8 August 1969.

4 *Seek First*, No. 36, April 1969, pp. 1–3. See also the reaction reported in *Seek First*, No. 37, pp. 1–2.

5 The best account to be published at this stage was authored by Philip Crowe: see the *Church of England Newspaper*, 2 May 1969, p. 8.

6 *Memorandum from the Staff of Tyndale Hall*, dated 28 March 1969, p. 2.

7 The petition had been drawn up by John Gwyn-Thomas, Peter Dale and Richard T. France, who were all then in parish positions in Cambridge.

8 See 'Re-tooling the Clergy Factories', *Churchman* 82 (1968), pp. 120–4, noting especially the comments on p. 122.

9 Richard Higginson, a part-time member of staff who taught in the field of pastoral studies, chose not to remain. He was subsequently replaced by Tony Baker, the new vicar of Redland.

10 Packer had been invited to deliver the Rhodes Lectures in Christchurch, New Zealand, and the Gunther Lectures in Sydney, Australia.

11 Richard James to Alec Motyer, 26 October 1969.

12 Both meetings were at Tyndale Hall. The working party consisted of two representatives of the BCMS General Committee (Canon R.C. Craston and the Revd M.J. Saward); the principal-designate and all present and forthcoming members of the Hall's teaching staff; two members of the Tyndale Hall Council (P. Lefroy-Owen and G. Ross-Cornes); a member of the Church Assembly; a former student (the Revd Dr Paul Dale); and a representative of Dalton House (Miss J. Baldwin).

13 Note that a meeting of the twenty-eight students at the Hall, held on Wednesday 22 October 1969, had unanimously affirmed the 'prime importance of studying theology'.

14 See the memorandum of Colin Brown, for discussion on 5 February 1970.

15 Note that not all evangelicals or Anglo-Catholics opposed the scheme of union; the point being made here is that the two major groupings who were opposed were evangelical and Anglo-Catholic in their orientation.

16 See Samuel's criticial review of *Growing into Union* in *The Evangelical Magazine*, November 1970, pp. 2–12. For Packer's response, see *The Evangelical Magazine*, April 1971, pp. 1–10.

17 It must be noted that Samuel was not among these; his criticisms related to Packer's application of evangelical principles, which he considered to be inconsistent. See his further contribution in *The Evangelical Magazine*, June 1971, pp. 2–6.

18 For an explanation and defence of Lloyd-Jones's perspective, see Iain H. Murray, *D. Martyn Lloyd-Jones: The Fight of Faith 1939–1981* (Edinburgh: Banner of Truth, 1990), pp. 656–8; 793–4.

19 Circular letter of June 1959.

20 There is a fascinating parallel here with C.S. Lewis's *Screwtape Letters.* Originally published in article form in a small Christian journal (*The Guardian*), they only achieved their great prominence on publication in book form.

21 *The Evangelical Anglican Identity Problem*, Latimer Study No. 1 (Oxford: Latimer House, 1978); *A Kind of Noah's Ark? The Anglican Commitment to Comprehensiveness*, Latimer Study No. 10 (Oxford: Latimer House, 1981).

22 *A Kind of Noah's Ark?*, p. 10.

23 *A Kind of Noah's Ark?*, p. 36.

24 *A Kind of Noah's Ark?*, pp. 37–8.

25 Clifton Theological College, Bristol; Cranmer Hall, Durham; London College of Divinity; Ridley Hall, Cambridge; Tyndale Hall, Bristol; Oak Hill College, Southgate; and Wycliffe Hall, Oxford.

26 Memorandum of a Meeting of Representatives of Evangelical Theological Colleges, 12 March 1970, pp. 1–2.

27 This was confirmed when Packer attempted to get the university to compound the existing theological teaching at Tyndale so that it might lead to a Bristol Bachelor of Theology degree. Grayston wanted nothing to do with the proposal. See Principal's Report, September 1970.

28 It should be noted that Wesley College, Bristol (the Methodist institution in question) only came into being in 1967 as the result of a merger of two colleges of very different backgrounds. The merger was tense and difficult, and it is likely that difficulties which were internal to the college heavily influenced its policies concerning external relations at this point.

29 Ridley Hall, Cambridge, decided not to take part in the exercise, apparently on account of internal difficulties arising from the recent resignation of its principal.

30 Circular letter to past and present students, and members of the Tyndale Hall Association, September 1970.

31 *The Future of the Evangelical Theological Colleges* (Unpublished Document), pp. 14–19. The Bristol situation was by far the most complex issue addressed by the group.

32 *Report of the Commission* (Unpublished Report for Internal Circulation), p. 12.

33 Packer to O'Neill, 5 November 1970.

34 At its meeting on Tuesday 3 November, the Wycliffe Hall Council had resolved to accept the Runcie recommendation, and to write immediately to Clifton to open negotiations. The Clifton decision reflected knowledge of the Wycliffe willingness to negotiate over this matter.

35 In the event, Wycliffe Hall failed to provide a representative, due to a misunderstanding over the date of the meeting.

36 St John's College Council wrote to Tyndale Hall to report their view that it 'does not feel that the proposed move of Tyndale Hall to Nottingham is a viable proposition, and is unable therefore to recommend that it be pursued'.

37 See document *GS 20 Reorganization of the Theological Colleges: A Report of the House of Bishops* (London: Church Information Office, 1971).

38 The issue dominated the *Church of England Newspaper* of 5 February and 12 February 1971.

39 Packer to Archbishop of Canterbury, 4 February 1971.

40 See Packer to Tomkins, 3 February 1979 (following up on the conversation).

41 Michael Clark and David Atkinson, dated 8 February 1971.

42 'Notes of a Meeting', dated 11 March 1971.

43 *Report of Proceedings* (London: Church Information Office, 1971), p. 181.

44 For his comments, see Packer, 'On from Runcie', *Tyndale Hall Topic*, 1971, p. 28.

45 Some suggested that the name was now more appropriate, given that there would be three, rather than just two, merging institutions. The implicit tritheism of this comment will interest some readers of this work.

46 Tomkins, private 'Occasional Journal', February 1971.

47 Packer had long been a champion of 'every-member ministry in the body of Christ', and saw the proposed triumvirate as a way of applying this New Testament principle to the leadership of a theological college. See his essay 'Towards a Corporate Presbyterate', pp. 15–16.

48 Tomkins to members of the Councils of Clifton, Tyndale and Dalton, dated 13 May 1971.

49 Packer was asked to contribute a memorandum setting out his views on this matter. See his 'Notes on the 3-Dean Structure', dated July 1971, which formed the basis of the opening discussion on 3 August.

50 Tomkins, private 'Occasional Journal', 3 August 1971.

51 The meeting had two memoranda before it, prepared by Motyer and Packer, outlining possible responses to the Clifton Council's scheme.

52 Minutes of the Interim Council of Trinity College, 14 October 1971.

53 This version was drawn up by Tomkins for the meeting on 3 August 1971.

54 In fact, the number of students was eighty-one for 1971–2, and rose
to 132 for 1980–81 (the final year of Motyer's principalship).

Chapter 9: Bristol: Trinity College, 1972–9

1 Michael Smout, 'What is an Evangelical Anglican?', in E. Neale et al.,
77 Notts Untied (London: Lakeland, 1977), pp. 20–66; quote at pp.
31–2. The unusual title of this work involves a pun on the title of J. C.
Ryle's famous work of 1877, *Knots Untied*, with 'Notts.', the standard
abbreviation for 'Nottinghamshire'.
2 Packer's title often caused confusion. Most theological colleges used
the title 'vice-principal' to refer to the senior member of staff who was
directly subordinate to the principal. The agreed structure of Trinity
College, as we have seen, was grounded in the idea of the principal as
a *primus inter decanos.* The term 'associate principal' was intended to
articulate this notion of shared leadership. However, Packer was widely
referred to as the 'vice-principal' of Trinity Hall, simply because the
term 'associate principal' was unfamiliar. British reprints of *Evangelism
and the Sovereignty of God* dating from after the formation of Trinity
College illustrate this point. Thus the 1977 reprint correctly refers
to Packer as 'Associate Principal, Trinity College, Bristol' on its title
page, but as 'Vice-Principal' on its back cover.
3 See his later pamphlet *The Thirty-nine Articles: Their Place and Use Today*
(Oxford: Latimer House, 1984). An earlier pamphlet should also be
noted: *The Thirty-nine Articles* (London: Falcon, 1961).
4 One of the most significant consequences of Packer's move to
Vancouver, to teach in a transdenominational school of theology,
was that he was no longer obliged to teach in such a specifically
Anglican and English manner.
5 That is, Gregory of Nazianzus, Gregory of Nyssa, and Basil the
Great.
6 Packer would eventually comply; the result was *Keep in Step with
the Spirit.*
7 Something of the story is told in Edward England, *An Unfading
Vision: The Adventure of Books* (London: Hodder & Stoughton, 1982),
pp. 152–3.
8 As of January 1992, Hodder & Stoughton had over 233, 000 copies
in print, and InterVarsity Press 736,000. Foreign translations account
for the remainder of the million.
9 *Knowing God*, p. 41.
10 Isaiah 49:16 'See, I have engraved you on the palms of my hands'
(NIV). The King James Version uses the older term 'graven'; Packer
here alludes to this classic translation.

11 Packer, 'On Knowing God', *Tenth: An Evangelical Quarterly*, July 1975, pp. 11–25.

12 For an introduction to the origins and development of this major work, see Alister E. McGrath, *A Life of John Calvin* (Oxford/Cambridge, Mass: Blackwell, 1990), pp. 136–74.

13 In Calvin's case, the book in question was the *Institutes of the Christian Religion*.

14 Packer used the term himself as early as 1968, seeing it as a close modern equivalent to the Puritan notion of the 'application' of Christian truth to life: 'Retooling the Clergy Factories', *Churchman* 82 (1968), pp. 120–4.

15 Packer, 'Questions about IVF', *Breakthrough* 11 (May 1962), p. 15.

16 For full documentation, see George M. Marsden, *Reforming Fundamentalism: Fuller Seminary and the New Evangelicalism* (Grand Rapids, Mich.: Eerdmans, 1987).

17 Other European attendees included Donald Wiseman and Andrew Walls (UK) and Hermann Ridderbos (The Netherlands).

18 Harold Lindsell, *The Battle for the Bible*, (Grand Rapids, Mich.: Zondervan, 1976).

19 See his later *The Bible in the Balance* (Grand Rapids, Mich.: Zondervan, 1979), especially the concluding comments at pp. 319–22.

20 Packer's own account of the debate may be found in his article 'Thirty Years' War: The Doctrine of Holy Scripture', in H. Conn (ed.), *Practical Theology and the Ministry of the Church* (Phillipsburg, NJ: Presbyterian and Reformed, 1990), pp. 25–44.

21 A suggestion put forward by Glenn T. Sheppard, in *Union Seminary Quarterly Review*, 32 (1977), pp. 81–94.

22 These may be found reprinted in the 1988 edition of *God has Spoken* (Grand Rapids, Mich.: Baker Book House, 1988), pp. 149–55; 163–72.

23 *God has Spoken*, p. 152.

24 *Evangelical Anglican Identity Problem*, p. 5.

25 *God has Spoken*, pp. 170–1. On Calvin's approach here, see Alister E. McGrath, *A Life of John Calvin* (Oxford/Cambridge, Mass.: Blackwell, 1990), pp. 253–7.

26 *God has Spoken*, p. 153.

27 Packer, 'Biblical Authority: What It Means Today', in *Biblical Authority for Today* (Basic Baptist Beliefs 3 (photocopied)) p. 9.

28 Citations from photocopied handout for lecture 12, 'Notes on Biblical Inerrancy'. For a brief synopsis, see his article 'Infallibility and Inerrancy of the Bible', in S.B. Ferguson and D.F. Wright (eds), *New Dictionary of Theology* (Leicester, Inter-Varsity Press, 1988), pp. 337–9.

29 Lindsell, *Battle for the Bible*, pp. 174–6.

30 Packer, 'Battling for the Bible', *Regent College Bulletin*, 9/4 (Fall, 1979), no page.

31 G.W.H. Lampe, 'The Atonement: Law and Love', in A. R. Vidler, *Soundings* (Cambridge: Cambridge University Press, 1962), pp. 173–91.

32 An important defence of the classic evangelical position was provided by the Australian writer Leon Morris, *The Cross in the New Testament* (London: Tyndale Press, 1955).

33 *The Nottingham Statement* (London: Falcon, 1977), p. 13.

34 Packer, 'What did the Cross Achieve?', *Tyndale Bulletin* 25 (1974), pp. 3–45. Of particular interest is the way in which Packer interacts with the new interest in the nature of theological language at this time, evident in works such as Ian T. Ramsey, *Religious Language* (London: SCM Press, 1957) and John Macquarrie, *God-Talk* (London: SCM Press, 1967).

35 Readers wishing to have an introduction to these approaches may consult Alister E. McGrath, *Christian Theology: An Introduction* 2nd edn (Oxford/Cambridge, Mass.: Blackwell, 1996), pp. 390–412.

36 *Christian Believing* (London: SPCK, 1976), p. 3.

37 Packer, *The Evangelical Anglican Identity Problem*, p. 4. A particularly severe criticism of *Christian Believing* by John Wenham (Packer's former colleague at Tyndale Hall, Bristol), suggesting that Packer had failed to defend central evangelical beliefs, was published in the December 1975 edition of *The Christian Graduate*. For reasons that remain unclear, the journal failed to publish Packer's response of January 1976; indeed, they did not even acknowledge it until 28 June. For Packer, the point at issue was simple. If the report was to be a 'non-judgmental description' of views that were held within the church, it was important that the conservative evangelical position was faithfully represented (Packer to O. Saenoir, 6 January 1976). Packer had explained his position in some detail to Wenham, and was concerned that his review failed to take account of (or quite misunderstood) that discussion (Packer to Wenham, 7 January 1976).

38 Adrian Hastings, *A History of English Christianity 1920–1985* (London: Collins, 1986), pp. 650–1.

39 Hastings, *A History of English Christianity*, p. 545.

40 Text and background in Teddy Saunders and Hugh Sansom, *David Watson: A Biography* (London: Hodder & Stoughton, 1992), p. 186.

41 Bruce Kaye (ed), *Obeying Christ in a Changing World: The Changing World* (London: Collins, 1977), p. 9.

42 Eddie Neale, 'Nottingham 77', in *77 Notts Untied*, pp. 1–19; quote at p. 15.

43 For the statement, see *The Nottingham Statement* (London: Falcon, 1977). For a comment on the event, see Trevor Lloyd, *Evangelicals, Obedience and Change* (Bramcote: Grove Books, 1977).

44 David F. Wells, 'On Being Evangelical', in M.A. Noll, D.W. Bebbington and G.A. Rawlyk, *Evangelicalism: Comparative Studies of Popular Protestantism in North America, The British Isles, and Beyond 1700–1990* (New York: Oxford University Press, 1994), pp. 389–410; quote at p. 398.

45 See his 1971 essay 'Biblical Authority, Hermeneutics and Inerrancy' in E.R. Geeham (ed.) *Jerusalem and Athens* (Philadelphia: Presbyterian and Reformed, 1971), pp. 141–53.

46 Michael Smout, 'What is an Evangelical Anglican?', in E. Neale et al., *77 Notts Untied*, pp. 20–66; quote at pp. 35–6.

Chapter 10: Vancouver: Regent College, 1979–96

1 For background, the reader is referred to Robert Burkinshaw, *Strangers and Pilgrims in Lotus Land: Conservative Protestantism in British Columbia, 1917–1981* (Montreal and Kingston: McGill–Queen's University Press, 1995).

2 The article which sets outs the committee's findings was authored by John Cochrane, but was endorsed by the committee as a whole: John Cochrane, 'The Effect of Increased Education – and a Proposal!', *Calling* (Fall, 1965), pp. 9–11. (*Calling* was a quarterly Brethren periodical founded in 1958 by Sheppard.)

3 Cochrane, 'Effect of Increased Education', p. 10.

4 See Arthur Dicken Thomas Jr, 'James M. Houston: Pioneering Spiritual Director to Evangelicals', *Crux* 29/2 (1993), pp. 2–10.

5 F.F. Bruce, *In Retrospect: Remembrance of Things Past* (London: Pickering & Inglis, 1980), pp. 250–1.

6 It is not clear where this idea of a 'Bible school' (along the lines of Prairie Bible Institute or Briercrest Bible College) came from. All the documentation suggests that the original committee was clearly committed to a graduate-level seminary model. It is possible that Houston's British background led to some confusion about the status of the various North American models available.

7 See the following unpublished memoranda held in the archives at Regent College: James M. Houston, 'The History and Assumptions of Regent College' (1974); W. Ward Gasque, 'A History of Regent College' (1984) (included as the opening section of a self-assessment report entitled 'Report on Institutional Self-Study', which was prepared as part of the process for obtaining accreditation by the Association of Theological Schools in 1985). A further

memorandum by James M. Houston, entitled 'The Inside Story of Regent College' (undated) has also been used, although this appears to differ slightly at points concerning the original vision for Regent College.

8 The importance of this point must be stressed. At the time, this was an innovative concept; indeed, the model of a three-week summer school would be widely imitated. Even at this early stage, Regent proved to be a leader in what was to become a major trend in North American theological education.

9 About fifty attended in 1968; nearly 100 in 1969.

10 For some of the issues, see Houston, 'The Importance of Being on a University Campus', *Regent College Bulletin* 1 (Spring 1971).

11 Note that Regent College used British terminology for its senior faculty in its opening phase. One of the most interesting aspects of the evolution of the college was the way in which it mingled British and North American models of education. In retrospect, this may well have contributed to its growing international appeal.

12 Three part-time appointments were made: Ian S. Rennie and John A. Toews (church history); Samuel J. Mikolaski (theology).

13 For a useful survey, see Robert K. Johnston, 'Clark H. Pinnock', in W.A. Elwell (ed.), *Handbook of Evangelical Theologians* (Grand Rapids, Mich.: Baker, 1993), pp. 427–44.

14 The original house no longer exists; it was demolished after the Packers moved out to a smaller house in the 1990s.

15 The designations of these courses varied from year to year. The 1995–7 catalogue (which can be seen as reflecting the final recension of this material on Packer's 70th birthday), designates these four courses as THEO 601, 602, 603 and 604. The descriptions provided in the text are taken from this catalogue. See *Catalogue 1995–1997*, pp. 63–4. Each lecture course consisted of between twenty-two and twenty-four lectures. Audio recordings of each of these lecture series are available: see p. 291 for details.

16 Mark Noll, 'J.I. Packer and the Shaping of American Evangelicalism', in D. Lewis and A. McGrath (eds), *Doing Theology for the People of God* (Downers Grove, Ill.: InterVarsity, 1996), pp. 191–206.

17 'Let's Stop Making Women Presbyters', *Christianity Today*, 11 February 1991, pp. 18–21.

18 See *Christianity Today*, 29 April 1991, p. 8.

19 See R. M. Anderson, *Vision of the Disinherited: The Making of American Pentecostalism* (Oxford: Oxford University Press, 1980). For more recent developments, see Richard Quebedeaux, *The New Charismatics: The Origins, Developments and Significance of Neo-Pentecostalism* (New York: Doubleday, 1976).

20 P.E. Hughes, Editorial, *The Churchman* 76 (1962), pp. 131–5. This editorial was reprinted in pamphlet form, and is estimated to have sold some 39,000 copies.

21 For its impact on the ministry of David Watson, see Teddy Saunders and Hugh Sansom, *David Watson: A Biography* (London: Hodder & Stoughton, 1992), pp. 68–85.

22 See Saunders and Sansom, *David Watson: A Biography*, pp. 70–2.

23 See his early article 'The Holy Spirit and the Local Congregation', *Churchman* 78 (1964), pp. 98–108. The text of the 'Gospel and Spirit' statement can be found in Michael Harper, *This is the Day: A Fresh Look at Christian Unity* (London: Hodder & Stoughton, 1979), pp. 131–49.

24 The lecture focused especially on John Owen's *Discourse of Spiritual Gifts*, which was probably published posthumously in 1693.

25 'Theological Reflections on the Charismatic Movement', *Churchman* (1980), pp. 7–25; 108–25. For a more accessible version of this important study, see his *Keep in Step with the Spirit* (Old Tappan, NJ: Fleming H. Revell, 1984), pp. 200–34.

26 The title of the book derives from Paul's telling phrase in Galatians 5:25: 'if we live by the Spirit, let us also walk by the Spirit'.

27 Packer, *'Fundamentalism' and the Word of God* (London: Inter-Varsity Press, 1958), p. 48.

28 Mark A. Noll, 'The Last Puritan', *Christianity Today*, 16 September 1996, p. 53.

29 For a critical assessment of the theology that lay behind these 'altar calls', see David L. Weddle, *The Law as Gospel: Revival and Reform in the Theology of Charles Finney* (London: Scarecrow, 1985).

30 *A Kind of Noah's Ark?*, pp. 35–6.

31 John H. Crook, *Evolution of Human Consciousness* (Oxford: Oxford University Press, 1980), p. 361.

32 The influence of James Orr's classic *The Progress of Dogma* (London: James Clarke, 1901) will be evident here.

33 See Packer's 1965 commencement address at Westminster Theological Seminary, 'Ministry of the Word Today', *The Presbyterian Guardian* (July-August 1965), pp. 87–90.

34 See the interview 'Packer on Preaching', *New Horizons* 8/1 (January 1987), pp. 1–3.

35 Packer, 'Some Perspectives on Preaching', *Ashland Theological Journal* 21 (1990), pp. 42–64.

36 Packer, 'To make our Theology serve our Godliness', *Leadership* (Tokyo Christian Institute) Spring-Summer 1987, pp. 1–2.

37 'An Introduction to Systematic Spirituality', *Crux* 26/1 (March 1990), pp. 2–8.

38 Packer takes this definition from Henry Rack, *Twentieth Century Spirituality* (London: Epworth Press, 1969), p. 2.

39 The lectures were delivered over the period 11–14 May 1965, with the titles: 1. 'Motives and Forms of Universalism'; 2. 'Human Destiny'; 3. 'Grace Triumphant'; 4. 'Universalism and the Gospel'.

40 'The Problem of Universalism Today', *Theological Review* 5/3 (November 1969), pp. 16–24.

41 '"Good Pagans" and God's Kingdom', *Christianity Today*, 17 January 1986.

42 For an early and brief analysis, see Millard J. Erickson, 'Is Universalistic Thinking Now Appearing Among Evangelicals?', *United Evangelical Action* 48/5 (September-October 1989), pp. 4–6. A useful survey can be found in Tony Gray, 'Destroyed for Ever: An Examination of the Debates Concerning Annihilation and Conditional Immortality', *Themelios* 21 No. 2 (January 1996), pp. 14–18.

43 I take this definition from a lecture by John Wenham, 'The Case for Conditional Immortality', delivered at Rutherford House, Edinburgh, Scotland, on 29 August 1991.

44 David L. Edwards with John R.W. Stott, *Essentials* (London: Hodder & Stoughton, 1988), pp. 312–39; quote at p. 319. Stott has subsequently indicated that, although he is inclined towards annihilationism, he ultimately remains agnostic on the issue.

45 Wenham, 'Case for Conditional Immortality', p. 2.

46 See Clark H. Pinnock, *A Wideness in God's Mercy* (Grand Rapids, Mich.: Zondervan, 1992), and especially his earlier article 'The Destruction of the Finally Impenitent', *Criswell Theological Review* 4 (1990), pp. 243–59.

47 I use the term 'Roman Catholicism', following a long-standing tradition, but note that the term 'Catholicism' is preferred by many members of the church referred to in this way.

48 Its fifteen members were made up as follows. On the Catholic side, Juan Diaz-Vilar, SJ; Avery Dulles, SJ; Bishop Francis George; Msgr William Murphy; Richard John Neuhaus; Archbishop Francis Stafford; George Weigel. On the evangelical side, Charles Colson; Kent Hill; Richard Land; Larry Lewis; Jesse Miranda; Brian O'Connell; Herbert Schlossberg; John White.

49 Packer, 'Crosscurrents among Evangelicals', in C. Colson and R.J. Neuhaus (eds), *Evangelicals and Catholics Together: Toward a Common Mission* (Dallas: Word, 1995), pp. 147–74. See also the important essay 'Why I Signed It', *Christianity Today*, 12 December 1994, pp. 34–7.

50 C.S. Lewis, *Christian Reflections* (London: Bles, 1967), p. vii.

51 Richard Land and Larry Lewis withdrew their signatures to the statement in April 1995, following concern that their action had

created the impression that the Southern Baptist Convention had officially endorsed the document. At this stage, Land was serving on the Christian Life Commission of the Convention, and Lewis was on its Home Mission Board. Both indicated their continuing personal endorsement of the document.

52 The statement can be studied in Colson and Neuhaus, *Evangelicals and Catholics Together: Toward a Common Mission*, pp. xv-xxxiii.

53 See his 'On from Orr: Cultural Crisis, Rational Realism and Incarnational Ontology', *Crux* 32, No. 3 (September 1996), pp. 12–26.

54 It is not without significance that Iain H. Murray, one of Lloyd-Jones's advisers, and a leading critic of Packer during the 1970s, should weigh in against ECT: '"Evangelicals and Catholics Together": A Movement of "Watershed Significance"?', *Churchman* 110 (1996), pp. 217–29.

55 See especially 'On from Orr: Cultural Crisis, Rational Realism and Incarnational Ontology'.

56 See the trenchant criticism (particularly directed against Packer) in R.C. Sproul, *Faith Alone: The Evangelical Doctrine of Justification* (Grand Rapids, Mich.: Baker, 1995), pp. 183–92. 'The Alliance of Confessing Evangelicals', founded in April 1996, reflected similar concerns. See J.M. Boice and B.S. Sasse, *Here We Stand: A Call from Confessing Evangelicals* (Grand Rapids, Mich.: Baker, 1996).

57 John Ankerberg, Michael Horton, D. James Kennedy, John MacArthur, and R.C. Sproul. Joe Stowell chaired, and John Woodbridge was present as an adviser.

58 See John G. Stackhouse, Jr., *Canadian Evangelicalism in the Twentieth Century* (Toronto: University of Toronto Press, 1993). This study is of major importance in its reappraisal of the strength, character and significance of Canadian evangelicalism, and is a 'must-read' on the subject.

59 For the papers and declaration, see G. Egerton (ed.), *Anglican Essentials: Reclaiming the Faith within the Anglican Church of Canada* (Toronto: Anglican Book Centre, 1995).

60 See the assessment of Mark A. Noll, 'J.I. Packer and the Shaping of American Evangelicalism', in D. Lewis and A. McGrath (eds), *Doing Theology for the People of God* (Downers Grove, Ill.: InterVarsity, 1995), pp. 191–205, especially p. 197.

61 The phrase comes from the 1996 essay 'On from Orr: Cultural Crisis, Rational Realism and Incarnational Ontology'.

62 See Packer, 'The Gospel Bassoon', *Christianity Today*, 28 October 1996, p. 24.

Chapter 11: James I. Packer: An Assessment

1 See the analysis in *Christianity Today,* 16 September 1996.
2 See especially the major 1995 essay 'On from Orr: Cultural Crisis, Rational Realism and Incarnational Ontology'. As an Anglican, Packer has long felt that the Thirty-nine Articles and the Book of Common Prayer express this great tradition in a classical form.
3 David F. Wells, *No Place for Truth; or, Whatever Happened to Evangelical Theology?* (Grand Rapids, Mich.: Eerdmans, 1993; Leicester: Inter-Varsity Press, 1995); Mark A. Noll, *The Scandal of the Evangelical Mind* (Grand Rapids, Mich.: Eerdmans, and Leicester: Inter-Varsity Press, 1994). See also the comments in Alister E. McGrath, *A Passion for Truth: The Intellectual Coherence of Evangelicalism* (Leicester: Inter-Varsity Press and Downers Grove, Ill.: InterVarsity Press, 1995).
4 Edward Farley, *Theologia: The Fragmentation and Unity of Theological Education* (Philadelphia: Fortress Press, 1983), pp. x, 7. The debate which resulted may be followed in works such as J.C. Hough and J.B. Cobb Jr (eds), *Christian Identity and Theological Education* (Chico, Calif.: Scholar's Press, 1985); Charles M. Wood, *Vision and Discernment: An Orientation in Theological Study* (Atlanta: Scholar's Press, 1985); Farley, *The Fragility of Knowledge: Theological Education in the Church and University* (Philadelphia: Fortress Press, 1988).
5 According to David Lowes Watson, 'Spiritual Formation in Ministry Training', *Christian Century* 101 (6–13 February 1991), pp. 122–4.
6 See Walter L. Liefield and Linda M. Cannell, 'Spiritual Formation and Theological Education', in J.I. Packer and L. Wilkinson (eds.), *Alive to God: Studies in Spirituality* (Downers Grove, Ill.: InterVarsity, 1992), pp. 239–52.
7 On Calvin's understanding of the dialectic between theology and experience, see Wilhelm Balke, 'The Word of God and *Experientia* according to Calvin', in W. H. Neuser (ed.), *Calvinus Ecclesiae Doctor* (Kampen: Kok, 1978), pp. 19–31.
8 For an analysis, see Alister E. McGrath, *Evangelicalism and the Future of Christianity* (London: Hodder & Stoughton, 1994, and Downers Grove, Ill.: InterVarsity Press, 1995).
9 J. I. Packer, *The Evangelical Anglican Identity Problem: An Analysis* (Oxford: Latimer House, 1978), p. 29 (adapted). The quotation originally specifically refers to 'Anglican evangelicals'; nevertheless, the point being made applies to the movement as a whole.

Index